Ball of Fire

BALL OF FIRE

The Tumultuous Life
and Comic Art of
Lucille Ball

STEFAN KANFER

ALFRED A. KNOPF   NEW YORK   2003

THIS IS A BORZOI BOOK
PUBLISHED BY ALFRED A. KNOPF

Library of Congress Cataloging-in-Publication Data
Kanfer, Stefan.
Ball of fire : the tumultuous life and comic art of
Lucille Ball / Stefan Kanfer.
p.   cm.
Includes bibliographical references and index.
ISBN 0-375-41315-4
1. Ball, Lucille, 1911–1989
2. Entertainers—United States—Biography.   I. Title.

PN2287.B16 K36 2003
791.45'028'092—dc21
[B]   2002043090

Manufactured in the United States of America
Published August 22, 2003
Reprinted Once
Third Printing, August 2003

For Bip

Caritas omnia potest

Contents

Preface: Why Lucy? Why Now?

LUCILLE BALL made her final exit more than a decade ago. In 2001, commemorating the fiftieth anniversary of the *I Love Lucy* debut, cable and network stations ran several documentaries concerned with her life and career. Videotapes of her best films, and almost all of the *Lucy* episodes, are available. Internet surfers can carom from site to site devoted to Lucille Ball. There is a posthumous autobiography introduced by her daughter. There are numerous authorized and unauthorized accounts of her life; her husband Desi Arnaz's candid view of their marriage and intertwined careers; and several volumes about her company, Desilu Productions. Yet despite this wealth of material, the Lucille Ball story is far from complete.

For one thing, almost all personalities suffer a decline in reputation after death. Not Ball. Each year she has grown in significance and popularity. Some of this increase is prompted by the longing for a simpler time, an epoch when television and politics were presented in unsubtle shades of black and white. That desire became more pronounced after the atrocities of September 11, 2001. The sudden vulnerability of the United States sharpened viewers' appetite for a secure past, and *I Love Lucy* reruns earned extraordinarily high ratings on such cable channels as Nickelodeon and TV Land.

But there is more to the phenomenon than nostalgia for the commercial and moral certainties of the Eisenhower era. Lucille Ball was the first woman with major economic power in postwar Hollywood. (Mary Pickford, who rose from star performer to cofounder of United Artists, preceded her in the silent era.) As president of Desilu, Ball took on the new identity of feminist icon. It was a role she abjured; she liked to say she was too busy succeeding to think of joining women's lib. That response hides more than it reveals. She knew her own history very well and, as we will see, was keenly aware that she had spent much of her life showing deference to men. Thus the garment of feminism was uncomfortable, and she refused to wear it.

Still, some part of Lucille Ball was always independent. It was this component that kept her going from a difficult childhood to the day the middle-aged divorcée found herself CEO of Hollywood's most important television studio. Here, as with so many challenges in her life and career, she had to change or go under. In this she was rather like Katharine Graham, the publisher of the *Washington Post,* who took control of a communications empire upon the death of her husband, Philip. Mrs. Graham had always been in his shadow, and a weaker soul might have collapsed under the pressure, sold the paper, and retired in comfort. Instead, the newly widowed, middle-aged woman forced herself to master the newspaper business. She hired the right editors, learned how to use or delegate authority, and in time became a prominent, respected, and, on occasion, feared publisher. Similarly, Mrs. Arnaz, who had left the biggest financial decisions to Desi, made herself into a powerful, esteemed, and, on occasion, feared personage in a harsh and unforgiving trade. Up to now this aspect of her life has not received enough commentary and analysis.

In addition to the other facets there is Lucille Ball's burgeoning reputation as a comic influence. She was funny as a girl, funnier as a young stage actress and as a Hollywood starlet. She was professionally hilarious in films, yet never achieved iconic status until she was reduced in size. As a sixty-foot image on the screen, the actress was only a journeywoman performer; as a sixteen-inch TV image, she turned into a superstar. This paradox has also needed examination.

In tracing the long arc of her life and career, I found that people tended to see Lucille Ball in terms of their own lives, their marriages, and their occupations. A toy collector I spoke with is typical; he views her as a *matryoshka*—one of those Russian dolls concealing a person inside a person inside a person, and so on. I suppose I tend to view her that way, too, envisioning Lucille Ball as a woman who was a novelist manqué. She was the subject of her own unwritten book. It featured a central character who began in an orderly fashion and then ran away with the story, as colorful personalities frequently do in defiance of those who invent them. In this nonfiction novel, the protagonist starts as one kind of individual and grows, in and on stages, to end as a pantheon figure and an enduring influence—a status she never envisioned. It is the object of this book to tell her extraordinary story, begun in 1911 and, to use the Hollywood phrase, still in development after all these years.

BALL OF FIRE

Introduction

EVEN BY Beltway standards the entire weekend had been bizarre. The six winners of the 1986 Kennedy Center Awards were treated to brunch at the Jockey Club, where their aggressively genial host was John Coleman, owner of the Ritz-Carlton. That hotel was about to file for Chapter 11 bankruptcy. At a more formal occasion the six honorees were saluted by a beaming secretary of state. George Schultz made no mention of the just-unearthed Washington scandal—U.S. arms for Iran had been illegally diverted to the contras in Nicaragua. In November, in response to journalistic and popular outcry, President Ronald Reagan's national security adviser, Admiral John M. Poindexter, had resigned, and Poindexter's aide, Lieutenant Colonel Oliver North, had been fired. Now, in the second week of December, aftershocks still reverberated along the Potomac.

Nevertheless, the President and his staff welcomed the half-dozen honorees to the White House, blithely pointing out the seasonal tinsel and poinsettias as they attempted to chat up their visitors. The atmosphere remained as frosty inside the White House as it was outdoors; small talk was slow and laughter strained. Conditions were not markedly improved by the President's wife Nancy, who wore a fixed, unconvincing smile as she clutched a handkerchief behind her back for the next hour.

Then, about a third of the way through the presentation ceremony, a noticeable thaw occurred. In the presence of fellow performers Reagan began to relax for the first time in days, and when he did his attitude seemed to put everyone but Nancy at ease. When the President congratulated violinist Yehudi Menuhin for a lifetime of rave reviews—"I know from experience that good notices don't come too easily"—the relief was palpable. Five others also basked in the Chief's increasingly warm praise: singer Ray Charles, the veteran Broadway couple Jessica Tandy and Hume Cronyn, English choreographer Antony Tudor, and actress–comedienne–producer–studio executive Lucille Ball. Each was treated with esteem, but somehow Lucy seemed first among equals. Partly this was because, as the centerpiece of the celebrated situation comedy *I Love Lucy,* she was the most recognizable. Even the formidable Ray Charles, whose records had gone platinum so many times he had lost count, was not so familiar a face.

Partly it was because everyone in the White House audience knew that Lucy's ex-husband and longtime partner, Desi Arnaz, had died only five days before.

And partly it was because her entrance had topped all the others:

> *I'm your Vita-veeda-vigee-vat girl. Are you tired, run down, listless? Do you pop out at parties—are you unpoopular? Well, are you? The answer to ALLLLL your problems is in this li'l ole bottle. Vita-meata-vegemin. (She looks pleased with herself for getting it right) Contains vitamins, meat, metagable, and vinerals. With—(She looks at the bottle) Vitameatavegemin you can spoon your way to health. All you do is take one of these full (She holds up the spoon) Vita-meedy-mega-meenie-moe-a-mis . . . after every meal. (She has a lot of difficulty getting the spoon under the neck of the bottle, keeps pouring so that it doesn't hit the spoon but goes on the table. Finally, she puts the spoon down on the table, takes the bottle with both hands and pours it into*

the spoon. She puts the bottle down, looks at the spoon to see that it's full, beams back at the audience, turns back to the table, picks up the bottle, and drinks out of it. As she puts the bottle down, she notices the spoon again, picks it up, and puts it in her mouth. She forgets to take it out. With spoon in her mouth) It tastes like candy. (She takes the spoon out of her mouth. By now, she is leaning, practically sitting on the table) So why don't you join the thousands of happy, peppy people and get a great big bottle. (She opens her mouth but realizes that she'd better not try it again. Holds up the bottle) This stuff . . .

From the moment the seventy-five-year-old Lucy stepped into the room, she became the embodiment of Jenny Joseph's poem "Warning," "When I am an old woman I shall wear purple / With a red hat which doesn't go." Dressed in deep purple chiffon and matching shoes, her hair dyed a carrot hue, she stirred her colleagues and dazzled the onlookers.

Lucy's merry expression lasted until the President spoke. "Others in life have seen to our material needs," he intoned, "built our roads, constructed our cities, given us our daily bread. But these six are artists, and as such they have performed a different and singular task—to see to the needs of the heart." By the time he addressed Lucy directly, her mascaraed eyes were wet. "It's no secret that Nancy and I are friends of Lucy," he said, "and I think this redheaded bundle may be the finest comedienne ever."

The words were from the heart. Ronald Reagan and Lucille Ball shared many things, including a birth year, 1911. They had struggled in Hollywood at about the same time, grinding through the B movies that were supposed to lead them picture by picture to the upper level—yet, for one reason or another, never did.

I was queen of the B-pluses. I went from one-liners to these sort of mediocre B-plus pictures. I would do anything, though. I was in the only Tracy-Hepburn flop ever made, and I got good reviews. What you were encouraged to do at the studios was to become a flapper girl, a glamour girl or some type. You were that type of girl belonging to that type of picture. It was very limiting, and I was really stuck. . . .

Later on (much later, in Reagan's case), they both received a celebrity beyond anything either could possibly have envisioned. The speaker burbled on. President or not, he insisted, he was no different from the common fan: "Like millions of Americans and people around the world, I still love Lucy." Following the appreciative murmur, he added, "I know Miss Ball would want us to pay tribute to the man who produced *I Love Lucy* and starred in it with her, the late Desi Arnaz."

I kept Desi driving up and down the coastline visiting spots I had seen in my seven years in California, from San Francisco to Tijuana, below the Mexican border. I wanted to share every experience with him, the past included. I even took him to Big Bear Mountain, where we had filmed Having Wonderful Time. *I was in slacks, shirt and bandanna; Desi was in an open-necked shirt, tanned the color of mahogany. We looked like a couple of tourists.*

Desi ordered a ham-and-cheese sandwich at Barney's, the local bar-café, and then disappeared to wash his hands. The waitress looked at me and then at Desi's retreating back. "Hey," she said disapprovingly, glancing from my red curls to Desi's blue-black hair, "is he Indian? Because we're not allowed to serve liquor to Indians."

Nobody could picture us as a couple, even a tourist-hardened waitress. . . .

Lucy took a couple of deep breaths. They were not sufficient to keep her emotions in check. Robert Stack, who had starred in *The Untouchables,* a Desilu production, read a letter from Arnaz, written in his last hours. The signoff elicited little broken cries from the audience: "P.S. 'I Love Lucy' was never just a title." Lucille Ball nodded in private agreement; the tears were flowing more copiously now. She had been married to her second husband, comedian Gary Morton, for six years longer than she had been married to her first. The numbers hardly mattered. Desi had been not only the father of Lucy's two children, but her business partner, her costar, the cocreator of her image, the cofounder of her wealth and reputation, and, *au fond,* the object of her obsessive affection. Hardly a day went by when Lucy failed to acknowledge that without Desi she would have been one more actress who never realized her potential, the star that never was.

The day I filed for the divorce, on the grounds of "extreme mental cruelty," we were filming an hour show with Ernie Kovacs and his wife, Edie Adams. In this episode, Lucy tries to get Ricky on Ernie's TV show. To disguise myself, I wore a chauffeur's uniform with cap and mustache. In the final scene, Desi was supposed to pull me into an embrace, mustache and all, and kiss me.

When the scene arrived and the cameras closed in for that final embrace, we just looked at each other, and then Desi kissed me, and we both cried. It marked the end of so many things. . . .

The years after Desi amounted to epilogue—the solace of an attentive second husband, the consolations of money, the exercise of power as the head of a major studio, but also, inescapably, the sense of having stayed onstage too long, followed by professional disappointments and the downhill process of aging.

After Lucy *ended, I thought, "I'll live a few more years, and then I'll die." I didn't plan to live this long. I didn't want to. I don't know why. I didn't want people waiting around for me to die just because I've got a few bucks. . . .*

During the Desi period came the sense of mutual struggle, then small victories, and then vindication when *I Love Lucy* altered the history of television and turned their lives around. The *Hollywood Reporter* was the first to catch the dream. The review was pasted in the scrapbook and permanently entered in Lucy's memory:

Every once in a great while a new TV show comes along that fulfills, in its own particular niche, every promise of the often harassed new medium. Such a show, it is a genuine pleasure to report, is I Love Lucy, *starring Lucille Ball and Desi Arnaz in a filmed domestic comedy series for Philip Morris, which should bounce to the top of the rating heap in no time at all. If it doesn't, the entire structure of the American entertainment business should be overhauled from top to bottom.*

The outstanding pertinent fact about I Love Lucy *is the emergence, long suspected, of Lucille Ball as America's No. 1 comedienne in her own right. She combines the facial mobility of Red Skelton, the innate pixie quality of Harpo Marx, and the daffily jointless abandon of the Patchwork Girl of Oz, all rolled into one. She is a consummate artist, born for television.*

Half a step behind her comes her husband, Desi Arnaz, the perfect foil for her screwball antics and possessing comic abilities of his own more than sufficient to make this a genuine comedy team rather than the one-woman tour de force it almost becomes. . . .

And before Desi? Before him was a climb so desperate and odd that Lucille Ball often had trouble confronting the past. President Reagan had been much too kind, she realized; people always exaggerated at these award things. It was not true that everybody loved Lucy, not when she dominated American entertainment, not when she was a striver in New York and Hollywood, not when she was a child.

You have to understand. I am from a suburb of Jamestown, New York. Not Jamestown itself, but a suburb, yet. You think Cleveland or Cincinnati is bad, Jamestown is only a place to be from. *To be* from *only. . . .*

Lucy had read enough of the gossip books, the speculative magazine bios, to know that the world was not composed of Lucille Ball fan clubs. The gossip had come back to her for years, so much of it false or twisted out of shape: she had ties with the Mafia, she had shot a little boy back in upstate New York and the family had paid to shut it up, she had slept her way to film roles, she was an ungrateful bitch, a shrew on the set, hell to work for.

I am not funny. My writers were funny. My direction was funny. The situations were funny. But I am not funny. I am not funny. What I am is brave. . . .

A little
world out
of nothing

*F*EW INTIMATIONS of Lucille Ball's character and career can be found on her family tree. Hers is a classic instance of the comic talent that surfaces without genetic antecedent. There have been, of course, many such "sports" in show business, performers who sprang from generations of laborers or small-time entrepreneurs. But most often these comedians and clowns were first-generation Americans, breaking out from the poverty, illiteracy, and prejudice that still afflicted their parents. Moreover, the great majority of them came from the streets of New York City, where demonic energy was the only résumé they needed, and where opportunity lay all around them—from larceny and murder to medicine, law, and entertainment.

Lucille had little in common with the generation that was to beget laughter in vaudeville, in the legitimate theater, and on the sound stages of the 1930s. Compared to them she is a bloodline aristocrat. "My mother, Desirée Hunt," her account proudly states, "was of French-English descent, with a touch of Irish from her father's side that showed in her porcelain-fine English complexion and auburn hair." Lucille's father, Henry Durrell Ball, was descended from landed gentry in England; some of the family came to the New World as early as the seventeenth century. She was delighted to note that there was "some Ball blood in George Washington" since "his mother's maiden name was Mary Ball." If there were any deeper investigations of the Ball genealogy, Lucille did not record them. Actually, George Washington's relationship with his mother was one that grew increasingly unpleasant and embarrassing. Hardly had George left home when Mary began to complain publicly about her son's neglect. Rather than take pride in his early career, she used it as a lever to pry favors from him. During the French and Indian War, for example, he suffered terrible privations in the service of King George III. Mary displayed little interest in his ordeal; her letters demanded more butter and a new house servant. Irritation between parent and child remained until her death in 1789.

Evidently a number of Mary's descendants were working folk and farmers, scattered about the United States, with little in the way of wealth or prospects. For one of them, fate intervened in 1865, when oil was discovered in the appropriately named town of Pithole, Pennsylvania. Clinton Ball, Lucy's great-grandfather, had property in the vicinity, accepted the enormous bid of $750,000, and headed for the progressive, gaslit village of Fredonia, New York. There he built a large house and acquired an additional four hundred acres. Clinton must have found Protestant fundamentalism to his liking; he donated generous sums to local churches, but made certain that anyone who preached there hewed to his literal interpretation of the Bible. Unsurprisingly, he looked upon city life as licentious and went so far as to forbid any of his six children to dance.

Five of them obeyed; the sixth was an adventurer who wanted something more than received wisdom. Jasper Ball—"Jap," as he preferred to be called—married young and became a father soon afterward. He settled the family in Jamestown, New York, and began to invest his savings in the newfangled telephone business. When the hinterlands proved inhospitable to the invention he sought employment out west. The Securities Home Telephone Company of Missoula, Montana, hired him as manager, and for many years he shuttled between work and family, from the towns and villages of Montana to his home in upstate New York. In time Jap's admiring son Henry Durrell Ball

("Had" to family and friends) came to Missoula and signed on as a line-man for the phone company. In 1910 Had returned to Jamestown to visit his mother and sisters, and while he was there someone intro-duced him to the eighteen-year-old Desirée Evelyn Hunt, the daughter of a professional midwife and a man who had worked at a number of trades, including hotel management, mail delivery, and furniture con-struction. (She chose the Frenchified spelling; "Desire" was the name on her birth certificate.) The twenty-four-year-old Had qualified as an attractive older man. Several months later, on September 1, 1910, the two were married at the two-story gabled home of Frederick and Flora Belle Hunt. Some 140 guests witnessed the ceremony, conducted by the Reverend Charles D. Reed, pastor of the Calgary Baptist Church. It was the biggest social event of the season. Contemporary pho-tographs show a pale, conventionally pretty young woman, and a hus-band so lean he appears to be two profiles in search of a face.

Laden with gifts of silver, linen, and furniture, the couple boarded a train and headed toward the sunset. They settled in the little town of Anaconda, Montana, about twenty-five miles from Butte. A couple of months later Desirée became pregnant. She expressed a desire to have the baby back home in Jamestown, where her mother could act as mid-wife. Had consented, and the couple went east in the summer of 1911. On August 6, Lucille Desirée was born.

Once Flora had pronounced her granddaughter fit for travel, the Balls returned to Montana—only to turn around and head back east. Securities Home Telephone had recently acquired the Michigan Tele-phone Company, and the company needed experienced linemen. The little family resettled in Wyandotte, outside Detroit, a town just far enough from the automobile industry to offer quiet tree-lined streets and clean air. Had regarded it as a fine place to raise a family, and pretty soon Desirée was pregnant again. Everything went well: Had was making five dollars a week, a good salary in those days, and the doctor said that Desirée was the ideal age and weight to bear a second child. As for little Lucille, she was an active, healthy youngster, fond of her mother and crazy about roughhousing with her father—she would scream with delight when he tossed her into the air and caught her inches from the floor.

All this was to change in the awful winter of 1915. In January, cases of typhoid fever were reported in the Detroit area. Public health offi-cials warned citizens to boil their water and to stay away from unpasteurized dairy products. Desirée scrupulously followed their instructions. Had went along for a while, but in early January he treated himself to a dish of ice cream. A week later he began to suffer from sleeplessness, then intestinal problems, and finally he developed a fever of 104 degrees accompanied by delirium. Physicians made a grim diagnosis and nailed a sign to the Balls' front door: KEEP OUT — HEALTH AUTHORITIES. Neighbors shut their windows and drew the curtains; there was no vaccine at the time. The family doctor could do little beyond making Had comfortable and preparing Desirée for the end.

Distraught and overburdened, she kept Lucille out of the sickroom and in the fresh air for hours at a time. To ease her mind she tied one end of a rope around the child's waist, the other end to a steel runner on the backyard clothesline. As long as she heard the metal squeal, Desirée knew that her little daughter was running like a trolley from the back of the yard to the front. Whenever the noise stopped for longer than a few minutes she ran outside to see if Lucille had slipped the knot. The three-and-a-half-year-old never did escape, but on at least one occasion she tried. After an ominous silence Desirée found her batting her eyes and negotiating with a milkman: "Mister, help me. I got caught up in this silly clothesline. Can you help me out?"

Had died on February 28, 1915. He was twenty-eight years old. Lucille retained only fleeting memories of that day, all of them traumatic. A picture fell from the wall; a bird flew in the window and became trapped inside the house. From that time forward she suffered from a bird phobia. Even as an adult, she refused to stay in any hotel room that displayed framed pictures of birds or had wallpaper with an avian theme.

Had's widow was twenty-two. She was five months pregnant, with a dependent child, little insurance, and no professional skills. Somehow she summoned the strength to make funeral arrangements in two cities: Wyandotte, where her late husband was embalmed, and Jamestown, where he was to be interred. In order to get a little peace, Desirée enlisted the aid of a sympathetic grocer. Six decades later, Lucille gratefully summoned up images of Mr. Flower: "He let me prance up and down his counter, reciting little pieces my parents had taught me. My favorite was apparently a frog routine where I hopped up and down harrumphing. Then I'd gleefully accept the pennies or candy Mr. Flower's customers would give me—my first professional appearance!" Those gifts came from customers who would rather donate money than pay condolence calls to a quarantined house.

Several days later Desirée and Lucille accompanied Had's body on the long train ride to upstate New York. On the chill, iron-gray morning of March 5, Had was buried at Lake View Cemetery in Jamestown. Lucille looked on blankly, oblivious to the glances in her direction. At the last moment, as Had's casket was lowered into the grave, the loss suddenly hit home. The little girl was led away screaming to her grandparents' house on Buffalo Street in Jamestown. Mother and child had no other refuge.

So an autonomous nuclear family backslid to total dependence, as Desirée returned to the adolescence she had fled, reliant on her parents for food and shelter. Still, Fred and Flora Belle Hunt were kind and undemanding folks; they did everything possible to make their daughter and granddaughter feel wanted and comfortable. The Hunts had lost their own son, Harold, at the age of eighteen, and when Desirée presented them with a grandson on July 17, 1915, they were deeply gratified. When she announced that she would christen him Frederick, after Grandpa Hunt, they were beside themselves. To all appearances, Lucille was once again in an affectionate and secure household.

But she was not satisfied with appearances. "I was largely ignored," she remembered, "and I became very jealous." Lucille had been struck two terrible and inexplicable blows. As she interpreted them, a beloved father had abandoned her without so much as a good-bye. Five months later she had been displaced by a wailing rival who absorbed 100 percent of her mother's love and attention. Confused, anxious about her own mortality, the child became fixated on her grandparents, a pair whose idiosyncrasies she came to cherish. Fred Hunt was an imposing figure, overweight and garrulous, with a wardrobe of three-piece suits that had seen better days. He stoked his omnipresent pipe with Prince Albert tobacco, played popular tunes on the parlor piano, whittled toys for his grandchildren, and palavered incessantly about the sorry condition of the Working Man in America. Hunt's favorite philosopher was Eugene V. Debs, and he was forever booming the virtues of that fighter against economic injustice—a man "baptised in Socialism."

As for Flora Belle, she had been a hotel maid in her youth and she retained both a winsome air and a vivid physical presence; Lucille was to remember her Grandma Flora as "a real pioneer woman." Together, the Hunts encouraged Lucille to learn the piano and to take pleasure in the familiar. These included free visits to the local amusement center. A five-cent streetcar ride brought her to Celoron Park, and admission was free. There Lucille Ball became an upstate Dorothy Gale, "dazzled by the brilliance of the Wonderful City," with Celoron as her Oz. Four-decker picnic boats floated along the twenty miles of Lake Chautauqua; stands offered pink cotton candy on a stick; strollers could gawk at a bearded lady, a strong man, a snake charmer, a fortune-teller. As the wide-eyed children shrieked and giggled, the Phoenix Wheel took them a hundred feet in the air before descending to street level. A ramp let them slide deleriously into the shallows of the lake. John Philip Sousa's men blared away on the bandstand. And a zoological garden allowed glimpses of exotic tigers, as well as the chance to ride Shetland ponies around a little track. Best of all were the nickelodeons, with their joyous two-reelers of Charlie Chaplin and the cliff-hanging serials of Pearl White.

It was as if Lucille had been granted compensation for all the losses of the last year—and a new kind of freedom was still to come. Desirée, brought low by Had's early death, suffered from postpartum depression. Nothing seemed to lighten her burden, and after a few months Fred and Flora Belle determined that the only cure would be a complete change of scene. They bought their daughter a round-trip railroad ticket to California and took over the raising of the children. Two active youngsters were one too many for the aging couple; they entrusted Lucille to her mother's sister, Lola, then operating Jamestown's busiest beauty salon. The move turned out to be one of the happiest periods in Lucille's life. Aunt Lola had just married a Greek immigrant, George Mandicos, and the couple had eyes only for each other. Their charge came and went as she pleased, making faces in the wide glittering mirrors, nourishing a harmless crush on her uncle George, getting pats and compliments from her aunt's customers. Looking back on those halcyon days, Lucille recalled: "Once again I was an only child, with a mother *and* a father, and it was such a happy, relaxed time for me."

She was never again to enjoy that status. Desirée came back restored and balanced. Of all the things she had seen out west, only one incident remained in her now placid mind. She had been riding on the same train as Douglas Fairbanks, and as it drew into Los Angeles the actor jumped from the train, vaulted a low barrier, and leaped into the arms of his wife, Mary Pickford, waiting for him in a baby-blue convertible. It was like a dream, Desirée told her parents; she never expected to see movie stars up close again.

When World War I began, Desirée found work in a local assembly plant. There she caught the attention of the strapping, thirty-one-year-old Ed Peterson, a foreman in the sheet metal department. Ed's large features were a mixture of the ungainly and the attractive, and he seemed surprisingly intelligent and well read. Not many eligible men lived in Jamestown; Desirée overlooked the foreman's reputation for drinking to excess. Their courtship was brief; the pair announced wedding plans in the summer, and got married on September 17, 1918.

Lucille fancied that Ed would simply slide into her father's place and make the family whole again. Her dreams were dashed when she sidled over to the groom on his wedding day.

Taking his hand tightly, the seven-year-old inquired in her most flirtatious tone, "Are you our new daddy?"

Peterson frowned down and pulled loose from her grip. "Call me Ed," he instructed.

*L*ucille and little Freddy scarcely got to know Ed Peterson before he and Desirée took off for Detroit in search of well-paying jobs. Once again Lucille was farmed out. Ed thought it best if the outspoken little girl got some lessons in deportment, so this time she was sent to the home of *his* parents. There could have been no greater contrast than the indulgent Mandicoses and the severe and elderly Petersons. Grandpa Peterson was to remain a shadowy character, but Grandma let it be known early on that she would brook no backtalk or misbehavior. Sophia Peterson was something of a pioneer woman herself. The Swedish immigrant believed in the literal truth of the Bible, with emphasis on the seven deadly sins as off-ramps to Purgatory. To keep her granddaughter busy she ordered her to hand-roll linen toweling—a difficult assignment for small hands—and to wash the dinner dishes over and over again until Sophia was satisfied that they were spotless. As if these character-building exercises were not sufficient, Lucille was also forbidden any traces of vanity. Sophia spoke derisively about her granddaughter's oversize feet, ungainly posture, squeaky voice,

maloccluded teeth. The house had but one mirror, in the bathroom.
When Lucille was caught examining her face in it she was sent to bed
early. It was summer, and in her autobiography she bitterly recollected
the sounds of neighborhood children playing outdoors while she tossed
restlessly. Yet these restrictions failed to suppress the girl's spirit, reason enough for Grandma Peterson to regard her grandchild as "nervous," "sassy," "bold," and "silly," words she repeated when she
complained about Lucille to the Hunts.

Like many children similarly traumatized and oppressed, Lucille
sought refuge in fantasy. When Grandma Peterson was off tending her
garden, her step-granddaughter played with clothespin dolls, assigning
them personalities and speaking to them like intimates. She invented
several playmates to console her. Sassafrassa was a smooth amalgam of
the silent film actresses Pearl White and Pola Negri. Madeline was a
cowgirl inspired by the heroine of Zane Grey's pulp western *The Light
of Western Stars*. At the library Lucille read what she could find about
the state of Montana, a place her mother always spoke of with powerful nostalgia. Lucille tried to imagine what life might have been like
had the family stayed in the West. Perhaps her father would not have
gotten sick and died. Perhaps she could have become a cowgirl. To her
fanciful intimates she confided her miseries and her aspirations—
among them the wish to visit the far-off Wonderland she had heard
Fred Hunt mention in glowing terms, New York City.

Lucille was not friendless at school; still, the notion that she was
poorer than her classmates kept her withdrawn and self-conscious.
More than once she left the room for a drink of water and kept on
going toward what she thought was Manhattan until someone spotted
the child and brought her back. There was a touch of Cinderella in all
this, except that there was no handsome prince to ride up and rescue
the waif. All the ingredients for misery were now in place: self-doubt,
obsessive-compulsive behavior, insecurity—the sort of psychological
afflictions that attend a deprived childhood. As we will see, one way or
another she carried these difficulties intact, from her early years into
old age. Yet in her nervous accommodations with the past she came to
regard this period as the Making of Lucille Ball. Looking around at the
celebrities of business, entertainment, and politics, she concluded that
society's followers were the ones with happy beginnings. Its leaders
were those who had endured early emotional and physical misfortune.

The worst of those hardships ended in 1919, when Desirée returned with her second husband to reclaim the children. Lucille's ordeal had lasted little more than a year; even so, it was to transfigure the rest of her life. (For children it is not the length of the pain and discomfiture that matters, but the intensity. A century before, the respectable clerk John Dickens was sent to debtors' prison and his young son forced to work long hours in a blacking factory. Charles's stay was only a few months, but one way or another the humiliating experience was to echo in every novel.) Lucille took to calling Grandpa Fred Hunt "Daddy," just as her mother did, trying always to keep him within sight, cheering his every idea. Her favorite was the one about moving the entire family under one roof. In Grandpa Fred's opinion, that roof had to be over a much larger dwelling, and to everyone's surprise he made good on his notion early in 1920. On February 1, he sold the old house and bought a two-story dwelling on Eighth Street in Celoron, moving everyone closer to the enchanted amusement park. The assets of the new house included lilac bushes and a coop full of chickens in the backyard. Inside were plenty of mirrors, large bedrooms, and the luxury of two toilets, one in a half-bathroom downstairs, one in the full bathroom upstairs.

Lucille was to remember the Celoron household as a version of the George S. Kaufman and Moss Hart play *You Can't Take It With You*. That comedy concerned a family as freewheeling and odd as her own—except that hers had no curtain that could descend when things got out of hand. In addition to the elder Hunts, there were Ed and Desirée Peterson (she was now called DeDe, a nickname Lucille and Freddy used in addressing her), plus Aunt Lola Mandicos, who had just separated from her husband, and Lola's three-year-old daughter, Cleo. To stay afloat Grandpa Fred ran a lathe in a furniture factory, Ed labored in whatever local plant would have him, Desirée took a job selling hats at an upscale dress shop in Jamestown, and Lola ran her beauty parlor in the house. The children were given specific assignments: Cleo dusted, Freddy made beds, and Lucille led the other two in the dishwashing and table-setting chores. That left Grandma Flora, whose strange mood swings bewildered the children. Where once she had been smiling and indulgent, she was now edgy and critical. A piano sat in the parlor, and Desirée, convinced that Lucille possessed musical talent, had hired a piano teacher. In the beginning, Flora loved to hear her granddaughter practice the scales and attempt new pieces. Now, mysteriously, the sounds seemed to grate on her nerves. Lucille was finally told the truth: Flora was very ill. She had been diagnosed with uterine cancer. The girl watched her grandmother grow weaker and smaller until, toward the end, the patient was confined to a big mahogany bed placed in the front parlor. When Flora died, the adults thought it better to keep the children away from what would be another traumatic funeral. Lucille disobeyed the order to stay at home. Taking Cleo and Fred by the hand, she led them down the streets of the little town until she spotted a procession to the graveyard. The three children followed at a distance, their silence broken only by the older girl's sobs.

Grandma Flora's death signaled the end of supervision. No adult remained in the house during the day, and at the age of eleven Lucille found herself in charge. School took up the weekday mornings and early afternoons. After that, freedom reigned until about 6 p.m., when the clang of a streetcar bell indicated the approach of Desirée. This was the moment for Freddy to set the table while Lucille and Cleo frantically made all the beds. DeDe was undeceived by this last-minute activity: a thousand dust motes danced in the air. Upon seeing them she generally made a wry remark or two, and these let the children know that they had not fooled her—but that they would not be punished for the tardy cleanup.

Between the end of the school day and DeDe's arrival, the children liked to fill the hours by playacting, with Lucille as the leader. Their dramas and comedies started out as miniature versions of the two-reelers she had seen at Celoron Park. Later they reflected the influence of monologists who had enchanted her at a local theater.

As much as she found Ed Peterson unlikable and remote, Lucille conceded that it was he who introduced her to Chautauqua. This was an institution that began in 1874 in upstate New York as a summer retreat for Sunday-school teachers, then grew into a series of year-round venues for lecturers, musicians, and actors. Lucille liked to reminisce about the winter evening "a monologist named Julian Eltinge was appearing. A female impersonator, yet. Ed insisted I go." Eltinge used to get into fistfights—most of them staged—to scotch any rumor of effeminacy, and though he used rouge, lipstick, and yards of female costumery, he kept his material resolutely clean and simple. Lucille watched as a solitary figure amused audiences with nothing more than a bare lightbulb, a table, a glass of water, and his extraordinary skills at mimicry. She was equally impressed by another soloist, Julius Tannen, who went on to major character roles in Preston Sturges films. Tannen affected the air of a peering, self-involved businessman complete with pince-nez and a pompous manner. A vaudeville historian remembered his "fine command of English" and the way he liked "to switch in the middle of his monologue to 'dese, dose and dems'—maybe just show he was the same kind of a guy that was sitting up in the gallery." No one could squelch hecklers with a lighter touch. Razzed by one, he replied simply: "Save your breath, you may want it to clean your glasses later." Tannen favored word pictures; he said that using a paper cup reminded him of drinking out of a letter, and he excused himself for being late by saying he had squeezed out too much toothpaste and couldn't get it all back in the tube. To Lucille he was pure enchantment: "Just this voice, and this magnificent man enthralling you with his stories, his intonations, which I never, never forgot. *He* changed my *life*. I knew it was a very serious, wonderful thing to be able to make people laugh and/or cry, to be able to play on their emotions."

Ed Peterson did more than take Lucille to events on the Chautauqua circuit. He was a Shriner, and when his organization needed female entertainers for the chorus line of their next show, he encouraged his twelve-year-old stepdaughter to audition. Her enthusiasm outran her ungainliness; they awarded her the part. Onstage she understood what Tannen and Eltinge felt: the energy of performance and the assurance of applause. This could be more than a kick, Lucille decided. This could be a vocation.

Empowered by her little triumph, Lucille tried out for a musical produced by the Jamestown Masonic club; she won a role in that as well. During rehearsals, a partner threw her across the stage so vigorously that she dislocated a shoulder. Rather than discourage her, the accident only provided a goad. Next time out she appeared in a straight play, and a local critic compared her to Jeanne Eagles. The family assured Lucille that the notice was flattering; she had never heard of the silent-film star. The following year, with DeDe's approval, she took a bus to New York and went to an open call for the chorus line of an upcoming Shubert musical, *Stepping Stones*. Her bright blue eyes and long legs attracted the attention of the choreographer, and Lucille thought that if this was all it took to crack Broadway, conquering show business was going to be a snap. Before rehearsals began it was discovered that the dancer was thirteen years old. She was unceremoniously sent back to Celoron. More than three decades would pass before

Lucille Ball took a bow on Broadway. Nevertheless, the appetite for recognition had been awakened. It would take few naps from now on.

The mixture of Hunts and Petersons was a lot merrier from the outside than within. The effects of Prohibition had reached upstate New York. With the closing of the public bars, many of the hotels around Lake Chautauqua lost their clientele and shut their doors for the last time. Tourism began to dry up on the shorefront and in the towns. Along with many of his neighbors, Ed hung around the local speakeasy, and he returned drunk on too many evenings. DeDe kept her voice down when she bawled him out; Ed was not so discreet, and Lucille overheard their arguments. She was distressed but not surprised to see her mother come home early on certain afternoons, laid low by the pains of a migraine headache. DeDe would draw the shades and remain bedridden, unable to move or talk until the pain had lifted. Fred Hunt no longer seemed his cheerful and anecdotal self; since the death of Flora he had spent hours at the Crescent Tool Company griping about conditions and urging workers to demand a bigger piece of the pie. DeDe heard about the agitation and disapproved. Stirring up trouble might well be a firing offense, and the loss of his salary would mean a backslide to penury.

Lucille watched all this and said nothing. But she began to spend more time away from the house, performing stunts and taking dares from her new friends in high school, roller-skating across the freshly varnished school gymnasium floor, sitting on the front radiator of a classmate's jalopy as it roared through the streets of Celoron, playing hooky whenever she was in a vagabond mood. She was a difficult student, bright but distracted. She fought with other girls—and sometimes with boys—and once got so angry with a teacher she threw a typewriter at her.

But Lucille had absorbed too much moral training to go completely wild. She yearned for some direction in her life, and when it was not forthcoming at home or school, she imposed it on herself. One of her cronies, Pauline Lopus, was to remain in Jamestown for most of her life. More in awe than envy, she liked to look back to the days of 1925 when Lucille called her Sassafrassa for some reason, when her new friend seemed to be "the first girl in town who dared to talk aloud about her dreams—about one day being able to have nice cars, nice clothes, a nice home; about one day doing something and being somebody *special*."

Along with Pauline and another pal, Violet Robbins, Lucille founded a musical group called the Gloom Chasers Union. Pauline conducted, Violet played the piano, and Lucille provided the rhythm on a set of borrowed drums. It was not a success. Egged on by their leader, the girls then recruited two more members and founded an acting company. Their most memorable production was a version of *Charley's Aunt,* adapted and directed by Lucille. She not only gave the story another spin by starring as a man who impersonates a woman, she dragged furniture from her house to use as scenery, sold the homemade tickets for twenty-five cents apiece, put makeup on the cast, and persuaded the school principal, Mr. Drake, to let them have the gym for the evening. The prompter was DeDe, who got so caught up in the plot and gags that she kept laughing, applauding, and losing her place in the script.

Although tourism was off that summer, Celoron Park still needed extra help to get through July and August. Lucille talked her way into a job as short-order cook. "Look out! Look out!" went her spiel. "Don't step there!" When the startled passerby stopped, one foot in the air as he stared worriedly at the ground, Lucille closed the sale: "Step over *here* and get yourself a delicious hamburger!" Off-hours were spent experimenting with makeup and fashion. Passing a shop window one day, she stopped to admire a leather hat in black and white. Over dinner she bargained with DeDe: the hat for hours and hours of extra work around the house. Her mother refused at first, then gave in to the entreaties. The delighted teenager wore the hat everywhere, including the kitchen as she washed and dried the dishes.

DeDe's response was not so lenient after Lucille attended her first dance at the Celoron Pier Ballroom. For the occasion DeDe made a taffeta dress and trimmed the hem with real fur, prompting envious sighs when Lucille's classmates first clapped eyes on it. At the end of the dance, a drably dressed classmate went out of her way to admire the outfit. The next day Lucille presented it to her. DeDe remonstrated when she learned about the gift. Her daughter's explanation—the donee came from a poor family and had never owned a decent dress before—left her unmoved. Weeks went by before DeDe forgave Lucille.

The teenage Lucille was aware that women dressed to please the opposite sex, but she knew next to nothing about that sex. Because of her daughter's innocence, DeDe allowed her only a few tentative experiments with lipstick and makeup. The colors widened Lucille's mouth and accentuated her bright blue eyes so effectively that some laws had to be laid down. Lucille was strictly forbidden, for example, ever to go canoeing with any young male except her brother. Predictably, she could hardly wait to paddle around the shallows with a local boy. When he tried some amateurish overtures, however, she managed to tip the canoe, tossing them both overboard. "I got wet," she recorded proudly, "but I was still virtuous!"

That state was not to last much longer. In time she bobbed her brown hair and shortened her skirts, thereby advertising an interest not only in fashion but in young men. Lucille was tall, willowy, physically mature, and emotionally undeveloped. "Maybe I was still searching for a father," she was to speculate. There was no maybe about it. When the DeVita sisters introduced Lucille to their big brother Johnny at Celoron Park, she was instantly beguiled. A bit shorter than her five foot seven, much heavier than her weight of just under one hundred pounds, Johnny wore an unflattering moustache, and his hairline was already beginning to recede. But he had acquired a reputation as a local hood, someone who gambled, trafficked booze, and carried a gun. As if these enticements were not enough, he owned his own car and had a closetful of expensively tailored suits. Best of all, he was an adult. Johnny DeVita's driver's license offered proof: he had recently passed his twenty-first birthday. Lucille was fourteen.

CHAPTER
TWO

"This girl's fulla hell"

𝒥OHNNY'S SWAGGER did not derive from movies or pulp fiction. He was the son of Louis DeVita, a nouveau riche who sold insurance and produce to Italian immigrants. On the side, it was rumored, he was involved with prohibited booze and illegal gambling. As Louis's chauffeur and heir apparent Johnny had the use of several automobiles, not to mention a steady income and a status enjoyed by few men his age. He and his new romance became the object of lurid high school gossip, a situation that Lucille found immensely pleasing: once again she was on center stage. The adult response was not so pleasurable, particularly when it issued from DeDe. Lucille protested that her boyfriend was from an honest and caring family; she reminded her mother of all the times Louis had given her dishes of pasta and bags of vegetables to bring home. As for Johnny himself, she went on, her young man was not an irresponsible playboy; he was going to medical school in a year or two. DeDe bought none of this but did nothing, on the assumption that the affair would burn itself out in a few weeks. When the weeks turned into months she took Johnny aside and asked him to stay away from her daughter. He refused to do it. They were in love. What right had she to interfere?

After a year of soul-searching, and some painful ransacking of her bank account, DeDe saw a way out. Lucille liked to talk about the vaudeville acts Johnny took her to see at the local houses, Shea's and the Palace. When she spoke of those evenings her voice thrummed and her eyes took on a glitter that Johnny himself could not evoke. Clearly she yearned to be in a real spotlight. And who could tell? With Lucille's background in amateur theatrics, perhaps she had a chance to be a chorine or a soubrette. Everyone said she had talent—even Mr. Drake had proclaimed as much, on the night of *Charley's Aunt*. Still, the fifteen-year-old needed professional instruction, and such lessons were not available in upstate New York. For those, Lucille would have to go to Manhattan, geographically six hundred miles and emotionally light-years away from the small-town life in Chautauqua County.

At the time, the Robert Minton–John Murray Anderson School of Drama on East Fifty-eighth Street in Manhattan was the most prominent institution of its kind, and one of the most demanding, financially as well as psychologically; in 1926 the tuition was $180 per five-month term for a playwriting course, $270 for scenic and costume design, $350 for drama lessons, $390 for musical comedy, and $500 for motion picture acting, a fee that included a screen test. The faculty and advisers included such luminaries as choreographer Martha Graham, composer Jerome Kern, actor Otis Skinner, writers Christopher Morley and Don Marquis—as well as the founders themselves. Anderson was a longtime producer of the hugely successful *Greenwich Village Follies,* and Minton had directed a number of breakthrough symbolic pieces, including the afterlife drama *Outward Bound* and the Russian allegory *He Who Gets Slapped*.

DeDe cobbled together enough money for the first semester and persuaded some friends in Manhattan to board her daughter. This seemed too rare an opportunity to pass up. Lucille was to characterize herself at that time as "struck by the lightning of show business"—a flash that Johnny could not hope to outshine. He was philosophical about it; he drove his young inamorata to the station in Buffalo and saw her off on the train to New York. She carried a small valise full of clothing deemed proper for the city, $50 sewn into her underwear, and a passage she had copied from a Julius Tannen routine. The monologist had inspired her in upstate New York, and now he brought her luck in Manhattan. The other girls auditioned with stilted deliveries of Shakespearean verse. With her vaudeville turn, the fifteen-year-old from Jamestown gave the impression of originality and freshness. Alas, from that moment everything went downhill.

"Ridicule," Lucille was to recall acrimoniously, "seemed to be part of the curriculum." In an elocution class, Minton mocked his student for what he called her "midwestern" pronunciations of "wawter" and "hawrses." She retreated into silence. Lucille hoped for a better time in dancing class, where she could let her legs do the talking. The pupil was promptly informed that she had "two left feet." In another period the school might have carried her for a second term, until she acquired some polish and timing. But it was Lucille's misfortune to be there at the same moment another young actress was making her mark. Bette Davis arrived as a powerhouse with more gifts than the rest of the pupils combined. Anderson questioned Lucille's instructors, received negative reports from all of them, and sent a letter to DeDe informing her that she was only wasting her money. Little comfort came from the knowledge that her daughter was not alone: of an entering class of seventy, only twelve survived the first term. Lucille never forgave her teachers. "All I learned in drama school," she claimed later, "was how to be frightened."

Back in Jamestown Lucille tried to put a good face on her failure by dismissing the New York City experience as a waste of time, resuming the romance with Johnny, and throwing herself back into high school activities with a will. She became a football cheerleader, played center on the girls' basketball team, ice-skated in the winter, and rode horseback in the spring. Most of her classmates were unaware of her humiliation in drama school; they knew only that Lucille had dared to skip town on her own. Years afterward, when Lucille had become a global celebrity, she was topic A for her former high school classmates. They vied with each other for the clearest memory of the young, hyperkinetic adolescent who seemed in perpetual motion, pounding downstairs two at a time, flashing elegant legs as she whirled in her pleated skirt. At sixteen Lucille was back in good spirits, comely, and popular. By the time the school year ended she was having too good a time to obsess about cracking show business. The summer of 1927 looked to be the best of them all.

In July 1927, Freddy Ball would turn twelve, and Grandpa Hunt thought the Glorious Fourth might be a perfect moment to salute the season, the nation, and the boy. The day before the national holiday he presented the boy with a long, thin, mysterious package. Freddy impatiently peeled off the brown wrapping paper and gave out whoops of delight. Grandpa let him carry on; not every lad got a .22 caliber rifle on his birthday. Yet when Freddy headed outdoors to shoot some crows, he was forbidden to use the firearm. "Tomorrow," Grandpa promised, "I'll show you how."

According to Lucille, July 4 dawned bright and hot, with the aroma of lilacs and clover wafting over the backyard. Rehired as a short-order cook at Celoron Park, Lucille was about to go off to work, but she lingered to watch Freddy's shooting lesson. Before Grandpa Fred set up a tin can in the backyard he gave a brief lecture about guns and safety, emphasizing that behind the target were open fields with no houses or people. "Besides me," Lucille was to write about this occasion, "there were Cleo and Johanna, a girl Freddy's age who was visiting someone in the neighborhood." The company also included an unexpected visitor. "There was an eight-year-old boy who lived at the corner whose name was Warner Erickson. Every once in a while you would hear his mother shriek, 'War-ner! Get home!' and Warner would streak for his yard since his mother spanked him for the slightest infraction. This Fourth of July weekend he had wandered into our yard and was peeking around the corner of our house watching the target practice." At first no one noticed the boy; then Grandpa Hunt spotted Warner and ordered him to sit down and stay out of the way. From her back stoop, a safe distance away, Pauline Lopus watched the action unfold. Freddy took a number of shots at the tin can; then it was Johanna's turn. She picked up the .22 and held it to her shoulder, one eye closed. At that very instant came the strident voice of Mrs. Erickson: "War-*ner*, get home this minute!" The boy rose and bolted in the direction of his home, crossing in front of the rifle just as Johanna pulled the trigger. The pressure of her finger was to change everything that Lucille knew and cherished. She watched in silent horror as Warner fell spread-eagled into a lilac bush.

"I'm shot! I'm shot!" he screamed.

Grandpa Hunt refused to believe what he had just witnessed. "No you're not," he insisted. "Get up."

Then, Lucille recalled, "we saw the spreading red stain on Warner's shirt, right in the middle of his back. Cleo screamed, and I took her into my arms. The slam of a screen door told me that Pauline was running to tell her mother." Grandpa Hunt lifted Warner and, accompanied by Lucille and Freddy and Cleo, carried him the hundred yards to his house as the boy murmured, "Mama, I am dying." Before they could arrive, Warner's mother burst out of the house shouting, "They've shot my son! They've shot my son!"

They implied the entire group, but within an hour everyone knew that a child had done the shooting and that an adult had been responsible for the tragedy. On July 5, the Jamestown *Post-Journal* told the story: "Warner Erickson, eight years old, of Celoron, is still in critical condition at Jamestown General Hospital as a result of being shot in the back. The Erickson lad stepped out in the range as Johanna Ottinger, a young girl, fired at about the same time, the bullet entering the boy's back and passing through his lungs, lodging in the chest. Mr. Hunt, grandfather of the Ball children, was watching the target practice." In fact, the wound was even worse than originally reported. The slug had severed Warner's spinal cord, paralyzing him below the waist.

About a fortnight later the invalid returned, permanently bound to a wheelchair. Almost every day Mrs. Erickson wheeled her son up and down the block, moving very slowly as she passed the Hunt house. The children were told to ignore her but Cleo kept peeking out and crying. Mrs. Erickson's gesture was only the beginning. A lawsuit got under way, accusing Fred Hunt of Eighth Street, Celoron, New York, of negligence in the wounding and paralysis of the eight-year-old victim. The plaintiffs' lawyers asked for $5,000 plus court costs and insisted that the sum was, if anything, too low to cover Warner's medical expenses. (In this they were correct; the boy lived for six more years and needed care for the rest of his short life.) In any case, the sum represented more than Fred Hunt's savings. He declared bankruptcy. The only asset left was the house, and he deeded that to his daughters. The plaintiffs sued once more, claiming that Hunt's maneuver was "fraudulent, designed to delay and defraud his creditors." Again the court agreed. The sheriff foreclosed on the house. Over the course of a year Fred Hunt lost everything. He was sixty-two, and, as Lucille observed, with the two court judgments "the heart went out of him." Without a cent, bereft of a job and a place to call his own, he became totally dependent on DeDe. Distant relatives allowed him to board at their upstate farm, where he subsisted on a diet of their main crop: strawberries. This meant strawberries for breakfast, lunch, and supper.

Lucille, Freddy, DeDe, and Ed moved into a bleak ground-floor apartment on East Fifth Street in Jamestown, and Lucille was transferred to Jamestown High School. There she was an unhappy stranger, outside of the cliques and clubs that had enlivened her days in Celoron. Lola abandoned any plans to reopen her beauty parlor and enrolled in a nursing program far from Jamestown. Cleo went to live with her father, George Mandicos. The family would never be whole again.

*A*fter the "the Breakup," as DeDe bitterly called it, long-dormant urges reawakened in Lucille. Upstate again came to represent mediocrity, and Broadway the main chance. No matter how devoted she was to Johnny, or how sorry she felt for Fred Hunt, she had to test herself in New York City, to prove John Murray Anderson wrong. To that end she would often leave school for a week or more without bothering to get permission from any authority other than DeDe. On the bus she would practice her locution and work out a plan of attack. Once in Manhattan she would head to a cheap rooming house on Columbus Circle, buy a copy of *Variety*, read the notices for open calls, and go to the auditions. Nineteen twenty-eight was not a bad time to be looking in the musical theater. In those flush times audiences paid top prices to see the *Ziegfeld Follies*, Earl Carroll's *Vanities*, and whatever musicals the Shuberts were presenting in their theaters. All of these shows employed chorus lines made up of girls in feathers and furs. The trouble was, producers wanted dancers with experience, and Lucille was as green as the lawns of Jamestown.

After a few weeks of total frustration, she presented them with an audacious new persona. Instead of encountering Lucille Ball of upstate New York, they saw a fresh-faced newcomer, "Diane Belmont" of Butte, Montana. (The surname was taken from a racetrack just outside New York City, and the locale was a bow to the place where Had and Desirée had once been young and happy.) To get her story straight, Lucille had written to the Montana chamber of commerce asking for literature. Poring over the booklets and brochures, she committed statistics to memory, in case producers inquired about her background. They rarely did, and once in a great while Miss Belmont from Butte actually landed in the third company of a revue.

The assignment never lasted. For one thing, Lucille met unexpected hostility from members of the chorus line. The Shubert girls, for example, turned out to be an insular, backbiting group that closed ranks against outsiders. For another, the seventeen-year-old lacked basic technique. The producer of the revue *Stepping Stones* kept her on for five weeks—a new record for Lucille. She was preparing to write home with the good news when late one night her benefactor told the cast: "We're going to add some ballet, girls. Anybody who can't do toe work is out of the show." He made a point of addressing Lucille privately: "You're a nice kid but you just don't have it. Why don't you go home to Montana and raise a big family?"

Out of luck and money, Lucille took any job she could find. (For a week she jerked sodas at a midtown fountain, only to be fired when her mind wandered and she forgot to put the banana in a banana split.) She began to patrol short-order joints, seeking a "one-doughnut man"—an individual who sat at a counter, ordered doughnuts and coffee, downed the cup, and left a nickel tip after eating only one doughnut. "I'd do a fast slide onto his stool," she said, "yell for a cup of coffee, pay for it with his nickel, and eat the other doughnut." Her finances touched bottom the day she reached into her purse and found four cents, one short of the subway fare. "So I panhandled for a penny. One well-dressed older man stopped to listen, then offered me a ten-dollar bill. 'Listen, mister,' I told him with a withering look, 'all I want is *one* penny.' " Thoughts of suicide entered her head. "I thought, 'I'll get killed faster in Central Park because cars go faster there. But I want to get hit by a big car—with a handsome man in it.' Then I had a flash of sanity. I said to myself, 'If I'm thinking this way, maybe I don't want to die.' So I regrouped my forces."

The Sunday papers were full of want ads. Lucille chose one seeking attractive young women to model overcoats. If I'm good-looking enough to be a chorus girl, she reasoned, maybe I can at least be a clotheshorse. The stores and boutiques liked what they saw, and thus she began a freelance career. It was slow at first, but the other young models were a refreshing change from the Broadway felines. They told her which stores were hiring, arranged blind dates, and taught her a few tricks to use at restaurants. One evening, as the waiter moved away from the table, she watched a fellow mannequin put a linen table napkin into her handbag, followed by several buttered rolls, celery and olives, a large slice of roast beef, and a French pastry. Lucille followed suit. These cadged meals did not provide enough to get by, however, and she did some posing for photographers. These pictures she later came to regret: a topless shot was to remain in circulation for the next sixty years.

Then, late in 1928, Lucille's luck changed. At about the same time she started using her real name again, a cameraman passed the word that coat models were needed at Hattie Carnegie's. Lucille dropped by the East Forty-ninth Street salon. The proprietress looked her over and noticed a fleeting resemblance between the newcomer's willowy figure and that of Constance Bennett, second wife of the Marquis de la Falaise (his first was Gloria Swanson). The blonde celebrity had yet to make her mark as a light comedienne, but she was already famous as an international party girl and trend-setter. Lucille was ordered to drastically lighten her own brunette hair. She obediently showed up the next day as a peroxide blonde; no one ever said no to Hattie Carnegie.

This was the first truly powerful woman Lucille had ever met. Born Henriette Kannengiser in Vienna, Hattie arrived in the United States in 1886 at the age of six. In 1904 she quit the Lower East Side ghetto and started working in overdrive, first as a messenger at Macy's, and five years later as the owner and operator of a stylish Greenwich Village boutique. By this time she had taken the name of another immigrant who was not afraid to follow his dream: Andrew Carnegie. Her well-tailored merchandise attracted the attention of rich window-shoppers, including Mrs. Randolph Hearst. The publisher's wife passed the word to friends, and by 1923 Hattie Carnegie was prosperous enough to move her salon to a town house, where she catered to duchesses, society folk, and film celebrities.

"Hattie," Lucille gratefully noted, "taught me how to slouch properly in a $1,000 hand-sewn sequin dress and how to wear a $40,000 sable coat as casually as rabbit." A *New Yorker* profile described Miss Carnegie as a small, fashionably haggard boss-lady with hair rather more reddish-gold than her age would suggest, and possessing "the temper of a termagant." Her youngest model readily endorsed that opinion. Soon after signing on, she found herself covered with bruises where Hattie had kicked her in the shins or pinched her in the ribs— reminders that a Carnegie model must watch her posture at all times. These souvenirs were invisible to customers; Lucille was always swathed in long-sleeved, sweeping gowns. Typically, she made twenty to thirty costume changes a day, hustling into the back room, kicking off whatever shoes went with the ensembles she was wearing, and cramming her feet into another pair to match the next outfit. By night-fall she was footsore and shopworn. She was also considerably richer: her salary was $35 a week, a very decent wage in 1929.

She also got to go to significant places and meet important people. In addition to Constance Bennett and her sister Joan, Lucille showed Carnegie styles to Joan Crawford, Gloria Swanson, and the Woolworth heiress Barbara Hutton; paraded before debutantes at the Plaza and Pierre Hotel fashion shows; and went out to horse shows on Long Island to model the latest Carnegie garments. It was at one of those affairs that she saw the Gish sisters, Lillian and Dorothy, sitting in a box with their dates. Presently Lillian went off with both gentlemen, leaving Dorothy to amuse herself. She did exactly that, tearing tiny bits off her bright red program. When the trio returned, they saw that Dorothy had stuck the particles to her face like measles spots. All four dissolved in laughter, and Lucille made a mental note to try the Gish trick sometime.

Not every outing was a triumph or a learning experience. Once, Lucille wore a disastrously tight Paris import to an outdoor show on Long Island. The dress was made of organza with a hand-painted fish-scale design. A sudden squall ruined the afternoon, and rain made the scales slip from the textile and onto Lucille's skin. She spent the rest of the day trying not to look like a drowned mermaid. And then there was the persistent clannishness of the other models—an echo of that other closed society, the chorines of Broadway. The Carnegie mannequins deliberately froze Lucille out, speaking an unintelligible jargon to one another and discomfiting the new employee.

She dated from time to time, but none of the young men seemed as exciting or, in a curious way, as comfortable as Johnny, and none of the restaurant meals seemed as restorative as the ones DeDe prepared. Homesickness kept eating away at her, and early in 1929 she said a reluctant good-bye to Hattie, put her modeling career on hold, and returned to the compensations of home and family. Almost overnight Lucille went from the high glamour of Manhattan to the backwater milieu of upstate New York, from imitating Constance Bennett to aping the styles of the other girls in Jamestown High School. The brown roots of her hair grew longer. She resumed the pleated skirts and inane chatter of adolescence. It had all come to nothing.

Lucille made only one good friend in high school, Marion Strong, who envied her air of self-reliance. Many years later Marion remembered the months when she and Lucille were inseparable, attending double features, looking up at the screen with wide eyes, then fantasizing endlessly about life's possibilities at the local teen hangout. Many times the search was for gainful employment. Even before the Depression hit with full force, the Ball and Hunt families barely got by. Lucille never asked for money; she just went out and took whatever job was available for as long as it lasted. She sold cosmetics, concocted malteds at the Walgreens soda fountain, ran an elevator at Lerner's department store. Together she and Marion adopted a terrier puppy, named it Whoopee after a new film starring an ex-vaudevillian, Eddie Cantor, and presented it to Mrs. Peterson, the grandmother Lucille wasn't afraid of anymore.

The two girls watched firemen battle the blaze that took down the old Celoron Pier Ballroom, and subsequently went to the Jamestown Players Club, where a director was auditioning candidates for the featured role of Aggie Lynch in Bayard Veiller's melodrama *Within the Law*. The play about a wronged woman's revenge had already been given the silent-movie treatment, most recently in 1923 with Norma Talmadge in the starring role. It was now in the repertory of theater groups throughout the country. A well-connected attorney's wife had nailed down the Talmadge part and sought a supporting cast of at least minimal professionalism. She inquired into the background of this brash young brunette, and when she learned that Lucille had washed out of drama school—a school in Manhattan, however—she felt safe enough to secure her the part of a tough-talking, gold-hearted thief. Miss Ball might be just good enough to remember her lines, but she would offer no threat to the female lead.

After a one-shot performance at the Nordic Temple in Jamestown, the production moved on to the Chautauqua Institution's Norton Auditorium. Lucille had done well enough in her debut, but this time she ran off with the show, ringing every laugh out of lines like "I only said a few words in passin' to my brother Jim. And he ain't no common pickpocket. Hully Gee! He's the best dip in the business!" The *Jamestown Morning Post* praised Lucille's comic relief, "so necessary in the play of the intensity of *Within the Law*." And the *Chautauqua Daily* was rhapsodic: Miss Ball, said the critic, "lived the part of the underworld girl with as much realism as if it were her regular existence. It was her sparkling action and lines that brought continued applause from her audience." At the finale of *Within the Law,* continued the review, she "played with even more enthusiasm than before and put her part across to the audience in the best manner of the evening. In a role that required action, and a good deal of it, she exhibited remarkable maturity and poise."

The coltish performer of the past had vanished. "It was funny," Lucille later wrote, "to think how awkward and tongue-tied I had been in drama school; here in my beloved Jamestown I didn't have a shred of self-consciousness." She had less than two months to enjoy her euphoria. In August 1930, Aunt Lola died after having been kicked in the stomach by a mentally disturbed patient in the hospital where she was working. The little family was reduced yet again. DeDe and her second husband had not been getting along, and Lola's death seemed to push their marriage over the edge. DeDe arranged to get a job at a department store in Washington, D.C.; Ed remained in Jamestown. Lucille was left entirely on her own, melancholy about her aunt and unsure of her future.

One thing was certain: Lucille's romance with Johnny was just about over. She had finally begun, after four years, to see him for what he was, a provincial charmer and a thug in the making. A month after Lola's death Johnny was arrested for transporting whiskey. Other charges followed, including illegal gun possession and running a gambling establishment. In the winter of 1931 Louis DeVita, Johnny's father and mentor, was shot and killed just after he emerged from church services. The assassin was said to have been a foreign-looking man in a brown overcoat. There was not enough evidence to make an arrest. There would never be enough.

By then Lucille was living in New York City once more. For a brief period she shared a room at the Kimberly Hotel with her Jamestown crony, Marion Strong. Emboldened by Lucille's tales of the city, Marion had taken the bus to Manhattan and talked herself into a job as a secretary to an antiques dealer at $20 a week. Lucille did better. Hattie Carnegie welcomed her back; Constance Bennett had remained one of Carnegie's best customers, and the designer was glad to have the look-alike on board again. Lucille's salary was boosted to about $2,000 a year, supplemented by occasional freelance work for commercial photographers—this at a time when most New York City dwellers brought home an annual income of $1,200.

In an effort to replace Johnny, Lucille dated some prominent men, including the public relations counselor Pat di Cicco, who would one day marry Gloria Vanderbilt; and Sailing Baruch, nephew of President Franklin D. Roosevelt's financial adviser, Bernard Baruch. If others were not so well known, they all had enough money to treat a pretty girl to a night on the town. What they failed to appreciate was Lucille's yokel mannerisms. At a high-toned nightclub, her escort introduced some friends. As he spoke, Lucille vigorously smacked one of them in the face. A mosquito, Lucille explained, had just landed on the lady's forehead. The young man never called again.

As countrified and robust as she appeared, Lucille was growing pale beneath the makeup. The demanding schedule, social pressures, and increasingly acute pangs of homesickness all took their toll. Her health failed late in 1930; pneumonia forced her to leave work for a couple of weeks. She returned too early—and immediately regretted it. As she stood on the dais for a fitting, both her legs suddenly felt inflamed. The pain was so severe she sank to the floor, clutching her calves. Amid the chatter and panic Hattie Carnegie kept order. She summoned her own physician and he took Lucille to his office. An instant diagnosis was offered: she had some violent form of arthritis. There were many varieties of the disease. The one to worry about right now was rheumatoid. If she had that she was likely to be crippled for life. In any case, she had to go to a hospital at once. Lucille thought of her last bank statement. "I have eighty-five dollars to my name," she moaned. Very well then, the doctor responded tersely, she must go to a clinic serving the poor of New York. That night Lucille waited three hours to see a specialist donating his services in Harlem. He offered a new and radical injection of serum made from horse urine. Lucille could barely choke out her consent. For several weeks she stayed in her room; periodically the doctor stopped by to administer an injection. A month later the money ran out and she arranged to be taken to the train station in a wheelchair. Once more Lucille went home, unable to break the thread that kept tugging her back to Jamestown—permanently, it seemed. By then Grandpa Fred and DeDe had also returned. Together the family worked on Lucille's morale and aided in her intensive physical therapy.

Ultimately there came a day when, with the support of Grandpa Fred and the doctor, Lucille got to her feet and tried a few tentative steps. Something was very wrong. Her left leg was marginally shorter than her right, and it pulled sideways, unbalancing her gait. To correct the imbalance she had to wear black orthopedic shoes, with a twenty-pound weight in the left one. The metal device was oppressive, cold and as ugly as the footwear. To boost her declining spirits Lucille took to wearing heavy blue satin pajamas. She was one of the first women in Jamestown with the audacity to wear slacks outside the house.

After her recovery Lucille used to speak about the nature of her affliction. Sometimes she referred to a mysterious automobile accident that had occurred in New York City—she had been thrown into a snowbank where she had suffered from frostbite. No record of a car crash involving Lucille Ball, or, for that matter, "Diane Belmont," ever surfaced, but that did not keep early biographers from printing the story. Sometimes she spoke of a hard-won victory over rheumatoid arthritis. That was also untrue; Lucille did not suffer permanent muscle and nerve damage, almost always the case with rheumatoid cases. Kathleen Brady, Lucille's investigative biographer, wonders if Lucille might have had a bout of rheumatic fever, cured, eventually, by a then experimental sulfa drug. It is not beyond possibility, given all that had gone before, that the failed actress and overstrained model suffered from a psychogenic illness only time would heal.

In any event, once she was literally and emotionally back on her feet Lucille felt ready to give New York City one last try. She would have to find a different confidante—Marion Strong had eloped with her high school sweetheart and set up house in Jamestown. Never mind; Lucille was the one who had gone over the wall so often she had lost count, and for local girls who yearned for a bigger life she represented glamour and audacity. Years afterward, a young hairdresser named Gertrude Foote spoke ruefully about the day she decided to follow Lucille to Manhattan. Lucille dropped into the beauty parlor and announced an intention to quit Jamestown and head for Manhattan. The envious "Footie" hesitated a moment, then quixotically left the job and joined her friend on a new escapade.

The romance of Depression New York failed to ignite Footie's imagination. Lucille went right back to work as a model, but her friend had to scramble for low-paid work at a beauty parlor. Still, in the trough of the Depression they did well enough. Lucille cheerfully paid most of the rent at the Kimberly Hotel and picked up the bill whenever the roommates ate together. Lucille's magnanimity was more than a way of caring for a pal without much money or ambition. The would-be actress had made few friends in Jamestown, and of those few only Footie had been bold enought to buy a ticket to New York. Buying dinners was Lucille's way of saying thank-you without being maudlin.

Nevertheless, there was no shortage of men who wanted to take Lucille out and show her the town—including several gang members. Indeed, she picked up the nickname "Two Gun" in the ensuing months when a mishap occurred in her bathroom at the Kimberly. As she explained it, "A gang war was going on around the corner. I didn't hear the bullet whang into the tub, but the water began to disappear. I got out and tried to mop the floor. That's all there is to the story." Not everyone believed that explanation, and the nickname took her a while to shake off.

Hard times intensified in the early 1930s, and even with two salaries Lucille and Gertrude sometimes had trouble making ends meet. There came a day when both paychecks were delayed, and all the young women had between them was twenty-five cents. They walked along in a melancholy state, Gertrude expressing the wish to get some food before she fainted dead away, Lucille wondering if there was any chance for her to get work in this unyielding town.

Between them they had exactly twenty-five cents. A gardenia seller passed by, offering flowers for a quarter. Without hesitation Lucille bought the blossom. Even at that desperate juncture, she preferred to please the eye rather than the stomach.

Yet flowers could do only so much. Lucille needed something more, something she had done without for too long: her family. There was no going back now; although Hattie Carnegie had let many models go, she had kept Lucille on, paying her a salary no upstate employer could match. The solution was to send for Jamestown. Separated from Ed Peterson, DeDe was only too glad to accept the invitation. "My friends in Jamestown thought I was crazy to move there," DeDe said later. "But we all wanted to be with Lucy. We sold my father's house, and he came too—he and Freddy and Cleo. I worked as a buyer for Stern Brothers' store. Lucy modeled, and Fred and Cleo went to school. Our bathroom looked like a Chinese laundry every night—Freddy even washed and ironed his own shirts. But the main thing was that we were together. I didn't realize how briefly." Only Grandpa had trouble adjusting to the new situation. Too old to find a job, he wandered the slums for hours at a time. He had never witnessed such massive desperation and he began wondering aloud whether America could survive the economic crisis without radical alterations.

In the meantime, Lucille gave the lie to all that Fred Hunt had witnessed. After living on the margin she suddenly found herself in demand for freelance assignments and showroom work. By the spring of 1933 she was grossing $100 a week. Breadlines stretched for blocks, one-third of the nation was ill-clothed, ill-housed, and ill-fed, but for Lucille, Recovery was well under way. The only real drawback to her life in Manhattan was Manhattan. She had never been comfortable there. "New York City," she was to write, "scared me to death. It had something to do with all that cold concrete and steel instead of grass and trees."

That place of concrete and steel was all the more forbidding in the summer of that year. In the times before air-conditioning, the city baked and shimmered in the heat. The air felt heavy and dirty; the sun's glare bounced off store windows and hurt the eyes; asphalt stuck to women's high heels when they crossed the streets. On her lunch break Lucille walked to midtown, looking for a brief change of scene— as well as a glimpse of herself enlarged to giant size.

A few weeks earlier she had been freelancing in the showroom of Mrs. E. A. Jackson, whose principal designer was Rosie Roth, a former associate of Hattie Carnegie. Roth was fond of her best model, but hated to show it. While she draped and tucked and pleated, Lucille made faces, bent herself out of shape, and produced funny noises. Roth rose to the bait. "This girl's fulla hell," the designer complained, turning on the model. "You got flair, you got personality, a beautiful body you got. So why so aggravating? You make my ulcer ache. You're fired." That night she called Lucille and rehired her, throwing in an offer to let her borrow whatever gown she liked. Several days later Lucille did indeed wear one of Roth's dresses when she posed for a Liggett & Myers ad. Dressed in a flowing chiffon number, flanked by Russian wolfhounds and holding a Chesterfield cigarette in slim fingers, she seemed the epitome of sophistication. Within weeks her picture was everywhere, including a large billboard at Times Square. On that epochal summer afternoon Lucille was looking up at herself, comparing the immense image with the smaller, far more important ones of real actors in the Palace Theatre lobby. A voice interrupted her reverie.

"Lucille Ball! What are you doing in New York in July?" The speaker was Sylvia Hahlo, a theatrical agent who had a nodding acquaintance with leading models. Lucille responded quite logically by reminding her that New York was where the jobs were. Not true, Hahlo said. "How'd you like to go to California?"

Forget it, Lucille said. "What would I do in California?"

"You're the Chesterfield Girl, aren't you? Well, Sam Goldwyn needs a dozen well-known poster girls for a new Eddie Cantor movie. He had all twelve picked. But one just backed out.' "

Hahlo told her to see Jim Mulvey, Goldwyn's New York agent. His office was right here, in the Palace Theatre building. What the hell— Lucille ascended the stairs and presented herself to Mulvey. He looked her over. Tall. Thin legs, and not much frontage; uncapped teeth but maybe she could keep her mouth shut when she smiled. A lively face with sharp blue eyes. She photographed pretty in still pictures, like all models. But what about movies? And could she act? He would have to take a long shot. If it didn't work out, the chief would have a fit. Mulvey rummaged through his desk for a contract.

That was on a Wednesday. On Saturday Lucille Ball departed for Hollywood on the Super Chief, MGM's legal document in hand, already wrinkled and creased from close readings by everyone in the family. It guaranteed the newest Goldwyn Girl $125 a week for six weeks, plus free transportation. She left with the blessings of Grandpa, DeDe, and Freddy, and Carnegie, Jackson, and Roth. After all, the whole thing would take only a month and a half. She used the same phrase to reassure each of them. The granddaughter, the daughter, the sister, the model would be "back in New York before the maple leaves flamed in Central Park." They had her word on it.

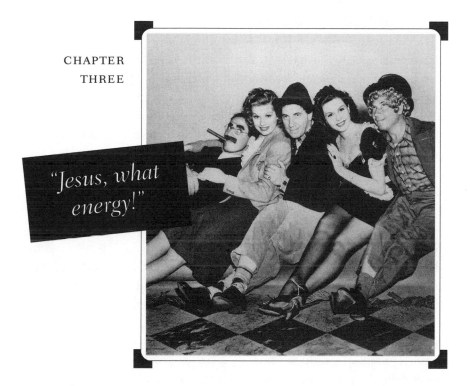

"Jesus, what energy!"

$\mathcal{A}$ T THE TRAIN station Lucille was picked up by studio limousine and chauffeured from Pasadena to Hollywood, in 1933 a relatively small town with groves of orange and olive trees, flocks of birds, and unsaturated air. The United Artists studio, distributor of Samuel Goldwyn productions, found her a one-room apartment on Formosa Street. It had a Murphy bed, a kitchen, and an ideal location—about three blocks from the film studio. She could save money by cooking at home, and she could save even more by walking to work. This was going to be a profitable sojourn.

Lucille had barely checked into the apartment when she received a notice to report for work. At the studio the next morning, she and her fellow chorines were issued skimpy jersey bathing suits and told to line up. As the others primped and prepared, Lucille extracted a piece of red crepe paper from her purse. She had been carrying the fragment around, waiting for an opportunity to use it for maximum comic effect. This was her chance. As Eddie Cantor began his inspection she tore the paper into small dots and applied them to her face, Dorothy Gish–style. The other girls filled out their bathing suits more voluptuously (at five-foot-nine Lucille weighed 111 pounds), and some of them had theatrical experience, but not one of them elicited the reaction she did. Cantor walked down the line, casually giving each new Goldwyn Girl the once-over until he came to Lucille. When he confronted the bogus case of measles he tried to keep a straight face. It was no good. The comedian's famous exophthalmic eyes bulged and he dissolved in laughter. Cantor asked Lucille to identify herself, then proceeded down the line chuckling about "that Ball dame—she's a riot." For the first time since Lucille boarded the Super Chief, she lightened up. Working for Eddie was going to be a lot easier than modeling for Hattie.

As Mick LaSalle points out in *Complicated Women,* a history of Hollywood before the censors moved in, "Pre-Code musicals were often daring. One reason is that, just by their nature, musicals featured lots of young chorus girls. But perhaps more important is that audiences were more ready to relax their standards when music was playing. . . . Pre-Code musicals tell audiences how great it is to be young." *Roman Scandals* was just such a production, with all the vital ingredients on hand: a comic star, comely chorines, a few melodies, and a happy ending to take the public mind away from the Depression for an hour and a half. Producer Sam Goldwyn intended his picture to be the biggest musical of 1933, and United Artists did not stint on production values or talent. At forty-one, Eddie Cantor had gone from headliner in the *Ziegfeld Follies* to Hollywood star, as big a draw as Will Rogers, Clark Gable, or Jean Harlow. Eddie's previous film, *The Kid from Spain,* had been a smash, and *Roman Scandals* was expected to exceed its grosses. George S. Kaufman and Robert E. Sherwood, each of whom would become a Pulitzer Prize winner in a few years, had been assigned to do the scenario. Dissatisfied with their dialogue, Goldwyn hired two of the Marx Brothers' most inventive writers, Arthur Sheekman and Nat Perrin, to add gags and visual business. The cinematographer was Gregg Toland, who would go on to make *Citizen Kane.* Busby Berkeley, master choreographer of the 1930s, supervised the dances. The songs were written by Harry Warren and Al Dubin, later known for their score for *42nd Street.* The cast included the popular singer Ruth Etting and character actors Edward Arnold and Alan Mowbray.

If the plot was less than original, at least it borrowed from prime sources: Mark Twain's *A Connecticut Yankee in King Arthur's Court* and George Bernard Shaw's *Androcles and the Lion*. Cantor, as a whimsical delivery boy named Eddie in West Rome, Oklahoma, falls asleep on the job. In a dream he is projected back to ancient Rome, where he serves as official food taster to the wicked emperor Valerius (Arnold). Before Cantor awakens, there are songs, anachronistic gags (for example, a slavemaster is disabled by fits of mirth when he inhales lava gas), an attempt to overthrow Valerius followed by a prolonged chase scene, a love story, and, predictably, many close-ups of scantily clad slave girls locked in chains as they await the emperor's pleasure.

Lucille played one of the slaves, and she learned the hard way that filmmaking was neither as amusing nor as easy as it looked from the outside. Back in the 1930s the actor's workday knew no limits. Sometimes shooting went on until 3 a.m. Even more demanding than the oppressive schedule, in Lucille's view, was the studio's decree that all the girls must resemble Harlow, the blonde luminary whose eyebrows were represented by two carefully penciled-in crescents. Accordingly, Lucy shaved off her eyebrows—and found to her distress that they never quite grew back. Every morning from that day to the end of her life, the first item she reached for upon rising was her eyebrow pencil.

Sam Goldwyn had a notorious predilection for ladies with fuller figures. He found little to admire in Lucille's understated torso and tried to convince Berkeley to release the new girl. The choreographer held firm; true, this scrawny blonde radiated little sensuality, but there was something different and appealing about her. Not that the choreographer gave Lucille any breaks. He was a hard taskmaster, sometimes drunk and always demanding, rehearsing dances over and over again until she could barely walk home. The next day, though, she would be back on the job, looking for a way to insinuate herself into a scene, lobbying the writers for additional camera time. Perrin admired her willingness to do anything for a laugh; when Cantor wanted to restate the old custard-pie-in-the-face gag with mud taking the place of the pie, none of the girls wanted any part of it except Lucille. She also volunteered to get gummed by a trained crocodile. Perrin rewarded her with a couple of lines.

The weeks stretched out to months. Goldwyn was forced to extend the Lucille Ball contract, and she made herself at home in Hollywood. While the movie ground away, she discovered that Darryl F. Zanuck's fledgling company, Twentieth Century–Fox, had leased studio space from Sam Goldwyn. During her downtime she hitched rides with trucks making their way onto various Fox sets, where she'd ask if anybody needed a walk-on. For two of Zanuck's productions, small parts did become available, and Lucille was there to grab them. Before *Scandals* was released, moviegoers saw her, unbilled, in *Broadway Thru a Keyhole* and *Blood Money*. One of Goldwyn's executives described her apprenticeship: "She sweated out every goddamn break she got. She was one of dozens of girls at the studio watching and waiting for *the* opportunity. The difference was that she was a worker. That, and Jesus, what energy!" Lucille's unique amalgam of vigor and humor caught the eye of a touring New York journalist, Walter Winchell, who gave her a few modest plugs in his column. These were duly noted by studio executives and helped her keep her job. The trouble was that her job was little more than human decoration, a cut above those faceless players who filled out crowd scenes.

While Lucille caromed from Fox to United Artists and back again playing small parts, she expended very few ergs on romance. Only one of the men she dated expressed any long-term interest: an actor named Ralph Forbes, who had just been divorced from the stage actress Ruth Chatterton. Forbes's elegant carriage and English accent dazzled Lucille—until he proposed marriage. Lucille immediately dropped him. "I'm not the crooked-finger-and-teacup type," she explained. But the breakup had nothing to do with two people separated by a common language. It was simply that romantic commitment terrified her. She was more at ease with blithe, emotionally uninvolving dates, like the ones she had with Mack Grey. Né Max Greenberg, the former boxing manager served as factotum and bodyguard for George Raft, an ex-hoofer, now middle-level movie star who had trouble separating his tough-guy roles from real life. Both men had risen from the streets of Manhattan, both were known to carry guns and slap people around—although when Raft did the slapping it was usually while Grey held the victim's arms behind his back. Yet Raft had a sentimental side. He took an avuncular interest in Lucille, encouraged by Carole Lombard, his current flame. The blonde actress could be every bit as foulmouthed as her date, if not more so. (Groucho Marx described her with admiration: "She talked like a man, used words men use with other men. She was a gutsy dame. She was a real show business girl.") Even though Lucille's vocabulary was comparatively chaste, the real show business girl recognized a sister under the skin. Carole began to advise her new friend on what she called "studio behavior": how to speak to producers, staying genial without actually winding up on the casting couch; how to negotiate for bigger parts; and how to drop names.

The twenty-three-year-old Lucille worked in a succession of pictures, but despite the sagacious advice, casting directors assigned her to roles so small she went unlisted in the credits. Besides appearing in *Roman Scandals,* she was in three bottom-of-the-bill pictures released by United Artists: first *Broadway Thru a Keyhole,* then *The Bowery* and *Blood Money.* She also had a bit part in the film version of *Nana,* Émile Zola's naturalistic novel about the life of a demimondaine. Sam Goldwyn's inflated production was a critical failure and a box office bomb. "In all these pictures," Lucille would wryly and accurately note, "I was just part of the scenery, strolling past the camera in chiffon and feathers." She briefly became a stand-in for Constance Bennett, and she tried to strike up a conversation with the actress, only to learn that Bennett could not remember meeting the young Hattie Carnegie model. Lombard urged Lucille to try out for comedy, but Goldwyn and United Artists displayed little interest in the genre and even less in Lucille, beyond offering a modest extension of her contract. All things considered, it was not a bad deal. After all, of the dozen Goldwyn Girls who had started out together, only four were still in town.

Every week or so Lucille felt pangs of homesickness. To allay them she called home, pleading with her mother, brother, and grandfather to come out to California and live with her. The weather was ideal, she assured them: no more upstate New York winters—no winter at all, in fact. They could play in the sun, sit on the porch as long as they liked. The job market was beginning to pick up; maybe they could nab some sort of assignment at one of the studios. Even if they couldn't, she was making $150 a week. And once she got a screen credit, who knew how high her salary might go? Quite sensibly, DeDe asked where Lucille intended to put the family—surely not in her tiny apartment.

Lucille's answer came in the spring of 1934, when she took an expensive rental about half a mile from the studio. The financial aid came from Raft—money that would take six years to pay back. The new dwelling place at 1344 North Ogden Drive was little more than a bungalow, with three small bedrooms and a yard wide enough for a garden, but it was enough. Freddy was the first family member to come west, and he wasted no time landing a job as a page boy at the Tro-cadero supper club. One of Lucille's colleagues, actress Ann Sothern, helped her decorate her place. When Lucille was satisfied with the look, she issued an invitation to DeDe and Grandpa Fred Hunt.

While she was feeling energized, Lucille hammered away at Sam Goldwyn to let her do comedy. Beyond making a halfhearted move on her, Goldwyn had nothing to offer beyond another minuscule and unbilled part in *Kid Millions,* the new Eddie Cantor movie. Lucille accepted the role and promptly became a major pain on the set. The demanding Busby Berkeley was in charge again, and he gave the cast very short breaks. After each one, Lucille was the last to appear. Over the public address speakers would come the message: "Miss Ball . . . Miss Ball . . . On set, please." The film's second lead, George Murphy, whispered: "Honey, I don't understand you. One of these days they'll fire you." Lucille conceded that he might be right. "But one thing you can be sure of," she added. "They'll know who I am."

A snappy comeback, Murphy had to admit, but not one likely to advance her career. Indeed, by the end of 1934 Lucille had appeared in ten films without acquiring a single screen credit. "It galled her that schleps with no talent were getting billing while she wasn't," recalled a colleague from those days. Manifestly she had to get out of the shadow of Goldwyn and United Artists. The trouble was, she had nothing to bargain with—no credits, no reputation, no friends, no luck. All that was to change late in 1934 when the comedy writers Arthur Sheekman and Nat Perrin learned that their agent, Bill Perlberg, had just been hired as casting director of Columbia Studios. He asked his former clients if they knew any performers he should look at. Both mentioned Lucille's off-camera clowning on the set of *Roman Scandals.* "We didn't mention her as an actress," Perrin would recall, "because we knew her as a personality. We told him she was funny and amusing."

On the strength of their recommendation, Perlberg offered Lucille a contract at $75 a week, half what she had been making with Goldwyn. She sighed and she signed—anything for a crack at comedy. "I wanted to learn," she was to write. "And my forte, I figured, was that. I didn't know what I was getting into."

That was not quite true. Everyone in Hollywood knew about Columbia and its Neanderthal head of production, Harry Cohn. With his brother Jack, and Joel Brandt, a pal from New York, the high school dropout and former song-plugger had founded Cohn-Brandt-Cohn Film Sales in 1919. While Jack and Joel stayed in the East, Harry moved to Los Angeles. There he leased studio space for CBC on Gower Street, known to the movie colony as Poverty Row because it housed so many companies specializing in low-budget, "quickie" productions. Cohn-Brandt-Cohn was typical; it turned out so many cheap, slam-bang comedies that actors said "CBC" stood for Corned Beef and Cabbage—reason enough for Harry to change the name to Columbia Pictures.

Beneath the new sign the Cohn philosophy remained the same: low budgets and fast schedules. A number of talented actors and directors chose to work with Columbia anyway. The reason was as basic as Cohn himself. Although he refused to underwrite expensive sets or locations, he respected established talents and gave them the freedom they required. Director Frank Capra was one of those who stayed with Columbia despite offers from bigger studios, and when Lucille entered the place, Carole Lombard and John Barrymore were busy on the same lot. The difference was that Lombard and Barrymore were cast in *Twentieth Century* while Lucille was capering with the Three Stooges. Cohn had decreed that his new contract player would be perfect as the dumb blonde foil in Larry, Moe, and Curly's latest effort, *Three Little Pigskins*. The farce about college football used her mainly as a target. Again she maintained, "I didn't know what I was getting into," and again this was not quite accurate. The Stooges' pratfall reputation preceded them, and not a soul in Hollywood expected them to be anything short of gross. Lucille dutifully allowed them to pelt her with lemon meringue and squirt soda in her face. All she learned from the trio, she insisted, was that "seltzer up the nose really hurts." But all affronts to her dignity vanished when she was rewarded with something money could not buy: a screen credit. Lucille Ball was no longer an elevated extra, a supernumerary glamour girl. Heartened by the prospect of more film comedies, she wired money for the rest of the family to take the Super Chief to L.A. The reunion was only days away.

It was during those days that Harry Cohn made one of his periodic slashes of the Columbia budget. More than a dozen performers were summarily fired. Lucille remembered the collective feelings of shock and fear. "One night at six o'clock, *Boom!* We were on the streets, going, 'What *happened?*' Nobody knew. They just—got rid of everybody." Lucille had a date that night with Dick Green, brother of Johnny Green, a studio musician and composer of such hits as "Body and Soul" and "Out of Nowhere." He took note of the glum face. "Lost my job," Lucille snuffled: Dede and her brother and grandfather were coming to stay at the house in Gower. But now—

He cut her off. It so happened that there *was* an opportunity. Why, this very evening RKO had an open call for showgirls.

Lucille put her tongue in her cheek.

No, Green insisted: this new Astaire-Rogers film really needed chorines.

They're auditioning them after dark? she demanded.

Yes, she was assured, in the p.m.

Lucille showed up for the casting call, invented a long history of modeling for Bergdorf Goodman in New York, and was offered a job. The salary seemed insultingly low, as if she was backsliding rather than rising in Hollywood—$50 a week. She signed immediately.

Informed that she was going by bus to meet her mother and grandfather at the railroad station, George Raft was appalled. That was no way to greet the family. He advanced Lucille $65 and gave her the use of his limousine for the day so that she could arrive in style. As soon as DeDe laid eyes on the house on North Ogden she started to cry, moved by her daughter's success. What seemed a striver's dwelling to Lucille was paradise to her mother.

DeDe kept weeping at intervals throughout the day. In the evening the two went for a drive around town. They parked at the top of Mulholland Drive, the local lovers' lane. Lights from the San Fernando Valley and the Los Angeles basin twinkled below them. The sentimental DeDe began to cry again and Lucille put her arm around her mother. "We sat there for a few minutes," Lucille would recall, "when all of a sudden there was a cop next to us. He banged his nightstick against the running board and said, 'Okay, you dames. None of that stuff up here. Run along, butch.' I don't think my mother had ever heard the word 'lesbian' and when I told her what it meant and that the cop thought we were necking, she cried all the way home."

Grandpa Fred worked hard at adjusting to the new climate and the new house. Lucille eased the way as best she could, calling him Daddy, deferring to him in little matters, and creating a small studio for him in the garage. Seated behind a desk, Fred Hunt gave political lectures to his new friends, the milkman, the trash collector, and various retirees he met on his Ogden Drive constitutionals. Overhearing the talks, his granddaughter was amused to see that the old man's radical leanings had been brought to Los Angeles intact. Harmless, she thought, and very good for Daddy to exercise his opinions as well as his body.

Not that she could spare much time for the family once everyone had settled in. Lucille was, after all, a contract player with RKO Pictures, and she was determined not to lose this job.

The company letters stood for Radio-Keith-Orpheum, vestiges of the company's vaudeville origins. At one time it had been under the control of the financial shark Joseph P. Kennedy, now the head of the Securities and Exchange Commission, and David Sarnoff, president of the Radio Corporation of America. The executives had believed in the future of talking pictures, and attempted to create a rival to Warner Brothers, acknowledged leader of the revolution in sound. But that was before the Depression gutted the parent company, which fell into the hands of the receivers. Kennedy and Sarnoff were back in New York, and RKO Pictures was left to founder on its own. In the early 1930s it did better than anyone had dared to predict. No genre was left untouched. A series of revolving-door executives experimented with special effects, as in *King Kong;* dramas featuring the high-toned young actress Katharine Hepburn, who won an Academy Award with her third picture, *Morning Glory;* and adaptations of Broadway musicals, including *Roberta,* starring Irene Dunne and a newly popular dance team, Fred Astaire and Ginger Rogers.

It was for this last film that Lucille was hired, specifically as an onscreen clothes model. *Roberta* is set in Paris, where Dunne plays a White Russian princess turned couturier, Rogers is an American singer posing as an Eastern European aristocrat, and Astaire is a fellow American undeceived by Rogers's bogus accent. Lucille again tried to lobby the writers for more work, but it was no use: she was supposed to be Parisian, and French intonations were totally beyond her. Rather than give the actress additional dialogue, the director William A. Seiter excised her only speech. All that remained in the finished film was a walk-on, with Lucille striding around in ostrich plumes and silk.

The event was disappointing rather than dispiriting. Lucille was the first to acknowledge that she had a lot to learn. She would begin by devoting herself to the task at hand—any task at all. According to her testimony: "I adopted RKO as my studio family. I talked to everyone I met, from office boys to executives—possibly because of that urgent need I'd always had to make people like me—and I posed for every cheesecake picture they asked for. I could never say no."

These frantic efforts were to pay large dividends. During the first few months she caught the eye of Pandro S. Berman. Nine years her senior, Berman had risen from editor to RKO's most important executive, overseeing Katharine Hepburn's films and the Astaire-Rogers musicals. He was surrounded by beautiful women on the lot and around town, but somehow, this year, 1934, he preferred Lucille's fresh and audacious style. For her part, Lucille thought him attractive enough; since the days of her crush on Uncle George Mandicos, and through four years with Johnny DeVita, she had shown a distinct preference for swarthy Mediterranean types—even if they were married. Berman fit the mold. They started to see each other, and within a month Lucille became Topic A among the studio gossips.

This could scarcely be called a casting couch stratagem. Beguiled though he was, Berman knew the actress's limitations and offered her no major roles. All the same, studio folk knew of the involvement and treated Miss Ball with extreme politesse. She had only one line in *I Dream Too Much*, a vehicle built for the talents of soprano Lily Pons. As an American parvenu touring Paris, Lucille denounces the city's attractions: "Culture is making my feet hurt." A larger role came with *Chatterbox,* where she played a combative actress. This was followed by minor roles in two subsequent Astaire-Rogers features, as a dancer in *Follow the Fleet* and a flower seller in *Top Hat.*

Manifestly, her connection with the boss was not enough to elevate Lucille from the bottom rungs of RKO, a situation she discussed at a commissary lunch with Margaret Hamilton. The beaky character actress would become an icon when she played the Wicked Witch of the West in *The Wizard of Oz,* but at the time she was just another RKO performer punching the clock like the rest. "Am I ever going to succeed?" Lucille demanded. "I have financial responsibilities for my mother and I need to make money." Hamilton could only provide a sympathetic ear; she had no counsel, and no inside information. Still, there *was* one avenue as yet unexplored.

One of the clichés of Hollywood, Lucille was to observe, is "Behind every successful actress is a hairdresser and a mother." "Hairdressers come and go," she wrote, "but Ginger Rogers has only one fabulous mother, a woman who played mother to many of us on the way up." In order to further her daughter's career, and to give herself something to do, the restless Lela Rogers had founded an acting school on the RKO lot. Lucille made a point of matriculating at this institution, headed by a most unusual woman.

Lela Rogers had several ex-husbands but only one child, and she resolved to make that girl famous. The goal required concentration and discipline, two attributes Lela had acquired as a female Marine during World War I. Returned to civilian life, Lela applied them to her daughter, training the child for a career in show business. At fourteen Ginger won a Charleston contest in Dallas; after that there was no stopping mother or daughter. Lela hired some dancers, wrote original songs and special material, and arranged a vaudeville contract for Ginger Rogers and Her Redheads. On the road she served as Ginger's press agent and tutored her in academic subjects. The troupe played the circuits until Lela pronounced the appealing little blonde ready for New York. In 1929, at the age of eighteen, Ginger Rogers made her debut in a Broadway musical; the following year she appeared in her first film, *Young Man of Manhattan*. At RKO, with Lela's backing, she sang and danced in the films that would make her reputation as Fred Astaire's partner, doing everything he did, as she liked to point out, backward and in high heels.

When Ginger was not on the set, she polished her craft in Lela's acting classes. Lucille joined the group of apprentices and found herself in a position of considerable delicacy. She wanted to improve her skills, to secure larger roles, to become *somebody*. At the same time, Lucille could not threaten Ginger, the focus of all this schooling, by letting her ambition show. The humble attitude worked so well that after one class Lela took Lucille aside.

"What would you give to be a star in two years?" the older woman demanded. "Would you give me every breath you draw for two years? Will you work seven days a week? Will you sacrifice all your social life?"

Lucille nodded her assurance.

"Okay, let's start."

For Lucille, the Lela Rogers regimen meant getting her teeth straightened, wearing dresses instead of slacks and shirts, reading English literature to improve her vocabulary and get a better understanding of character, taking elocution lessons in order to lower her voice by four tones. Of all the counsel Lela dispensed, Lucille had trouble with only one piece of advice: to her instructor, sex was "more of a hindrance than a help to a would-be star." More actresses, she insisted, "have made it to the top without obvious sex appeal than with it." This contradicted all that Lucille had experienced, but what Lela wanted Lela got: her young pupil learned the value of subtlety in performance and deportment.

These lessons were not absorbed all at once; there were times when Lucille forgot she was a lady and reverted to Jamestown rebel. Early one morning she was preparing for yet another publicity photograph when Mary, Queen of Scots, strode into the makeup room. The staff whisked Lucille to the adjoining wardrobe department as Katharine Hepburn, dressed as Mary, studied her script and settled luxuriously into the chair. Lucille peeked through a small window and saw that she had left behind in the makeup room a box of caps for her teeth. She tried to catch the eye of the makeup man; he deliberately snubbed her. Furious, Lucille grabbed a container of coffee and hurled it through the window at him. The missile missed its target and hit a chair, spattering coffee over Hepburn's costume. *Mary of Scotland* would not be filmed that day. The postponement cost RKO several thousand dollars and infuriated the front office. But Hepburn, forever skirmishing with RKO management, refused to blame Lucille. Pandro Berman argued that it was just an accident that could have happened to anyone, and Lela advised the bosses that Lucille Ball happened to be the most promising student in her class. The transgression was overlooked, but unforgiven; Lucille would have to work twice as hard merely to stay in place.

She understood the situation and applied herself to acting and cultural lessons. There was no point in playing office politics; studio executives seemed to come and go with the seasons. Drawing on past experience and present lessons, she was creditable as the second lead in another Lily Pons film, *That Girl from Paris,* and garnered her first rave review from a New York paper. The *Daily Mirror* accurately termed her a "capable actress" and mistakenly judged her "an agile dancer" before getting to her real strength: "Miss Ball plays it quite straight, intensifying the comedy of each disaster. She rates, thereby, more conspicuous roles and more intense promotion. She is a comedienne, which is always a 'find.' " As a brunette gangster's moll in *Don't Tell the Wife,* she was funnier between takes than when the cameras rolled, but even as a practical joker she attracted an unusual amount of attention. In the middle of one ad-lib routine Lucille was approached by a heavy, hard-breathing old gentleman. He whispered, "Young lady, if you play your cards right, you can be one of the greatest comediennes in the business." She responded with a wry look and stepped away. "I figured he was one of the guys who came around measuring the starlets for tights," she later remarked. Too late, she learned that the speaker was not on the make and that he had meant what he said. He was Edward Sedgwick, the retired comedy director who had been responsible for many Keystone Kops and Buster Keaton movies.

Late in 1936 the studio acquired the rights to George S. Kaufman and Edna Ferber's *Stage Door,* a Broadway hit about the rivalries and friendships of ingenues. Every actress under the age of thirty ached to be in the cast, and Lucille lobbied Berman for a part—any part. His endorsement was not enough. Leland Hayward, Kaufman's agent, believed there were at least a dozen more adept performers at RKO and he vetoed her. Never mind, Berman consoled Lucille, there might be another way into the project. He knew of a straight play bound for Broadway. If she could win a role and appear on the Main Stem for a couple of months, she might yet persuade these provincial New Yorkers that Lucille Ball had the talent and experience for *Stage Door.*

The name of the play was *Hey Diddle Diddle.* Written by an unknown playwright, Bartlett Cormack, it would be directed and coproduced by Anne Nichols, author of *Abie's Irish Rose.* That comedy of intermarriage opened to scathing reviews (the *New Yorker* ran a contest for the most amusing pan, won by Harpo Marx: "No worse than a bad cold") and proceeded to run for a record-breaking 2,327 performances. Now wealthy and immune to criticism, Nichols was persuaded to hire Lucille. She would play one of a trio of roommates trying to make a career in show business.

An eager young actor, Keenan Wynn, son of the comedian Ed Wynn, was also in the cast. The lead was the silent-movie veteran Conway Tearle, whose last film had been *Romeo and Juliet,* with Leslie Howard and Norma Shearer as the lovers. Rehearsals augured well and *Hey Diddle Diddle* opened to an enthusiastic crowd late in January 1937, at the McCarter Theater in Princeton, New Jersey. The *Variety* critic reported: "Miss Ball fattens a fat part and almost walks off with the play. She outlines a consistent character and continually gives it logical substance. Has a sense of timing and, with a few exceptions, keeps her comedy under control." The notice was not a fluke. After a performance in Washington, D.C., the *Washington Post* reviewer expressed dissatisfaction with the play, but not with its comedienne: "If there is one young person who is going to add to her professional stature in *Hey Diddle Diddle* it is Lucille Ball, just about the slickest trick you ever saw in slacks." Lucille read the notices and mused about the future. Let Hollywood treat her as a clownish newcomer; she would become a headliner in the place she belonged—the legitimate theater.

It was not to be. Conway Tearle, succumbing to the illness that would cause his death a few months later, was forced to leave the play. In less than a month *Hey Diddle Diddle* was due to open at the Vanderbilt Theatre on Broadway. There was barely enough time to find another suitable lead and make the extensive revisions that Nichols demanded. Both alternatives were within reach, until Cormack announced that his work needed no drastic rewrites; he thought the script required only a few minor brush strokes. The argument escalated from shouting match to power struggle. Nichols settled matters several days later by closing the production out of town.

Disappointed and at loose ends, Lucille returned to RKO hoping that someone important had seen her out-of-town reviews. Someone had. Armed with the reviews, Pandro Berman convinced the higher-ups that Lucille belonged in the cast of *Stage Door*. The director, Gregory La Cava, gave way, and with that decision Lucille found herself in an A picture for the first time. She played Judy Canfield, one of a group of aspiring actresses hell-bent on stage careers. Compared with the others, Lucille's part was not large. Katharine Hepburn won the central role of the haughty debutante Terry Randall. Ginger Rogers, who considered herself Hepburn's number one rival in the rising-star category, was determined to outshine everyone as Jean Maitland, a sarcastic girl from the wrong side of the tracks. Other actresses regarded this film as their big break, including Eve Arden (as Eve), who specialized in the wry comeback, Andrea Leeds (as the doomed Kaye Hamilton), whom La Cava considered "the best natural actress" he had ever worked with, and Ann Miller (as Annie, a long-legged dancer), who looked several years older than her real age. Lucille had seen Miller on the stage in San Francisco; she knew that the girl was actually fourteen, but she assured RKO executives that Ann was eighteen and therefore outside the New Deal's child labor laws.

Throughout the filming La Cava aimed for realism. He all but dismissed the wardrobe department; the women were to wear their own clothes instead of the usual studio ensembles. (Lucille complied, but audaciously sent her clothing bills to RKO. The studio refused to pick up the tab.) Despite the fact that *Stage Door* had thrived on Broadway, La Cava determined that the film adaptation would be an extempore affair. Actors would ad-lib their scenes around certain agreed-upon lines; scenarists would fill the gaps with smart gags and backchat. Making up dialogue was difficult enough for Lucille; working with Hepburn was excruciating. "She was s-o-o-o highbrow that I never really knew exactly what she was saying, but I'd nod my head and agree with her," Lucille told a friend. "She'd never talk to anyone directly, she'd address you looking all around you but never at you. I was riveted to her when she was around. She wasn't really standoffish. She ignored everyone equally."

La Cava was not so easily intimidated. At opportune times he reminded Hepburn that RKO considered her "box office poison," and made her recite an affected line she had been trying to forget. "The calla lillies are in bloom again" was from *The Lake*, a Broadway flop that had prompted Dorothy Parker to issue the widely quoted appraisal, "she [Hepburn] runs the gamut of emotions from A to B." At La Cava's insistence Hepburn spoke those words again in *Stage Door*, and thenceforward impersonators made sure she never forgot them.

The director was no more benign with others in the cast. Lucille felt that La Cava disliked her in particular. If that was the case, he did not allow his personal feelings to interfere with the filming. He and the scenarists saw to it that her character, Judy Canfield, remained the realist of the group, an appealing Seattlite who eventually chucks her stage career and heads west to marry a lumberjack. En route, Ball has several indelible encounters, including a defining one with Leeds and Arden:

LEEDS
I actually saw one manager. It wasn't an interview. I just saw him as he rushed out of his office.

BALL
Well, at least you know there is such an animal. What did he look like?

LEEDS
Like any other animal. He had on pants, a tie and collar.

ARDEN
Did smoke come out of his nose?

BALL
Did he say "Man, man" when you squeezed him?

LEEDS
I didn't get that close to him.

ARDEN
You didn't see a manager, dearie. What you saw was a mirage.

Of all the films released in 1937, *Stage Door* received the best word-of-mouth and the most glowing reviews. It was honored with Academy Award nominations. Katharine Hepburn's reputation was restored, and the New York film critics vindicated La Cava's methods by naming him best director of the year.

On the strength of her new screen credit Lucille signed with Zeppo Marx, the Marx brother who had dropped out of the comedy act in 1933 to become an influential agent. He drove her salary up to $1,000 a week and negotiated for better billing in B movies like *Having Wonderful Time,* with Ginger Rogers and Douglas Fairbanks Jr., and *The Affairs of Annabel,* a light satire of Hollywood in which Lucille headlined with Jack Oakie. The latter movie proved so popular that the studio offered a second *Annabel* feature. The *New York Times* preferred her to the film; Lucille Ball, said the reviewer, was "one of our brightest comediennes."

With this rush of recognition she relaxed enough to enjoy her home, and to expand her social life. By now Cleo had joined the group at North Ogden Drive; it was as if Lucille had finally brought the entire emotional structure of Jamestown west, brick by brick. Everyone seemed happier now—save for Grandpa Fred Hunt. A recent stroke seemed to propel him backward in time. Although the country was in Recovery, he acted as if the Depression had just begun. To anyone who

would listen, and to many who would not, he again boomed the virtues
of socialism, Eugene V. Debs–style.

Flush with her grand new salary, Lucille hired a maid. Unlike most
of her career moves, this one happened quite by accident. She was
straightening the house and idly listening to a radio program presenting a series of job-seekers. Prospective employers were invited to call
in. A young woman, Harriet McCain, spoke glowingly about her
mother, who had been Jack Benny's maid for fourteen happy years.
Harriet had enjoyed a brief fling in show business; now she was ready
to follow in Mama's profession. On a whim Lucy called in, and the
next day a plump, cheerful African American presented herself. "When
I interviewed Harriet," Lucille said, "I didn't ask for any references, to
her surprise. After about five minutes' talk, I decided I liked her looks
and manner and asked, 'What size uniform do you wear?' and that was
that."

It did not take long for Grandpa Fred to agitate the new worker with
lines like "You're being exploited by your employers!" These exhorta-
tions annoyed Lucille, but could hardly have been a surprise. Ever
since his arrival in Los Angeles Fred Hunt had been espousing radical
causes, lecturing on street corners, quoting his favorite periodical, the
Daily Worker, and joining most of the left-wing organizations in town,
frequently signing up other members of the family without their
knowledge. His arguments against the Roosevelt administration's
defense of capitalism grew so fierce and choleric that Lucille feared for
his health. It was to placate the old man that she, her brother, and her
mother followed his lead and registered as Communists for one pri-
mary. "I remember feeling quite foxy [about that day]," Lucille said in
later years. After all, what was the harm of signing up as an L.A. Bol-
shevik? "I always felt I would be all right if I didn't vote it."

Between assignments at the studio and domestic chores, she
allowed herself a limited social life. The involvement with Berman
waned when his wife gave birth and Lucille saw herself in the unaccustomed role of temptress. "I knew what it was like to lose a beloved
father early in life," she declared later. "No child was going to be put
through that torture because of me." She was not alone for long.
Another exotic type came along: Cesar Romero, a well-established
Latin star. Lucille thought him "the best dancer in the world." She
recalled: "One night we both went to Mocambo, and we both had too

much to drink. I thought maybe he'd make a pass after all the times we went out, but he didn't. As we danced, he started to cry. I asked him what was the matter, and he just said, 'I'm strange.' I told him that we were all a little strange, and then he really broke down."

Stranger still was Oscar Levant, the deadpan pianist-composer-actor who made a career of his neuroticism. On a lark Lucille agreed to have dinner with him. He picked her up at the house, then drove to the top of Mulholland Drive. Lucille mused, "If that cop came back, at least I was with a man this time." After an interminable silence, Levant extinguished his fourth cigarette. "Well, I guess you're wondering why I haven't made a pass at you."

"I just looked at him," Lucille went on. "I didn't know what to say. If I said yes, I thought he'd kiss me and I'd scream, and if I said no he'd do it anyway and I'd scream. Then he said, 'Well, don't worry. I'm not going to make a pass at you. I have syphilis.' I don't know if he was kidding or not, but that was the end of it. He started the car and took me home without another word."

She also dated Henry Fonda, who had appeared with her in *I Dream Too Much*. Their association was extremely short-lived. One evening Lucille and Ginger Rogers double-dated with Fonda and his roommate, Jimmy Stewart. They danced at the Cocoanut Grove nightclub until about 5 a.m. before stopping off at Barney's Beanery to sober up with coffee and a light breakfast. The quartet hit the street at sunrise. Both actresses had spent a long time choosing their ensembles and applying heavy makeup, false eyelashes, and dark mascara. As long as the lighting was dim, they were the epitome of glamour. In the harsh morning glare, they suddenly looked like dime store mannequins. Fonda did a double take as he examined his companion, uttered one syllable—"Yuck!"—and took her home. There were no further dates.

RKO publicists had no idea how to sell Lucille Ball. They could hardly merchandise her dalliance with Berman, nor could they make much of her casual evenings with Broderick Crawford, fresh from his role as Lennie in the Broadway play *Of Mice and Men;* with comedian Milton Berle; or with screenwriter Gene Markey, whose chief distinction was a brief marriage to Joan Bennett.

So they invented a new Lucille Ball for their own use. Just as later publicists concocted a Joan Crawford who adored staying home in the kitchen with her daughter, or a Rock Hudson who was an unrestrained ladies' man, the studio put together a Lucille who was a woman of multiple talents, an admixture of Amelia Earhart, Eleanor Roosevelt, and Aphrodite. With a straight face RKO offered the official biography to newspapers throughout the country. Among other things, it claimed: "She once took an open-cockpit plane up in weather 20 degrees below freezing to effect the rescue of a schoolboy; she plays a fast game of polo, has a hobby of woodcarving, owns a profitable florist shop, and is one of Hollywood's best-dressed actresses."

Lucille did not know how to fly, was not a horsewoman, had no financial interest in any flower shop, and dressed well but not as well as a hundred more successful actresses with their own couturiers. Not that this mattered. What was important was to convince editors that her RKO films were worth coverage. Image was everything. Accuracy had nothing to do with it.

The cumulative assault had an effect not only on editors and writers, but on studio executives as well. "Eventually," she claimed, "they started sending me scripts and asked me if I'd like to do this or that. It was a big thrill. One day I saw a casting sheet that said, 'A Lucille Ball type.' I went to the casting office and said I'd be available in a week." She took a screen test, only to be turned down by the producer. He said she was wrong for the role.

"I'll call you
Dizzy"

Rummaging through souvenirs of the late 1930s, Lucille reminisced to a friend, "I was very happy being Queen of the B's." Bestowed by derisive studio folk, the title was accepted with equanimity. "Actually, that's one of my problems," she admitted. "I'm very happy in my nice little ruts."

This particular rut turned out to be long, profitable, and almost entirely devoid of glamour. For a time Lucille and Eve Arden competed for minor wisecracking roles: "One of us would be the lady executive and the other would be the 'other woman.' They were the same roles. We'd walk through a room, drop a smart remark, and exit. I called us the 'drop-gag girls.' "

Next came screwball comedies like *The Next Time I Marry* and *Beauty for the Asking.* In the former Lucille plays a potential heiress. The good news is that she has fallen in love with a handsome foreigner. The bad news is that she can inherit $20 million only if she marries an American. To outwit the estate lawyers, Lucille marries the first eligible Yankee in sight, and the couple sets off for Reno and a quickie divorce, only to find through various calamities and arguments that they cannot live without each other. In the latter movie she plays a young woman thrown over by a young man in search of a dowry. Fueled by resentment, she invents a beauty cream that women find irresistible. The cosmetic becomes a national sensation, whereupon the fortune hunter finds that Lucille *is* rather fetching after all.

A glance at Lucille Ball's films from this period shows a wide range of parts, almost all of them in bottom-of-the-bill movies. In the comedy *That's Right, You're Wrong* she is cast as a starlet helping bandleader Kay Kyser and his Kollege of Musical Knowledge pass their screen test; in the flagwaver *The Marines Fly High* she portrays a cocoa-plantation owner kidnapped by bandits and rescued by daring pilots; in the melodramatic *Panama Lady* she plays a conniving cabaret dancer out to separate an alcoholic oilman from his money. Buried in that sump of cinematic clichés, she still managed to attract critical attention: The New York *Daily News* critic deemed *Panama Lady* "another minor triumph for Lucille Ball . . . It is high time RKO recognized her potential and put her in something more deserving of her ability than the last things she has appeared in. I don't contend that she is a Duse, but she is one of the most up-and-coming players around."

The comer did win a role in *Room Service,* playing an aspiring actress and straight woman to the Marx Brothers. In theory, the Marx Brothers feature should have been her breakthrough. Pandro Berman thought so highly of the Brothers he paid half a million dollars for the rights to film the stage hit. That money included the salaries of Groucho, Chico, and Harpo, borrowed for this occasion from Metro-Goldwyn-Mayer. Unfortunately, the producer failed to notice something vital: every one of the previous seven Marx Brothers movies had been built from the ground up, the scenario carefully shaped to their talents and idiosyncrasies. *Room Service* was a Broadway comedy hastily rejiggered to fit the trio. The plot concerns a theatrical con man who refuses to leave his hotel room until he can find a backer rich enough to pay his bills and underwrite a new play. Audiences and critics were more tolerant than Groucho. "It was the first time we tried doing a play we hadn't created ourselves," he complained later. "We can't do that. We've got to originate the characters and situations ourselves. Then we can do them. Then they're us. We can't do gags or play characters that aren't ours. We tried it and we'll never do it again."

Lucille learned only one skill from her Marx Brothers experience: how to eat an exotic vegetable. At a dinner at Sam Goldwyn's palatial home she was seated next to Harpo. When an artichoke was placed before her, Lucille panicked. She had never encountered one before, and thought to go at it with knife and fork until Harpo quietly showed her how to peel the leaves one by one. Harpo's kindness was not duplicated by his younger brother. Privately, Groucho appraised Lucille Ball as "an actress, not a comedienne. There's a difference. I've never found her to be funny on her own. She's always needed a script."

Here the usually astute comedian was wrong. Granted, Lucille would never be as furiously amusing as the Brothers, who could turn any occasion into a comic sketch. They were already notorious for squatting nude and roasting potatoes in Irving Thalberg's faux fireplace when the production chief was late for a meeting. During the filming of *Room Service* they picked up where they had left off at MGM. RKO had promised to close the set of the movie, then reneged. Angry that visitors were on the way, Groucho, Chico, and Harpo prepared themselves for a scene in which they were to run after Lucille. That they did—but they had removed every stitch of clothing. The astonished tour group, composed of priests and nuns, averted their eyes.

But if Lucille could not match the Brothers for bare lunacy, she was not above making some memorable mischief of her own. Frank Albertson, who had played the hapless playwright in *Room Service,* booked himself into a local hospital. There he underwent a long-delayed hemorrhoid operation. Painfully recuperating, Albertson looked up one afternoon to see a group of his fellow performers, led by Lucille. She had talked the head nurse into allowing a visit. They were on a lunch break, she lied, and had only an hour before shooting resumed. They would be the very essence of sympathy and dignity.

Frank "knew we were up to no good the minute he saw us," Lucille said, "and he begged us to leave. Well, that's all we needed." At her instigation, the callers did everything they could to break him up. "He shut his eyes as tightly as he could, trying to pretend we weren't there, but it didn't work. He bit his lip so hard it turned purple. He finally gave in, alternating screams of laughter with screams of pain. The nurse came running in like a sketch nurse in a vaudeville scene, and threw us all out on the spot. As I was leaving, Frank looked at me with the purplest face I've ever seen and said, 'I never knew my eyelids were connected to my asshole.' "

.   .   .

$\mathcal{B}$y mid-1939 Lucille was forced to acknowledge what everyone else already knew: Ginger Rogers had risen to become RKO's A-picture star, and Lucille Ball had fallen into the category of B-picture comedienne, a rut from which there seemed no exit. Given these conditions, she considered other career opportunities. Nostalgic for the energy that came across the footlights from a live audience, Lucille thought about doing a legitimate play or working in the dying medium of vaudeville and the immensely vigorous one of radio. "In pictures," she noted, "by the time they get around to the close-up, the comedy is gone." She heard that the Jack Haley and Phil Baker radio programs, both top-rated shows, were looking for actresses, and she auditioned for and won both jobs. She made the most of them. After one successful show *Variety* commented: "[Lucille Ball's] material was only so-so, but her timing and knock 'em dead emphasis on the tags italicized the humor. Her withering style of always belittlin' was particularly well suited to go with Baker's fooling."

This emphasis on humor came to overshadow every assignment and audition, no matter how serious the intent. During the season she was establishing herself as a foil, Lucille (like almost every other Hollywood actress under thirty not actively employed in a brothel) was asked to test for David O. Selznik. The producer was on a widely publicized search for an actress to play Scarlett O'Hara in his much-ballyhooed production of *Gone With the Wind*. Lucille suspected that she was wrong for the role, but no performer ever refused a command from Mr. Selznick. And besides, stranger things had happened in Hollywood. Mindful that this could be a lifetime opportunity, Lucille bought a new outfit reminiscent of the Old South, complete with flower-printed wide skirt and matching broad-brimmed hat. Her plan was to approach the Selznik studio in a big convertible, passing through the gate like a superstar. En route an unpredicted downpour soaked Culver City. The convertible failed to convert, and by the time Lucille reached her destination she and the dress were waterlogged.

A sympathetic secretary told her that Selznik was running behind schedule. That gave the actress a chance to dry out in the boss's office. "She took a decanter of brandy off his desk and offered me a glass," Lucille remembered. "I was shaking so much and so chilled that I took it and downed it in one gulp. She offered me another, and I downed that, too. By the time Selznik came in, I was smashed." He smiled reassurance and asked her to do the scene she had prepared. "I read Scarlett's speech to Ashley, the one where they don't see Rhett on the sofa, looking like I went over Niagara Falls in a barrel." When she finished, the producer offered congratulations on her ingenuity; it was very daring to make such a choice. "I didn't know what he was talking about. Selznik said, 'To do the scene on your knees like that!' I was kneeling the whole time, and never even knew it."

While she strove for name recognition, Lucille kept earnest suitors at bay. As she saw it, her career progress had been slow enough without the encumbrance of marriage. When Alexander Hall came along, he provided an easy choice for a long-term, emotionally uninvolving liaison. Hall, a director best known for guiding Shirley Temple in *Little Miss Marker,* had already been divorced twice and had no intention of marrying again. He was middle-aged, dour, and physically unattractive, but he had been a child star in vaudeville, had great stories about the old days, and knew almost every local and visiting comedian. Hall introduced Lucille to radio headliner Fred Allen and his wife, Portland Hoffa, and to George Burns and Gracie Allen. He also cleared up an old misunderstanding when he brought Lucille to meet Ed and Ebba Sedgwick. Several years before, Lucille had snubbed Edward Sedgwick, convinced that the Keystone Kops director was just another dirty old man. Now she realized that he was a true believer, an expert in knockabout farce who thought Lucille Ball could become as big a luminary in her day as Mabel Normand and Constance Talmadge were in theirs.

Like any other actress, Lucille doted on praise, but she knew better than to rely on the flattery of an emeritus director. Work was the important thing, whether it was in light comedy or in such melodramas as *Five Came Back.* Directed by John Farrow from a script by Nathanael West and Dalton Trumbo, this was a suspense film about a plane crash in the jungles of South America. Of a dozen passengers who survive, only five will avoid the tribe of headhunters who surround them. Lucille Ball, playing a world-weary trollop, is one of the five—a plum role in what seemed to be a cursed production. First, torrential rains delayed the shooting. Then one character actor, John Carradine, fell ill. Another, Chester Morris, confused his costar Lucille's on-screen role with her private life and kept pawing her whenever she let down her guard. Farrow displayed his sadistic side, arguing with and humiliating whatever cast member got in his way on a given day. Lucille became his unwitting victim one afternoon when she leaned on some tropical vegetation brought to the set for verisimilitude. It housed two tarantulas, and both fell onto her hair. She had hysterics and had to be assisted to her dressing room, much to the derisive amusement of the director.

A few months later Lucille found it in her heart to forgive him. Farrow had bullied his cast into tense, convincing performances, and *Five Came Back* turned into the sleeper of 1939. The *New York Times* called it "as exciting as a pinwheel" and singled out Lucille Ball for her "gripping realism." The front office began to regard Lucille in a different way. Studio press agents came around, hinting that big things were in store—perhaps the A films she had been striving for. In December she was sent east to make a series of personal appearances in New York. While in the city, she was told, it would be a good idea to see the new Richard Rodgers and Lorenz Hart musical. RKO had just bought *Too Many Girls,* and casting would begin just after New Year's Day. Was this the studio's way of telling her that Lucille Ball was at long last an A-picture talent?

Because of her own foolhardiness, two weeks went by before she got tickets to the show. Studio publicists had set up a shoot with Lucille skating at the rink in Rockefeller Center. They asked her to do a pratfall and she obliged them: anything for a laugh. "After so many years in California," she reflected, "I guess I'd forgotten how hard ice can be. I landed with a slight crack on my sacroiliac." She was carried off on a stretcher and spent the next ten days of her holiday in a hospital. Friends dropped in and told her about *Too Many Girls.* It was not much on plot, they said, but how could you beat songs like "I Didn't Know What Time It Was" and "I Like to Recognize the Tune"? And the cast wasn't half bad. There was an outstanding new comedian, Eddie Bracken; a promising blond chorus boy, Van Johnson; and a good-looking Cuban kid who stopped the show with a conga dance at the end of act 1. As soon as she could walk, the visitors urged, Lucille had to go down to the Imperial Theatre and catch Desi Arnaz in person.

*L*ucille hobbled to her orchestra seat, made herself as comfortable as possible, and waited to be entertained. The opening scenes were amusing rather than entrancing; she wondered what all the fuss was about until the first big number, "Tempt Me Not." "I couldn't take my eyes off this Desi Arnaz," she was to write. "A striped football jersey hugged his big shoulders and chest, while those narrow hips in tight football pants swayed to the catchy rhythms of the bongo drum he was carrying. I recognized the kind of electrifying charm that can never be faked: star quality." And this was before Desi had spoken a line.

Lucille momentarily toyed with the idea of pursuing him, then reconsidered. The program said Arnaz was twenty-two, almost six years her junior, and she had a comfortable relationship with an older man. Besides, she had to get back to the Coast, where her next film, *Dance, Girl, Dance,* was already under way. The plum part of Judy, the prima ballerina, had gone to Maureen O'Hara. Lucille, thanks to typecasting, was assigned to play her rival, Bubbles, a salty, hard-bitten stripper. Turning blonde again, Lucille took well-publicized tours of strip joints in downtown L.A., allegedly to pick up pointers on bumping and grinding.

During the first few months of shooting, RKO patted itself on the back for liberality, pointing out that the cast was being directed by a woman, Dorothy Arzner. The first female member of the Directors Guild of America, Arzner had previously been responsible for Samuel Goldwyn's pretentious failure *Nana,* as well as the sentimental box office smash *Craig's Wife.* (Studio handouts failed to mention that Arzner was RKO's second choice, hired after Roy del Ruth withdrew from the project.) Fitfully, her work on the bromidic feature showed what might have been. A smackdown between Bubbles and Judy, for example, was spectacular in rehearsal. The encounter was so eagerly anticipated that the stars charged admission, with proceeds to be turned over to charity. Aided by fight choreographers, they went at it in the film's most galvanic scene. To demonstrate that there were no hard feelings afterward, Maureen O'Hara and Lucille Ball went off to lunch together, chuckling all the way to the commissary.

Caparisoned in a slinky gold lamé dress slit halfway up the thigh, her bleached tresses falling over a bogus black eye, Lucille stopped by a table to say hello to George Abbott, the director of *Too Many Girls,* then in rehearsal. At Abbott's side were several musicians and actors, including one he had brought west for the film version. Over the years biographers and journalists have compared the next few moments to such epochal meetings as the one between Romeo and Juliet ("She speaks, yet she says nothing"), and Sherlock Holmes and Dr. Watson ("You have been in Afghanistan, I perceive"). In fact, neither participant thought much of it at the time and neither was dressed to impress.

Outfitted in the striped jersey and scuffed tights of a college football player, Desi stood up, mumbled his name in a heavy Cuban accent, and flashed a perfunctory smile. He thought Lucille "looked like a two-dollar whore who had been badly beaten by her pimp." She found him quite different from the charismatic actor she had seen onstage—the one with the strange Spanish name—what was it again?

After Lucille returned to her table, Desi asked Abbott, "Who the hell is that?"

He was informed that Lucille was the actress assigned to play the part of the ingenue in *Too Many Girls*. Desi shook his head. The skills of the makeup artists notwithstanding, it would be impossible to change this run-down hooker into a coed.

That night the young actor, cleaned up and wearing a new outfit, was rehearsing the Rodgers and Hart song "She Could Shake the Maracas" when Lucille walked in. She had showered and exchanged her costume for a yellow sweater and a pair of tight-fitting beige slacks. In a heavy Cuban accent Desi whispered to the piano player, "Man, that is a honk of woman!"

"You met her today," the pianist reminded him.

Lucille strolled by and said hello.

"Miss Ball?" Desi inquired, just to make certain there was no mistake.

"Why don't you call me Lucille?" she offered. "And I'll call you Dizzy."

*A*t the time he and Lucille met, Desi was engaged to a dark-haired dancer named Renée de Marco, the partner and estranged wife of Tony de Marco. Renée had been treated brutally by her husband; she was grateful for the attentions of this boyish Cuban. Some of Desi's friends said Renée was rather like his mother, Lolita Arnaz—dark, beautiful, willful. He paid them no mind. To him, Renée was "a jewel, a rare and unique find." That was before the encounter with Lucille Ball.

For two years Lucille had enjoyed Al Hall's company, his advice and guidance. That was before she got a closer look at Desi Arnaz. Ann Miller was in the room when the meeting took place. Love at first sight is one of those phenomena, like sunrises, that occur daily but are watched by few. Miller was one of the observant. "When Desi first was introduced to Lucille," she claimed, "his eyes just lit up. He was the cutest thing around. God, he was attractive." Seven hours after the studio lunch the couple went dancing at a Mexican restaurant on Sunset Boulevard. Two days later they broke off relations with their former lovers. "A Cuban skyrocket," Lucille wrote, had "burst over my horizon." In Desi's words, "those damned big beautiful blue eyes" had trivialized everything and everyone else.

Love is an autobiographical passion, and during their first few dates the couple related their life stories. Lucille's, as we have seen, provided a winding and unusual narrative; Desi's tale was a good deal more exotic. Those who thought him a slum kid from the streets of Havana (and Lucille was one of them) were astonished by the news that Desi had been a child of privilege. Desiderio Alberto Arnaz y de Acha III was the only son of a prominent and moneyed Cuban politician. Desiderio II was not only the mayor of Santiago, a major port city; he also owned three large ranches with scores of employees. Desi's maternal grandfather was a cofounder of the Bacardi Rum company. The boy was expected to attend college and law school, and eventually to take over the family business. The summer of 1933 changed everything. It was in the month of August that Fulgencio Batista led the Cuban army in revolt against the corrupt regime of El Presidente Gerardo Machado. Politicians who had been close to the president were marked for execution or imprisonment, and their lands were confiscated. Desiderio II was placed under arrest and jailed, but in the chaos of *la revolución*, Desi and his mother, uncle, and cousin escaped the newly empowered Batista police force. The Arnazes had only the clothes they wore, a few pesos, a car, and a tank of gas—enough to get them to a port city in the western part of the island. En route, they pretended to be fervent supporters of the new regime, shouting *"Viva la Revolución!"* whenever they saw figures of authority. A day later the four made their escape on a ferry headed for Key West. On the voyage to Florida, Desi played and replayed in his mind the years of ease and the days of fear. Among his last sights of Cuba was the explosion of a bomb released from an open-cockpit plane; the bomb missed its target and blew the arm off a young bystander. The final image of his autobiographical account describes "a man's head stuck on a long pole and hung in front of his house. The rest of the body was hung two doors down in front of his father's house."

With an increasing number of barrios rising in Miami, the family could have retreated into an insular, resentful life of poverty and rage. But they refused to give in to circumstance. Six months after Desiderio II was incarcerated, strings were pulled and he was released, penniless but physically unharmed. He made his way to the beach city and attempted to set himself up in business.

Desi III tried to earn his own way, cleaning cages for a canary breeder, driving taxis, clerking in stores. On his parents' insistence, the youth attended a Catholic high school part-time. His closest friend at St. Patrick's was a boy he called Sonny. Desi never mentioned Sonny's absent father, although he knew the old man's identity and his whereabouts: Alcatraz. One morning Desi read that the old man had been paroled. He called Sonny and heard a strange speaker.

"He had a very high voice," Desi wrote, "almost a soprano.

" 'May I speak to Sonny please?' I asked.

" 'Who's this?'

" 'Who am I talking to?'

" 'This is Al, his father.'

" 'Oh, Mr. Capone!' Jesus Christ, I was talking to Al Capone."

The association was not one that met with the approval of the elder Arnazes, who still had plans to send their son to college (Notre Dame was their first choice). It was not to be. In the winter of 1936 Desi got a temporary gig singing and playing the guitar with a pickup rhumba band at the Roney Plaza Hotel in Miami Beach. The salary was more than he had ever earned in his life: $39 a week. A month later, the most prominent Latin musician in America dropped by. Xavier Cugat summoned Desi to his table. Satisfied that the young Cuban was properly deferential and naive about money, Cugat hired him to sing and play with his band. Salary: only $30 a week—but it offered the chance to travel, all expenses paid. Desi pounced. The tour started in Cleveland and wound up in Saratoga at the height of the racing season. On the way to the bandstand for a second set, he stopped to gawk at a patron. Bing Crosby greeted him in Spanish, invited the awed singer to hoist a glass, and asked about his salary. Desi told the truth.

"That cheap crook. Come on, let's talk to him."

As Cugat approached the table, Crosby spoke out: "Listen, you cheap Spaniard, what do you mean paying this fine Cuban singer thirty dollars a week?"

"He's just starting, Bingo."

"Never mind the Bingo stuff. Give him a raise. One of these days you are going to be asking him for a job."

"Okay, okay. How about singing a song with the band, Bing?"

"Will you give him a raise?"

"Of course."

Crosby performed many songs that night, some with his new friend. "He sang in Spanish, which was pretty good," Desi was to write, "and then I sang in English, which was pretty bad. The next time I saw Bing was when I was a guest on his Kraft Music Hall radio show. It was the very first time I appeared on national radio.

"The first thing he asked me was, 'Did you ever get that raise?'

" 'You bet. The following week he raised me to thirty-five dollars, and the only thing extra I had to do was walk his dogs until they completed their business.' "

Desi's offhand charm and intriguing accent made him an audience favorite, and in six months he felt confident enough to break away from Cugat and tour with his own band. Yet he remained insecure enough to want a safety net—a twenty-one-year-old singer-bandleader was unlikely to attract crowds without some sort of gimmick. He presented an idea to the conductor: what if he billed himself and a band of pickup musicians as "Desi Arnaz and His Xavier Cugat Orchestra"? That way Cugat would receive free publicity and Arnaz could get bookings. The boss agreed with one proviso. The brash young man had to pay him a royalty of $25 a week for the use of the Cugat brand name, work or no work.

Desi found himself in the black before the first note sounded. Mother Kelly's Club in Miami, impressed by the band's association with a headliner, offered $650 a week with a guarantee of three months' playing time. Then came opening night. Underrehearsed and cacophonous, the musicians displeased the audience and infuriated the owner. This was not even road-company Cugat, this was Amateur Night. Desi was fired on the spot. He begged for one more chance and received it only because no other talent could be found to replace the band on such short notice. The next evening, under the shaky baton of their leader and arranger, the orchestra offered "La Conga." Here was a

Cuban dance so elemental that Desi had never thought to play it in America. He illustrated the number with a brief demonstration: "It's very simple: one . . . two . . . three . . . KICK. One . . . two . . . three . . . KICK." As he watched, a conga line of listeners began to form, with the musicians showing them the way, kicking backward in unison as they made their way around the room. In a week, audiences were forming conga lines around the block. The craze that was to sweep America had begun.

The U.S. fascination with Latin American music was hardly a new phenomenon. It could be seen and heard in the 1933 Astaire-Rogers film *Flying Down to Rio;* in Al Jolson's mocking number, "She's a Latin from Manhattan" ("You can tell by her mañana / She's a Latin from Manhattan / and not Havana"); in the rhumba standard "South American Way"; and, of course, in the glib syncopations of Xavier Cugat's orchestra. But this was something new: a dance that could be appreciated by the tone-deaf and performed by the flat-footed. Mother Kelly's was renamed La Conga, and there Desi reigned supreme. At the age of twenty-two he traded Miami for New York City, leading his band at a new midtown nightery, also called La Conga. It was here that he embraced his first redhead. She was sitting with another beautiful young woman and an older woman with a husky and resonant voice. The place was noisy; Desi barely managed to catch the elder's name: Polly Adler. He had never heard of New York's most notorious madam, and when she invited him to have breakfast at her place he politely assented. There, after he had enjoyed caviar, sturgeon, scrambled eggs, and champagne, Polly gestured to a redhead at the end of the long table. She asked if the guest liked her. By now Desi realized that he had stumbled into a very high-priced whorehouse. The young lady's fee, he suspected, would bankrupt him. Adler looked at the guest's melancholy face, boomed her famous contralto laugh, and assured him, "That's all right, sonny. This one's on the house."

Desi's charmed life continued that way throughout 1939. Wherever he went, celebrities cottoned to him. He became the great and good friend of Brenda Frazier, an unruly debutante whose notorious antics were parodied by in a song by Richard Rodgers and Lorenz Hart:

> *I'll buy everything I wear at Sax,*
> *I'll cheat plenty on my income tax,*
> *Swear like a trooper,*

Live in a stupor. . . .
Swimming in highballs,
Stewed to the eyeballs,
Just disgustingly rich,
Too disgustingly rich!

Adler and Frazier brought hundreds of new customers to La Conga. These ranged from out-of-town businessmen to society divas and their dates, all looking for someplace new to spend an evening. Between sets, Desi whiled away the hours with Brenda Frazier's crowd, or hung around at Polly Adler's. Working at night, sleeping most of the day, he lived an animal existence with no plan beyond the approaching meal and the next coition. When Rodgers and Hart dropped by his dressing room one night, he thought it was just another pair of Broadway celebrities making a pit stop. He had no idea his life was about to be changed forever.

Months before, Hart had seen Desi cavorting in the Miami club. Watching him on a New York stage, the lyricist saw new possibilities in the young Cuban. He might be right to play a Latin football player called Manuelito in the new Rodgers and Hart musical, *Too Many Girls*. The trouble was, Desi had never played a part other than his ebullient self. Hart took him in hand, taught him the rudiments of auditioning, and slipped him a script—in direct violation of director George Abbott's policy. Abbott liked actors to undergo cold readings so that he could evaluate their talents while they squirmed and struggled. Upon hearing Desi sing, Abbott gave Hart an instant evaluation: "Well, he's loud enough." Desi was then handed a script and ordered to read the part where a young Argentinian football player is recruited by an American college. The Latino agrees to go, provided the institution has a superabundance of senoritas.

"Oh," says the talent scout. "You mean coeducational."

"Tha's it," replies Manuelito. "Cooperational."

Desi seemed ideal for the part, all right. A little too ideal. He read the rest of the lines flawlessly, and as Abbott and Rodgers exchanged looks Hart tiptoed up the aisle toward the exit.

"Larry!" Abbott called. "You gave him the script, didn't you?"

Hart sputtered, "Who? Me? How? Why?"

"Because he hasn't looked at one goddamned word of that scene. He did the whole thing like a big ham, emoting and waving all over the place. You taught him, didn't you? And, I may add, you did a bad job of it."

Hart broke down and confessed, and Desi sheepishly admitted his part in the plot. Abbott, less out of charity than out of a sense that Desi really was right for Manuelito, forgave the composer and the actor and signed up the man he addressed as "Dizzy" from then on. Desi did more than charm his director. The first-act finale, "Look Out," was built on a shave-and-a-haircut tempo that mentioned the names of college football teams. Rodgers wrote it as a march, and Desi had trouble adapting to the four-quarter time. He kept imposing his own conga beat, to the conductor's intense annoyance. In the middle of the rehearsal Rodgers came in and heard about the contretemps.

"What's the matter with your guys?" he asked the musicians. "We'll have the first chorus straight, and then when Desi starts the conga beat, we'll change it to fit his thing. To tell you the truth, I like it better his way."

Rodgers's instinct for the *note juste* was infallible. During rehearsals Desi's beat gradually took over the entire number, the young Cuban banging out the rhythm on his drum while Diosa Costello sang and wiggled on the beat as the chorus wove a serpentine line around the stage. *Too Many Girls* opened on October 14, 1939, at the Imperial Theatre. Desi had never attended a Broadway show. Now he was starring in one created by some of the most dazzling talents in the musical theater. In the end, it was naivete that kept him from being nervous. He recited his lines without error, ended the first act with that triumphant dance, and got a standing ovation for his efforts. The song he delivered with Costello was to take on another meaning in later years:

> *She could shake the maracas*
> *He could play the guitar,*
> *But he lived in Havana*
> *And she down in Rio del Mar.*
> *And she shook her maracas*
> *In a Portuguese bar*
> *While he strummed in Havana.*
> *The distance between them was far.*
> *By and by*
> *He got a job with a band in Harlem.*
> *She got a job with a band in Harlem.*

Ay! Ay! Ay!
He said, "I'm the attraction!"
She said, "I am the star!"
But they finally married
And now see how happy they are.
So shake your maracas,
Play your guitar!

When the curtain came down Desi walked to La Conga and did the midnight show as if nothing unusual had occurred. The last set ended at 4 a.m. At last he could cool down and chat with Richard and Dorothy Rodgers, George Abbott, and Larry Hart. "About half an hour later," Desi ecstatically wrote, "I saw Polly Adler heading for our table. She had all the newspapers in her hands, and as she approached she hollered in that big, deep voice of hers, 'Cuban, you are the biggest fucking hit in town!'" Within a few weeks Walter Winchell had dubbed the conga line "the Desi Chain," and young Arnaz became a New York fixture whose celebrity seemed to increase with each performance. There were offers to appear in other shows, other nightclubs, films.

Only one faux pas was committed in this period, and that was made not by Desi but by his mother, Lolita. At a party at Desi's new apartment, a duplex overlooking Central Park, Larry Hart's mother was enthusing about her son. Suddenly Lolita reached out and sat Larry on her lap. Hart was something of a faun in appearance, five feet tall and excruciatingly self-conscious about his diminutive height and build. Lolita held the lyricist in place, laughing uproariously as he attempted to shake loose from her maternal grasp. Helpless and humiliated, he started to cry.

Desi was to remember 1939 as one of the most triumphant years imaginable—but also as one of the saddest. For during that year his father filed for divorce, a rare event for Catholic Cubans, and unthinkable when it involved two people who had seemed so devoted to each other. When Desiderio II called his son to explain the situation, Desi hung up on him. The two were not to reconcile for many years, and during that time Desi assumed the role of guardian for Lolita, a dispirited woman exhibiting some unattractive aspects of middle age.

While his father moved in with a younger woman, Desi and Lolita lived in Desi's duplex, an ideal bachelor pad before the bad news arrived, but now an unnaturally quiet place. Desi thought his mother needed an attentive listener, and he curtailed his tomcat prowls. But this devotion only served to increase Lolita's dependence on her only child. She spent most evenings at La Conga, beaming at her son from a front table. It was all too much for the young, charged-up performer, and he sought the classic exit from a suffocating family arrangement: marriage. Most recently he had been seeing Renée de Marco, and together they made the necessary arrangements. Desi would accept a Hollywood offer to appear in the film version of *Too Many Girls,* driving cross-country and meeting Renée on the Coast as soon as she received her divorce. Everything went according to plan—until that fateful evening when the "honk of woman" entered Desi's orbit. From that moment, all bets were off.

𝒟esi started calling his new flame Lucy a day after they met. The reason was less aesthetic than proprietary. "I didn't like the name Lucille," he commented. "That name had been used by other men. 'Lucy' was mine alone."

Hollywood is a town that runs on rumor, and the Desi-Lucy romance had barely begun when studio gossips started odds-making. Unsolicited advice issued from Lucy's friends and acquaintances: "He's flashy and egotistical." "He's Catholic and you're Protestant." "He's immature—almost six years younger than you are." "He dumped Renée de Marco without a backward glance. You'll be the next." And indeed, apart from the obvious physical attraction they felt for each other, there seemed no reason to believe the affair would be any more than a brief, passionate fling destined to burn itself out, as studio Cassandras forecast, in six months. Even in little matters Desi's impulsive character seemed at odds with Lucy's calculating one. He would take her for rides in his Buick Roadmaster convertible, pushing down on the gas pedal until they reached a speed of a hundred miles an hour on the straightaway. At one point Lucy began to scream uncontrollably.

"What's wrong?" Desi shouted.

Nothing, she claimed; she had been instructed to lower her voice an octave or two, and Katharine Hepburn said that screaming was the best way.

"Okay," Desi replied. "You scream and I'll drive."

On the set of *Too Many Girls,* Lucy paid close attention to the advice of director George Abbott. In contrast, according to Garson Kanin, who was assisting Abbott, "Desi came on strong, bossy, and a pain in the ass." The Arnaz charm went a very short way, not only with Kanin but with many other Anglos of the period, men and women. A few years prior to Desi's first Hollywood role, Helen Lawrenson had written a widely quoted article that appeared in *Esquire,* "Latins Are Lousy Lovers." Many a jealous suitor and disappointed paramour could recite passages by heart, particularly the one about Cubans: "God knows, the Cuban man spends enough time on the subject of sex. He devotes his life to it. He talks of it, dreams it, reads it, sings it, dances it, eats it, sleeps it—does everything but do it. That last is not literally true, but it is a fact that they spend far more time in words than in action. . . . According to them, they always had their first affair at the age of two. This may account for their being worn out at twenty-three."

Lucy was familiar with all the objections and well aware that Desi was not winning friends and influencing people at the studio. She was too smitten to care. For the first time since her arrival in town, she dated at the end of a workday, and on weekends she and Desi escaped the heat by motoring to Palm Springs. Saturdays and Sundays brimmed with passionate declarations, but very heat of their affair made meltdowns inevitable. Almost every Sunday night ended with a furious argument about each other's intentions and infidelities. By nightfall Desi would drop Lucy off at the apartment she kept on North Laurel Avenue and announce hotly that he was going home to look after his mother. Lucy would plead for him not to go so soon—there was still so much left unsaid. It happened that two of the town's greatest magpies witnessed many of the quarrels. F. Scott Fitzgerald and his inamorata, columnist Sheilah Graham, used to watch the spats from Fitzgerald's balcony. "She always seemed to be asking him not to drive away," Graham wrote. "We couldn't understand his reluctance and sometimes made bets on the outcome. No matter which of us lost, we were both pleased when Lucille won."

Sexual jealousy was omnipresent. When the two were on the road, Desi plugging *Too Many Girls* and Lucy publicizing *Dance, Girl, Dance,* they kept in touch by phone. He tended to open the conversation with tart demands, like "Where were you when I called you last time? Who the hell were you having dinner with?" With that as an opener, the colloquy could only go downhill. Desi remembered one particular call from Lucy. Before he could get settled in his chair, she shouted, "You Cuban sonofabitch, where were you all last night? What are you trying to do, lay every goddamned one of those chorus girls in *Too Many Girls*? No wonder they picked you for the show."

As a matter of fact, Desi was trying to do exactly that, and he felt that his best defense was a counteraccusation. When he saw a newspaper picture of a young, good-looking Milwaukee politician, he decided that Lucy was in that city for one purpose only. "I know why you're staying there," he yelled. "You're screwing the Mayor." Desi later commented, "How the hell we survived this period and still had the guts to marry I'll never understand."

Everyone else was similarly puzzled, with the exception of Desi's mother, who spoke no English and smiled upon Lucy because of her kind face and good manners, and Lucy's family, who welcomed Desi because he was what Lucy wanted. Whatever her cousin desired, Cleo maintained, "was accepted by one and all. We knew why she liked him. He was adorable looking. Lucy was a mature person. I suppose DeDe was delighted she had fallen head over heels and was confident she could handle it." "Daddy," as usual, was something of an exception. Fred Hunt whispered to Lucy that Desi "seems a nice fellow, but he doesn't speak so good and he's a little dark, isn't he?" These objections did not stop Hunt from propagandizing his granddaughter's newest beau. "Couldn't get in the door without his reading all those *People's World* editorials," Desi would write. The Cuban needed no advice about revolutions; he had seen one at close range. "I told Fred Hunt to cut it out or I'd teach him to rhumba."

Published more than thirty-five years later, Desi's memoir states that he was in Manhattan in November 1940 when Lucy "finally finished her Milwaukee deal and came to New York. I was wrong about her screwing the Mayor—I think—and I was madly in love with her, and I knew she was in love with me." He was doing five shows a day at the Roxy, and between appearances he made a few out-of-town phone calls, then taxied over to the Hotel Pierre, where Lucy had a suite. He found her in the middle of an interview with a magazine writer. The journalist had provisionally titled her article "Why Lucille Ball Prefers to Remain a Bachelor Girl," and Lucy was enumerating the reasons for staying single. The questioner had just moved to the subject of Desi. As he listened, Lucy assured the journalist that while the couple would see each other in New York—after all, he was here right now—marriage was out of the question. There were too many cultural, professional, and emotional barriers between them. Even the geography made no sense. Desi was committed to a life on the road, a life of nightclubs and theater work; she was rooted in Hollywood. With growing impatience, Desi sat and twitched until the interviewer departed.

"This girl is going to have a hell of a time with that story," he predicted.

Really, Lucy remarked. And why was that?

"Because I have everything arranged to marry you tomorrow morning, if you would like to marry me."

"Where?"

"In Connecticut."

"You're kidding, right?"

"No, I'm not kidding. I want to marry you and I want to marry you tomorrow."

"Why couldn't we just live together?"

"No, I don't want to just live together. I want to marry you and I want to have some children with you and I want to have a home. I am not like the image you have of me."

The final sentence was his acknowledgment that there were two Desis: the handsome, inconstant Latin lover and the devoted family man. Yes, he had made many vows of love before only to go back on them, but this, he swore, was different. If a man was in love—truly in love—he could change, thoroughly, completely, forever. Of that Desi was certain. What better way to prove it than with a bout of intense lovemaking? But there was no time left—he had to race back to the Roxy to perform his fourth show of the day.

When Desi returned he found Lucy going over contracts with George Schaefer, the president of RKO. He was gratified to hear that they were discussing business, and not the impending nuptials; Desi wanted to break that news himself. As he made ready to speak, Schaeffer tried to attract his attention: Desi's fly was open, and in his haste to dress he had forgotten to put on underwear.

Lucy caught the gesture and explained to Schaeffer, "He believes in advertising."

Desi also believed—correctly, it turned out—that Lucy was about to change her mind. Her self-doubt expressed itself in hesitations and evasions, all of which Desi refused to acknowledge, talking fast and thinking later. Skating over thin ice, his safety was in his speed. He picked Lucy up the next morning at eight and headed for Greenwich, Connecticut, in a limousine driven by his business manager. The bride, still irresolute, still confused, wore black. A wool dress was all she had with her; the rest of her clothing had not yet been sent on from Milwaukee. Not that it mattered to Desi. As the car roared up the Merritt Parkway he smiled and necked with his intended, and when he came up for air, he serenaded her with songs in Spanish. She noticed the sheen of his dark eyes, and the adoring smile that softened his face. She also observed that the groom's hands were trembling.

"The hair is
brown but the
soul is on fire"

*I*N HIS HASTE Desi had neglected a few items. Connecticut law required couples to observe a five-day waiting period before taking marriage vows. In order to get around the law, he and Lucy had to round up a judge to make an official exception. Once that was done, they still were short of a vital, if sentimental, item. Desi had neglected to purchase a wedding band. While the couple fretted, Desi's manager ran into a local Woolworth's and bought a brass ring from the costume jewelry counter. On November 30, 1940, Justice of the Peace John P. O'Brien agreed to conduct a ceremony at the Byram River Beagle Club. After that, the couple ate their wedding breakfast before the glowing fireplace in the club lounge, kissed each other, and then kissed the marriage certificate. (Decades later, when the paper had begun to show signs of age, Lucy's lipstick still glowed red upon the surface.)

By now word had leaked out, and local reporters gathered in the lounge. Desi consulted his watch. It was nearly noon, and he was due to lead his band at the Roxy Theatre in midtown Manhattan. He made his way to a pay phone, called the theater manager, and identified himself.

"You're on in five minutes," came the annoyed reply.

"That's what I called you about," said Desi. "I'm in Connecticut."

"You *can't* be in Connecticut."

"I know. But I am. I been marrying Lucy."

On their way back to New York the couple heard a radio announcer read a bulletin: actress Lucille Ball and band leader Desi Arnaz had wed. DeDe, in California, received the news from the same coast-to-coast broadcast. A knot of boisterous fans waited outside the Roxy, greeting the new Arnazes with a clamorous ovation. Desi brought his bride onstage to another chorus of cheers. That night, calls to relatives and friends reassured Desi and Lucy. Everyone seemed ecstatic—with the sole exception of Harriet McCain. Lucy's maid had never been certain about this Cuban courtier, and when Lucy phoned to ask about the wardrobe, Harriet inquired, "*Who* did we marry?"

It was a shrewder question than she knew. The charmer and devoted lover had many hidden traits that were to emerge in subsequent years. He turned out, for example, to be a possessive and dictatorial male in the much-caricatured Latin tradition. Desi was not as extreme as Fernando Lamas, who refused to see Esther Williams's children because they were evidence that she had slept with another man. Yet Desi wasted no time staking out his territory and making his demands clear. On the wedding night, for example, he shook Lucy awake because he was thirsty. "I was out of bed and running the tap in the bathroom," she remembered, "before I woke up sufficiently to wonder why in the hell he didn't get it himself." He also refused to let his wife ride in a taxi alone, because it would place her in close proximity to an unknown male. And it was his taste in food that determined what was on the menu (arroz con pollo, picadillo, rice and black beans) and not her meat-and-potatoes preferences. Nevertheless, Lucy warmed to the role of married woman. If marriage called for her to play a supporting role to the star, so be it.

The Roxy engagement ended a week later, and the couple traveled home on the Super Chief to Los Angeles. Desi had arranged for adjoining bedrooms, opening the door between them to fashion a rolling honeymoon suite. Between passionate embraces he sat in a corner mumbling to himself while he strummed a guitar. Lucy wrote about her primal fear at the time: "My God, he's already tired of me." In fact,

her new husband was simply composing a love song in her honor.
When it was completed he serenaded the bride, playing it over and
over for the rest of the journey:

> When I looked into your eyes
> And then you softly said "I do,"
> I suddenly realized I had a new world
> A world with you
> A world where life is worth living
> A world that is so new to me
> A world of taking and giving
> Like God meant the world to be
> Where good times will find two to greet
> Where hard times will find two to beat
> I found my new world with you, darling
> When you softly said "I do."

Back in Los Angeles the Arnazes set up living quarters in Lucy's
apartment, each fully aware that this could be only a temporary
arrangement. Each had grown up in a house; both wanted four walls
and a patch of earth they could call their own. Lucy had been friends
with Jack Oakie since their days on the *Annabel* films. Early one
evening the comedian welcomed the couple to his house at
Chatsworth in the San Fernando Valley. A local developer had built
small ranch houses on five-acre plots surrounded by gently sloping
mountains, and Oakie invited them to look around. Within an hour the
Arnazes found a spread with a large grove of orange trees and a swimming pool. Negotiations got under way. The asking price was $14,500,
to be paid up front. That was more than the Arnazes wanted to
advance. There was a brief hesitation, then the developer relented.
After all, the prospective buyers were recognizable Hollywood names;
perhaps he could use their celebrity to attract others. Lucy and Desi
were allowed to make the purchase for a minuscule down payment of
$1,500 and a ten-year mortgage.

Friends showered them with presents and congratulatory dinners,
topped by a champagne supper at Chasen's given by Carole Lombard
and her new superstar husband, Clark Gable. All that was missing was
a name for the Arnaz property. "We had heard of Pickfair, Mary Pickford and Douglas Fairbanks's elegant million-dollar estate, so why

shouldn't we have one?" Desi wrote. "Our place looked like a million to us. We tried Arnaball (no good), Ballarnaz (ugh), Lucy's Des (no), Desi's Ball (definitely not), Ludesi (not quite), Desilu—BINGO!" It was the first time he had received top billing over Lucy. She offered no objection; it was part of her role as second fiddle. Besides, they were both thrilled with Thornton Wilder's judgment. The playwright and novelist was spending some time in town as a screenwriter; he heard of the name for their home and told them "Desilu" sounded like the past participle of a French verb.

For a short, delirious time, the bucolic appeal of Desilu helped to divert the newlyweds' attention from Hollywood reality. The calf and the chickens they'd acquired, the orange grove, the vegetable garden gave the couple a strong sense of well-being. While Lucy was newly beguiled by the land, she remained enthralled with her husband. In *Collier's* magazine, Kyle Crichton, biographer of the Marx Brothers, noted: "You start interviewing Miss Lucille Ball and then Mr. Desi Arnaz enters and Miss Ball leaves. It is not that she leaves in person, she merely leaves in spirit. Miss Lucille Ball looked at Mr. Desi Arnaz as if he were something that had floated down from above on a cloud."

Yet the professional situation could not be ignored for much longer. Desi's accent had slowed his rise in pictures. When RKO got around to offering him a part, it was the dual role of prince and commoner in the hack farce *Four Jacks and a Jill,* ineptly directed by former film editor Jack Hively. Desi labeled it a lesson in "how not to do comedy," called the director a broken-down bum, threatened him with bodily harm, and predicted box office disaster. His prediction was accurate. Notwithstanding, the studio had no patience for Latin temperament. Desi was next assigned the very minor role of singing stowaway in *Father Takes a Wife,* with Adolphe Menjou and the faded star Gloria Swanson. As a crowning irony, Desi's version of the song "Perfidia" was dubbed by an operatic tenor. Later, he observed, "I received letters from Latin America, Spain, and especially Cuba, asking me, 'What the hell were you trying to do with "Perfidia" and where did you pick up that Italian accent?' "

Lucy's career was nearly as uncertain. Rattled by several recent turkeys, RKO hired pollsters to question the public about the studio's

contract players. The results were not good news for Lucille Ball: only
58 percent of those questioned recognized her name, and she and Desi
were among forty-five performers who were long shots to become box
office draws. Still, she did appear irregularly on Rudy Vallee's and
Edgar Bergen's radio programs, and that made her exploitable in the
short term. Early in 1941 Lucy played Bergen's love interest in *Look
Who's Laughing,* a modest hit built around such radio personalities as
Fibber McGee and Molly, and Harold Peary, better known to listeners
as the Great Gildersleeve. That fall she was assigned to appear as a
restaurant owner in a second-rate "oater" called *Valley of the Sun,* starring James Craig as a federal agent.

Desi briefly visited the set in New Mexico before setting off to pro-
mote his own film, back on the road with a band—no "Mr. Ball" for
him, he indignantly proclaimed. Following the Western fiasco (*Variety*
labeled her as "low-voltage marquee strength"), Lucy was told to report
for work as the second lead in *Strictly Dynamite.* She declined to play
in Betty Grable's shadow—and immediately went on suspension. "This
shows how her career was being handled," observed a prominent
agent. "Her studio wasn't interested in building her into a long-range
star. They were content to make a quick buck on a loan-out, even
though it would have been bad for her career."

As the Arnazes' marriage approached the one-year mark it became
distinguished not by the annealing passion Desi had promised but by
the separations he had chosen. Their relationship was largely maintained via telephone. In those days, Lucy said, "We spent a lot of
money on the word 'what.' When Desi was calling me or I was calling
him, the connection was always so bad we couldn't hear each other.
That's why 'what' was so expensive." A week after their first anniversary
Desi and his band were booked into New York. For once he would be
in a large city for at least a fortnight. Lucy flew to his side. "I knew he
was fooling around with somebody," she grumbled, "and I couldn't do
anything about it long distance. Also I knew I couldn't get pregnant
over the telephone." In New York all sexual and professional skirmishes
seemed to dissipate in the crisp December air. A friend loaned them
his apartment, and one Sunday the Arnazes took over the place, enjoying brunch in bed, kissing and embracing as they listened to a football
game. Early in the afternoon a terse announcement put an end to the
fun and games: Japanese planes had attacked Pearl Harbor. New York

suddenly seemed like alien territory, an arena of bad news. The Arnazes left for their ranch the next morning.

Conscription touched the lives of nearly everyone around Lucy and Desi—at the studio, in the stores, on the street. Lucy miscarried early in her first pregnancy, but there was no point in feeling sorry for themselves; many of their friends and acquaintances had suffered much more painful losses. During a war bond drive in January 1942, Lucy's pal and mentor, Carole Lombard, perished in a plane crash outside Las Vegas. And all around the Arnazes were reminders of the war: the dispiriting headlines, the lonely wives, the men in uniform getting ready for combat duty overseas. At twenty-five Desi was within draft age; the Selective Service notice was due to arrive any day. He wanted to go on the road to take his mind off the situation—and, Lucy suspected, to prove his masculinity and professional viability. She tried to talk him out of it, but in the spring of 1942 he signed on to the Victory Caravan, effectively removing himself from the Hollywood scene without really leaving it. This group of fund-raisers for army and navy relief included Bob Hope, James Cagney, Mickey Rooney, and Olivia de Havilland; along with some eighteen others, they acted, sang, joked, and gave speeches as they traversed the country in a railroad car. As Robert S. Sennett details in *Hollywood Hoopla,* the stars of the Caravan "may have been genuinely interested in helping the war effort, but they were flushed out of their private hiding places by necessity. The war had destroyed the foreign market for films, and domestic sales needed tremendous boosting. Glittering premieres with fancy cars and floodlights were disallowed. There was nothing for the stars to do but roll up their sleeves and go to work like everybody else."

When he was not working like everybody else, Desi went in avid pursuit of anything in skirts, a pastime that provoked comment even among such spirited seducers as Rooney. Word got back to Lucy, who hit the ceiling—and then persuaded herself that Desi was just reflecting the strain and craziness of the war, and his inability to catch on in Hollywood. The best thing to do in the interim was to keep busy. At this moment of great distress an unusual opportunity came her way.

The film was *The Big Street,* based on a Damon Runyon story. Lucy had met Runyon at least twice, once when Walter Winchell introduced them, and again when the creator of Sky Masterson and Nicely-Nicely Johnson came to RKO as a producer. In the previous year

Carole Lombard had recommended Lucy for the role of the mean, manipulative nightclub singer, Gloria, in a screen adaptation of Runyon's short story "Little Pinks." Runyon remembered the suggestion and sent Lucy a copy of the script.

One reading convinced Lucy that Gloria was the part of a lifetime, "a girl with a foolish, unhealthy obsession which made her more ruthless than Scarlett O'Hara. It was anything but a sympathetic part, but it was exciting because it was so meaty—so rich in humor, pathos and tragedy." Even so, she hesitated to sign the contract. "It was the only time," Desi was to remark, "that I'd seen her afraid to tackle a role." Lucy could hardly be blamed for her concern. Gloria is wheelchairbound, thanks to a brutal attack by her ex-lover, and brimming with hostility to men. In her view, "Love gives you a one-room apartment, two chins, and a long wash line." She vents her hostility on the one soul who truly loves her, a shy busboy called Little Pinks, to be played by Henry Fonda. Fonda had grown several cubits in stature as an actor since their date, and Lucy was edgy about working with a bona fide leading man—something she had never done before. Of greater concern were the disagreeable aspects of her on-screen character. She whispered her doubts to a respected acquaintance, Charles Laughton. Much to her astonishment, the English actor agreed to scan the scenario. That night he summoned the young woman to his house. His counsel was direct and highly professional. She was not to fall back on her familiar "drop-gag" persona. The role needed a vixen, not a pussycat.

Easy for him to say; Lucy was not so sure. Only after heated discussion with friends and family did she agree to do the part as written, hoping that Fonda would help her delineate the character of Gloria. No such luck. This was the last RKO picture in Fonda's contract, and as far as he was concerned it was good riddance to bad celluloid. He came to the set aloof, and remained so for the duration of the filming, totally absorbed in his own interpretation of Little Pinks. After the first day Lucy realized she was on her own, and made the best of it. Director Irving Reis professed delight in her performance. Runyon was so moved by Lucy's interpretation that when the movie was completed he watched it in the privacy of a screening room, where he hoped no one would see him snuffling. He had forgotten about the projectionist.

But the film seemed to sail under a curse. Just after *The Big Street* wrapped, Runyon left the studio, Reis joined the army and was thus unavailable for postproduction refinements, and the editor, William Hamilton, died of a heart attack while cutting the picture. With all this going against it, *The Big Street* had little chance at the box office, even though it earned the best notices Lucy had ever received. The *New York Herald Tribune* reviewer wrote: "Lucille Ball gives one of the best portrayals of her career as the ever-grasping, selfish Gloria who takes keen delight in kicking the hapless Pinks about." *Life* magazine concurred: "Ball's performance is superb—the girl can really act." And in *Time* James Agee offered a review that was particularly gratifying because he detested Fonda's work (to him Little Pinks possessed all "the dignity of a wax grape of wrath"), whereas "pretty Lucille Ball, who was born for the parts Ginger Rogers sweats over, tackles her 'emotional' role as if it were sirloin and she didn't care who was looking."

In Hollywood, then as now, reviews ran a far second to profits, and *The Big Street* barely broke even. In June 1942, less than a week after Lucy completed her last scene for the Runyon film, she was back in harness. The B musical *Seven Days' Leave* costarred Victor Mature as a soldier who must marry an already engaged woman (Lucille Ball) in order to inherit a fortune. The movie featured a few good tunes by Frank Loesser and Jimmy McHugh, but the plot was banal and so was Mature, on loan from Twentieth Century–Fox and resenting every minute of it. At the time he was carrying on with Rita Hayworth and wanted her as his costar. Harry Cohn, boss of Columbia Pictures, refused to loan Hayworth out. Petulantly, Mature blamed it all on Lucille. He gave an even more subaqueous performance than usual, and during love scenes he held his costar painfully close. While he groped her he kept up a steady stream of invective just out of microphone range. Sometimes Lucille screamed at him; on other occasions she just ran to her dressing room and bawled.

As shooting wound down, RKO's new president summoned Lucy to his office and gave her the straight story. The studio brass no longer regarded the actress Lucille Ball as a comer. Good notices were all very well, but public response had never been impressive and now she was bumping her head on the ceiling. "For your own good," Charles Koerner told Lucy, "you should get up the gumption to leave. A couple of other studios have been asking for you since *The Big Street*. I'll share your contract with Metro or Paramount. Which do you want?"

She chose Metro-Goldwyn-Mayer, principally because it was considered the Cadillac of studios (her salary was increased to $2,000 a week), but also because it gave her a chance to rub shoulders and other parts with the most impressive names in the industry. In a sense, the jump was intimidating. She would have to compete with such established personalities as Irene Dunne, Greer Garson, and Margaret Sullavan, as well as with relative newcomers like Kathryn Grayson, Esther Williams, and the young Lana Turner, eleven years younger than the thirty-one-year-old Lucy. Yet it was also exhilarating: MGM's leading men included Clark Gable, Spencer Tracy, and Jimmy Stewart.

If Lucy was not in their stratum, neither was she a cipher. Louis B. Mayer agreed to sign Lucille Ball because he knew her to be a thoroughgoing professional, able to deliver a comic line with flair, pretty enough to be in A pictures, and devoid of star temperament. He saw to it that she got the dressing room that had once been Norma Shearer's in the grand old days when Shearer was married to MGM's late production genius Irving Thalberg. And he made sure that Lucy would be tested for MGM's flattering Technicolor process.

She was preparing for that test when a momentous decision was made. It would enhance her professional life in more ways than she could count, though at the time she regarded the alteration as a nuisance. Sydney Guilaroff, Metro's chief hair stylist, took a look at the newest addition to the stable and proclaimed, "The hair is brown but the soul is on fire." Accordingly, he had Lucy's hair dyed "Tango Red," a shade between carrot and strawberry. Guilaroff, Lucy wrote, "also changed the style of my hair from long and loose and flowing to up and laquered, until I had to take the crust off it at night by cracking it with a brush."

Uncomfortably, gingerly, Lucy took a big step up. Her first project for MGM was a carefully scrubbed adaptation of Cole Porter's risqué musical *Du Barry Was a Lady,* with a cast that included Red Skelton, as the comic lead; a young dancer named Gene Kelly; and comedian Zero Mostel, making his film debut.

Events in Lucy's private life did not correspond with those on her résumé. Grandpa Fred was obviously failing. Her brother Freddy seemed to be dogged with bad luck since the beginning of the war. He was hired on the night shift for Vega aircraft—and then dismissed without notice, coldly informed that he was not a good citizen. Freddy was no longer a wide-eyed innocent; he suspected that this was payback for registering as a Communist in that long-ago election. He assembled a sheaf of letters testifying to his good character. Employers nodded sympathetically but refused to hire him. He left Los Angeles and found work with airplane companies in Wichita, Kansas, where the tolerance for "security risks" was evidently higher than on the Coast. But the stigma would not go away. Frederick Ball was drafted, only to be deferred—something in his background, Selective Service hinted, although its representatives would not be more precise. Returning to L.A., Freddy opened a roller-skating rink. When he was away from his place of business Lucy bought hundreds of admission tickets and gave them to her friends. Nothing helped; despite all this surreptitious aid the rink failed. "The only money it was taking in," Lucy remarked, "was the money I was sending in."

Added to these difficulties was the unending problem of Desi. Interludes of domesticity were broken by his tours, and these always seemed to lead to more womanizing. When he did get a break, it revealed the ugly underside of casting. Since the early days, Latin leading men—Ramón Navarro, Gilbert Roland, Cesar Romero—had found a place in Hollywood, but that place was precarious. In his description of a Latin band, Raymond Chandler caught the attitude of the time: "Whatever they play, it all sounds the same. They always sing the same song, and it always has nice open vowels and a drawn-out sugary lilt, and the guy who sings it always strums on a guitar and has a lot to say about *amor, mi corazón,* and a lady who is *'linda,'* but very hard to convince, and he always has too long and too oily hair and when he isn't making with the love stuff he looks as if his knife work in an alley would be efficient and economical."

That viewpoint was much in evidence when Louis B. Mayer caught Desi's act at a live show in Hollywood, Ken Murray's *Blackouts.* The executive asked the singer to drop by sometime. Thrilled, Desi showed up the next day. "You remind me of Busher," Mayer informed him. Busher was the top racehorse in Mayer's stable, and Desi took this as a compliment until the studio chief elaborated: "Busher looks very common when he's around the barn, but when they put a saddle on him, and he goes around the track, you know he's a champion. The same thing happens to you when you hang that drum around your shoulder. Up to that point you're just another Mexican."

"Not Mexican, sir. Cuban."

"Well, one of those Latin fellows."

Mayer's verbal affront was followed by a financial one. Desi did something he had never done before. He swallowed the insults, humbly signing with MGM for $650 a week, less than half what Lucy was making. Now he had two choices: he could play househusband—gardening, straightening up, waiting each day for Lucy to come home from work—or he could go back on the road raising money for the USO. As Lucy expected, he signed up for the next available trip. In what amounted to a challenge, she went out on her own brief USO journey, flying cross-country even though she had been terrified of planes since the death of Carole Lombard. Her Hollywood group included Betty Grable, Marie "the Body" McDonald, Ann Sheridan, and the vaudeville and theater performer Frank Fay. "Fay lusted after Marie McDonald like nothing I've ever seen," Lucy later recounted. "But he went about it in the most disgusting ways possible. He would back her into a corner and say, 'I'm going to fuck you.' Or he'd call her hotel room in the middle of the night and say, 'I'd love to see the back of your belly.' "

As the plane circled the field one evening, Fay sat across the aisle from McDonald, lasciviously appraising her bodice. "Suddenly," Lucy went on, "we hit the worst turbulence I ever felt in my life, and the plane was all over the sky. Up and down. Up and down. I was sure we were going to crash. All I could think about was Carole. I looked over at Marie bouncing around in her seat and everybody's screaming except Frank Fay, who can't get his eyes off Marie's tits. She was clutching the armrest, and her face was white as a sheet. She looked over at Frank and said, 'So you want to fuck me?' Frank shook his head yes. McDonald grabbed him and said, 'Okay . . . NOW!' "

With Desi away so much of the time, Lucy threw herself into the making of *Du Barry Was a Lady*. Her voice was deemed inadequate, and a singer was hired to do the songs while the redhead mouthed them. Lucy had trouble with her footwork, but this inadequacy was addressed by dance director Charles Walters, who spent weeks getting the steps right, and by Robert Alton, who oversaw the musical portions and the lip-synching. In addition, Buster Keaton, the old silent farceur, was on the set to give pointers about physical comedy.

The plot of *Du Barry* revolved around Red Skelton as a coat-checker yearning for a nightclub singer, played by Lucille Ball. Someone slips him a Mickey Finn and his fevered brain propels him back to the eighteenth century. He becomes Louis XIV and Lucy metamorphoses into Madame Du Barry. Their wooing comes to involve lords and ladies-in-waiting, servants and jesters, as well as the entire Tommy Dorsey band. With most of the racier material excised, the humor was labored and obvious, save for a bit with a celery stalk conceived by Keaton.

Even though Skelton and Ball knew their way around a funny line, the two stars never enjoyed a close rapport. The comedian tried for big moments; the comedienne shrank from them. On the set, nothing seemed to work in her favor. Hours spent rehearsing on a trampoline made her seasick. Her newly tinted hair was buried beneath mounds of white wigs, and her figure obscured by vast, unflattering hoopskirts. She disliked the exaggerated mouth movements she had to make while pretending to sing, and, burdened by heavy costumes in every scene, she found the Technicolor lighting hot, harsh, and intimidating. But the experience was not a total waste. When Lucy saw the dailies, she was dazzled by the way everyone looked. The German cameraman Karl Freund had found a way to make the cast—especially Lucy—blithe and glamorous. She remembered his name above all the other technicians and actors; clearly, this was a man to cultivate.

A crew from *Life* came to the filming; a story in the magazine showed Lucy on the trampoline and, recalling her performance in *The Big Street,* called her "almost a Damon Runyon character." It continued: "She is ambitious, hard, flamboyant and luxury-loving. Yet paradoxically, she is generous, funny and extremely sensitive."

Lucy's teeth, apparently, were among her most sensitive parts. A few days after a dentist put in some temporary fillings she heard music inside her convertible. She swiveled the dial on the car radio, then realized that the sound was not issuing from the loudspeaker. It was coming from inside her mouth: the fillings were picking up a broadcast from a local station. Some days later, an odd rhythm sounded in her molars again. No music this time—it seemed to be Morse code. She reported the incident to MGM's security officers, and they dutifully passed the word to the FBI. To the studio's astonishment, investigators canvassed the area and discovered an underground radio station run by a Japanese gardener. Lucy dined out on the story for months. She related the incident to Ethel Merman—the stage Du Barry—and Merman passed it on to Cole Porter. It became part of the plot of his next Broadway show, *Something for the Boys.*

· · ·

$\mathcal{D}$esi had gone missing for several days—no word, no wire, no telephone call. Frantic, Lucy traced him with the help of Pentagon officials. They located her husband on tour in St. Thomas, part of the American Virgin Islands. He was about to go on at a hotel when she had him paged. He ran to the phone convinced that something terrible had happened.

"Lucy, don't tell me," he shouted. "You're dead."

"Can't you hear me?" she yelled back. "I'm alive!"

"Mother is dead."

Lucy told him Lolita Arnaz was still among the living.

"*Your* mother is dead. The house burned down!"

"Just listen—"

"You may not be dead, but if you found me here, you must be dying!"

"None of those things. Get your ass back here. You're wanted to star in *Bataan!*"

Louis B. Mayer had found a part in MGM's big war movie of 1943, a role the chief thought would make Desi more than "just another Mexican." He was to play Felix Ramirez, a Hispanic GI condemned to die in defense of a bridge. Robert Taylor led the cast, perishing heroically in the last scene. Others to be killed by enemy fire included George Murphy, Lloyd Nolan, Thomas Mitchell, and Robert Walker. Desi's finish was nowhere near as dramatic. Ramirez was to perish of malaria, vibrating with fever. It was not the way Desi preferred to go but he seized the opportunity with both hands, arguing that the mosquito net would be in the way of his big scene, and that Ramirez would not speak English. He would go back to his childhood and dramatically recite the Act of Contrition in Latin, as Desi had done in Jesuit school.

Garnett thought it over. The suggestions seemed reasonable enough; if the star agreed he would go along. Taylor offered no objection and the scene was played as proposed. An unexpected change came over Desi. Now that he had been in an A picture and had even improved his role, Lucy's higher salary struck him as irrelevant. After he completed work on *Bataan,* Desi threw himself into domesticity. He and Lucy acquired five dogs and innumerable cats, raised egg-laying hens, nurtured a much-beloved cow and a pig with the idea of providing meat at a time of rationing. When slaughter time came around, though, the gentleman farmer and his lady didn't have the heart to kill either mammal; both the cow and the pig died later of natural causes. The couple produced home movies of themselves in casual clothes, Lucy pretending to be Scarlett O'Hara, Desi posing as the lord of the manor, gesturing toward his swimming pool; his garden of corn, artichokes, and strawberries; his bright red convertible. The family came around: Fred Hunt, enfeebled but still capable of wandering the estate with cranky awe along with DeDe and Freddy; Lolita Arnaz, proud of her son but intimidated by his surroundings. Friends dropped in— Desi's pals played Cuban melodies, Lucy's colleagues stepped to the music of the square dance, and the two genres never quite met. Lucy's friends, most of them in show business, vied with each other in Monopoly, Scrabble, and the Game, a fierce version of charades.

On an evening in 1944, one special version of the Game featured Lucy; her cousin Cleo and Cleo's new husband, Ken Morgan; Keenan Wynn and his wife; the burly actor Laird Cregar, who had just made a name for himself as Jack the Ripper in *The Lodger;* and several other performers. The group laughed, drank, and played hard, and finished the evening by jumping into the pool en masse. The following day as Lucy drove to the studio she heard that Cregar had died of a massive heart attack that very evening—probably a few minutes after he got home. It was a long time before she could play Hollywood charades again.

Card games were another matter. Lucy never stopped playing them, and revealing an unpleasant part of her nature in the process. Players who made mistakes were chewed out in public, and often reduced to tears. Lucy's quick temper indicated more than an aggressive streak. The Arnazes had resumed their quarrels and jealousies, and she acted out her frustrations at the card table. From various clues and rumors Lucy knew that Desi was involved with other women; meanwhile, he convinced himself that she was being unfaithful. On weekends, for example, Clark Gable, still in mourning for Carole Lombard, would come by on his motorcycle, driving the Harley-Davidson recklessly, as if in search of an accident. There was a time when Lucy thought the actor "handsome but such a lump." Now she spent hours encouraging him to talk out his sorrow, encouraging Gable to stay off the bike and come for a drive. Desi stayed behind, wondering whether Lucy was becoming more than a good listener.

And matters were about to worsen on the professional front. Lucy's and Desi's recent movies were both box office smashes. *Du Barry Was a Lady* grossed almost $3.5 million, and *Bataan,* in addition to receiving good notices and big box office receipts, won Desi the *Photoplay* award for best performance of the month. ("It wasn't the Academy Award," he allowed, "but damn good enough for me.") Yet this was to be his last big moment at MGM. Mayer had no plans to put the Latin fellow in any upcoming feature, whereas Lucy was already in rehearsal for *Best Foot Forward,* replacing the pregnant Lana Turner. That film about a fading star and a young cadet was of little moment—which was why the studio cast an actress who could neither sing nor dance in a musical. Still, *Best Foot Forward* kept Lucille Ball's name before the public and gave her a chance to work with such promising newcomers as June Allyson and Gloria De Haven. As she worked, the distance between her and Desi widened. June Allyson paid Lucy a visit during this period and expressed envy at the house and garden, and all the other signs she mistook for happiness. Lucy let slip a remark about the situation: "We're not ships that pass in the night so much as cars that pass in the morning. This is supposed to be married life?"

The Arnazes' troubles might have gone public had Lucy's star continued to rise and had Desi continued to be a bandleader on the road to nowhere. But in May 1943, the draft notice finally arrived. Desi planned to enter the air force and with his flair for self-dramatization spoke about becoming a bombardier, making hazardous forays deep into enemy territory. The day before he was to report for duty, Desi joined a pickup team and played baseball at the Arlington Reception Center near Riverside, California. His first time up, he swung at a ball, missed, and tore the cartilage in his good knee. The other one bore the scars of operations done during his adolescence in Cuba, and this new accident put him out of commission. Desi spent weeks in a hospital, and when he was released doctors pronounced him unfit for bombardier school. He entered the infantry as a private. After basic training he was assigned to the Army Medical Corps, not as a technician but as an entertainer. Looking at the bright side, Desi saw himself entertaining the troops overseas. Then one evening Lucy received a call.

"I'm going to be in Birmingham, honey," declared her husband.

"Gee, that's great," she responded. "I'm leaving for a bond tour in the East next week and I'll come to Alabama to see you."

"Birmingham, California," he groaned. *That* Birmingham was less

than five miles from the Desilu ranch. At a base hospital Desi worked
with wounded soldiers returned from Corregidor, Tarawa, and, ironically enough, Bataan. He taught English to illiterate draftees, rounded
up books and radios, ran films, acquired sports equipment. In his spare
moments he put on one-man shows. Once in a while he brought in
Lucy for some offhand comedy. Nevertheless, she was to note, it was
obvious that Desi was restless and unhappy. "It galled him not to be
overseas himself. He was allowed to leave the hospital every night and
weekends, which turned out to be unfortunate. He was too close to
Hollywood." For in the early 1940s, the tone of Hollywood's social life
was set by the studio chiefs. Louis B. Mayer had just left his wife and
moved into a mansion formerly occupied by Marion Davies. Once the
town's most powerful executive showed the way, many other middle-
aged producers abandoned their spouses and, along with Mayer, took
up yachting, horse breeding, gambling, and the pursuit of younger
women. Parties went on every weekend, and Desi wangled invitations
to most of them. All the while Lucy kept working in pictures, caroming
from *Meet the People,* a musical starring Dick Powell, to *As Thousands
Cheer,* a morale builder with MGM stars playing themselves in a show
for GIs headed overseas.

Lucy shied away from the parties, warning Desi that his pursuit of
immediate gratification could be a costly error, and not only because of
what it was doing to her: "No one approves of an actor enjoying wild
parties and late nights; it's too exhausting and shows up immediately in
the face and the voice before a camera." She repeatedly reminded her
husband that his hosts were also his employers, "and they would have
no respect for his ability and talents as an actor if all they ever saw was
a charming irresponsible playboy."

He ignored the tocsins, and as a result Lucy spent many lonely
weekends with no other company than her maid and confidante, Harriet McCain. One unhappy day she clipped a picture of a baby from a
women's magazine and pasted it in her scrapbook side by side with the
movie reviews. Underneath she scrawled a caption in the infant's
imagined voice: "I don't see any pictures of me in this book and this is
your third year of marriage—quit kiddin.' "

· · ·

*E*arly in January 1944, Lucy and Desi briefly appeared together to mourn the passing of Grandpa Fred Hunt, who died at the age of seventy-eight. "We never even considered burying him in Hollywood," Lucy said. "He belonged next to Flora Belle in the elm-shaded Hunt family plot in Jamestown."

She took the body back and stayed in the old Jamestown Hotel alone, a visiting celebrity whose visit was heavily covered in the local press. It was no accident that the reporters turned out; MGM had sent a publicity man along to make sure everyone in town knew that Lucille Ball, screen star, was back. The adventurous adolescent turned Goldwyn Girl was now a bona fide movie personality, and wherever she went crowds followed her, from the hotel to the cemetery and back. She saw old girlfriends, reminisced about her favorite teachers, visited Johnny DeVita and his mother. Not an ember of the amour remained. Dutifully she stopped by the local defense plant and attended a bond rally. Then she was off on a train for Philadelphia to sell war bonds at yet another rally. Wrapped in silver fox, her red hair coiffed and her makeup, lipstick, and eyebrows artfully applied, the epitome of glamour looked back and waved to a fervent crowd. Jamestown receded into memory. The place seemed so small and irrelevant these days, as if what occurred in the 1920s had happened to someone else, someone in a forgotten bottom-of-the-bill movie released long, long ago.

Lucy returned to Hollywood, where she took a small part in an overblown and inconsequential film, *Ziegfeld Follies*. That led to a major supporting role in *Without Love,* starring Katharine Hepburn and Spencer Tracy. Wherever she went, reporters asked about Desi. The reply was always the same: everything was fine, rumors about their difficulties were pure fiction created by malicious columnists or jealous actresses. The only bad feature of 1944, she told a reporter, was: "I haven't had Desi. I don't begrudge him to the Service, but I miss him. When Desi comes back, I don't believe there's any doubt but that MGM will realize they have one of the biggest bets in the business." Unmentioned was the fact that in the summer of that year her husband stopped coming home altogether. The scurrilous *Confidential* magazine ran a feature about Desi's Palm Springs weekend with another woman, and that story, along with Hollywood's unending rumor machine, pushed Lucy over the edge.

In the afternoon of the first day's shooting on *Without Love,* she drove to Domestic Relations Court in Santa Monica and filed for divorce. The charge was mental cruelty. Even now, however, she refused to say anything specific about Desi's extramarital capers. She told Judge Stanley Mosk that the Arnazes' differences were mainly about money. "When we argued about it, he became angry and went away," she claimed. "That was a habit of his—going away whenever we had an argument. He always ran out on me rather than stay to talk the matter out. It left me a nervous wreck. I got no rest at night at all."

Desi did not plan to contest the decree; he knew that Lucy had him dead to rights and that she could have gone into damaging detail if she chose to. But the evening before she was due to appear in court to sign the final papers, he took one last chance and dialed the number at Chatsworth.

"What are you doing tonight?" he asked.

"Nothing particular. You know I'm divorcing you tomorrow morning."

"Yeah, I know that. But what are you doing tonight?"

"Nothing special."

"Well, would you like to have dinner with me?"

Lucy sighed. "All right."

Desi wheedled a twenty-four-hour pass from his commanding officer, picked up his wife, and took her to a Beverly Hills restaurant. Afterward, they returned to an apartment Lucy had borrowed for the occasion. Desi wrote about the next few hours:

"We had a beautiful night. At seven-thirty in the morning she got up and said, 'Oh, my God, I'm late. I've got to go.'

" 'What do you mean?' I asked. 'Where are you going?'

" 'I told you I'm divorcing you this morning.'

" 'Yeah. I know you told me but you're not going through with it now, are you?'

" 'I gotta go through with it,' she answered. 'All the newspaper people are down there. I got a new suit and a new hat. I gotta go.'

"She went to court, got the divorce, came right back and joined me in bed. This, of course, annulled the divorce immediately because in California in those days there was a one-year waiting period between the interlocutory and final decree, and if during that period the principals got together and had an affair, the divorce was automatically null and void."

Reconciled against all odds, the couple vowed to be different from now on. Desi and Lucy swore to work on the marriage: he would do no more straying, she would do no more complaining. Both would curb their tempers. In fact, neither did much in the way of adjustment. Desi's concession to Lucy consisted in sleeping with the windows open because Lucy liked it that way, and occasionally joining her friends in a square dance instead of confining himself to Cuban music with his friends. As for Lucy, as she wrote later, "I closed my eyes, put blinders on, and ignored what was too painful to think about." Since the divorce didn't work out, marriage would have to. But it would not bear examining. Work was the main thing now; she would concentrate on that.

"How can you conceive on the telephone?"

SERGEANT Desiderio Alberto Arnaz, U.S. Army 392-956-43, was discharged in November 1945, three months after V-J Day. During the war, film studios had come to a collective arrangement. Those in the service would not be paid salaries while they were away, but upon their return they would be granted one large raise. This was intended to acknowledge the periodic increases that would have accrued had they been working all along. Desi's salary was $650 a week just before he was drafted; with the raise his weekly paycheck now came to $1,000.

Desi knew the MGM scuttlebutt about the beautiful swimmer Esther Williams ("Wet, she was a star"), but he also knew that she was a big box office attraction. When he heard that a Williams movie was in development at MGM, and that the script called for a Latin leading man, Desi went to the producer and offered himself for the role.

Jack Cummings was succinct: "I've already got someone else."

Desi asked the name of this other Latin lover.

"Ricardo Montalban."

"Ricardo who?"

"Montalban. A Mexican actor. He's going to play the lead opposite Esther."

"I have been in the army for two and a half years," Desi reminded him. "This is a perfect part for me and you are going to give it to someone else who's not even under contract to the studio?"

"It's already done."

With those three words Desi Arnaz's film career effectively ended. Montalban was the new boy on the block, MGM's official Latin stud—twenty-six years old, skilled in comedy and drama, unconventionally handsome. The spurned veteran tried to be philosophical, but his acrimony could not be masked: "I guess it was out of sight out of mind. I had been gone two and a half years and they had forgotten what they had hired me for."

There was more bad news: Desi had been lax about various financial responsibilities before the war. The Internal Revenue Service calculated that he owed $30,000 in back taxes.

In the past, whenever Desi had experienced a reversal—professional, marital, emotional—he had turned to the one arena that had never let him down: music. In the 1930s he had observed Xavier Cugat closely, watched the way the Rhumba King managed musicians, bargained hard with nightclub owners, and squeezed profits out of short engagements as well as long ones. Now was the time to use what he had learned. Desi organized a group of instrumentalists and persuaded the manager of Ciro's on Sunset Strip to book the Desi Arnaz Orchestra in the club's first black-tie opening since the war. The leader played his specialties, featuring the bogus native incantation "Babalu":

> *Jungle drums were madly beating*
> *In the glare of eerie lights*
> *While the natives kept repeating*
> *Ancient jungle rites.*
> *All at once the dusky warriors began to*
> *Raise their arms to skies above*
> *And a native then stepped forward to chant to*
> *His Voodoo goddess of love*

And the more genial "Cuban Pete":

They call me Cuban Pete
I'm the King of the Rhumba beat.
When I play the maracas
I go chicky-chicky-boom
Chick-chicky-boom.
Si, Senorita, I know that you will like
the chicky-boom-chick
'Cause it's the dance of Latin romance.

A self-mockery attended these numbers; Desi became a caricature of the Latin fellow Louis B. Mayer had dismissed so airily. No matter; the smiling Cuban was willing to do whatever it took to reestablish his name. Mugging, rolling his eyes, and swaying with the music, he basked in applause and celebrity, paying conspicuous attention to the likes of Humphrey Bogart and Errol Flynn, who chatted with him between sets and stayed until the finale. Opening night was a grand success. But in that triumph were the seeds of more domestic misery.

Lucy was busy at MGM, working in comic trivia like *Abbott and Costello in Hollywood* and *Easy to Wed* with Keenan Wynn, and then loaned out to Twentieth Century–Fox for the melodrama *The Dark Corner*, with Mark Stevens as a detective and Lucy as his loyal, tough-minded secretary. Her scrapbook was getting fat with encomia. The *New York Times* verdict on *Without Love:* "Lucille Ball throws wisecracks like baseballs." The New York *Sun* on *Easy to Wed:* Wynn and Ball "make it clear that they are the funniest comic team on the screen just now—and by a big margin." The Hollywood Press Club had named Danny Kaye the King of Comedy, and Lucy the Queen. This recognition provided meager compensation for a home life that, once again, was deteriorating.

MGM required actresses to be at the studio hairdresser promptly at 6 a.m., and Desi's schedule called for him to be at the club until the small hours of the morning. The couple would meet at the top of Coldwater Canyon as she was driving off to work and he was returning to the ranch for some sleep. On many mornings they merely waved as they passed. Sometimes they would park side by side and chat. If Desi was feeling especially amorous he would board Lucy's car and neck with his wife before driving home. At the other end of the day the process reversed itself: she returned to bed as he headed off to work.

On weekends Lucy would stop by Ciro's, trying to rekindle what remained of their marriage.

Inevitably the group had to go on tour, and Lucy persuaded Desi to hire her brother Freddy as the band manager. But Freddy was a man who checked receipts, not beds; if she expected a report on Desi's notorious prowling she was to be disappointed. One evening Lucy spent an entire phone call accusing her husband of disloyalty, and he yelled at her for being oversuspicious. She slammed down the phone. It rang in her room and she picked up the receiver, ready to resume her argument. The voice was not Desi's; it was the operator's. She had eavesdropped on the conversation. "Why haven't you called him back?" she demanded. "I know he's in his room feeling miserable, waiting for you to call him. He didn't mean any of the things he said and I'm sure you didn't either, so why don't you call him back and make up with him? He's just a baby." Lucy laughed, melted, and did as asked. For that evening, at least, the conversation was filled with apologies and pledges of commitment.

After crossing the country in a series of split weeks and one-night stands, the Desi Arnaz Orchestra settled in for a long engagement at the Copacabana in New York City. Lucy took a few days off and flew into town. A visit to the club aroused new misgivings. On display were the Copa chorus girls, beautiful, highly publicized young women who embodied temptation. Lucy accused her husband of carrying on with the chorines. Desi protested that he never chased the women he worked with. She didn't believe a word he said. In an interview with *Look* magazine, she attempted to adopt her husband's cavalier manner. Desi's macho style didn't bother her in the least, said Lucy, and went on to boast, "I like to play games, too." This was pure bravado, putting a good face on a melancholy situation. The journalist bought the line, but Lucy knew she was faking it.

The only thing the couple could agree upon was their unhappiness. She was running in place at MGM, as she had once done at RKO, even though the pay was better. Desi was improving as a musician; jazz historian Will Friedwald was to note, "Arnaz had virtually the only success story of any new band launched after the war." Yet as a husband Desi was an abject failure and in low moments he acknowledged the fact.

As if to underline the speed of the passing years, MGM released Lucy in the summer of 1946. It was a good time for the studios: more people went out to the movies than ever before. The war was over;

peace dividends included a renewed economy, veterans' housing, and a great national hunger for entertainment. Lucy should have been part of it, but somehow her timing was off. She had been born too late or too soon, had passed through various phases at the studio—glamour girl, rising star, comedienne, second lead—without finding a screen identity. Audiences knew who she was and liked her, but without taking her to their hearts. Louis B. Mayer had had enough. Just as there were newer Latin actors to replace Desi, there were fresher talents to replace a thirty-six-year-old redhead.

During this period Lucy began to decline physically and emotionally. She actually began to stutter, something she had never done before, even in childhood. Lucy blamed some of the difficulties on her current agent, Arthur Lyons, and fired him. That left her without representation. On the other hand, she may have thought, what was left to represent?

During the weeks that Lucy was in mourning for her career an influential agent named Kurt Frings made a surprise visit to Chatsworth. He had heard about the trouble at MGM from a vigorously independent client, Olivia de Havilland, who had gone through her own battles with studios, sometimes refusing roles and going on suspension. The actress admired Lucy's work, and when she heard about her travail, she pushed Frings to represent this gifted redhead. "I hardly knew Olivia except to say hello," Lucy later wrote. "I was bowled over by her kindness."

Frings told his new client that she was unlikely to land a long-term contract. Still, current conditions might work in her favor. Why not freelance, he suggested, go wherever the jobs were? As a matter of fact, there was a picture about to get under way at Universal, *Lover Come Back,* costarring the suave Irish-American actor George Brent. Lucy would be ideal for the part of a comically jealous wife. "I can't, I can't," Lucy responded. "All I can do is stut-stut-stutter." Frings dismissed her fears; the actress was simply tired and out-of-sorts. What Lucy had to do was learn new lines instead of going over old grievances. She remained unconvinced until the director of the film, William Seiter, phoned with his encouragement: "You're a great gal. We need you. Come over to Universal and go to work."

She protested: "I c-c-can't read a l-l-line."

The director knew better: "Of course you can."

For several days Lucy struggled with the role, stammering through rehearsal. By the fifth day she began to recover her normal rhythm and tone. *Lover Come Back* might more accurately have been called "Lucy Come Back." The picture was universally panned, but the critics were kind to the female lead. "Our sympathy to Miss Ball, "who is fetching in Travis Banton's gowns in spite of the plot's ennui," said the *New York Herald Tribune*. The *New York Times* reviewer also preferred the apparel to the scenario: "Miss Ball wears a wardrobe of costumes and acts as if she really had a script. The poor lady is sadly deluded, she is completely without support."

Poor as the film was, it saved Lucy and rescued her marriage in the process. She came back into play just as Desi began to prosper in New York. As the mobile one, she came to Manhattan, and the Arnazes took up residence in the Delmonico Hotel at Park Avenue and Fifty-ninth Street. To all appearances they were a happily reunited, hand-holding couple.

Gossip columnists suspected otherwise. Stories occasionally appeared about Desi's wanderlust and Lucy's accusations. Sheilah Graham paid particular attention. After a tip from a hotel employee, Graham wrote an item that riled Lucy's mother in California. DeDe telephoned that night: "It says here you lock Desi out of the bedroom and he pounds on the door and shouts and hollers." Lucy traced the columnist to her home and went on the attack. She had accidentally locked Desi *in* the bedroom, not out of it. And what business was it of Graham's anyway? By now Lucy had worked herself into a rage. In a sudden flare-up she gave away more than she realized: "You've got two children and you don't care. You say things like this about me and I will never have children!"

So there it was. She had withstood loneliness, Desi's infidelities, being cut loose from MGM. From the age of three, when she lost her father, Lucy had idealized the notion of family. Nothing hurt so much as the feeling that biology had caught up with her, that she was on the cusp of a sterile middle age. Lucy was not one to keep her misery to herself, and when some of her listeners asked why she didn't adopt a child she wailed, "I want Desi's baby."

$\mathcal{A}$t the end of the year Desi appeared in his last film for MGM, *Cuban Pete,* a hastily fabricated musical, capitalizing on the postwar craze for Latin music. The best notice came from *Variety,* and it was tepid: "Arnaz tries hard, and his songs and music are an aid." From Hollywood he went back to bandleading as Lucy resumed her film work.

Now it was Desi's turn to express jealousy as Lucy appeared with a series of attractive leading men. The Russian-English actor George Sanders, whose reputation as a seducer extended to two continents, played the romantic lead to Lucy's taxi dancer in *Lured.* There were those, among them Zsa Zsa Gabor, later Sanders' wife, who were convinced that George and Lucy had an affair during the filming. If they did, discretion marked their intimacy; the town's most relentless gossip columnists could never find the incriminating evidence they needed for a scoop. So they switched direction and boosted the marriage. Louella Parsons went so far as to say Lucy was little more than a lovesick slave, wearing a bracelet that read, "My name is Lucille Ball. If lost, return me to my master, Desi Arnaz." Hedda Hopper had a different take: "About once every six months someone notifies me that Lucy and Desi Arnaz are separating. I've learned to doubt the reports, but dutifully get on the phone; and we have a long amiable conversation. Doubtless they have their spats, as which couple doesn't." Hopper added inaccurately, "Lucille is Irish and Desi is Latin—a combination that occasionally makes for some spectacular fireworks; but it's nothing serious."

The fact was, though, that the couple *had* blackslid on their promises and obligations. Lucy prevailed on Bob Hope to hire Desi as music director for his radio show; what caused the comedian to consent became a matter of salacious Hollywood speculation. Whatever the case, Desi got the job. A lot of good it did Lucy; when he was not on the radio bandstand he was touring the United States and Canada with scant attention paid to his wife—except for expressions of jealousy when she filmed *Her Husband's Affairs,* opposite the dashing Franchot Tone. Edward Everett Horton, who supplied the comic relief for that movie, proclaimed that Lucy had "more talent than these people realize." "These people" were the executives at Columbia. The picture did not thrive, and the studio offered her no other roles.

During an unhappy time Lucy played host to June Havoc, a serious actress with a long and famous background in entertainment—her older sister, Gypsy Rose Lee, had become the most celebrated striptease dancer in America. According to Lucy, Havoc suddenly announced: "I know you're going stir-crazy! Why don't you take a big

chunk of time—now that Desi's away and you're free-lancing—and
tour the country with a play?"

The whole encounter may well have been a setup, for shortly thereafter the men who ran the Princeton Drama Festival paid a call. Lucy
allowed them to talk her into appearing in the title role of Elmer Rice's
Dream Girl. Almost a decade before, she had starred in *Hey Diddle
Diddle* at the same theater. Her memories of that occasion, if not of the
end results, were happy ones. What she failed to take into account was
the piece itself. Of all the legitimate theater works in 1947, this was far
and away the most demanding. A modernist fantasy, it called for the
central character, Georgina Allerton, to escape from her everyday existence in a bookshop to a universe of dreams. In separate episodes in
her imagination she gives birth to twin babies and becomes a murder-
ess, a Shakespearean heroine, and a suicidal prostitute before finding
true love in the real world.

The part required Lucy to be onstage for almost the entire play, and
the feat of memory was prodigious. She suffered an occasional lapse in
rehearsals, and even on opening night, but she recovered quickly
enough to impress her producers, the audience, and the critics. Rice
later wrote that of all those who had portrayed Georgina—including
the original Broadway performer, Betty Field—"the only actress whose
performance really delighted me was Lucille Ball." Lucy "lacked tender wistfulness, but her vivid personality and expert timing kept the
play bright and alive."

The reaction that gave her the biggest lift came from two authoritative figures who dropped backstage during the tour. They were familiar
to Lucy; both were on the faculty of the Robert Minton–John Murray
Anderson School of Drama. The pair oozed compliments, which she
accepted with a polite curtsey. Lucy was kind enough not to remind
them that the school had rejected her as unpromising.

Dream Girl toured the Midwest and headed to California, pleasing
audiences and critics wherever it went. Toward the end of the year,
however, a virus began to work its way through the cast. By the time
the show hit Los Angeles, Lucy was barely able to stand. Somehow she
got through opening night. No one out front knew how sick she was;
the Los Angeles critic went out of his way to praise her energy and
skill: "Here is a young lady of the films who could, if she would, have a
dazzling footlight career. And what is more—though this may be a
brash statement to make—she is, in a sense, wasting her talents in pic-

tures. Miss Ball is a striking presence in the footlight world. She has efficiency as a comedienne. She can tinge a scene delicately with pathos. She has special facility in dealing with sharp-edged repartee." The review meant more to the entertainment industry than it did to Lucy. She went through one matinee with a fever of 102 degrees and ultimately had to be hospitalized. There was no understudy; after a week the show folded ingloriously.

At one point during this period, Harry Ackerman, a vice president of the Columbia Broadcasting System, was airborne, shuttling from New York to Los Angeles. In the 1940s coast-to-coast air travel could take more than ten hours, and on his flight Ackerman idly perused *Mr. and Mrs. Cugat: The Record of a Happy Marriage*. Isabel Scott Rorick's recently published novel centered on a young executive and the light-headed wife who kept placing him in awkward social situations, but who, in the end, proved to be as lovable as she was frenetic. Ackerman saw commercial possibilities in these characters. In Hollywood he met with Don Sharpe, an astute agent-packager in the Kurt Frings office. Sharpe had already designed radio shows featuring such film stars as Dick Powell (*Richard Diamond, Private Eye*) and Cary Grant (*Mr. Blandings Builds His Dream House*); he sparked to the property Ackerman had brought him. They began to develop *Mr. and Mrs. Cugat* as a radio comedy series, selling the idea to Hubbell Robinson, CBS vice president of programming. Robinson in turn brought it to Lucy.

"I was interested," she was to recall, "especially if Desi could co-star." Even though the fictive couple's name suggested Xavier Cugat's, and thus an indeterminate Hispanic background, Robinson thought Desi was hardly the type to play the part of a typical American spouse. "But he *is* my husband," Lucy insisted, "and I think it helps make a domestic comedy more believable when the audience knows the couple are actually married." She added that the demands of radio broadcasting were much less intrusive than those of every other entertainment medium, "a fact borne out by the experiences of such happily married radio greats as Mary Livingstone and Jack Benny, Fred Allen and Portland Hoffa, Gracie Allen and George Burns, and Harriet and Ozzie Nelson." CBS turned her down cold. She would play opposite a man of their choice or she could forget about a radio series; it was as simple as that. Lucy gave way.

Originally the experienced stage and radio actor Lee Bowman was slated to be Mr. Cugat, but CBS delayed the opening when sponsorship failed to materialize. By the time the network agreed to back the program with its own funds, Bowman had signed for another show. Another well-known actor, Richard Denning, took his place. The ingratiating star of B pictures had a resonant voice capable of conveying Mr. Cugat's stuffiness without making him unsympathetic. The next change was in the name of the characters: Mr. and Mrs. Cugat metamorphosed into the unambiguously WASP Liz and George Cooper, and the title changed to *My Favorite Husband*.

With everything and everyone in place, CBS still hesitated to go on the air; the dialogue was judged to be insufficiently funny and credible. Comedian Steve Allen learned of the difficulties—and so did his writers. Two of them, Madelyn Pugh and Bob Carroll Jr., were in their twenties and restless. They submitted a script, received an offer within days, and traded the security of an established program for the challenges of an untried one. Carroll was a bearded, Mephistophelian character who had learned how to construct situations and gags, and Pugh was a pert brunette who knew how to make feminine characters credible. They were novices, however, and Lucy rode all over their work. The smiling lady, so amiable when they first met, proved to be a tyrant in script conferences. Carroll was confused by Lucy's tempests, and now and then Pugh was reduced to tears. The CBS brass liked their ideas, but it was clear that a firmer presence had to be added to the mix. A veteran comedy writer and producer was brought in.

At the age of thirty-five, Jess Oppenheimer had already written for Fred Astaire, Edgar Bergen, and, most significantly, Fanny Brice. One of the most skilled dialect comedians in America, Brice had headlined in vaudeville and the *Ziegfeld Follies,* and, after some false starts, found a home in radio as the voice of "Baby Snooks." Oppenheimer wrote that show, taking advantage of Brice's hilarious yammer, but always eschewing cheap gags for a credible relationship of father and child. In a typical episode, Snooks misbehaves and Daddy (Hanley Stafford) administers a spanking. The brat speaks up:

> SNOOKS
> I don't want you to be my father no more.
>
> DADDY
> What kind of talk is that?

SNOOKS
You hate me.

DADDY
Nonsense. I spanked you this morning because I love you.

SNOOKS
You got a funny way of showing it.

DADDY
If I had hated you, you know what I would have done?

SNOOKS
Yeah. You would have killed me.

DADDY
No. I would have left you alone to grow up into a selfish, greedy girl who always has to have her own way. How would you like that?

SNOOKS
(*Wisely*) I'd like it.

DADDY
Oh, what's the use? Will you at least talk to me?

SNOOKS
No. You spanked me, and I'm sore at you.

DADDY
Look, Snooks, I spanked you, in the first place, for your own good. And in the second place, you're not "sore." You're angry. Do you understand?

SNOOKS
Yeah, I'm angry in the second place.

DADDY
Right. Now come over and sit down.

SNOOKS
No.

DADDY
Why not?

SNOOKS
'Cause I'm sore in the first place!

Carroll and Pugh had followed the outline of *Mr. and Mrs. Cugat.* In their introduction, George Cooper was portrayed as a man of substance in his thirties, newly married to "the socially prominent Elizabeth." After the honeymoon, "George sold his polo pony, bought a stylish suburban home, took the first job that came along—fifth vice president of a bank—and now they're just George and Liz, two people who live together and like it." Audiences had no problem with wealthy protagonists: during the 1930s Fred Astaire and Ginger Rogers had become Hollywood royalty by dancing their way through the Depression in dinner jackets and gowns. The 1940s called for some changes in approach and personality. In a memoir Oppenheimer said, "I decided to make Liz a little bit less sophisticated, a little bit more childish and impulsive, than the character who appeared in the first few shows—in short, more like Baby Snooks. She would be a stagestruck schemer with an overactive imagination that got her into embarrassing situations. This would give me an excuse to engage Lucy in some broad slapstick comedy."

During the last months of 1948, as the scripts went in for revisions, Lucy began working on a new film with Bob Hope, *Sorrowful Jones,* based on yet another Damon Runyon tale. Filming during the day and rehearsing at night frazzled her nerves and upset her judgment. As one deadline approached, the story line was still in trouble. "Bob and Madelyn and I worked practically all night," Oppenheimer wrote. "We were confident that we had saved the script. We weren't too proud of the very last line, but the rest of it was good, and we had all day to work on that one last line." At daybreak Lucy and Don Sharpe arrived. She sank into an overstuffed chair and went through the script, laughing at regular intervals as she turned the pages. According to Oppenheimer, "I thought we were home free, until she came to that last line. Well, Dr. Jekyll and Mr. Hyde were identical twins compared to the transformation Lucy served up." She arose, threw the script across the room, and yelled, "I won't do this shit!" Oppenheimer waited for her to finish. Then he responded: "I thought we had a team effort going here. We're happy to stay up all night or all week, and break our butts to make the script right for you. But not if you're going to ignore a major rewrite, which you loved, and crucify us over one little line, which can easily be fixed. We need quite a bit more respect than that." He took Lucy's hand and shook it. "I can't say that it's been a pleasant experience working for you, but at least it's over."

Oppenheimer left the building. About halfway down the block he heard the clatter of rapid footsteps. Don Sharpe caught up with him and made a short-winded appeal: "She's crying and hysterical. She knows she was wrong. She agrees with you and wants to apologize." They went back into the building and Lucy said and did all the right things, which included making a small act of contrition for Carroll and Pugh, who had not seen her Jekyll-and-Hyde act. "I've been a shit," she told them. After Lucy had walked away Pugh asked, "What the hell was that all about?" It was about establishing modes of behavior and regard, and about understanding that Lucy's outbursts were signs not of certainty but of an insecurity that had been with her since childhood. Oppenheimer, Pugh, and Carroll would have to bear that in mind from now on.

Within weeks Oppenheimer wrought other changes in the scripts. He used the technique of the long-running Howard Lindsay and Russell Crouse play *Life with Father,* wherein Mother Day (Vinnie) uses her ditsy feminine arithmetic on Father:

> FATHER
> Vinnie, whatever happened to that six dollars?
>
> VINNIE
> What six dollars?
>
> FATHER
> I gave you six dollars to buy a new coffeepot and now I find that you apparently got one at Lewis & Conger's

and charged it. Here's their bill: "One coffeepot—five dollars."

VINNIE
So you owe me a dollar and you can hand it right over.

In *My Favorite Husband,* Oppenheimer slyly modernized and reworked the dialogue:

LIZ
You should be glad I bought that dress, George. I made twenty dollars by doing it.

GEORGE
You made twenty dollars?

LIZ
Absolutely. I bought the dress on sale at Cramer's for thirty-nine dollars and the identical dress is selling for fifty-nine fifty—so I made twenty dollars!

GEORGE
But you don't have that twenty dollars.

LIZ
I know I don't. I spent it on a hat to go with the dress!

Oppenheimer also made two emendations that were to have profound impact on the history of situation comedy. He felt that Lucille Ball and Richard Denning could not support a thirty-minute show by themselves. They needed comic support, and early in 1949 he supplied it by bringing on another, older couple. These were the Atterburys— Rudolph, George's boss at the bank (Gale Gordon), and his scatter-brained wife, Iris (Bea Benaderet). Both actors were seasoned radio farceurs, and a few weeks after they were introduced on the air their presence allowed scripts to develop in new directions. Gordon's Rudolph came across as a decent but hopelessly pompous banker, thereby humanizing George; Benaderet's Iris supplied a partner for all of Liz's harmless, funny schemes, usually in contrivances that pitted the wives against their husbands. Even with all this backup Lucy was having trouble making the comedy work to its full potential. Oppenheimer brought in a live audience to laugh at the jokes, and that helped somewhat. Still, he felt that something else was needed. During one rehearsal he handed Lucy tickets to Jack Benny's radio show.

She looked at him blankly. "What are these for?"

"I want you to go to school."

The Benny show provided her postgraduate course in pace and delivery. "Oh, my God, Jess," she said when she came back. "I didn't realize!" For the first time, she understood how Benny could make a funny remark and then, simply by gazing deadpan at the audience, sustain the laughter for twenty-five seconds. The exposure to a master of timing made all the difference. Lucy began to relate to the audience—often to the point of mugging—and it roared its approval. Sponsors signed on; *My Favorite Husband* rose in the ratings.

There was only part of the show that displeased Lucy: she was required to do a Jell-O commercial at the end of every program. When she performed the spots in her own voice she sounded so uncomfortable that Oppenheimer rewrote them as nursery rhymes—Jack and Jill, Goldilocks, Little Miss Muffet and the Spider:

> ANNOUNCER
> She was just about to eat her next dish when along came a spider and sat down besider . . . and what do you think he said?
>
> LUCY
> He said—wait till I find my spider voice—(*In different character*) "Pardon me, but isn't that Jell-O Orange Coconut Tapioca—an exciting new combination of refreshing orange and tropical coconut?"

That "spider voice" came out as a high-pitched nasal tone. Audiences found it irresistible. She quickly adapted the character to regular portions of the show, where laughter frequently began before she finished the punch line. "SPIDER," a private note scrawled in the margin, came to mean her trademark reaction to being discovered mid-plot against George or Rudolph. The success of her vocal tricks and timing settled Lucy down. Very gradually she came to trust the writers, and then to lean on them to an almost pathological degree. Although Carroll and Pugh dated briefly, they were only interested in each other professionally. "Once, when we came back from Europe," Carroll was to recollect, "Lucy said, 'Did you get married?' We said no. She said, 'Well, don't do me any favors.' She was furious."

*W*hile *My Favorite Husband* developed and grew in 1949, Lucy continued a parallel life in motion pictures. Early in the filming of *Sorrowful Jones,* Hope received a rare lesson in acting from his costar. "Bob at first was rather afraid of the straight scenes," Lucy remembered wistfully. "He was feeling his way and so was I. But after a few days, when he still seemed uneasy, I found the courage to take him aside and say, 'Don't be afraid to play it straight. If you believe in the scene, the audience will, too.' " Using a mixture of credible pathos and all-out comedy, the stars made *Sorrowful Jones* a commercial and critical hit. To most reviewers Lucille was the big surprise. *Newsweek:* "Lucille Ball, who has played a Runyon doll before (*The Big Street,* 1942), makes as delightful a one as any guy could hope to find between Times Square and Lindy's." After that film she unwisely chose to make *Easy Living* for RKO. This second feature costarred Victor Mature, whose past rudeness she had never forgiven, and Lizabeth Scott, who offered weak support. It quickly disappeared from neighborhood theaters.

Some fifteen years back, Lucy had been dismissed from Columbia Pictures. Since the Neanderthal Harry Cohn was still in charge of production, she saw no reason why the studio would be interested in her. She had failed to consider Buster Keaton and Ed Sedgwick, two of her longtime fans. Groucho Marx and many of his fellow comedians considered the alcoholic Keaton to be as obsolete as the Keystone Kops. Sedgwick had directed Keaton in two-reelers, and he, too, was widely regarded as a fossil from the silent era. Nevertheless, both men had worked their way onto the Columbia lot as advisers, and both believed that Lucille Ball had yet to show the range of her comic talent on the screen. They persuaded Columbia to sign her for the title role of Eleanor Grant, secretary, in *Miss Grant Takes Richmond.* With William Holden as her costar and sometimes foil, she played a wide-eyed secretary who believes that she's working for a real estate office when in fact the place is a bookie joint. Eleanor's gradual enlightenment, and her ability to siphon illegal gambling funds to a worthy housing project, gave Lucy an opportunity to mug and to play a few farcical scenes with unexpected panache.

Finally, when Lucy made *The Fuller Brush Girl* in 1950, her gifts for physical comedy went on full display. This follow-up to Red Skelton's comedy hit *The Fuller Brush Man* was written by Frank Tashlin. The former gagman for the Hal Roach comedies and director of animated cartoons went for the outrageous, the incongruous, and the obvious and got away with it because he knew more about comic construction than anyone else at the studio. Lucy gamely went along with the scenario, playing Sally Elliot, the bright fiancée of a clueless executive, Humphrey (Eddie Albert). In order to earn enough money to get married, Sally signs on as a door-to-door saleswoman. Customers treat her rudely, brats tie her up with rope, and, eventually, one of her customers is murdered and she's suspected of the crime—all giving Lucy a chance to react. Before Sally can prove her innocence she gets chased by a posse of bald women, hung up on a clothesline, and banged around by a TV roof antenna; she founders in a forest of banana peels, impersonates a bump-and-grind burlesque queen, and becomes the target of the real killers in a wine cellar—providing Lucy with an opportunity for her first drunk scene.

Standing just offscreen, Buster Keaton dispensed advice. His reward, and Lucy's, was the review in *Variety:* "If there were any doubts as to Miss Ball's forte, *Fuller Brush Girl* dispels them. She is an excellent comedienne and in this rowdy incoherent yarn, with its Keystone Kop overtones, she garners major laurels."

It has become a commonplace to observe that the sharpest humor springs not from funny things, but from such complex sources as emotional deprivation, anger, humiliation, and envy. Like so many of her fellow comedians, ranging back to Charlie Chaplin and Keaton himself, Lucy was deeply unhappy even as she cavorted blithely on the set. Her brother Freddy and her cousin Cleo (whom she tended to regard as a younger sister) each had married and become a parent while she remained childless. She would repeatedly ask friends, "How can you conceive on the telephone?" And she would moan about Desi's peripatetic life with the band. Even when he was around, Desi seemed preoccupied with a bunch of hangers-on who arrived early and stayed late. Lucy maintained her own circle of friends, among them Rory Calhoun and his wife Lita, Farley Granger, Priscilla Lane, Eve Arden, and the

Czech actor Francis Lederer and his wife Marion. They all could see
how restive and melancholy she had become. Lucy tried to lose herself
in various avocations and expenditures: she studied Shakespeare, tried
to learn Spanish, took up oil painting with a special emphasis on the
snowy landscapes she remembered from Jamestown, cooked, ordered
dresses that sat in her closet, tried a new hairstyle every week.

Lolita Arnaz thought she knew why Lucy and Desi had failed to
become parents. Granted, her boy was not the best-behaved man in
the world. And there was the business of the couple's conflicting
schedules. But the real trouble, according to Lolita, was that Lucy and
Desi remained unmarried in the eyes of the Catholic Church. Desi listened to his mother for the first time in years. He acknowledged that
he wanted a son desperately; if getting married in a ceremony would
make things right he would do it—if only Lucy would agree. She
would, with certain provisos: "Desi and I sat in our cabbage-rose-
papered living room and talked far into the night. We finally decided
that Desi would give up his cross-country tours and only take local
engagements with his band. We would both consult doctors to see why
we did not have children.

"And we would 'kick out the bums'—drinking, brawling, constantly
dropping in, they gave us no peace. We had to take over our home
again, losing the parasites for good."

On June 19, 1949, in the local cathedral of Our Lady of the Valley,
Father Michael Hurley officiated at the Roman Catholic wedding of
Desiderio and Lucille Arnaz, with Lucy in a blue satin wedding dress
and matching hat, and Desi in a bright white suit. Eight years after the
first Arnaz marriage, with DeDe and Cleo looking on and wiping away
tears, Ed Sedgwick gave the bride away. Desi's mother was matron of
honor, and Captain Ken Morgan, Cleo's husband, served as best man.
Looking back many years later, Lucy noted: "It was a beautiful ceremony and I believed in it. At the time, I seriously intended to become
a Catholic. I took instruction for a long time, but lost the inspiration
when I realized that Catholicism did not seem to help Desi in his life."

By now slapstick had become Lucy's natural comic mode. As Miss
Grant, and as the Fuller Brush girl, she had often gone over the top.
The trouble was that her laughs came at a cost. By the end of *The*

Fuller Brush Girl, Lucy was deep in the throes of migraine headaches reminiscent of the ones her mother had experienced thirty years before. In addition, she had sprained both wrists and displaced six vertebrae, irritated her sciatic nerve by pacing ankles-inward for a long drunken walk, come down with a severe cold when she was dunked in a wine vat for three straight days, found her eyeballs temporarily paralyzed when a wind machine accidentally blew a cloud of talcum powder directly into her face, and, for good measure, been severely bruised by several tons of cascading coffee beans during a chase scene. On the last day of shooting she gamely appeared at Hollywood and Vine for publicity shots on behalf of the local tuberculosis society. A mobile X-ray machine sat at the curb, and as she coughed and wheezed a technician asked her to step inside for a free examination. Shortly afterward, he emerged with the news that Lucy had walking pneumonia. She spent the next nine days in the hospital.

Restored to health late that summer, she began work on another Bob Hope movie, *Fancy Pants*. This remake of *Ruggles of Red Gap* starred Lucy as an American arriviste and Hope as an unemployed actor posing as her butler. Lucy sustained more injuries in the making of this film: a horse stomped on one of her feet, and the two-hundred-pound Bruce Cabot accidentally stepped on the other one. More therapy was needed, but the treatments did little to boost her sagging spirits.

In December, however, there occurred some heartening news: she was pregnant. Lucy and Desi made plans for a nursery; she watched her diet and measured her days, careful to get enough sleep, enough protein, enough quiet time. The measures were insufficient. She began bleeding one night at Chatsworth, and Desi drove her to Cedars of Lebanon Hospital praying that this was only a minor problem. In the morning the doctor gave them the sad report: she had lost the baby. But he also presented them with some encouraging information: after her first miscarriage, an inept physician had closed off one of Lucy's fallopian tubes. The team at Cedars had repaired the problem; all she and Desi needed to do was wait three months before trying to conceive again.

The story of Lucy's miscarriage could not be kept secret. When it made the papers, sympathetic listeners of *My Favorite Husband* wrote 2,867 letters of consolation. Over the course of the next six months Lucy answered every one of them.

By the time she signed the last letter Lucy felt fully recuperated and ready to begin again. But begin on what? She felt numb when someone told her yet again that Hollywood producers were looking for someone to play a "Lucille Ball–type role"; she had been on that treadmill too long. Radio was easy and, judging by the fan mail, it had renewed her popularity. But it still kept her from Desi, whose only skill was music, a field that would always take him away from her. Why couldn't they work together on something—a radio show maybe, or a routine with the band?

She consulted Don Sharpe, as always a fount of ideas. Doing a Lucy-Desi act was an intriguing notion, in his view, but such a project should not be cobbled together overnight. The show needed writers, planning, booking. To that end, the Arnazes formed an official legal partnership, Desilu Productions, and put Jess Oppenheimer, Bob Carroll, and Madelyn Pugh on the payroll.

Lucy also sought the advice of Pepito Perez, a skillful Spanish clown who had appeared with Desi, and Buster Keaton, who, despite a downhill alcoholic spiral, had never lost his ability to devise comic bits with inanimate objects. Among these objects was a trick cello. Its various hiding places contained flowers, a step stool, and a toilet plunger. Once Lucy learned how to operate it, she and Desi started to work on a carefully timed routine. When it was ready they tried it out before an audience. He played the straight man, earnestly attempting to conduct his orchestra. She was the baggy-pants clown in white tie and tails, her hair hidden beneath a battered fedora. In the middle of a musical number she loudly barged down the aisle demanding to be heard.

"What's going out there?" Desi inquired in a bewildered manner. "Please put the lights on."

The spotlight hit Lucy and her cello. "Where is Dizzy Arnazzy?"

The bandleader corrected her. "Desi Arnaz."

"That's what I say. Dizzy Arnazzy."

"Look, mister, what is it you want?"

"I want a job with your orchestra."

"Oh, are you a musician?"

"That's right."

To prove her claim she would do off-key solos on the cello, wringing laughter from all the props, then play the xylophone in the manner of a trained seal. Later she would appear in a provocative outfit, swinging a purse and singing, her lyrics interrupted by the drummer's rim shots.

> They call me Sally Sweet
> I'm the queen of Delancey Street
> When I start to dance everything goes
> Chick, chicky boom
> Chick, chicky boom
> Chick, chick boom.

With the ultimate "boom" she would do an exaggerated hip-swinging bump and knock the straw hat off Desi's head. Then the two would join in a wild rhumba, exiting into the wings. Lucy's manic routines, plus a short he-and-she sketch written by the team from *My Favorite Husband,* made up the act.

Lucy and Desi appeared in a few army camps before making an official debut at the Paramount in Chicago, where live performers alternated with first-run films. That hot June week in 1950, every gag seemed to work, and word quickly spread that the Arnazes had a hit on their hands. Offers came in from theaters around the country, and from the Palladium in London. While they were in Chicago their hotel room was robbed; Lucy lost almost all of her jewelry, but refused to be distracted. She was high on the news that audiences and critics loved the show, and higher on the suspicion that she might be pregnant. "I was elated, nearly delirious," she maintained, "but I was also frightened. Now I was scared to do my act because it was so physically strenuous. In my seal act, I had to do a real belly whacker, flip over on my stomach three times, and slither offstage. But I had six months' worth of contracts to fulfill. And I was so happy to be working with Desi again that I hated to call anything off until I was sure."

When the week was up they headed for New York, where Desi and Lucy were booked at the Roxy. She arrived on Friday and made clandestine arrangements for a pregnancy test, using her hairdresser's name to avoid publicity. That Sunday night she and Desi were relaxing in their dressing room. Desi fell asleep to the clack of Lucy's knitting needles and the staccato of Walter Winchell doing his radio broadcast. The next few moments were right out of a vaudeville skit, but they were real.

"After ten childless years of marriage," said Winchell, "Lucille Ball and Desi Arnaz are infanticipating!"

Lucy dropped her knitting and woke up her husband. "We're going to have a baby!"

Desi rubbed his eyes. "How d'ya know? We aren't supposed to hear until tomorrow."

"Winchell just told me."

"How d'ya like *dat?*"

Actually, they were delighted, even though the couple resented Winchell's notorious practice of bribing doctors, nurses, and medical technicians to get inside information on ailing or pregnant celebrities. The Arnazes finished out the week, canceled the rest of their bookings, and went home to Chatsworth. With a contractor Desi began work on a $23,000 addition to their $14,500 house. It would include two bedrooms, a patio, and a white tile room Lucy called "the Lab," to be outfitted with the latest cooking and laundry appliances. As a final touch Desi added an outside door at the far end of the playroom. No doubt remembering his own youth, he told Lucy, "When our son's a teenager, he'll need a private entrance."

Everything went well for the first two months of the pregnancy, but before the trimester ended Lucy was back in Cedars of Lebanon Hospital with acute pain and bleeding. She miscarried five days later. "They kept me in the hospital for a week," Lucy remembered, "doped with sedatives. I cried and cried, but the doctors assured me that I still had a chance to become a mother." She took them at their word and returned to work, determined not to succumb to melancholy. In the next three months she made six round trips to New York for guest shots on television variety shows, continued with *My Favorite Husband,* and had an agonizing kidney stone removed. All the while she kept at Don Sharpe, reminding him that audiences accepted the Cuban and the Redhead as a couple. Surely he could find some way for them to appear in the same radio program—or perhaps something in the burgeoning new medium of television. His replies were not encouraging.

That October she received good news for the first time since the miscarriage. Through her agent, Cecil B. DeMille had offered Lucy a part as the elephant trainer in his new circus picture, *The Greatest Show on Earth.* Her costars would include Jimmy Stewart, Charlton Heston, Cornel Wilde, and Dorothy Lamour. Lucy was thirty-nine, and she knew this was her last chance at a big-budget A picture. She accepted without hesitation. There was only one snag. The actress Lucille Ball was still under contract to Columbia and its ogre Harry Cohn. Lucy begged to be released from her obligation to the studio.

Cohn not only refused, he sent her the script of *The Magic Carpet.*

In that harem melodrama Lucy would be cast as a temptress "whose lips and temper are hotter than the desert sands." The producer was Sam Katzman, known in Hollywood for making "lease breakers." Katzman productions, in Lucy's words, were "strictly class E. Anyone of any stature was supposed to say, 'Over my dead body! I'll never do *that!'*" Having made a legitimate offer, Harry Cohn could then cancel the player's contract without paying her off. He had reckoned without Lucy's resolve. She phoned Cohn and was put right through. He expected outrage; instead he got sweetness. "I've just read the Sam Katzman script," she cooed. "I think it's *marvelous*! I'd be delighted to do it."

To the production chief's distress—as well as that of Sam Katzman, who had to pay her $85,000, a large part of his budget—Lucy showed up on the set five weeks later, her harem pants and jacket fitting snugly. A little too snugly, for she was pregnant again. This time she kept her condition totally secret, not only to beat the jinx but because there was a subclause about pregnancy in the fine print. If Cohn had tumbled to the news he could have canceled Lucy's contract overnight. On the set, everyone was kept from the truth except for Harriet McCain. Each night she let out the waist on Lucy's harem pants a notch or two. "I collected eighty-five grand for a total of five days' work," the actress was to crow, "and got out of my Columbia contract very nicely."

Then she and Desi got an audience with C. B. There, in the great man's office, Lucy went public with a formal announcement: "Mr. DeMille, I cannot do your picture, because I'm going to have a baby."

Decades later Lucy told the story as if it had happened the day before. DeMille did not react immediately. He paused, as if he were the central actor in one of his biblical epics.

Aware that Lucy ached to be in *The Greatest Show on Earth,* he also knew that she was nearly forty and that this might be her last chance at motherhood. At last he turned to Desi and delivered a line that Lucy was to treasure for the rest of her life: "Congratulations. You are the only person in the world to screw Harry Cohn, Columbia Pictures, Paramount, Cecil D. DeMille, and your wife, all at the same time."

CHAPTER
SEVEN

"How can I possibly sell this?"

$\mathcal{F}$OLLOWING a broadcast of *My Favorite Husband,* the *Hollywood Reporter* told readers it was "too bad that that Lucille Ball's funny grimaces and gestures aren't visible on the radio." The line was too provocative to be ignored. So were the notices that Desi and Lucy had received on their vaudeville tour. *Variety,* for example, had called their Chicago act "one of the best bills to play the house in recent months," and said: "If the red-headed gal wants to slide on her tummy for five or six shows a day past the initial five-week booking for this package, her agency should have no trouble lining up dates."

Bolstered by newspaper clips and their own enthusiasm, Don Sharpe and Jess Oppenheimer made a pitch to CBS. The network's radio division produced *My Favorite Husband,* and 1951 seemed the ideal time and place for Lucy and Desi to make the jump to prime-time television. The network thought otherwise. Sharpe and Oppenheimer pressed on. They found the sponsors of Lucy's radio show mildly receptive to the idea of a TV program centered on the Arnazes. Executives at General Foods' advertising agency, Young and Rubicam, called Lucy and Desi in and convinced them that CBS would never be persuaded by sales talk alone. The network needed proof that a Desi-and-Lucy comedy would work on the screen. "Produce your own audition program," counseled a Y&R vice president with a lot of experience in production and promotion. "That way you can sell it to the highest bidder."

Admen had a way of making the arduous sound simple; for Lucy and Desi such an audition program would mean a tangle of fiscal and emotional investments, and the word around the broadcasting business was far from encouraging. Executives warned that the public was not ready to see a Latino in a domestic role and that Lucy was far too glamorous to be accepted as a housewife. Desi wavered; not Lucy. "Look," she pointed out, "I was born in Jamestown, New York, and waited on tables and jerked sodas. You've been kicking around this country for seventeen years. Hell yes, we're average Americans. And we're going to do *I Love Lucy* even if we go broke." This despite the advice of friends who urged them to abandon the project. Studios, the Arnazes were reminded, did not look kindly on apostates. Desi could always lead a band, but what would happen to Lucy? She answered them by quoting the voice of Carole Lombard. Lucy insisted that her late friend had appeared in a dream, speaking ten magic words: "Honey, go ahead. Take a chance. Give it a whirl!"

Whirl they did. Because Oppenheimer, Carroll, and Pugh had exclusive contracts with CBS, Lucy and Desi were forced to commission scripts from outside teams. Every one of these was held at arm's length. Nevertheless, several were passed on to Don Sharpe, and he, in turn, shopped them around to the networks. One script contained just enough to intrigue programmers at NBC. In this scenario Desi played a successful bandleader, and Lucy his movie star wife. The plot revolved around their plans for a quiet wedding anniversary—until reporters and photographers from *Life* magazine crash the party. News of NBC's interest was carefully leaked to Harry Ackerman, CBS's executive in charge of radio and television production. The thought of losing Lucy was too alarming to ignore, and he capitulated—partway. Ackerman put Desi under contract as the master of ceremonies for a radio quiz show, *Tropical Trip*. (Another quiz show, to be called "Win

Your Vacation," had been planned for the same time slot. It would have starred a young comedian named Johnny Carson. He was deemed expendable.)

For the first time in her career Lucy stopped being a "gamer," ready and eager to go along with whatever the studio ordered. The independent spirit that animated her youth had been suppressed for years. The adolescent who had auditioned in New York City, and put red pieces of paper on her face to break up Eddie Cantor in Hollywood, had been missing for so long that people had forgotten her. But Lucy remembered Lucille. That audacious youth had been suppressed by the actress's need to work and the woman's desire to preserve two families—the one she began with, and the one she was trying to create with Desi. It was time for a reappearance.

Lucy sensed that she had the upper hand with CBS, and impudently refined her list of demands. The Lucy show, whatever it was, would have Jess Oppenheimer as its producer and head writer. A running part would be found for Desi. The show would be produced in Hollywood so that she could continue her film career. The newly created Desilu Productions was to own 50 percent of the program. CBS would pick up the tab for the audition film. Ackerman agreed to these conditions. Thus began a series of brainstorming sessions at CBS. "We were asking ourselves," Oppenheimer later wrote, "what do you do with a comedienne and a Cuban orchestra leader?" They began with the working title of "Lucy." Even that was to cause trouble when Desi demanded top billing. After about a week of negotiating, Oppenheimer recalled, "I had finally managed to convince him on the basis that it was the 'gallant' thing to do—to let the lady go first. But even then he had come back to me one more time, saying, 'I tell you what, Jess. Why don't we compromise and make it alphabetical?' "

In time Lucy and the writers arrived at the same conclusion: a situation comedy built around a supposedly famous bandleader and his celebrity wife was unworkable. In her words: "The general public doesn't think that movie stars have any problems. They think it's just party after party." Many meetings later Oppenheimer came up with a premise that he put in writing:

I LOVE LUCY

This is the title of an idea for a radio and/or television program incorporating characters named Lucy and Ricky Ricardo. He is a

Latin-American bandleader and singer. She is his wife. They are happily married and very much in love. The only bone of contention between them is her desire to get into show business, and his equally strong desire to keep her out of it. To Lucy, who was brought up in the humdrum sphere of a moderate, well-to-do, middle western, mercantile family, show business is the most glamorous field in the world. But Ricky, who was raised in show business, sees none of its glamour, only its deficiencies, and yearns to be an ordinary citizen, keeping regular hours and living a normal life. As show business is the only way he knows to make a living, and he makes a very good one, the closest he can get to this dream is having a wife who's out of show business and devotes herself to keeping as nearly a normal life as possible for him.

With this as armature, he and the writers constructed a different kind of comedy. The couple, Ricky and Lucy Ricardo, would be supported by Pepito the clown, and the actor Jerry Hausner, playing Ricky's agent. In 1951 television was such a novelty that when Hausner offered to buy his father a TV set, Hausner Sr., a Hungarian immigrant, declined. The old man had spent his Friday nights peering at wrestling matches through the window of a furniture store on Hollywood Boulevard. There, the only noise he could hear came from the traffic at his back. "Not yet," he told his son. "Just wait. Wait till they get *sound*. They'll figure it out one of these days. You'll see. Just like they did with the movies."

The *I Love Lucy* pilot went before cameras on March 2, 1951, Desi's thirty-fourth birthday. A kinescope—a film taken off the closed-circuit TV tube—was made during the proceedings. As technicians stood by in CBS Studio A, a meltdown occurred backstage. Lucy was now five months pregnant and showed it. Costumers outfitted her with loose-fitting pajamas and hoped for the best, while Desi and a network executive wrangled about the Arnazes' still-unsigned contract. With only a few seconds to go, the executive gave Desi a directive: "Sign the contract right now, as is, or the show will not go on."

Desi held his ground. "How much does the kinescope cost to shoot?"

"Nineteen thousand dollars."

"Okay," Desi yelled, "I'll pay for it myself, and it will belong to us."

The executive backed down. "We'll go ahead and shoot it now, and thrash out the details later."

After the kinescope was made, other details had to be thrashed out as well. To no one's surprise, the Lucy and Ricky Ricardo characters were convincingly funny. The clown and agent, however, seemed to diminish rather than augment the comedy. And the couple's locale, an apartment overlooking the Plaza Hotel at Central Park South, felt wrong, somehow. The show took a week of painstaking edits; even so, there were many rough spots and ill-timed moments. Upon viewing the kinescope, Hubbell Robinson, head of CBS programming in New York, phoned Oppenheimer and barked: "What are you sending me, Jess? This is the worst thing I've ever seen. How can I possibly sell this?" Two weeks later, without a buyer or sponsor for *I Love Lucy,* the final episode of *My Favorite Husband* was taped. When the last commercial was delivered, Lucy addressed the studio audience, unable to keep the desperation out of her voice when she spoke of the day when "we'll be able to come back on the air in the not-too-distant future." As she read the credits of all the people connected with the program for the last two and a half years she began to weep. Though she had become expert at turning on the tears, this was not an act. Lucy had good reason to feel that this time the dice were not going to come up in the Arnazes' favor.

Robinson shopped the kinescope around to various advertising agencies. The asking price was $26,000 for each episode, a bargain at a time when most shows cost upward of $50,000 to produce. He had no takers. Then, at the last moment, Milton Biow, head of the advertising agency that bore his name, evinced a mild interest. Biow's principal client, Philip Morris, had already backed two unsatisfactory programs: the television versions of *Truth or Consequences* and *Youth Opportunity* emceed by the bandleader Horace Heidt. The tobacco company was in the market for something to greet the new decade of the 1950s. Biow rolled the kinescope in his private screening room. He was quick to spot flaws and amateurisms, but he thought there might be something salvageable in the situation comedy of Lucy vs. Desi. Unwilling to trust his instincts, he called in his old friend Oscar Hammerstein II, one of Broadway's greatest lyricists and an expert on humorous scenes and characters. At a private screening the author of *Show Boat* and *Oklahoma!* chuckled at Lucy's antics and Desi's accent. Yes, he agreed, the kinescope was awkward and the premise needed work, but there was real potential here. That was good enough for Biow. He and Sharpe worked out an arrangement with Philip Morris, with Sharpe guaranteeing a stronger and more professional show by airtime. The cost of each episode was not to exceed $19,500. In the initial season of 1951–1952 there would be thirty-nine episodes, and then Philip Morris would have the option to continue the series or to cancel its sponsorship. By meeting's end, *I Love Lucy* had been guaranteed a network, a sponsor, and a time period—Monday night at nine o'clock. Desi was on a hot streak.

Guaranteed a season of employment, Oppenheimer, Pugh, and Carroll reexamined their handiwork. They agreed that having Ricky's agent as a main character would skew the program away from the couple and toward Desi. The character was dropped. They also looked back to their success with *My Favorite Husband,* in which Lucille Ball and Richard Denning played against, and with, an older couple. It was decided to change the locale from an expensive apartment building to a middle-class brownstone owned by Fred and Ethel Mertz—named for a couple who had lived on the same block with Pugh during her childhood in Indianapolis. The Mertzes could thus be landlords and second bananas at the same time. The logical choices for these parts were Gale Gordon and Bea Benaderet, the second leads on the radio show. The job offer came too late: by the time *I Love Lucy* was sold both character actors were booked for other assignments. The veteran character actor James Gleason was also considered until his salary demands were made known. At $3,500 a week, he had priced himself out of the game.

As an intense casting search began, Oppenheimer received a call from the East Coast. Milton Biow had just returned from a vacation in Europe and could scarcely contain his exuberance. "I was thinking about the show all the time I was away," he burbled. "I think it's going to be a great program." Oppenheimer was glad to hear it. Was there anything else? Well, there *was* one question: "When are you moving to New York?" The producer blanched. "New York? Who's moving to New York? Nobody told me anything about that! I thought the deal called for the show to originate from here—live—with kinnies for the cable, like *Burns and Allen* and *The Alan Young Show.*" He added that neither Lucy nor Desi nor their staff had any intentions of moving three thousand miles from their homes. "Jess," returned Biow, "I bought a show that's going to be done from New York. I am not about to put on a program where fifteen percent of the audience see it clearly and eighty-five percent see it through a piece of cheesecloth."

The adman was referring to the primitive state of television broadcasting in 1951. That year, when only 8 million Americans owned TV sets, shows were carried city-to-city via coaxial cable. It failed to reach even halfway across the country. Some 85 percent of viewers were located in the East and Midwest. Instead of seeing *I Love Lucy* live, they would be forced to see a kinescope made earlier—a blurred and, indeed, cheesy version of the show.

Desi consulted technical experts. They all told him the same thing. There was only one way out of his fix: put *I Love Lucy* on celluloid. Costly though the cinema process was, it would allow Desi to make as many prints as he wanted. These would be sent out to TV stations throughout the country, and each station would broadcast the same show with the identical first-quality footage. Biow expressed doubts about the process until he was reminded that it had already been done. The perennial radio favorite *Amos 'n' Andy* had been adapted for CBS television, with an all-black cast. Every episode was filmed instead of kinescoped. The executive screened a program, liked what he saw, and gave Desi the go-ahead—with certain ground rules. Keenly aware of why *My Favorite Husband* had garnered such high ratings, CBS insisted that *I Love Lucy* be shot before a live studio audience, and that the production price stay within reason. Desi, fluently talking through his hat, assured the network that he would have each episode shot with three or four 35mm motion picture cameras for a price he picked out of the air: $24,500 per. And, he went on, it would be no trouble to film *I Love Lucy* before a theaterful of "civilians"—this despite the fact that no situation comedy had ever been filmed in that way.

Desi's assurances came at a cost. In order to compensate for the additional expenses, the stars would have to take a pay cut. The Arnazes were slated to receive $5,000 each per show; instead they would receive $1,000 less, the money used to defray production costs. Now the businessman in Desi made itself heard. Since he had agreed to everything CBS wanted, he asked the network for one small favor. Desilu would take the pay reduction for the first thirty-nine shows—*if* his company could own those shows outright. Somewhat to Desi's astonishment there was no objection. In hindsight he wrote: "I think the reason CBS agreed is because they did not think filming the shows the way we wanted to was going to work. So what the hell? they probably thought. Let them struggle for a few episodes and they'll soon be glad to come to New York and do them live."

It was only to Lucy that Desi confessed his dilemma: he hadn't the slightest idea of how to proceed. "How about it," he asked in a private, desperate exchange. "Do you have any thoughts or ideas?"

She had one. "Well, it's going to be photographed on film, same as a motion picture—right?"

"*Sí, señora.*"

"Well then, *señor,* you better start by getting someone who knows how to photograph it."

Desi brightened. "You just gave me my first clue."

*I*n certain ways, Karl Freund's career paralleled Lucy's. He, too, had started out in show business at age fifteen. His first job was as a projectionist in his native Germany. Two years later he started working behind the camera, making newsreels and shorts. In the 1920s Freund worked on one of the most celebrated movies in Germany's Golden Age of cinema, *The Last Laugh.* In order to film one drunken scene, Freund strapped the camera to his chest and stumbled about like an inebriate. For the first time, the motion picture camera became a vital part of the narrative. When other filmmakers were satisfied to keep the action on one stage, Freund employed dollies and cranes. For the full-length documentary *Berlin, Symphony of a Great City,* he devised a special high-speed film stock and shot so quickly that no one spotted the camera. In 1929, the Technicolor Company lured him to the United States to work on its new color process. Two years later the cinematographer was hired by Universal Pictures, where he burnished his reputation by filming *Dracula* and *Murders in the Rue Morgue.* In 1938 he won an Academy Award for *The Good Earth,* and in the 1940s he developed a light meter that was still being used a generation later. But technology and stark imagery were not his only strengths; he also knew how to make women look glamorous on the screen. He was the favorite of Greta Garbo and Katharine Hepburn. Lucy knew why when she saw the luminous print of *Du Barry Was a Lady.*

Desi, who had often visited the set of that film, remembered Freund as "a big, fat, jolly man who waddled around all over the set carrying a Thermos full of martinis and giving orders in his thick German accent." His account continued: "I never saw him drunk, though, and he was a kind and brilliant man. Everybody called him Papa." Desi traced Papa to Washington, D.C., where the sixty-one-year-old was working for the government in its film research and development laboratory. Desi did a little research before stating his problem via telephone. There followed a conversation that was to alter the course of broadcasting. "I want to stage the show as a play," Desi explained, "film it in continuity in front of an audience of perhaps three hundred people, using three thirty-five-millimeter cameras and recording the audience's laughter and reactions simultaneously with our dialogue." All cameras would be synchronized on one sound track so that the film could be edited from master shot to medium shot to close-up without missing a beat.

Papa was concise. "You cannot do it."

Desi asked him to elaborate.

"Because, my dear boy, you must light for the master shot one way, light for the medium shot another way, and light for the close-ups in yet another way. You can't photograph all three angles at the same time and get any kind of good film quality. On top of that you want to do it in front of an audience."

"Well, I know that nobody has done it up to now, but I figured that if there was anybody in the world who could do it, it would be Karl Freund."

"That's very flattering."

With that reply as his cue, Desi turned on all the charm he possessed. "My God, Papa, you showed how to use a moving camera, you invented the light meter. . . . For such a genius, what I want you to do should be a pushover."

Pointing out that "Lucy's no chicken," Freund said he would have to "use special lighting, put gauze on the lens."

"I don't care what you have to do, Papa. I'll get you whatever you need."

A bit more wrangling and Papa ventured, "Okay, I come out and we talk and we look."

Freund came out, talked, looked, and signed on, consenting to work for basic union scale until *I Love Lucy* showed a profit. "Papa was loaded, anyway," Desi recalled. "He could buy and sell Lucy and me three or four times. The money he had made out of the light meter alone, plus a lot of acreage in orange trees he owned in the San Fernando Valley, made him a man of considerable means. The challenge was what got him, and that's what I was counting on."

Before the cinematographer could go to work, his new employer had to locate a workplace. Network facilities were measured and found insufficient for Freund's demands. Some studio sound stages looked promising, but they were for filming only. Fire laws forbade the seating of three hundred people in any of them, and no movie studio would permit architectural revisions to be made to accommodate a lowly TV show. After a long search Desi found the new home of Desilu Productions, the General Service Studios Stage 2 on Las Palmas Avenue. The abandoned building contained an arena large and airy enough for sets, technicians, and an audience. All that it required was $50,000 worth of work. The floor needed replacing, fire exits would have to be created, bleachers built, a sprinkler system installed. Desi presented CBS with a plan and a budget. Once again the network proved agreeable. With the money advanced, he gave an audible and grateful sigh, assuming that the last obstacle had been hurdled. He had forgotten Jess Oppenheimer.

The producer had designed the show, worked with the writers, created personnae. He had even arranged for a theme song by Disney arranger Eliot Daniel. The lyrics were as basic and functional as the tune:

> *I love Lucy and she loves me,*
> *We're as happy as two can be.*
> *Sometimes we quarrel, but then,*
> *How we love making up again.*
> *Lucy kisses like no one can,*
> *She's my missus and I'm her man,*
> *And life is heaven, you see,*
> *'Cause I love Lucy, yes, I love Lucy,*
> *And Lucy loves me.*

And yet Jess Oppenheimer had not been vouchsafed a look at his contract. He decided to speak to the boss about it, reminding Desi that Harry Ackerman—and therefore CBS, his employer—had promised Oppenheimer 20 percent of *I Love Lucy.* The network, however, had never informed Desi of this arrangement. "This can't be!" was the wounded reply. "Lucy and I own the package. How can CBS do this?

No way are we going to do the show. Forget the whole thing!" Storming off the lot, Desi drove home and, still steaming, told his wife, "The show is off." Lucy refused to go along. "We can't back out now," she argued. Desi was unmoved. In desperation she phoned Oppenheimer. "Jess, everyone knows we're doing it. If we don't go through with it, they'll say we failed. My entire career is at stake!"

Oppenheimer was as implacable as Desi. The only reason he agreed to do the audition program, he reminded Lucy, was because of the 20 percent understanding. If Desilu was going to renege he would back out of the show. Period. Furious negotiations began. Ultimately Desi conceded; he recognized that Oppenheimer was too integral to the writing and production. Sensing an advantage, Oppenheimer asked that percentages be given to Carroll and Pugh. This time it was Desi who refused to budge, and it was the producer who conceded. He made a private arrangement to share 5 percent with the writers, leaving him with 15 percent. With these financial arrangements made, the dust settled. All warring parties made peace and returned to their mutual task: casting the supporting players for *I Love Lucy*.

To find the right man to play Fred Mertz, Desi pored over casting directories and went through résumés. Along the way a call came in from William Frawley, a short, plump performer with long experience playing gruff but loveable characters. Desi looked him up. The sixty-four-year-old actor had been born in Burlington, Iowa. He and his handsomer brother, Paul, had kicked around vaudeville in the 1920s. When Paul's looks began to fade, so did his career. William went on solo or with a series of partners, one of them his wife, Edna Louise. The marriage lasted less than seven years; after that William opted for lifelong bachelorhood. His beefy, cantankerous character played well on Broadway, particularly as a profane and disillusioned press agent in the Ben Hecht–Charles MacArthur hit *Twentieth Century*. That success consolidated his reputation as a dependable character actor and brought him to Hollywood. Audiences saw Frawley in a variety of films, backing up the likes of Bing Crosby, Pat O'Brien, and James Cagney, and playing key roles in films as disparate as the Gary Cooper vehicle *The General Died at Dawn*, in which he played a gunrunner, and Charlie Chaplin's *Monsieur Verdoux*. In the latter movie he articulated a Chaplin line with autobiographical zest: "You know, it's a peculiar thing. At funerals one's inclined to laugh; and at weddings, weep."

But whiskey had slowly eroded his career, and as the 1950s began,

Frawley found himself at liberty. He lived alone or with one of his sisters, happy to sit and drink and watch Yankee games, dependably loyal, grouchy and uncomplicated, oblivious to his reputation as a boozer, wondering when someone would call and offer him another role. He did a lot of waiting.

Desi went over the films and liked what he saw. Then he began to ask around. "I checked with the CBS people, the sponsor, and the agency," he noted. "They all said 'Yeah, we know what he has done in the past, but what has he done lately? Besides, he's an alcoholic. You'd be out of your mind to hire him. There are a lot of actors who are much more dependable and can play that part.'" The contrarian in Desi became intrigued with these bad reviews and invited Frawley to lunch at Nickodell's, a restaurant on Melrose Avenue behind the RKO studios. While the two men enjoyed their preprandial drinks, Desi mentioned the rumors of insobriety, and the warnings that Frawley might be too drunk to show up for rehearsals, let alone filmings.

"Well, those bastards, those sonsabitches," responded the player. "They're always saying that about me. How the hell do they know, those bastards?"

"Look," Desi reassured him, "I don't give a damn whether you drink or not. I like to drink myself and I'll drink you under the table anytime you'd like to give it a try, except during working hours. But Lucy and I have everything going on this project. If we fail, I don't want it to be because some character like you loused it up."

A few drinks later Desi elaborated on the theme. "I have considered many good character actors for this part, especially Gale Gordon, who's very well liked by the agencies and the networks."

"What's he do that I can't?"

"Nothing, it's what you do that he *doesn't* do that louses you up. But I am convinced that there's no one better in the whole world to play Fred Mertz than William Frawley."

"All right, so what's your problem? William Frawley is now sitting next to you and willing to listen to the kind of proposition you are willing to offer him to make your show a success."

Desi made his proposal. "The first time you are not able to do your job, I'll try to work around you for that day. The second time, I'll try to manage again. But if you do it three times, then you are through, and I mean *through*, not only on our show, but you'll never work in this town again as long as you live. Is that fair enough?"

Frawley nodded, ordered another drink, and announced, "Okay, Cuban, we have a deal and we'll show all them bastards how wrong they are."

That left the part of Ethel Mertz to be filled. Desi had hired Marc Daniels, who had won awards for his use of multiple cameras in television drama, to direct the first season of *I Love Lucy*. Familiar with the work of a stage actress named Vivian Vance, Daniels pressed Desi and Jess Oppenheimer to catch her in a revival of John Van Druten's *The Voice of the Turtle* at the La Jolla Playouse. The star was the comelier Diana Lynn, but all three pairs of eyes were trained on Vance. She played a heart-of-gold whore who managed to be salty and touching at the same time. At the first-act intermission Desi turned to his colleagues and said, "I think we've found our Ethel."

There could have been no greater contrast between second bananas.

At thirty-nine, Vance had been married three times, and her latest marriage, to actor Philip Ober, was heading toward the rocks. Abused as a child, she had suffered from psychosomatic illnesses and a nervous breakdown before undergoing intensive psychotherapy. Yet even in her early years Vivian Roberta Jones was marked as a girl with promise. More promise, said her neighbors in Cherryvale, Kansas, than her playmate Louise Brooks, the silent-film star. "I always thought Vivian was ten times the actress Louise ever was," claimed one of them. There was no way to tell the accuracy of this appraisal; Brooks walked away from a film career at the age of thirty-two and thereafter became a symbol of the I-don't-care flapper, tossing her Dutch bob and heading into the wind. The Jones family moved to Albuquerque, where Vivian, like Lucy, starred in high school productions. The teenager then went on to seek a theatrical career, over the vociferous objections of her Protestant fundamentalist parents. She married to get away from home, was divorced two years later at the age of twenty-one, and was attractive and talented enough to make the chorus line of the Jerome Kern musical *Music in the Air* at twenty-three. Parts offered to her grew larger, and she began to garner a reputation as "the little Albuquerque bombshell." She also acquired a second husband, advanced to starring roles in straight plays, and eventually became, according to the New York critics, the onstage embodiment of a "hussy," "blonde menace," "alluring vixen," and "other woman." She took a lover during the second marriage, actor Philip Ober, who became husband number three after her divorce.

On the surface Vivian seemed a lighthearted, if fickle, personality. In fact she was continually hovering on the edge of emotional collapse, and finally she did suffer a nervous breakdown. It took years of therapy before she could acknowledge that from adolescence onward two opposing forces pulled her apart. As she came to understand, the first was "a compulsive, an irresistible urge to act. I could no more have fought it than I could have willed myself not to breathe." The second was "the deep-set, unshakeable conviction on the part of my mother and father, splendid folk but tempered in inflexible religious and moral dogma, that the stage was a sinful business."

During her slow recovery, the shaky actress appeared in several unmemorable films before returning, very tentatively, to the theater. It was in 1951 that she received a call from Mel Ferrer, who wanted her for the Van Druten drama. Five years before, in Chicago, she had played the same role and received rave reviews. She signed on, terrified but unwilling to relinquish her vocation. "In the wings," she recalled, "a moment before the curtain rose, I nearly fainted. Then I spoke my first line, and knew I was all right." Better than all right, Desi concluded. Informed of her problems, he pushed them aside. In his view, Vance, like Frawley, was worth the risk.

*M*eantime, Lucy had other things on her mind. The baby was two weeks overdue. She felt too bulky and uncomfortable to go down to the La Jolla Playhouse or to bother with any more hiring; all matters pertaining to the show were ceded to Desi. To her surprise, she would learn that the naming of the infant was also left to him. On July 17, 1951, twenty days before her fortieth birthday, Lucy went under anesthesia when doctors saw that she was about to have a breech birth. The parents had already agreed upon a name: Desi if the child was male, Susan if female. When Lucy awoke, she was informed that she had given birth to a girl. She demanded to see Susan. "You mean Lucie," corrected the nurse. No, came the answer, "*I'm* Lucy." She was shown the birth certificate. Desi had signed it while she was asleep, having decided that one Lucy in the family was not enough.

Six weeks after the delivery Lucy appeared at Stage 2 for the show's first rehearsal, wearing dark glasses and seeming ill at ease. She greeted Frawley with warmth. He looked and sounded right, and if the old boy could stay off the sauce, she reflected, he could be a perfect foil. Lucy was less sure about Vance. She had expected a female version of Frawley; instead she confronted an attractive blonde, her junior, it was said, by almost a year. "She doesn't look like a landlady," Lucy whispered to Daniels. Vance overheard the complaint. "I photograph dumpy," she assured them. In a disappointed voice Lucy blurted, "I expected you to look like Bill." Frawley took his cue from Lucy. As the hammering and sawing of set construction echoed around him, he motioned toward Vance and asked Desi, "Where did you get this bitch?" Vance had her own view of Frawley, and she made sure that he overheard it: "How can anyone believe I'm married to that old coot?" The cast of *I Love Lucy* was off and running.

Complicating the technical problems was Desi's dual role as actor and as president of Desilu Productions. During rehearsals, he would be approached in the middle of a comic scene and asked to make an executive decision. Having done so he was then required to dive back into the part of Ricky Ricardo with exactly the same brio as before. At the same time, Lucy was going into overdrive, puffing cigarette after cigarette, trying out props in a dozen different ways, badgering Al Simon, the production coordinator brought in from *Truth or Consequences,* a quiz show that utilized three cameras. ("You don't know how much this means to me. Can you really do it?") Lucy was operating at such a high tempo that at one point she enlisted the aid of Vance and some Bon Ami and cleaned the studio washrooms for want of something more creative to do. Annoyances cropped up in unexpected places: the letters I.L.L. on a script caused Lucy to explode: "I don't want a show that's ill." Desi explained what the initials meant, but she would not be placated. Sighing, he sent out a memo announcing that the only proper abbreviation from now on was "LUCY."

In the beginning Lucy had no feel for story lines. She concentrated instead on individual scenes, wringing every laugh she could out of objects, or being padded out to look twenty pounds overweight. Extra poundage was the essential gag in "The Diet," one of the first scripts filmed, but the third to be broadcast. All the basic elements of the program were contained within its two acts: Lucy Ricardo has ballooned in weight because of an unchecked appetite. One of the chorus girls in her husband's nightclub quits. Ever anxious to break into show business, Lucy auditions for the job. The casting director informs her that she can join the chorus—if she can shed the excess avoirdupois. How many pounds? Twelve. How long does she have? Four days. There follows a period of frantic exercise, but all she loses is a few ounces. Lucy presses on. At dinner, for example, she crunches a stalk of celery while Fred Mertz and Ricky enjoy a hearty meal, with second helpings. As the pounds begin to melt away, the diet begins to drive Lucy to distraction. She winds up stealing meat from the Mertzes' dog. With just hours left in which to lose the last five pounds, Lucy buys a portable steam cabinet, sweats away the remaining weight, and hastens to the nightclub. There she belts out a song—and faints dead away from malnutrition.

In all, six episodes were shot before *I Love Lucy* went on the air, and the first one to be filmed became the fourth to be shown. "Lucy Thinks Ricky Is Trying to Murder Her" assumes that the protagonist is one of world's most suggestible women. Having read the chilling *Mockingbird Murder Mystery,* Lucy overhears Ricky talking to his agent about getting rid of a singer. She misinterprets the conversation and believes that Ricky wants to do away with his wife. Her feelings are intensified by the dire fortune-telling of Ethel. Some hysterical maneuvers result, among them Lucy's strapping a skillet around her middle to shield her from bullets. Ricky, convinced that his wife has lost her reason, slips her a sleeping powder. Before Lucy can nod off, however, she barges into his nightclub, the Tropicana, where she intends to shoot him before he eliminates her—a plan foiled in the last five minutes when all becomes embarrassingly clear.

The episode was an audience-pleaser, an ideal way to display all the characters at high pitch. Lucy and Desi were as confident as possible under the circumstances—circumstances that included carpenters banging in the final nails; Desi's band tuning up endlessly; CBS and Philip Morris executives standing around, looking imperious; a line of potential audience members on the sidewalk outside; overanxious ushers borrowed from CBS to seat all the people in the new bleachers; and a distracted Karl Freund, still uncertain that his cameras would work simultaneously. Backstage, the Arnazes were going over last-minute changes with Frawley and Vance when Desi was pulled aside by an inspector from the Los Angeles health department.

"I don't think you can go on and do the show," he said.

Desi's blood froze. It wasn't enough to have opening night jitters. Now this civil servant, this nit-picking creep . . .

The inspector continued frostily: "According to our regulations, you have to have two bathrooms, one for ladies and another for men, within a certain prescribed distance from where the audience is sitting. You have one for the men within that distance, but none for the ladies. I cannot allow that audience in unless you have both."

A quick huddle occurred. Oppenheimer got wind of it and exploded, "We're about to go on and do our first show and you're looking for a *bathroom*?"

That they were, and the only one within the proper distance was the private john in Lucy's dressing room. She spoke up: "Tell the ladies to be my guests."

Desi turned to the inspector. *Now* would it be all right to let the audience into the theater? It would. But the delay had led to a new problem. The spectators were beginning to sound restive after their unscheduled half-hour wait. Oppenheimer pointed out: "We sure as hell don't want a grouchy, unhappy audience. They won't react well to our jokes." He appealed to Desi. "Why don't you go out there and warm them up?"

"What the hell does that mean, warm them up?"

"Oh, for Crissake, go out there, welcome them, make them feel at home, tell them about the technique we're using to film our shows, then tell them a few jokes to get them in the mood to laugh. After that, introduce the cast and we'll start filming."

Desi obeyed, welcoming the strangers and informing them that they were going to see a kind of stage play for television. He also warned them that there might be a moment or two when the cameras interfered with their line of vision. Then he hit a light note: "I was told to tell you a few funny stories to get you in the mood to laugh. I don't know many funny stories but there was an old vaudevillian with us for several weeks on our first theater tour. I heard this one so many times that I think I know it pretty good."

He told them about a beautiful seventeen-year-old girl who was innocently swimming in a lake when she heard a voice appealing to her. She saw no one but a little turtle on a rock.

"The young, beautiful girl said to the turtle, 'Are you the one who was calling me?'

" 'Yes, I was.'

" 'How come? You are a turtle and you can talk?'

" 'I was not always a turtle. I used to be an army sergeant, but some witch put a curse on me and turned me into a turtle. The reason I called you over here is because you can help me.'

"The girl asked, 'How can I help you?'

" 'If you take me home with you and let me sleep in your bed under your pillow, by tomorrow morning I'll be an army sergeant again.'

" 'I don't think I can do that.'

" 'Oh, please, you have to. I am so tired of being a turtle. I just have to get back into the army.'

" 'All right,' the young, beautiful girl said, 'I'll help you.' She took the little turtle home with her, took it to bed with her, and let it stay there for the night.

"The next morning her mother came into the room. The young girl was late getting up to go to school. And there in the bed, lying right next to her daughter, was this very handsome six-foot-two army sergeant.

"And do you know, to this very day that little girl's mother doesn't believe the story about the turtle?"

Desi got the desired response, and when the laughter died down introduced the cast. First came Frawley and Vance as the Mertzes, then he added with great fanfare: "Here's my favorite wife, the mother of my child, the vice president of Desilu, my favorite redhead, the girl who plays Lucy, Lucille Ball!" The power passed to Lucy as she embraced the supporting players and yelled at Desi, "How ya doing, you gorgeous Cuban?" She drew attention to the fact that her mother and Desi's were in the audience, blew kisses to everyone in sight, and created what Desi was to remember as "a happy, carnival type of feeling."

From the booth Daniels's voice broke into that carnival: "Please take your places for the first scene. Cameras get ready. Roll the sound. Roll the film. Now go on and do a good show for us tonight. Action!" They did do a good show. The cameras rolled noiselessly on the new floor, the audience chortled in the right places and the pacing seldom faltered. But what the audience saw as a miniplay was quite a different comedy on film. Observed in a screening room, many of the shots seemed mismatched, and the "flat" lighting that Freund had arranged so that all cameras were set to the same exposure caused harsher contrasts than expected. A specially designed Movieola editing machine

held multiple reels of film from three cameras, while a fourth component dealt with the sound. This contraption, dubbed "Desilu's Four-
headed Monster," allowed the editors to mix and match as they
pleased. Even so, it took nearly a month to pare the first episode to the
requisite twenty-two minutes, and meanwhile others were being written, rehearsed, and filmed. By now, the costs had gone over budget by
almost $250,000, and CBS executives were betting that *I Love Lucy*
would lose more than half a million dollars in its first year. The idea
of a second year was beyond their most malicious imaginations.
William S. Paley, president of the network, heard about the wagers and
fretted in his corner office.

Uncertain of just how the show would play, Desi tested "The Diet"
in a movie theater in Riverside in Orange County, some forty miles
from Los Angeles. There the episode provoked laughter so loud that it
sometimes drowned out the dialogue. The theater reception did much
to boost studio morale, but the second episode to be shot, "The Girls
Want to Go to a Nightclub," was judged to be technically superior. It
was the first "I Love Lucy" to reach the general public.

On October 15, 1951, 9 p.m. EST, *I Love Lucy* debuted on CBS, running against the highly rated dramatic program *Lights Out* on NBC,
featuring such players as Boris Karloff, Billie Burke, and Yvonne De
Carlo. *Curtain Up,* another dramatic series, ran on ABC, while the
smaller Dumont network featured professional wrestling. Comedy was
thought to play best at an earlier hour, and conventional wisdom held
this to be another strike against Desilu.

Earlier in the day the cast had been working through the script for
the seventh Lucy episode, "The Séance." Its plot centered around
Lucy and Ethel's obsession with the occult, and their belief that Desi's
career depends on the stars. This is the day, predicts his horoscope,
when he must answer "Yes" to every question. As the bandleader follows their instructions he is led deeper and deeper into comic catastrophe. The premise was weak, and required a great deal of rewriting,
and the cast and writers became so intensely involved that they nearly
forgot to watch the first episode. The Desliu studio was loaded with
fancy technical equipment, but no one had thought to supply the place
with a television set. It was thirty miles to the ranch; the Arnazes
would have to break the speed limit to get there in time. Marc Daniels
intervened. He invited everyone to his house in nearby Laurel Canyon.

There was still time for a quick bite, the director reminded them. No one expressed any appetite for dinner.

One actor was missing from the company. William Frawley, blasé as always, had opted to go home and listen to the heavyweight fights on radio. The other principals watched intensely, without cracking a smile. The only sound of amusement came from Vance's husband, Philip Ober. It was a mark of their deteriorating marriage that his loud, flat cackle seemed to annoy rather than please her. Lucy found him irritating as well: "He was a terrible man. Loved to embarrass her. He was nuts and he made her nuts. She was seeing all these shrinks. God, it was a mess. I told her to get rid of the guy, but if Vivian was one thing, it was loyal." As the show rolled on, the viewers at Daniels's house looked at each other in acute distress. An echo issued from the TV speaker, mangling the dialogue. Each CBS station had worked out a failsafe procedure: a 16mm backup print ran in synchronization with the pristine 35mm one. If anything went wrong, the station would simply make a switch. For reasons unknown, the Los Angeles outlet had inadvertently gone to the 16mm version while the preferred one was playing. To Oppenheimer, "with both sound tracks going at the same time, one playing three or four sprockets ahead of the other, the dialogue sounded as if it were being played over the public address system of Yankee stadium."

Hysterical inquiries ensued. Desi and Lucy learned to their relief, and everyone else's, that technical problems had occurred only on that one local station. Yet the next day, even though the 35mm print rolled without a hitch across the country, not all were pleased with what they saw. Perhaps the most discontented was the president of Philip Morris, one O. Parker McComas. After viewing the initial *I Love Lucy* he called the Biow agency to ask how much it would cost to cancel the show. The cigarette commercials came across well, he conceded, but as for the episode itself—in his view it was "unfunny, silly and totally boring." The advertising executives asked him to reconsider. At least wait for next week's show, they pleaded. McComas grudgingly told them he would go along, warning them that he spoke from experience. They were only putting off the inevitable.

$\mathcal{T}$HE NEXT morning the *New York Times* weighed in with some encouraging words: "*I Love Lucy* has the promise of providing a refreshing half-hour of video entertainment." Not all was well; the paper went on to pan the "poor second act" and to warn that Lucy's farcical situations might easily get out of hand. *Variety,* like many another paper, preferred the on-camera personnel to their gags: "As storyline comedies go it is the better part of appreciation not to ask yourself too many questions and just go along with what transpires on your screen."

By and large the viewers did exactly that, in increasing numbers as the weeks went on. By then the characters were firmly established, and Lucy and Ricky had worked out their marital and ethnic relationships. In "Be a Pal," the third show to be broadcast, Lucy fears that the honeymoon is over and that Ricky is losing interest in her. Even when she gets herself up in alluring outfits, he pays no attention. She takes Ethel into her confidence, and the landlady theorizes that the Latino is out of his element in New York. "Surround him with things that remind him of his childhood." In the next scene Lucy has filled the apartment with Latin American items, including two peons dressed in serapes and sombreros, plus a donkey and some fake palm trees. Lucy costumes herself in a hat full of fruit à la Carmen Miranda, and sings Miranda's signature number, "*Mamae Eu Quero.*" As she sings, five children appear—a reminder that Ricardo grew up in a large family. The bewildered Ricky demands to know what all this is about. Lucy explains, "I thought you were getting tired of me and if I reminded you of Cuba you might like me better." His response sets the tone for all the episodes to come: "Lucy, honey, if I wanted things Cuban I'd have stayed in Havana. That's the reason I married you, 'cause you're so different from everyone I'd known before." It was an endearing and valuable speech, but not so valuable as the time in which it was articulated.

For CBS had given Desilu the greatest gift of all: Monday nights. On television, Tuesdays were dominated by Milton Berle, "Uncle Milty" to the millions who watched his famously gross comic movements. Manic, tasteless, unsubtle, irrepressible, Berle was fond of appearing in drag, heavily lipsticked and girdled, or playing a grand piano until fireworks shot out from the instrument, or interfering with guest performers and unsettling the singers and dancers. Most viewers had never been exposed to the Borscht Belt from which Berle originated and thought of him as an exotic. They made his show number one throughout the country. Wednesdays belonged to *Your Show of Shows,* a variety program starring Sid Caesar, Imogene Coca, and Carl Reiner in brilliant freewheeling skits that parodied foreign films, sent up domestic crises, and regarded all human misbehavior as fair game. Mondays from 8 to 9 p.m. EST were the property of *Arthur Godfrey's Talent Scouts.* The show had been a hit on radio and transferred easily to TV, hosted by an easygoing freckle-faced redhead. (It would take years for audiences to realize that Godfrey's folksy manner hid an imperious and deeply self-involved personality.) Allegedly, *Talent Scouts* featured amateur performers looking for a show-business break. Actually, most of them were professionals on their way up. But this deception served the audience well; the level of performance was high, and the host was wise enough to let more talented people consume a goodly portion of time and space. *Talent Scouts* provided *Lucy* with the ideal lead-in. There were no remotes in 1951; in order to change the channel it was necessary to get out of the easy chair or couch, walk to the set, and turn a knob. Out of a mixture of indolence and curiosity the viewers stayed put as Godfrey's show gently led them to *I Love Lucy*. Once they got a glimpse of the Ricardos and their comic problems, they stayed to see how things worked out.

As the show established itself, Jess Oppenheimer discovered just how different Lucy and Desi were as performers and as individuals. Desi was painfully aware that CBS regarded him, in the words of one executive, as the Cuban caboose on Lucy's Twentieth Century train. He worked overtime to show that he was an intelligent, focused player as well as a responsible leader. Thus, on Monday mornings when the cast assembled to look over the new script, Desi made sure to absorb the material as soon as he read it, and he always delivered a solid reading the first time through. In contrast, Lucy needed many rehearsals to get the comedy right. Wrote Oppenheimer: "Lucy didn't know what she was doing—at the first reading. But after stumbling through, she would take the material to the mat. She fought with it, examined it, internalized it, and when it reappeared, she *owned* it." Those efforts came at a price. Lucy was querulous and demanding on the set, hardest of all on her fellow performers. The star's makeup man, Hal King, was appalled when Lucy "went over to Vivian Vance and pulled off Vivian's false eyelashes. Lucy said, 'Nobody wears false eyelashes on this show but *me.*'" In the beginning, before they got to know each other, recalled script clerk Maury Thompson, "Lucille gave Vivian a hard time. I mean a *really* hard time. One day I pulled Viv aside and I said, 'What are you going to do about her?' Vivian was very smart. She said, 'Maury, if by any chance this thing actually becomes a hit and goes anywhere, I'm gonna learn to love that bitch.'"

Desi tried to adjust his schedule to Lucy's, but that proved impossible. As the weeks went on he was forced to split his time between acting and making decisions for Desilu, leaving the set to sign papers or participate in meetings. As he prepared to depart Lucy would invariably beseech him, "But Desi, we need the rehearsal!" His answer remained the same: "What are you talking about? We know the words." In Oppenheimer's view, Desi "never could quite understand what was going on inside of Lucy's head"—a disability apparent to anyone who knew the Arnazes' calendar. With all of the efforts to create a nuclear family, Lucy spent much of the week alone with the baby, while Desi went to his thirty-eight-foot power cruiser *Desilu* and joined the roistering buddies who had been banished from the ranch. The growing popularity of *I Love Lucy* seemed to push the couple apart even as it

increased their influence. "Lucy needed to be dominated," Oppenheimer observed, "and Desi wasn't happy in a relationship where his
wife had a more powerful reputation than he did. He was deeply hurt
by all the publicity that said that the success of the show was entirely
due to her artistry."

The fact is, though, that it was *mainly* due to Lucy. As the producer
himself admitted, "Remove any other actor from the project and it
would be diminished. Take away Lucille Ball, and it would be demol-
ished." All the upstate eccentrics Lucy had known in Jamestown and
Celoron, all the society ladies she had observed in the months she had
modeled for Hattie Carnegie, all the timing she had picked up from
her stage work, all the tricks she had learned from the film farces and
dramas, from radio shows, from Damon Runyon, Buster Keaton, and
Jack Benny, were used to forge the character of Lucy Ricardo. The
writers created the situations, and Lucy embodied them. If she
schemed to get around Ricky and he discovered the plot, she spoke the
lie but expressed the truth in fluent body language. No comic situation
fazed her or appeared too extreme for her abilities. In the first series
she does variety turns, sings, gets herself twisted during a ballet
sequence, and, most memorably, auditions for the part of television
saleswoman, extolling the benefits of Vitameatavegamin, a tonic whose
principal ingredient is grain alcohol. Sampling a spoonful or two with
each take, she is soon unable to stand up straight, but not too sloshed
to keep pitching the product. Lucy later said, "While this may not be
my favorite episode per se, I think that Vitameatavegamin bit is the
best thing I ever did." It was unquestionably the funniest; even Desi
had to chew the inside of his cheeks to keep from laughing while she
performed.

In other situation comedies (most of them employing a single camera), scenes with the same backdrop were filmed together, often out of
sequence, over a three-day period. If someone came up with a new
idea it was impossible to rework the script—too many key exchanges of
dialogue had already been shot. *I Love Lucy* was different. Its complicated three-camera work allowed each episode to be filmed in
sequence at the end of the week. The delay allowed the writers, and
the star herself, to incorporate bits that had occurred to them during
the week. Lucy took advantage of the flexibility, sometimes at high, if
hilarious, cost. Two sequences illustrate the consequences of the program's extempore farce. For a candy-dipping sequence, Desi hired the

real thing after he saw Amanda Milligan working at the farmers' market on Fairfax Avenue. He thought the professional's deadpan movements would make her an ideal straight lady for Lucy's antics, and he hired Miss Milligan on the spot. As Lucy remembered it, "The only thing that this woman ever did her whole life was dip candy. I don't think she ever watched television, and she didn't have the faintest idea who the hell I was. We explained the scene to her a couple of times, and she thought we were all crazy. She never cracked a smile once. We began to think, 'Is this funny or isn't it?' " They rehearsed the sequence several times without chocolate in their hands, miming the movements. Lucy hit Amanda, but Amanda just tapped her in return. "She wouldn't give me the whack I needed to get the laugh. We hoped for the best when we filmed. We started the scene, and there was Amanda dipping the chocolate the way she had for the last thirty years. Well, it came time for me to hit her, which I did, and then for her to hit me, which she did! Bam! She gave me such a shot. I thought she had broken my nose. I almost called for a cut, and then I thought, no, we'd have to do it again, so I kept on going. But Lord, she really did bust me in the face. After the show, I said, 'Boy you really did hit me,' and she looked at me deadpan as ever and said, 'That's what you wanted, wasn't it?' "

Similarly, in the spirit of Sid Caesar and company, *I Love Lucy* did a parody of *neorealismo* Italian movies. In the episode Lucy is recruited by a foreign director, who intends her for the part of an American tourist. She mistakenly believes he wants to feature her as a grape stomper, producing juice for wine. By the early 1950s most California wineries were mechanized, but there were a few holdouts, and Desi managed to find one of the last remaining stompers. Her name was Teresa and she had no English, so a translator was brought on the set to convey the director's wishes. The amateur seemed to understand. "The time came for us to get in the vat, which was full of real grapes," Lucy remembered. "God, it was like stepping on eyeballs. We started stomping on the grapes, and I made a dance out of it, and then I slipped." As she did, she accidentally hit Teresa, a large woman, who believed that the sock was intentional and replied in kind, bopping Lucy on the cranium. "Down I went, with Teresa on top of me. My head was supposed to pop up and then my arm and then my leg, and nothing popped up. She just held me down, hitting me. I thought she was trying to kill me. I had grapes up my nose, up my ears. She was choking me. The audience thought it was part of the show, and they were hysterical. I started banging her back to get her off of me. Finally, I gave her one good shove and threw her off and yelled 'Cut.' I had to catch my breath. The director came over and calmed Teresa down and then calmed me down, and said we had to continue with the fight. The translator came over and explained it all again, and I thought it was okay. As soon as he yelled 'Action,' the fight was on again. I thought it was my last moment on earth."

Lucy's willingness to turn herself inside out for a laugh was almost—but not quite—enough to make her show a phenomenon. For that, she needed an exceptional cast and a series of fortunate circumstances. The most fortunate was public knowledge that Lucy and Ricky Ricardo were husband and wife in real life. Other real-life couples made radio or TV comedy their specialty, but none offered the strong contrast of a WASP wife with a Latino husband whose excited accent ran against her chirpy, uninflected speech. In the beginning, Ricky's botched pronunciations were mocked by other members of the troupe, but the jokes went over poorly with audiences. Soon, only Lucy was allowed to make fun of her husband, because the mockery was done with affection, especially when his malapropisms went over the top: "You can lead a horse to water, but you can't make him a drink." "I'll cross that bridge when I burn it." Added to those by-plays were little angry looks, furtive exchanges, swallowed smiles that no scriptwriter or director could have supplied. Moreover, Ricky Ricardo brought a touch of salsa to the bland fare of prime-time television. As a husband he was only a well-meaning greenhorn, barely able to understand (and head off) Lucy's grandiose and loony plans. But at the Tropicana Club he was shown as an impresario, a Cuban bandleader with ambition and authority. Watching him operate in situ, viewers understood what had attracted Lucille Ball to Desi Arnaz in real life.

As *I Love Lucy* proceeded to the top of the rating charts, certain rules and restrictions came into play. When Desi expressed discomfort with a scene it was usually changed, not because he was the boss but because, as Oppenheimer observed, "if he didn't like a piece of material he was simply incapable of performing it." There was, for example, a story line involving a surprise visit from an IRS auditor. The script called for Lucy to answer his questions truthfully—thereby revealing that her husband had fudged on some income tax deductions. Ricky was then called upon to do some fancy explaining, and ultimately to pay a fine for his lapses. Desi flatly refused to let the program go on as written. He granted that the premise was amusing; in his view, however, Ricky Ricardo would never attempt to cheat the U.S. government. "A short but lively discussion ensued," Oppenheimer recalled, "but there was no changing Desi's mind. In a matter of hours we came up with an entirely new second act in which Lucy's fibs unwittingly land her a job as a knife thrower's assistant (and target)."

As Lucy and Desi sculpted their personae, Vivian Vance and William Frawley also gave their characters dimension and personality. The fact that the actors disliked each other worked to the show's advantage. Fred and Ethel Mertz seemed to be an old married couple who could neither take nor leave their situation, and the tension between them became a risible battle of the sexes. Ethel was only too glad to live vicariously through Lucy's schemes to get around Ricky. And Fred radiated gratification every time he could foil their plans. Yet, in the rules of the show, the curmudgeon was intensely loyal: his back went up anytime an outsider criticized Ethel or Lucy—that was *his* job, and his alone.

What viewers saw on the screen was not very different from what the performers dealt with on the set. Upon presentation of the script, Frawley would take home only the pages marked FRED, in order to memorize his lines. "So sometimes," Desi recollected, "we would get to a joke and he would say to me, 'This is not funny.'

" 'What do you mean?' I'd ask. 'It's not funny? You haven't read the five other pages where we have been building up to your entrance.'

" 'What are you talking about?'

" 'You're just reading what you are supposed to say and we've been building up for you to come in and say, "Hello, Ethel," and get a big laugh.'

" 'You think "Hello, Ethel" is funny?'

" 'No, "Hello, Ethel" is not funny, but we've been building up this situation in which Ethel is inside a costume, representing the last half of a horse, and as you come in the door, she is bending down and facing away from you. All you can see is the last half of this horse—the horse's ass is all you can see—and you say, "Hello, Ethel," and *that* is funny.'

" 'Oh, yes, that *is* funny!' "

And yet Frawley continued to exhibit some unpredictable virtues. No matter how much he drank at night, he always showed up clear-eyed and sober. Not once was Desi forced to cover for him. Furthermore, the actor's years on the stage gave him an uncanny ability to ad-lib. Backstage, a list of *Lucy* performers was pinned to the wall, and next to each name a gold star appeared every time he or she came up with a funny, unrehearsed line. Frawley's line of stars far exceeded anyone else's.

Vance provided a striking contrast to her onscreen partner. After the first few months, according to Maury Thompson, the actress established herself as an instinctive editor. "She was like a story detector, and wasn't shy about bringing up points that didn't seem right to her. Around this time, Lucille began to take notice that most often Vivian was right. Lucille realized she had in Vivian a lot more than she thought, and she began to trust Viv's comedic instincts." By year's end, *I Love Lucy* had defined its personalities and solidified its comic style. New viewers dropped by each week, stayed for a half hour of laughter, and marked future Mondays at 9 p.m. as Lucy Time.

In the spring of 1952 CBS learned just how popular the program had become. For the first time in the history of television, a regularly scheduled TV program was being welcomed into 10 million homes. Lucille Ball was now outpulling Arthur Godfrey; in three months she had become Miss Monday Night. The American Research Bureau pointed out that *I Love Lucy* was more than simply the top-rated TV show in the nation. Because an average of 2.9 viewers watched each television set, each episode actually was seen by 30,740,000 individuals—nearly a fifth of the U.S. population. Partisans of Milton Berle pointed out that water use went down during his show because so few people used the toilet; Lucy fans claimed that she owned the new title of Queen of the John. (That battle was never truly settled.)

In the fall, Democratic strategists, thinking to tap into the show's popularity, preempted five minutes of *I Love Lucy* for their candidate, Adlai Stevenson. They realized their gaffe when thousands of outraged viewers wrote and phoned the network: how dare this *politician* take up valuable Ricardo time? In Chicago, Marshall Field's department store bowed to the latest trend. A sign on the front door read: WE LOVE LUCY TOO, SO FROM NOW ON WE WILL BE OPEN THURSDAY NIGHTS. Lucy was nominated for an Emmy Award in her first season, an unusual accolade, to be followed by an even more unusual one. When she lost out to Red Skelton, the comedian told the onlookers: "You gave this to the wrong redhead. I don't deserve this. It should go to Lucille Ball."

There was a good deal of truth behind his ostentatious modesty. In the first run of thirty-five episodes, Lucy had shown the world a rare versatility. Not since Carole Lombard had there been a glamorous woman so willing to make a fool of herself in pursuit of laughter. Lucy's routines included capering like a circus clown, mocking Ricky as a Cuban singer, getting flung around as an Apache dancer, and pretending to be a ballet star and getting a leg tangled in the barre. Not once did she keep herself glamorous at the cost of the comedy. For one bit she wore a goatee and then found that the makeup glue was impossible to remove, for another she locked herself in a meat freezer, and she capped the season off with the classic Vitameatavegamin commercial. In recognition, *Time* put her on its cover. Inside, the magazine raved about her show: "This is the sort of cheerful rowdiness that has been rare since the days of the silent movies' Keystone comedies. Lucille submits enthusiastically to being hit by pies; falls over furniture; gets locked in home freezers; is chased by knife-wielding fanatics. Tricked out as a ballerina or a Hindu maharani or a toothless hillbilly, she takes her assorted lumps and pratfalls with unflagging zest and good humor."

Led by Lucy, Desi honed his skills in timing and setting up gags. And, in response, the writers tried to elevate Ricky Ricardo from bandleader to nightclub manager in order to give him more comic moments. Among the most memorable—and one that could not have been played by anyone else in 1950s television—was "Lucy Hires an English Tutor." Distressed that Ricky's accent will hold them back, Lucy tries to teach her husband the fine points of English, demonstrating the difference between words that are spelled the same but pronounced differently, "rough," "through" and "cough," for instance. He pronounces them "row," "thruff," and "coo." When his errors are pointed out, Desi condemns Lucy's native tongue as "a crazy language," whereas Spanish makes complete sense. Lucy's solution: she will hire a tutor for Ricky. The instructor, Mr. Livermore (farceur Hans Conried), turns out to be a haughty and humorless pedant whose attempts to improve Ricky's English result in spectacular failure—in the end, the teacher, infected by Ricky's approach to communication, starts speaking with Cuban intonations and chanting the lyrics to "Babalu." Lucy surrenders: "It was a battle of the accents, and Mr. Livermore lost."

Pleasing as this interlude was, it departed from the show's mainstream comedy. To keep *I Love Lucy* consistent, Desi had to play second banana in almost every episode, setting up his wife's jokes and physical shtick. In the second season Lucy began to hear echoes of the 1940s, when they were the Bandleader and the Movie Star and nearly divorced. With that time in mind, she told any journalist who would listen that her husband was the real power of Desilu. Desi read the interviews, and persuaded himself that she was right. One morning he walked into Jess Oppenheimer's office and asked for a new credit: "What I really want to do is produce, but I need to build a reputation as a producer. How would you feel about letting me take 'executive producer' on the show?"

His question opened a new a clash of egos. Oppenheimer also sought to be recognized as a producer and had no intention of relinquishing his hard-won title. "I had made it clear at the outset," he later remarked, "that if I was going to be the producer, I would have to have ultimate control of all of the show's creative elements. My contract spelled that out." He suggested that Desi take the title of "executive in charge of production" or "coproducer." Desi refused. A period of bad feeling began and both men agreed to discuss the matter in a few weeks, after they had had time to consider alternatives.

Production resumed without further incident—until March 2, 1952, when the cast celebrated Desi's thirty-fifth birthday. By then Oppenheimer was exhausted with the preparation of so many shows produced under deadline. The notion of having Desi take over some of his duties exerted more appeal than it had when the subject was first broached. Sensing his vulnerability, the Arnazes double-teamed him. First Lucy privately asked him to let Desi have executive producer credit "as a personal favor in order to keep the peace" in their marriage. Then Desi assured him that the credit would have no effect whatsoever on the real producer's authority. Oppenheimer acceded to their wishes.

When the official ratings came in *I Love Lucy* was indeed the top television show in America, with some 23 million people tuning in every week. In honor of the occasion, Desi presented Oppenheimer with a trophy engraved "Jess Oppenheimer: *The Man Behind the Ball.* 4–18–52 #1 Nielsen." "It was a nice gesture by Desi," the producer noted gratefully. "I decided that I probably had been wrong to be so concerned about letting him have the executive producer credit."

That was on a Friday. The following Monday, Oppenheimer received an upsetting call from the Biow advertising agency. A column in the *Hollywood Reporter* was read aloud to him. It burbled about the new girl on the block, scattering credit for *I Love Lucy* like chocolates before a crowd of children. Don Sharpe was praised, as was Harry Ackerman "for never once throwing cold water on Desi's starry-eyed idea of not only filming the show but filming it before a live audience." Jess Oppenheimer and Karl Freund also received accolades. But the highest praise was reserved for Desi: "The crazy Cuban whom Oppenheimer insists has been the real producer all along and who in two weeks reluctantly starts taking screen credit as executive producer."

Livid, Oppenheimer presented himself in Desi's office, with the offending reportage in hand. "How can you quote me like that?" he demanded.

Desi replied blandly: "It's like I told you, amigo. I need to build a rep as a producer."

Shouts and recriminations followed; they led nowhere. Oppenheimer observed that "there was nothing I could do about the publicity without seriously damaging both the series and Lucy's precarious marriage. And I would never do anything to hurt Lucy or the show. I was stuck, and Desi and I both knew it." It was not a bad scene in which to be mired; the money was flowing in faster than anyone could count it. But the real producer never really forgave the usurper; years later he resentfully mentioned "Desi's habit of taking credit for other people's accomplishments." And sometime afterward, perhaps out of guilt, Desi corrected a story in *Cosmopolitan*. "Lucy's antics can't be underrated," the article maintained. "But no show is better than its producer, and Desi Arnaz is the producer." Desi sent a letter to the editor, begging to differ. "Actually I am executive producer. Jess Oppenheimer is the producer and also head writer, which means he does most of the work." All very well, but after that self-promotion in the *Hollywood Reporter* nothing was quite the same between the two men. Not that it mattered. The Arnazes were hardly a match made in heaven, and Vance and Frawley intensely disliked each other. As the Cuban proverb had it, the dogs yapped, the pageant traveled on.

*A*ssistants on the *I Love Lucy* set were quick to flash cue cards reading APPLAUSE. CHEERS. LAUGHTER. Only the first two were needed. Audiences came *in* laughing. They had waited patiently for a chance to see the show performed live before their very eyes, and everything said onstage rendered them helpless with mirth. Gratifying as this was, the writers, performers, and production crew had little time to enjoy their accomplishment. Hardly had they finished shooting one show when preparations for the next one began. Tuesdays were devoted to the script, as cast and writers sat at a long table going over the story line and the gags. Because *I Love Lucy* was perceived as family fare, plots had to be tasteful and credible. When some routine was deemed unacceptable, Pugh, Carroll, and Oppenheimer went back to work and began again under severe deadline pressure, often, though not always, emerging with something funnier than before. On Wednesdays an informal on set rehearsal took place, with actors expected to know their lines. The breaks were short, with the principals sitting back in director's chairs. One chair was marked "Desi Arnaz, Pres.," another "Lucille Ball, Vice Pres.," the third "Vivian Vance, Girl Actress," and the last "William Frawley, Boy Actor." No one appeared in costume for these occasions, and there were times when Lucy and Vivian made a point of dressing down. On a blazing summer day the two lounged in shorts and halters, while Desi and Bill lay on the floor in trousers and undershirts. At that unpropitious moment, a tour guide brought in a group of ladies. The visitors were greeted by an astonished quartet. "They were all be-ribboned, be-hatted, and be-orchided," Vance remembered. "Some of them even had gloves on. When the guide said, 'This is the *I Love Lucy* company,' you should have seen the unbelieving expressions on their faces. They're still probably talking about how awful we looked, and I don't blame them." Once the drop-ins had disappeared, work resumed in earnest and continued until the heat overtook them all.

Wednesday afternoons, Karl Freund supervised a camera run-through, carefully measuring distances to get the most from each take. On Thursday mornings, Freund worked on the lighting for four sets: two for the interior of the Ricardo apartment, one for Ricky's club, and one for all other scenes necessary to the plot. At noon the cast gathered and dress rehearsal commenced. Generally it lasted until 6 p.m. Friday there were final revisions, and at 8 p.m. filming took place before the live audience. Hardly had the cast and crew begun to relax when the whole process resumed.

As might be expected, the stress exacted the greatest price from Lucy. The get-along-and-go-along girl of film and radio had achieved something she had dreamed about for four decades, national renown.

The trouble was, everything she had ever cherished—her father, her immediate family, the little triumphs of her early career, her marriage, even her health—had all been stolen from her or jeopardized in some drastic manner. There was no reason to believe that *I Love Lucy* couldn't also be taken away, too. To guard against that possibility she became obsessive about story lines, technical details, personnel. More than ninety people were now involved in the production of the show, and she wanted every one of them to be super-efficient, loyal, and willing to work an eighty-hour week if that was what it took to keep the show number one.

But the person on whom she made the greatest demands was Lucille Ball herself. Nothing seemed to put her at ease anymore. Lucy consulted a psychiatrist, yet remained anxious and fearful—although she learned to present a different face to the world. The analyst, she later claimed, "only saw me for three weeks. Then she told me there was nothing psychologically wrong with me. I was just worn out from having a baby and a television show at the same time." As a result of the therapy, Lucy learned only "how to rest in a roomful of people, to hold my emotions in, instead of talking about them. That's why people sometimes complain that I'm staring at them deadpan. I'm trying to be deadpan inside, too, so that I won't fly apart."

*L*ucy would need all the centripetal force she could summon in the spring of 1952. First, she learned that investigators for the House Committee on Un-American Activities (HUAC) had unearthed a fact she had tried to forget: California voting records showed that a Lucille Ball had registered as a Communist back in 1936. This was no small item. In 1947, the Hollywood Ten, a group of screenwriters and one-time members of the Communist Party, had been blacklisted out of the business. At the urging of HUAC, studios initiated a campaign to rid themselves of all those with a radical past. The fear and intimidation soon spread to the broadcasting business.

In 1950, during the intense heat of the Korean War, a pamphlet entitled "Red Channels" landed on the desks of network officials. Privately printed, the pamphlet declared that "where there's red smoke there's usually Communist fire." Accompanying that declaration was a list of performers and directors who had "leftist" associations. Some familiar names were on the roster: Lillian Hellman, Dorothy Parker, Leonard Bernstein. But there were many unfamiliar ones as well. Some of the people named were Communists, some fellow travelers, and some had merely signed a petition or attended a single meeting of a suspect organization. All were charged with subversion. General Foods bowed to pressure and fired an actress named Jean Muir from *The Aldrich Family* because one unnamed witness, cited in "Red Channels," said she attended pro-Communist meetings. Irene Wicker, radio's "Singing Lady," was fired because "Red Channels" said she had sponsored the reelection of a Communist congressman. She protested that she had done nothing of the kind, that in fact she had allowed her only son to enlist in the Royal Canadian Air force in 1940, when Moscow was virulently antiwar. Eventually the publishers of "Red Channels" realized that they had made a false accusation, and they allowed Wicker to enter an anti-Communist statement in one of their other publications. But she was not rehired, after twenty-five years on the air. She had been at the center of controversy, and controversy now equaled sin.

Terrified of what might happen to their nascent television business, CBS instituted a loyalty oath "to make sure that the full confidence of our listeners is unimpaired." From then on, a climate of fear overtook television. Blacklisting organizations were hired to check the background of anyone involved in performance or production. First check: five dollars per name. Additional research: two dollars.

With talent so cheaply valued, all those who had attended meetings or signed petitions, no matter how long ago or under what circumstances, waited for the ax to fall. If it had fallen earlier, when Lucy appeared on *My Favorite Husband,* she might have been forced out of radio. But by the time HUAC caught up with her in April 1952, *I Love Lucy* was too big to suffer a frontal assault. Every courtesy was afforded the reigning star of situation comedy. She testified in secret, explaining her background as directly as possible: Grandpa Fred Hunt— "Daddy"—was an eccentric populist, a union organizer but hardly a Muscovite radical. And besides, Lucy and her brother had registered as Communists only to keep the old man from having a stroke. They had never actually *voted* in that long-ago election. The congressmen seemed satisfied with this family history and Lucy was excused without prejudice. No reporters were privy to the meeting, no stories appeared in the papers the next day. Lucy got the impression that HUAC had bigger flesh to fry.

$\mathcal{H}$ardly had that crisis passed when a new one arose. On one hand, this was a happy problem; on the other hand, it could lead to the demise of *I Love Lucy* just when it was destined to dominate television for the season of 1952–1953. At the age of forty-one, the star was pregnant again. An interesting bit of dialogue occurred when Desi conveyed the news to Jess Oppenheimer.

"Oh, my God," exclaimed the producer. "What are we going to do?"

Desi laughed. "What do you mean, what are we going to do? She's going to have a baby. Whatever there was to be done about it, Lucy and I have already done it."

"Yeah, but what about the show? You know how big she gets. There's no way we can hide it for more than a couple of months at the most."

"I know. So how about Lucy Ricardo having a baby as part of our shows this year?"

Bearing in mind the current network restrictions—no sexually suggestive language of any kind, no double beds for couples to sleep in, not even the use of the word "pregnant"—Oppenheimer warned the prospective father, "They'll never let you do that."

"Why won't they? And who are 'they'?"

"The sponsor, the network, the advertising agency."

"Lucy and Rick are married," Desi declared impatiently. "She's pregnant. There is no way we can hide that fact from the audience. We have already signed the contracts."

Oppenheimer was pensive. Then he brightened. "It'd be a hell of a gimmick."

So it would, but CBS wanted no part of the scheme. Nor did the sponsor, Philip Morris. Company executives insisted that the show go on without a mention of Lucy's condition. "Can't you hide her behind chairs or something?" became their favorite question. Desi refused. Finally they asked, "Can you just do one or two shows about it?" Again he said no. One show was to be devoted to Lucy's springing the news to Ricky. And then at least eight had to be devoted to the last six months of her pregnancy, with all the appropriate sentiment and humor.

No one bought his argument. Agitated beyond measure, Desi decided on one last effort before he gave up. He and Lucy had met Alfred Lyons, the British chairman of the board of Philip Morris. The old man had been extremely courteous and willing to entertain other points of view at the time. Perhaps he would listen to Desi's side of the debate. A letter—very sincere, but perhaps not in the most felicitous English—was airmailed to London, quite literally over the heads of the big shots in New York. After explaining the situation, Desi left the decision up to Lyons.

> You are the man who is paying the money for this show and I guess we will have to do whatever you decide. There's only one thing I want to make certain that you understand. We have given you the number-one show in the country and, up till now, the creative decisions have been in our hands. Your people are now telling us we cannot do this, so the only thing I want from you, if you agree with them, is that you must inform them that we will not accept them telling us what not to do unless, in the future, you will also tell us what to do. At that point, and if this is your decision, we will cease to be responsible to you for the show being the number-one show on television, and you will have to look to your people, to the network, and to the Biow agency for that responsibility.
>
> Thank you very much for all you have done for us in the past.

Within a fortnight the negative comments had stopped. Desi heard no more objections to Lucy's onscreen pregnancy, and no one, at either the network or the agency, insisted that the shows about her condition be limited to one or two. If Desi wanted eight or nine or more, that was his business, not theirs. Only later did he learn that the letter to Alfred Lyons had borne fruit. The Philip Morris president had sent a private memo to certain key employees. It read, in its entirety, "To whom it may concern: Don't fuck around with the Cuban! A. L."

Powerful as Lyons's words were, they could not alter the network's rigid internal law. Lucy could be "expecting" or "with child," but the word "pregnant" could not be uttered in prime time. After a series of unpleasant meetings Oppenheimer arrived at a solution. A priest, a rabbi, and a minister would vet each of the "baby show" scripts, and attend each of the screenings. If a phrase, a sequence, or even a word was found offensive it would be excised. "Everyone," he was pleased to report, "was enthusiastic about the idea of having the baby shows 'blessed' by local clergymen. The network executives were finally starting to get comfortable with what we had been telling them all along— we could deal humorously with pregnancy on a television show and at the same time keep the program on a high moral plane."

And so, with the editorial assistance of Monsignor Joseph Devlin, head of the Catholic Legion of Decency; Rabbi Alfred Wolf of the Wilshire Temple, and Reverend Clifton Moore of the Hollywood Presbyterian Church, *I Love Lucy* tiptoed into its second season. Because the baby would be born, like Lucie, by cesarean section, there was no mystery about the date of birth. Obstetricians scheduled the event for January 19, 1953. The shows dealing with Lucy's pregnancy could thus be counted backward, and begun on December 8, 1952. Before that historic episode, the show went on as if nothing untoward was about to occur. By now Lucy's expressions were so familiar that the writers referred to them in a kind of shorthand. "Puddling Up" meant a pause, watery eyes, followed by a loud wail. "Light Bulb" referred to a sudden (and ultimately disastrous) idea crossing her mind. "Credentials" signified righteous indignation.

The main difference from the first season—discernible to the cast and crew but not to the public—was a change in directors. The restless Marc Daniels had moved on, in part because, as *Variety* reported, Desilu "refused to meet his demands for upped coin." Daniels's place was taken by William Asher, the director who had brought Eve Arden's radio show, *Our Miss Brooks,* to television. Things did not begin well. Early on, Asher left the set to deal with some technical difficulties. Lucy and the cast went off by themselves. When they resumed the rehearsal, according to Asher, "everything was different and it was obvious that Lucy had redirected everything." He called her aside and firmly advised: "There can only one director, and that's me. If you want to direct, send me home and save yourself some money." Surprised by his own outburst, Asher took a half-hour break, which he spent in the men's room composing himself, talking to mirrors, and throwing wadded-up papers into wastebaskets. He returned to the stage to find Desi pacing furiously. "After I explained to him what had happened," Asher said, "he agreed I was right. He spoke to Lucy, and then brought me back into her dressing room." There followed the standard confrontation and retreat, familiar to those who knew Lucy's history with men she perceived as father figures. "She was crying, I was crying, and I said, 'Why don't we get back to work?' She agreed, and we never had another problem like this again."

The opening show, "Job Switching," was the fixture as before. In the continuing battle of the sexes, Desi and Fred complain about women's inability to stay within the budget. Lucy and Ethel decide to show their husbands how hard housewives really work. For a week the men are to stay home and do the chores while the women go out to jobs as candy dippers. Lucy finds herself unable to keep up with the assembly line and, as the intimidating supervisor enters, crams the extra chocolates in her mouth, in her cap, and down her neckline in a wild, dialogue-free routine worthy of Chaplin. "Job Switching" met with overnight approval. Jack Gould, the influential television critic of the *New York Times,* praised Lucy's "comic artistry" and continued: "Perhaps her greatest asset is one of those sublime senses of timing that are instinctive rather than acquired. Whether it is a gesture, a change of expression or delivery of a line, she performs with the split-second assurance that is the heart of real comedy."

Another pre-pregnancy program centers on Lucy's attempts to enter show business, this time by trying to play the saxophone in Ricky's band—a move that, predictably, infuriates him. As a high school student Lucy once did try to play the saxophone, and she enjoyed fooling around with the instrument on the set. Soon, camera coordinator Maury Thompson reported, "she couldn't leave it alone. Every day, when we weren't rehearsing the actual script, Lucille was blowing that damn saxophone. She was such a perfectionist, trying to play that thing, that she almost ruined the bit by becoming too good." Other segments included a witty operetta, with lyrics by Carroll, Pugh, and Oppenheimer; a furious argument between the Ricardos and the Mertzes during which Fred kicks in his neighbors' picture tube; and an episode featuring Ricky with laryngitis and Lucy seizing her big break in show business, ineptly staging a show at the Tropicana.

"Lucy Is Enceinte" ushered in a new period of television history. The very title indicated the inhibitions of 1950s television. Not only was the word "pregnant" expunged from dialogue, it could not be shown in the title. Nevertheless, for those who had an inkling of French, episode 45 announced that Lucy was with child. The script indicated how heavily the writers depended on the star's pantomimic skills. According to their stage directions, Lucy practices breaking the news to Ricky: "She puts her arms around an imaginary neck. This will be facing her away from the cameras toward the back of the set, which is the way this particular scene should be played, considering that Lucy has more talent in the back of her neck than most performers have in their whole bodies." The script called for Desi to be so elusive that Lucy finally decides to break the news to him in public, at the Tropicana.

RICKY

Thank you, ladies and gentlemen. The next number— (*The maitre d' walks onto the floor and hands Ricky a note. To audience*) Pardon me. (*He reads the note*) Oh, isn't this sweet. "Dear Mr. Ricardo: My husband and I are going to have a blessed event. I just found out about it today and I haven't told him yet. I heard you sing a number called 'We're Having a Baby, My Baby and Me.' If you will sing it for us now, it will be my way of breaking the news to him." (*To audience*) Oh, isn't that wonderful? I have an idea. I think they ought to come right up here on the floor and I'll sing it to them. (*The audience applauds*) Come on—who sent me the note? (*He is looking around the room*) Come on. We just want to wish you luck. (*He starts walking toward the tables and the piano player starts playing "Rock-a-Bye Baby." To first table on the side*) Was it you? (*The couple giggles and shakes their heads "No." Ricky starts to sing along with the piano and ask with his eyes as he comes to each table. Singing*) . . . in the treetop. Etc. Etc. (*He sees an elderly couple—the woman is 95. He starts to ask with his eyes and quickly turns to the next table. As he is doing this Lucy comes in and sits at the empty table. Ricky sees her when she gets to the table, gives her a pantomime "Hi" between the words of the song, and, as though this were a big joke, asks her, with his eyes and expression, "You?" Lucy slowly nods her head "Yes." Ricky gives her a wink, starts to look away as he sings the next verse of the song and then does a tremendous take. What???! Lucy again shakes her head "Yes." Ricky rushes back to the table, sits down next to her, and has a hurried*

whispered consultation with her. Whisper) Lucy, you aren't
kidding?

LUCY
No, I've been trying to tell—

RICKY
Why didn't you tell—

LUCY
You didn't give me a chance—

RICKY
Oh, darling. (*He kisses her*)

That is not quite the way the scene played out. Historian Geoffrey
Mark Fidelman notes in *The Lucy Book* that Desi flubbed the song
lyrics and when he arrived at Lucy's table, a strange thing happened.
Recalled Jess Oppenheimer, "suddenly they remembered their own
real emotions when they discovered that at last they were going to be
parents, and both of them began crying. We had to yell at Desi to keep
going and do the baby song."

Lucy and Desi were not the only ones to wipe tears from their eyes.
DeDe and Lolita attended this performance, and they cried as well.
Asher, who welled up despite his stony expression, called for a retake.
The audience, who had been weeping along with the others, cried out
"No!" A second version was shot anyway, with the lyrics well articu-
lated and the conclusion dry-eyed. The scene was crisp, well-timed,
funny, and utterly bogus. Desilu bowed to the audience's judgment.
For all the flaws, the first take had a validity and tenderness no second
performance could hope to reproduce.

By episode 46 CBS had relented enough to allow the P-word to be
used in the title "Pregnant Women Are Unpredictable," and shows
thereafter featured a cascade of predictable jokes about unusual crav-
ings (ice cream and sardines was a favorite), and other instances of
whimsical behavior. By episode 47 the condition of the star was beyond
hiding. In "Lucy's Show Biz Swan Song" she persuades Ethel to join
her in a rendition of "By the Light of the Silvery Moon," featuring Mrs.

Ricardo in a hoop skirt with pantaloons that drop on cue. Later in the show, Fred, Ethel, Ricky, and Lucy join in a barbershop rendition of "Sweet Adeline," with Lucy flatting most of her notes.

In his meticulous survey of every episode of *I Love Lucy*, Fidelman notes that the final commercial in that show was done by Philip Morris chief Alfred Lyons himself. "In it he practically blackmails the audience (whom he claims now number 32 million) with the notion that if more cigarettes are not purchased, the show (which is seen by more people than any other entertainment in show business history) might not be on the air much longer." Lyons's ominous message did not go unchallenged. Within days *Variety* reminded Philip Morris and the Biow agency: "Lucy is being paid for just one thing—to deliver an audience, which it is doing at the lowest cost per thousand viewers. If P. Morris can't sell this vast audience there's something wrong with the selling copy or the cigarette and certainly not with *Lucy*."

Episode 47 was also notable for Lucy's persistent, big, blue-eyed stare. At this stage of her pregnancy she tired easily. As exhaustion took over, her left eyelid had a tendency to droop. To counteract the appearance of fatigue she kept her penciled eyebrows at a high crescent, and the look of astonishment became the most photographed of Lucy's trademark expressions. In addition, "Swan Song" was notable for the nonstop acrimony between the second leads. Vivian Vance, still steaming years later, spoke of Frawley's inability to get the joke. He "insisted that he do the repeats in the 'Sweet Adeline' number, and somehow it became my job to pull him aside, and set him straight. I told him that Lucille was the star, and it would be funnier if she did them. He got loud with me, so I told him to shut up and that we had to do this thing the way we rehearsed it. He finally calmed down, but he growled at me, 'You know what she's going to sound like, don't you? Like putting a shovel full of shit on baked Alaska.' Which was exactly what she was *supposed* to sound like, but his ego couldn't see it that way."

As the countdown to January 19 continued, vital decisions had to be made. What would be the sex of Lucy's onscreen baby? What was to be its name? In the days before amniocentesis all that could be determined was that the real Lucy would give birth on a Monday, the same night as her show. She hoped for a boy, and Desi was keen to have one even if the boy was fictive. "Look," he told Oppenheimer, "Lucy gave me one girl. She might give me another. This is my only chance to be sure I get a son. You give me a boy on TV." Thus it was decided that Mr.

and Mrs. Ricardo would be the parents of Ricky Jr. no matter what happened in the maternity ward.

Feeling very much like "a cumulus cloud in a cloak," Lucy went into Cedars of Lebanon Hospital on the evening of January 18. The following morning she was taken to surgery and given a spinal anaesthetic, allowing her to remain conscious during the cesarean. Since this was turning out to be the most anticipated blessed event since the birth of Princess Elizabeth of Great Britain, hundreds of journalists lobbied to attend. After lengthy consultations with Desilu, a single reporter, Jim Bacon of the Associated Press, was permitted in the delivery room. At 8:15, as if responding to stage directions, Lucy gave birth to Desiderio Alberto Arnaz IV. Bacon heard the mother chortle that her baby's nose was "turned up so much he'll drown if it rains—oh, Desi will be so happy." Ecstatic would be more accurate. After a glimpse of his eight-pound-nine-ounce son, Desi winked at waiting reporters. "That's Lucy for you. Always does her best to cooperate."

Another newsworthy incident occurred in this period: General Dwight David Eisenhower was inaugurated as the thirty-fourth president of the United States, watched by a television audience of 29 million. Impressive, thought the White House press corps, until they read the statistics the next day: 44 million had watched *I Love Lucy* episode 51, "Lucy Goes to the Hospital."

As life and entertainment blended, flowers were sent to the Desilu studios and to Cedars of Lebanon. The bouquets at the hospital started at Lucy's room and overflowed to the corridor and the stairway leading to a lower floor. In all, Lucy received thirty thousand congratulatory letters. (There were also twenty-seven letters scolding her for having the bad taste to be pregnant on television.) The popularity of *I Love Lucy* reached a fever pitch that winter; there were "Ricky Junior" dolls, "I Love Lucy" nursery tables and chairs, movie offers, fan clubs, games, and costume jewelry. *Variety* described the profits from these ventures as "Desiloot" and inquired: "Aren't Lucille Ball and Desi Arnaz carrying their endorsements a little too far? Their caricatures even adorn 'potty' seats."

A good question. And there was a more pertinent one to be answered. In this heady time, Bob Carroll and Madelyn Pugh put up with Desi's techniques of persuasion, half genial, half drop-forged steel, simply because whatever the couple suggested turned out to be right. In the spirit of cooperation they hung a sign in their office: IT'S

ONLY A SHOW. But was it? A valentine had become the logo of *I Love Lucy*, and the program actually did have a heart beneath the gags. It starred two people who were married on the screen and off, whose genuine and sometimes raw emotions underlay the numbered episodes, people whose comic battles worked so well because they were miniatures of real domestic wrangles. The writers had no trouble separating actual truth from weekly fantasy; for their bosses the distinction was not always easy to make. In one episode Lucy looks at a photo album of the Ricardos' life together. She asks her husband whatever happened to the young couple. "Haven't you heard?" Ricky responds. "They lived happily ever after." No irony is discernible in their faces and voices; nevertheless, their sincerity did not make it so. Lorenz Hart, the man who wangled Desi his first important job, came closer to the truth in his lyrics for "I Wish I Were in Love Again." There he spoke wryly of "The furtive sigh / The blackened eye / The words 'I love you till the day I die' / The self-deception that believes the lie."

"The only thing red is the hair"

As FAR back as the 1930s Lucy had tried to liberate her comic style. As we have seen, her attempts met with sporadic success, but they had never elevated her to the status she hankered for. Yet in the half-hour format Lucille Ball abruptly metamorphosed into the dominant comedienne of her time, a performer whose virtuosity and timing were compared to those of the giants of silent movies.

How was it possible for a performer entering middle age to alter her character and approach so drastically? Some believed that she was a stage actress rather than a film personality: Lucy's true metier was performing before a live audience rather than a group of jaded technicians. Others said she had never felt free enough to be zany until she could control everything from the scripts to the lighting. No doubt these factors were important in her astonishing turnaround, but one component overshadowed all the others: Desi. The man who made Lucy uneasy as a wife also gave her assurance as a performer. Cousin Cleo believed that, in films, Lucy "didn't trust, really let go, put herself in someone's hands and do what they told her to do. But she had total trust in Desi. She thought he was just brilliant."

And so he was. He was also mercurial, devious, and self-destructive. Lucy had to balance her husband's assets and liabilities like a CPA, and this did little to settle her nerves. On the plus side, Desi, acting as a sure-handed catcher to his wife's lunatic leaps, allowed her to be fearless. "His talents as an actor never received the public recognition they deserved," observed Vivian Vance. "The contribution that Desi made! The secret lay in his Cuban point of view, which he brought to three clods, who didn't know what to make of it. That was the crux of so much of the laughter." Desi's supposed bewilderment, his comic stubbornness, his accent always gave the trio something to work against. Gradually his bewildered "You got some 'splainin' to do," his cry of "Loooooosey!" and his cascade of dropped g's and mispronunciations became almost as vital to the comedy as Lucy's physical shtick. The *Hollywood Reporter* belatedly recognized these contributions when the paper called Desi "the most underrated performer on network television."

In fact, as time went on performance became the least of Desi's qualifications. "He had great enthusiasm," Bob Carroll was pleased to note. As producer, "he never said no. He never said anything was too expensive. He would do anything, pay for anything." Madelyn Pugh agreed: "For some reason, people play down his part, like he was some lucky Cuban. I mean, he *was* a lucky Cuban, but he deserved it. He loved writers and he loved working with us. We never had arguments. We never had harsh words." Lucy remembered the morning her husband pored over the network's budget for the new season and found a glaring error. The following day he charged over to CBS and presented his findings: their accountants had made a million-dollar mistake. "That's impossible," he was informed in a patronizing tone. "Look, Desi, stick to your acting. We'll take care of the business details." Desi spread the papers and pointed out the inaccuracies: there actually was an extra million to be used by Desilu for production expenses. "From then on," Lucy wrote, "when he talked, they listened."

As an executive Desi moved from strength to strength, just as he had done in the old days when he caromed from conga lines to Broadway to Hollywood. "He's intuitive," Lucy observed. "He lives from minute to minute. But I call him Nostradamus—he seems to know what'll happen next. And he learned every job in our setup before he hired anybody else to do it."

Among Desi's most important hires were the people he had seen on the other side of the desk. He began by offering the executive vice presidency of Desilu to Martin Leeds, a hard-nosed network administrator. According to Desi, "That son of a bitch had given me so much trouble arguing about the CBS money we were spending on *I Love Lucy.* I figured it would be better to have him fighting on my side." Leeds knew a growth opportunity when he saw it, and he persuaded some of his network colleagues to join him at Desilu. Bernard Weitzman became vice president of business affairs and Edwin E. Holly eventually came over to control the company's purse strings.

Desilu then moved into high gear, producing Eve Arden's hit show about a wisecracking schoolteacher, *Our Miss Brooks,* for CBS. High as Desi rose, however, he was never too big to stoop down and pick up the small change. The network had given him expensive overhead lights for the *I Love Lucy* show. Now that he was filming *Our Miss Brooks,* he felt free to charge the network for the use of those lights—and CBS paid up.

Later he found a new opportunity to increase revenue, and this one became a trove. As historians Coyne Steven Sanders and Tom Gilbert report in *Desilu,* Desi had always disliked the jarring interval between the show and the commercials. Onscreen he and Lucy usually faded to black, followed by the harsh peddling of Philip Morris cigarettes. "Different music, different lighting, different everything," Holly stated. "Desi thought this was wrong. He thought the commercial should be done as part of the show." That meant new music and careful illumination to provide a bridge from *I Love Lucy* to the ads. Under ideal conditions there would be no more jarring sales talks; ads would be tailored to the show's look and tempo. "Desi insisted that as part of the Lucy deal with Philip Morris and CBS that we take their commercials and integrate them—for an additional fee, of course." The integration was so successful that other producers eventually demanded the same smooth transitions for their programs. Desilu was happy to offer its services—for an additional fee, of course.

Desilu grew exponentially throughout the 1952–1953 season. As *I Love Lucy* continued to hold first place in the ratings, Jack Benny arranged to have the studio produce five episodes of his program.

Danny Thomas, then beginning to rise as TV producer, chose Desilu to make the pilot for his own show, *Make Room for Daddy.* Remembering the audition for ABC, he described himself as "fortunate to have Desi as a boss for the pilot. He laughed so hard on the soundtrack that we sold the pilot in forty-eight hours." In addition, programs starring Ray Bolger and Loretta Young were filmed on the premises.

Some of Desilu's aborted projects were as intriguing as the ones that were produced. Nothing came of the full-length feature *Lucy Has a Baby,* composed of episodes strung together and edited by Lucy's old counselor Ed Sedgwick. Frank Sinatra planned to star in *Blue in the Night,* a dramatic series about a musician. It was called off when he won the career-saving role of Maggio in *From Here to Eternity.* Still, business was so good that Desilu relocated to a seven-acre lot on Cahuenga Boulevard. By the time construction was finished, there were nine sound stages and scores of offices for new and veteran employees. Desi calculated that by the end of 1953 Desilu would gross a minimum of $6 million. That year, he predicted, would bring the Arnazes "nothing but blessings, success, honors, and wealth." (Mindful of costs, Lucy and Desi kept their own salaries at $35,000 each, a liberal sum but nowhere near what they might have drawn.)

During 1953 the couple agreed to star in *The Long, Long Trailer,* a slapstick comedy about newlyweds living out of a trailer as they ply the roads of Southern California. The film would be produced by Lucy's long-extinguished old flame Pandro S. Berman, and directed by Vincente Minnelli. Lucy was promised Lana Turner's old dressing room; Desi would have Clark Gable's.

There were individual achievements as well. Lucy won an Emmy as Best Comedienne. Desi cut a 78 rpm disc, *I Love Lucy* (with his own composition "There's a Brand New Baby at Our House" on the flip side); overnight it rose to the top of the charts. To ice the cake, he made the list of Ten Best-Dressed Men in the United States, alongside Rex Harrison, Danny Kaye, and President Dwight D. Eisenhower. Looking at the Arnazes' period of prosperity, as well as the nation's, the *New York Times* remarked: "With Lucille Ball's baby and Ike in as scheduled, the American situation can now be said to be well in hand." Walter Winchell added his own quip: "The nation got a man and Lucy got a boy."

Rather than cheer Lucy, these triumphal moments seemed to make her more neurotic and apprehensive. "I developed a feeling I couldn't shake," she was to write. "All our good fortune was suddenly going to vanish. When I tore myself away from my babies in the morning, I had this terrible fear that they'd be gone when I returned at night." Yet the more she thought about them the more these terrors seemed irrational. Filming of *The Long, Long Trailer* went smoothly; the pace was so undemanding that Lucy commented, "I never realized how much tension I was under making TV shows." She made a great effort to relax that summer, settling into a rented beach house in Del Mar. The four Arnazes were accompanied by Desi's mother, a nurse, and a continual stream of drop-ins. Lucy laughed a lot, swam, played word games, walked on the beach, and finally let down her guard. It was then that the letter arrived from the House Committee on Un-American Activities.

Nothing to worry about, said an aide to Representative Donald L. Jackson, the HUAC chairman. "We simply want to go over the statements made at your previous appearance before our committee last year." Lucy knew better: the long climb from Jamestown, the career, the house, the show, Desilu itself would all go. Let the shrinks and the friends scoff at her little formless fears. Every time she had reached a peak, disaster beckoned. It was beckoning now.

Since her last interview, the blacklisting of "radicals, fellow-travelers, dupes" and those who had been "prematurely antifascist" had become ruthless in Hollywood and New York. The committeemen of HUAC were obviously after big names, and at this point Lucille Ball was one of the biggest. She returned to their turf and resubmitted her testimony, emphasizing that she and her brother had simply placated their crusty old grandfather by registering as Communists. How many times had Lucy chosen unwisely just to please men? She had lost count long ago. The best thing she could do at present was to please more men, answering all their questions without hesitation.

Lucy's memory was usually remarkable; she could recall places she had visited and conversations with friends years afterward. But before the congressmen she stumbled, like an auditioning actress who has lost her script. Lucy could not, for example, recall whether she had signed a petition supporting the Committee for the First Amendment, a group protesting the HUAC investigation of Hollywood back in 1947.

Perhaps she did; she couldn't swear she didn't. The whole business was so long ago, and besides, everybody signed things in those days—Humphrey Bogart, Danny Kaye, Frank Sinatra.

Her listeners were sympathetic. After two hours Lucy was allowed to submit an official statement: "I am not a Communist now. I never have been. I never wanted to be. Nothing in the world could ever change my mind. At no time in my life have I ever been in sympathy with anything that even faintly resembled it." She had worked out a rationale and submitted it for the record: the family had posed as radicals to soothe Fred Hunt's psyche, that's all. Politics had nothing to do with their actions. "It sounds a little weak and silly and corny now, but at the time it was very important because we knew we weren't going to have Daddy with us very long. But I was always conscious of the fact I could go just so far to make him happy. I tried not to go any farther. In those days that was not a big terrible thing to do. It was almost as terrible to be a Republican in those days."

She was dismissed with the comforting words of investigator William Wheeler: "I have no further questions. Thank you for your cooperation." She shook hands with him and made her exit, assured that she was in the clear and that her testimony would remain sealed this time as in the past.

That weekend she and the children returned to Chatsworth. Desi remained at Del Mar, where he had scheduled a poker game at the home of producer Irving Briskin. Lucy put Desi IV and Lucie to bed and turned on the radio. It was time for Walter Winchell. Shortly before the newsman signed off, he offered a blind item: "The top television comedienne has been confronted with her membership in the Communist Party." No name was mentioned, but it was clear that Winchell did not mean Imogene Coca, costar of *Your Show of Shows*, the only other TV comedienne of comparable stature. Despite guarantees, someone had leaked the news that Lucille Ball had been before HUAC.

In Del Mar, Desi received a call from Cleo's husband, Ken Morgan, recently elevated to the position of Desilu's public relations chief. Had Desi heard Winchell tonight? No, he had been too busy at cards. What was up? Desi was filled in. Acting on instinct rather than cogitation, the boss ordered Morgan to meet him in Chatsworth. It would be a good idea, Desi added, to bring MGM's head of publicity, Howard Strickling, along for the ride.

"I was driving the 130 miles or so from Del Mar to the ranch," Desi later wrote, "when it hit me that history was repeating itself in an ironic sort of way." Twenty years before, in Cuba, "I had been playing poker when I got a phone call from my uncle, telling me that a bunch of Communists (Bolsheviks in those days) were on their way to ransack our house and asking me to get my mother the hell out of there."

He arrived at the ranch at 2 a.m. to find Strickling and Morgan advising their confused and terrified client. Lucy was willing to do whatever they counseled. Strickling felt that the best policy was no policy: keep quiet and let the mini-scandal blow over. Morgan also saw no reason to call attention to the problem. Desi agreed. For several days the Arnazes walked on eggshells but saw no mention of Lucy's past in the newspapers or on television. *I Love Lucy* continued to rehearse on schedule and everyone breathed a little easier.

Then came Black Friday. The Arnazes woke to find a reporter and a photographer camped in their front yard. At noon the *Herald Express* hit the stands with an extra. Some investigative reporter had done his job; the paper carried a four-inch banner: LUCILLE BALL A RED. Under it was a photostat of the 1936 card indicating Lucille Ball's intention to vote the Communist Party ticket. Lucy began to cry and remained in tears for the most of the day. The feeding frenzy had begun.

On several occasions Desi had met J. Edgar Hoover at the Del Mar racetrack. Now Desi imposed on their acquaintanceship with a phone call. He explained the situation as best he could and asked if there were any other nasty surprises in Lucy's FBI file. Hoover had already checked it. "Absolutely nothing!" he declared. "She's one hundred percent clear as far as we are concerned." With that assurance Desi felt free to call Frank Stanton, head of CBS in New York, warning that a scandal was about to break and that there was not a shred of truth in it. "I am so goddam mad, I'm going to fight this like I've never fought before," Desi told him. "We are not going to get scared. What happened to Larry Parks is not going to happen to her."

Desi was referring to the young actor who had mimed Al Jolson's numbers in the 1946 blockbuster *The Jolson Story*, did it again three years later in *Jolson Sings Again*, rose to celebrity—and was then exposed as a former member of the Communist Party. Humiliation followed. Pressed by HUAC to give the names of the comrades in his cell, Parks resisted. "I am no longer fighting for myself, because I tell you frankly that I am probably the most completely ruined man that

you have ever seen. I am fighting for a principle . . . I don't think that
this is fair play. . . . These are not people that are a danger to this country." The committee was having no truck with the actor's plea. "If you
will just answer the question, please. . . . Who were the members of
the Communist Party cell to which you belonged?"

Parks capitulated: "Well, Morris Carnovsky, Joe Bromberg, Sam
Rossen, Anne Revere, Lee Cobb, Gale Sondergaard . . ."

The committee chairman, discomfited by this pocket theater of cruelty, let up on the witness now that he had abased himself. "You could
get some comfort out of the fact that the people whose names have
been mentioned have been subpoenaed, so that if they ever do appear
here it won't be as a result of anything that you have testified to." True
enough, but the testimony was enough to finish Parks in Hollywood,
on the right because he had once been a Communist Party member,
and on the left because he had given HUAC what it wanted. Desi
vowed not allow such a catastrophe to happen to Lucy. He called the
Philip Morris panjandrum Alfred Lyons and told him that he had
talked to Hoover and Stanton, and that if his company wanted to back
out, Desilu would sponsor the program itself. Desi treasured the harrumphing reply: " 'No, young man, I ain't pulling out,' said the nice old
bastard. 'Let's go get some good headlines!' "

The phone rang nonstop that afternoon, and Desi was selective
about whose calls he would take. Later he confided to Lucy that he
had spoken to columnist Hedda Hopper. "I told her the only thing red
about you is your hair, and even that is not legitimate." "You 'dint'!" said
Lucy, and as soon as she made fun of his accent Desi knew she had
regained enough humor and equilibrium for his next move.

Just before filming of the first show for the new season, Desi
stepped before the audience and said: "Ladies and gentlemen, I know
that you have read a lot of bad headlines about my wife. I came from
Cuba, but during my years in the United States Army I became an
American citizen, and one of the things I admire about this country is
that you are considered innocent until you are proven guilty." He told
them that the full story would come out the next day, introduced Fred
and Ethel, proclaimed Lucy as "American as J. Edgar Hoover and President Eisenhower," and once again used the line about her hair being
the only thing red about the star. The star of the show came on to a
standing ovation and the continued shout "We love you, Lucy."

By the time the crowd settled down, almost everyone in the place was snuffling, including many of the reporters seated in the front rows. The troupe went on with the episode, "Ricky's Life Story," with Lucy flawlessly executing a dance number and playing with Little Ricky (impersonated by twin child actors, Joseph and Michael Mayer), and earning, once again, resounding applause and cheers. The following day, newspapers ran Lucille Ball's exculpatory testimony before the committee and quoted HUAC chairman Jackson, "We love Lucy, too."

To emphasize Lucy's rehabilitation, Desi arranged a press conference on Sunday around the Arnaz swimming pool. Amid the beer and the ham-and-cheese sandwiches, Luci and Desi chatted up a group of invited journalists. In case anyone was unkind enough to mention Lucy's ancient interest in the Committee for the First Amendment, four press agents stood by to parry: Morgan and Strickling had been joined by PR men from CBS and Philip Morris.

During the conference, the doorbell rang. Desi excused himself, went inside, and attended to the latecomer. It was Larry Parks, holding a bunch of flowers. Desi thanked him profusely, and, he confessed later, "told him to get lost." Desi wrote: "I explained it wouldn't do him or Lucy any good to have a story about Larry Parks bringing Lucy red roses at that particular 'period of time.' Some sonofabitch would accuse them of belonging to the same cell. Larry, who had suffered enough from some of this same bad publicity and who had always been a perfect gentleman, understood. I really felt like a shit but I didn't care to take the chance." Returning to his guests, Desi used the illegitimate red hair gag yet again and got laughs with it. The atmosphere of strained levity could not hide the fact that the conference was a miniature version of the committee, with witnesses called upon to debase themselves. It remained for the host to encapsulate the moment. The late Fred Hunt, Desi said, was "a wonderful guy, a loveable guy—the kind of guy who wanted everybody in the world to be happy and have more money. In 1936 it was a kind of a joke, a kind of a light thing. If Grandpa was alive today, we might have to lock him in a back room."

That sufficed for the Hollywood press, a group who genuinely liked Lucy and found Desi an amusing and generous chap. They dispersed, and then wrote flattering items about the Arnazes and dismissed the notion that Lucille Ball was anything but a patriot.

Not so the reactionary press. The charge was led by Westbrook Pegler, a Hearst columnist notorious for his invective, for his loathing of the Roosevelts, Franklin and Eleanor, and for his withering appraisal of anything to his left. Lucille Ball, he wrote, had not "come clean" at all. She had to be "tracked down and exposed" before confessing her past politics. "The proposition that she was only 24 years old and that her grandfather was a family tyrant, a Socialist who made her do this, has no value at all with me. This Ball woman knew what she was doing when she registered with the Communists. . . . Socialist grandfather! That is a new variant on the whine of the crooked White Sox player who did it for the wife and kiddies." Pegler was gratified to find a warm response from devotees. His fellow Hearst columnist Lee Mortimer messaged: "Re Lucille Ball, as usual you're on the beam. It was wonderful. If she's OK they should clear all of the Hollywood commies and let [Alger] Hiss out of jail." One reader sent in a limerick:

> *How touching to hear Lucille bawl*
> *"Grandpa was the cause of it all,"*
> *When she was caught*
> *In the Communist plot*
> *Designed for Uncle Sam's downfall.*

Others wrote more conventional letters: "If Lucille Ball at 24 years of age didn't know what Communism was she was not sufficiently educated to vote." "Will you *please* keep after this case and do your very best to keep that hard, cold-blooded communist off the TV." "Congratulations on today's article re Lucille Ball. I was a former fan of hers but when things like these are proven I no longer patronize these individuals."

Hedda Hopper, who had been one of Lucy's staunch defenders, was unprepared for the small firestorm of protest from her own readers. A Gold Star Mother reminded the columnist, "My son didn't vote red to please his grandpa—but he did die in Korea for his Uncle Sam." This angry sentiment was echoed by like-minded readers. "So the only thing RED about Miss Ball is her hair, eh?" one demanded. "Hedda, how can you be so taken in—or are you TOO all part of this publicity stunt? Certainly convenient to have a dead grandpa, isn't it?" In Indianapolis, a group of World War II veterans signed a petition stating that they would stop smoking Philip Morris cigarettes until Lucy was taken off the air. "We intend to use our memberships in veterans' organizations," they warned, "to combat the appearance, on TV, stage or screen, of anyone supporting or belonging to any party supervised by the Soviets."

Lucy and Desi made no more public statements, going about their business as if nothing had happened, resentful of fair-weather friends and acquaintances who made themselves scarce, and grateful to the handful who went out of their way to express their support. First to pay a call was comedian Lou Costello. Lucy thought of him as an acquaintance more than a pal; she had only been on his radio show a few times. But there he was sitting in the garden, and when Lucy asked him why he was in evidence Costello replied: "You just go about your business. I'm just hanging out here for the day. I just thought you might need a friend about now." Jack Oakie, Lucy's costar in the old days, also showed up; so did Lionel Barrymore, crippled by arthritis, who visited in a wheelchair.

During the next week thousands of letters came in. Almost all of them spoke of their love for, and their belief in, Lucy. Syndicated columnist Royce Brier took on Pegler: "Surely every middle-aged citizen of this country (Miss Ball is 42) is not under moral obligation to arise publicly and confess his or her manifestations of immaturity or ignorance at 25." Ed Sullivan, the New York *Daily News* columnist who loathed Winchell, added his own message: "It's a singularly fortunate thing for Lucille Ball that she's been a weekly visitor to millions of American living rooms. In those Monday night visits, people have come to know her well. TV cameras being as revealing as they are, the Jury of Public Opinion is an informed jury as it renders its verdict on a silly thing she did 17 years ago." Pegler's own home paper, the *New York Journal–American,* conceded in an editorial, "We wish Miss Ball had not done those foolish things long ago, but we don't wish it one millionth as much as Miss Ball. Folly is regrettable, but none of us is immune to it, and let's distinguish between folly and real treacherous conspiracy." In the *New York Times,* Jack Gould added: "For once the accusation and the rebuttal became known simultaneously and the public had an opportunity to judge and act for itself." Walter Winchell was forced to go into reverse, changing his tune to Yankee-Doodle: "Donald Jackson of the House Un-American Activities Committee, and all its members, cleared Lucy 100%, and so did J. Edgar Hoover and the FBI, plus every newspaper in America and, tonight, Mr. Lincoln is drying his tears for making her go through this." Unmentioned was the fact that "this" had been ignited by Winchell himself.

There was one more hurdle to clear: the ratings. It was all very well for journalists to withdraw from the attack, and for more than two thousand fan letters to arrive in support of Lucy—as opposed to two dozen negative ones. It was quite another to expect the country at large to stay tuned to the show. The Neilsen and Trendex polls would reveal more about the political climate than any columnist or mailbag. And so on a Monday night an apprehensive Desi and Lucy awaited "overnights"—the fast reading of what viewers had watched between 9:00 and 9:30 EST. Four men were just as tense: William S. Paley, chairman of CBS; Alfred Lyons of Philip Morris; adman Milton Biow; and Louis B. Mayer of MGM, producer of *The Long, Long Trailer.* Shortly after midnight the results came in. *I Love Lucy* remained number one, a fact noted in a *Los Angeles Times* headline the next day: EVERYBODY STILL LOVES LUCY. The heartening results spilled over into other arenas. B'nai B'rith, acutely sensitive to the vagaries of American politics, gave its Woman of the Year award to Lucy because of her willingness to appear at charity benefits. Of greater consequence was the fact that the Arnazes, along with William Frawley and Vivian Vance, were summoned to the White House by special invitation. The troupe performed to more than polite applause, and then President Eisenhower summoned Desi and Lucy to his table. "So you're the young man that knocked me off the front pages," said Ike. Flustered, Desi could only babble, "They said a foreigner with an accent wouldn't be believable playing an average American husband." The chief executive put him at his ease: "Out in Kansas they said I'd never be president. You know what we are? A couple of walking miracles!"

Lucy could not be included in that category. Her escape from history was not a matter of miracle but an accident of timing. "I was one of the lucky ones," she was to realize later on. "For a long time, people in Hollywood couldn't get a job because of unfounded and vicious smear rumors. If news of my registration had been revealed during the worst witch-hunting days—between 1945 and 1950—my career would probably have been finished." As it was, she could and did go on. Lucy and Desi never mentioned HUAC again in public. No less than the president of the United States had given her a clean bill of political health, yet Lucy would remain scarred and insecure. She could never quite relax after her experience with the congressmen and the fallout that came from their investigation. A signature on an old piece of paper had been enough to justify her most pathological fears: one's livelihood and social position could indeed vanish overnight, and in the end neither money nor love nor public relations would be powerful enough to keep the jackals away.

G ranted a second chance, could Lucille Ball make it big on the big screen? As MGM (and the Arnazes) saw it, the only way was to have her play Lucy Ricardo in disguise—hence the characters and plot of *The Long, Long Trailer*. The scenario by the experienced farceurs Albert Hackett and Frances Goodrich sedulously copied the devices of television. A few critics went overboard: the *Newsweek* reviewer thought the comedy made "Mack Sennett look, in retrospect, like a reticent disciple of Ibsen." But most agreed with the *New York Times* reviewer, who thought the misfortunes of a honeymooning couple in car and trailer little more than an extended episode of *I Love Lucy.* Tacy, the wife, the reviewer wrote, "is a nitwit with a benign and vacant stare, and Nicky, the spouse, is a good sport with more patience than passion—or brains." *Trailer,* the review continued, "is a comedy of situation—straight situation—from beginning to end, and Vincente Minnelli has directed for nothing but quick, responsive yaks." These he got in overplus. The film had enough box office magic to open at Manhattan's most important movie house, Radio City Music Hall, where Lucy made a personal appearance, gushing to the audience about going to the Music Hall in the 1930s. Never, "in my wildest dreams," she told her fans, "did I imagine that I would one day be on this stage myself." *The Long, Long Trailer* racked up impressive grosses in New York, then opened nationwide to large crowds. By the end of the year it had earned some $4.5 million and a place among the top twenty moneymaking films of 1954.

Now it was Desi's turn to go into overdrive. He took charge of pilots for new Desilu shows, reordered schedules, oversaw scripts. As a result he became tired and cranky in the office and on the set, and not every-one indulged him. Jerry Hausner, featured in the pilot for *I Love Lucy* as Ricky's agent, had been with the show for two seasons. During one episode he was required to speak to Desi on a pay phone. The prop was at one end of the stage; Desi's phone was at the other. The instruments were supposed to be connected so that the actors could talk in normal voices and actually hear each other on their receivers. At show time the phones were still unconnected. Instead of ranting at the engineers, Desi cursed out Hausner before the cast, crew, and audience. "I couldn't believe it," said Hausner. "In all my professional career I had never been treated so badly. I was so upset that I walked over to Jess Oppenheimer and told him I would never again do the show. He understood. It was terrible when Desi and I had to do another scene together in the last act. I found it very difficult looking him in the face."

Desi paid for his hyperactivity with eye tics, headaches, and bad digestion. Worse things were in store, though a seemingly offhand remark by Frawley helped to delay them temporarily. "Remember when you led a band?" the actor asked between takes. "You just waved a stick and the boys took it from there. Why don't you develop faith in others?" For an unsubtle man, Frawley showed extraordinary discernment. By using the image of the band, he persuaded the boss to start thinking about delegating authority. Desi began to allow others to take over some of his duties. Morale improved and productivity rose. Among the shows under way at the Desilu studio were *December Bride,* starring the aging character actress Spring Byington; *Those Whiting Girls,* with singer Margaret Whiting and her sister Barbara; *Willy,* starring June Havoc; *The Jimmy Durante Show*; and *The Lineup,* a police drama. Some never made it to the screen, others had a half-life of one season. *December Bride* made up for them all, placing among prime time's Top Ten for five years. Desilu would do 229 half-hour shows in 1954. According to Desi's calculations, this would be the equivalent of some eighty feature films.

The pressure of the schedule showed on everyone. Desi and Lucy maintained a façade of mutual satisfaction. Their employees went along with it, but privately they noticed that Desi's face bore unusually deep lines for a man under forty, and that his hair was dyed jet-black to cover the premature gray. The marriage was correspondingly strained; asked about it, Lucy cheerfully told reporters that the couple's domestic arguments were used as material for the show, and that running Desilu was their substitute for counseling. And besides, she added, with a long-running program, plus two children to raise, she had no time to waste fretting.

Those children were shadow figures to most of the Desilu personnel—and in a sense to Lucy and Desi. After yearning so hard and so long for children, neither seemed willing to assume the duties of parenthood. In later years Lucie was to remark that her mother and father

Lucy as a top Hattie Carnegie
mannequin in New York, circa 1932,
decked out in the designer's famous
low-hemmed white sharkskin suit.

The first time she saw Desi drumming in *Too Many Girls* (1939), Lucy recalled, "I recognized the kind of electrifying charm that can never be faked: star quality."

From childhood onward, both Lucy and Desi were exceptionally devoted to their mothers: Lucille with DeDe Hunt; Desiderio with Lolita Arnaz.

In her starlet period Lucy was glad for any
assignment, no matter how ludicrous.
Here she cracks a rhinestone whip as the
cats dance in *The Ziegfeld Follies* (1946).

The Ricardos and the Mertzes
dress the part for their Christmas
program in 1951. *From left:* Vivian
Vance, Lucille Ball, Desi Arnaz,
William Frawley.

Give Lucy a situation
and she invariably
jumped into it headfirst:
"Lucy Gets in Pictures"
(*right*) in 1955, and "Lucy
and the Loving Cup"
(1956).

When the going was good: against the
backdrop of their Beverly Hills home, Desi
and Lucy pose for a family portrait in 1955
with Desi Jr., aged two, and Lucie, four.

Turning her breadstick into a cigar, Lucy poses as Charlie Chaplin, to whom she was often compared. The salute occurred on her 1962 New Year's show.

Modern Hollywood considered silent comedian Buster Keaton to be all washed up. Not Lucy, who played straight woman to her old adviser in a 1965 TV special.

Lucy's death in April 1989 was given front-page treatment in the mainstream and Latino papers. The latter understandably emphasized her marriage to Desi Arnaz.

Since 1995, Emmanuil Snitkovsky's bronze statue of Lucy has welcomed visitors to Palm Springs, California, where the Arnaz family spent many vacations.

Cathy Kelley of "Cathy's Closet," a booming Internet site based in Texas, with hundreds of Lucy items for sale, ranging from wristwatches to salt and pepper shakers.

In autumn 2001, Lucille Ball's older fans were treated to a glamorous and astute reappraisal in *Modern Maturity*, house organ of the American Association of Retired Persons.

america's largest circulation magazine

AARP

m
m o d e r n

Super memory secrets

CREATE A SOLID-GOLD NEST EGG

BEST WALKS IN THE WORLD

FIRED! A 58-Year-Old Fights Back

Why we still love **Lucy** 50th anniversary special

september | october 2001
www.modernmaturity.org $2.95

Lucille Ball, 1943

were "never as happy as when they were working. They weren't home. I was raised by my nanny, Willie Mae Barker, and my mother's mother, DeDe." Barker saw Lucie and Desi IV off to school, reminded them to brush their teeth and clean their rooms, and drove them to pediatricians' appointments. DeDe took them shopping for clothes. As for Desi: "He didn't come to my fifth-grade father-daughter dance—my uncle did. Do you think I've ever forgotten that?" Weekends were another matter; then Desi and Lucy were very much in evidence, but more as lawgivers than as hands-on parents. Lucie concluded: "I think they would have loved to have been the Ricardos. But they weren't."

In fact, during its fourth season more attention was spent on the show than on the kids. It needed intensive care. *I Love Lucy* was running out of ideas, as the critics were the first to notice. In the *New York Herald Tribune,* John Crosby complained: "Miss Ball is always trying to bust out of the house; Arnaz is trying to keep her in apron strings. The variations on the theme are infinite, but it's the same theme and I'm a mite tired of it." Across town, Jack Gould, his counterpart on the *New York Times,* regretfully noted a surfeit of "the most pedestrian and sophomoric slapstick." Perhaps, he ventured, "*Lucy* has run its course and has no choice but to press too hard."

The public disagreed, and ratings remained high. Even so, the president and vice president of Desilu knew that there was a great deal of truth in the newspaper laments. So did their producer and writers. A pair of seasoned writers, Robert Schiller and Robert Weiskopf, were brought in to assist Pugh and Carroll. The new men did the first draft, then the veterans rewrote it. A difficult period of adjustment ensued until Desi made a fortunate error. Examining a script, he barked at Jess Oppenheimer, "Jesus, I don't know if you chose the right ones, these two guys." Recalled Weiskopf: "But Bob and Madelyn had written it. That really saved our necks." To give *I Love Lucy* a fresh look, it was decided to "open up" the show and take it on the road. The Ricardos became a little more affluent—as did a preponderance of their listeners in the mid-1950s—and many episodes took them out of Manhattan. A series of famous guests made cameo appearances, boosting the ratings and giving the program a glamorous undertone.

Driving to California, for example, the Ricardos and the Mertzes are caught in a speed trap and forced to stay in Bent Fork, Tennessee. There they run into the popular folk singer "Tennessee Ernie" Ford. (In some of the crowd scenes was a bit player named Aaron Spelling, who carefully observed the way Desi ran things. Much would be heard of him in the ensuing decades.) When the couples reach their destination, Los Angeles, Lucy manages to meet, among other film stars, Cornel Wilde, Rock Hudson, Van Johnson, Harpo Marx, and William Holden.

The Holden episode, "L.A. at Last," was to become a favorite with devotees. At the Brown Derby restaurant, Lucy argues rudely with the star, who is dining alone at an adjoining booth. Later, Ricky brings a new friend to the Ricardos' hotel suite—William Holden. In the next room, Lucy, embarrassed to be revealed as the offender, hastily disguises herself with kerchief, glasses, and a false nose. She enters. The script called for Holden to light her cigarette, and for the nose to burn up. It took Oppenheimer a full week to convince Lucy that the whole prop would not burst into flames, that only the tip was flammable. The makeup man, he remembered, "used a putty nose that wouldn't burn and placed a candlewick in it, just to ensure her safety. Still, Lucy was extremely nervous about it all through the rehearsal and during the final shooting, and we all held our breath. When her putty nose caught fire, the script called for her to remove it and dunk it in her cup of coffee. Lucy ad-libbed and picked up the cup with both hands, dunking the end of her putty nose while it was still attached. It was an inspired moment, entirely hers."

In the episode built around Harpo Marx, conditions were reversed. Lucy had adored the comedian since they first met in 1937 on the set of *Room Service*. She was delighted to welcome him to her own show, where the two of them would reenact the famous mirror sequence done by Harpo and Groucho in *Duck Soup*. Lucy had forgotten that Harpo never repeated his motions. Each time, he added some new business. "That was deadly for this episode," recalled Maury Thompson, "because she had to be his mirror image. This is one occasion where we had to reshoot a scene over and over again after the audience left." When the routine was finally completed, Lucy threw a party; Harpo played his instrument and Vivian Vance sang pop tunes. Harpo was to look back on the occasion with nostalgia and rue: "I hadn't worked for a while before this show, because I'd had a heart attack." His physicians advised against the appearance, but Harpo wanted to get back onstage. "Lucille loved to rehearse, but I had done this stuff for thirty-five years. I had a great time. Right after the show, I had another heart attack."

For all their comic qualities, these Hollywood episodes displayed an unattractive schizoid character. So strong was Lucy's television persona that to most viewers she had become a member of the family. For them, nothing could violate the image of Mrs. Ricardo as an insular and naive housewife, forever attempting to worm her way into small-time show business. On the new programs Lucy continued to be presented as the ultimate celebrity freak, dumbstruck by the superstars she met. At the same time, the audience knew very well that Lucille Ball was herself a superstar, very much on a par with the likes of "Tennesse Ernie" or Van Heflin. This collision of fancy and fact tended to unbalance the show, and for the first time *I Love Lucy* took on a forced, artificial quality.

Still, the fans continued to tune in every Monday night, and as a result of their loyalty the ratings stayed astronomical. No one was willing to kill the golden goose quite yet. But it was time to start looking elsewhere for income and fame.

The Arnazes signed with MGM to do another picture, *Forever Darling,* with Desi in the dual role of actor and producer, under the banner of Zanra—"Arnaz" spelled backward. The script had been lying around for twelve years. Scenarist Helen Deutsch, whose credits included *I'll Cry Tomorrow* and *King Solomon's Mines,* had shaped her work for the talents of Spencer Tracy and Katharine Hepburn. Carroll and Pugh (uncredited onscreen) did what they could to retool the plot and comedy for their employers, but *Forever Darling* remained an inappropriate vehicle and the principals seemed uncomfortable in their roles as research chemist Lorenzo Xavier Vega and his bitchy wife Susan. The cast was not materially aided by Al Hall, Lucy's friend from the old studio days. According to Desilu executive Bernie Weitzman, Hall "was an old-time director who couldn't get a job with anybody else. Lucy made him the director because she liked him and he was nice to her when she was a nobody." The good deed did not go unpunished.

Desi's great concern was bringing in the picture under budget, and that goal, at least, was accomplished—the film was completed several days ahead of schedule at a cost of less than the agreed-upon $1.4 million. That ended the virtues of *Forever Darling.* Radio City Music Hall management judged it to be inadequate in style and substance. The next best option was the déclassé Loew's State Theatre, where the film opened early in 1956.

This time out, critics treated Lucy and Desi with open disdain.

Bosley Crowther of the *New York Times* was among the kindest when he only poked holes in the "thin, overdrawn, weak caper" of a couple "whose once-rosy marriage has deteriorated into bickering and boredom and then is saved through the intervention of the lady's 'guardian angel.' " He found James Mason, as the angel, a good deal more convincing than the earthly characters. Crowther concluded: " 'We had something that slipped away from us,' one of the disconsolate principals says early in the proceedings. A truer phrase was never coined." In later years Lucy acknowledged that the film was an unqualified dog, but she was also quick to say that the effort was worthwhile. "As corny as it sounds," she was to allow, "that movie was more than just a dumb fantasy. I kept hoping that *something* would come along and save my marriage."

No feature could have worked that miracle, but at least *Forever Darling* brought Lucy back to Jamestown, where she could introduce Desi to her girlhood friends for the first and last time. Some 25,000 fans turned out to greet the Arnazes, standing in a cold rainstorm for the privilege. Desi turned on the charm and kept it going for three days. During a party arranged by press agents, Lucy went around the room trying to recognize classmates she had not seen in more than a generation. There was some trouble identifying the guests by name, but in most cases she could recall something specific: "Your mother kept a red bowl on the sideboard." "You had a green bicycle." The last person in line, she wrote in her autobiography, was "a short, bald, sweet-faced man. He looked up shyly while my old friend Pauline Lopus smiled impishly by my side. I kept looking at this stranger, totally mystified. At last Pauline burst out, 'That's Vinnie.'

"Vinnie Myers! My eighth-grade beau! . . . I whooped, then hugged and kissed him; Desi . . . shook his hand and slapped him on the back. 'So you're the one I've been jealous of all these years!' It was quite the highlight of the trip."

During all this career chaos, Lucy and Desi decided to give up their ranch and move closer to town. A number of incidents precipitated their decision. First were the long hours at Desilu that strained their marriage almost to the breaking point. Then there was the sudden change of sponsorship that threatened the business. Without warning,

Philip Morris announced that it would not renew its sponsorship of *I Love Lucy*. The tobacco company had long been criticized for sponsoring a family program, and this was its response. Never before had a sponsor walked away from a top-rated show. In time General Foods was persuaded to fill the gap—after all, *I Love Lucy* was still number one, with an audience of millions. But the mini-crisis precipitated by Philip Morris demonstrated that nothing in television could be taken for granted, especially the promises of businessmen. And then there was a rumor that someone was out to kidnap their children. Police came up with nothing. The gossip may have been started by a crank or a prankster, but the Arnazes were unwilling to take a chance. Indeed, the threat underlined feelings they had left unexpressed for too long. Over the past several years developers had built hundreds upon hundreds of new houses in the San Fernando Valley, bringing in strangers, changing the character of the neighborhood, and making longtime residents feel crowded and vulnerable in ways they had never anticipated. Finally, there were the stories in the likes of *Whisper* magazine and *Hollywood Confidential*.

In another time Desi's infidelities would have been labeled "bimbo eruptions" and dealt with by adroit publicists. Here they were called an outrage, detailed in scandal sheets, and denied by no one. One article stated that Desi had "sprinkled his affections all over Los Angeles for a number of years." It went on to say that "quite a bit" of money had been bestowed on "vice dollies who were paid handsomely for loving Desi briefly but, presumably, as effectively as Lucy." According to the publication, Arnaz had spent time with a prostitute at the Beverly Hills Hotel and shared her with an unnamed male relative because a man, married or single, "should have as many girls as he has hair on the head." Desi's tomcat proclivities had never been a secret to Lucy. ("I was always giving Desi a second chance, third chance, fourth chance, hundredth chance," she was to recall.) This time, however, the secret was out in the open for all to read, and his denial—"a lot of baloney"—was as implausible as it was loud. The Arnazes had fights, some of them physical ones in which Desi was hit with a hammer and bopped with a bottle, and all of them bitter. A split was considered and rejected; there was too much at stake at Desilu and there were too many employees to put at risk.

But externally at least, conditions had to change. Lucy began to house-hunt in Beverly Hills, close to the action. As a real estate agent showed her around, Lucy's eye was caught by a large white Williamsburg-style house at 1000 North Roxbury Drive, next door to Jack Benny and Mary Livingstone. The agent looked up the property. It was not on the market. No matter, Lucy decided. She rang the front doorbell and was instantly recognized by the owner, a Mrs. Bang. Lucy complimented the older woman on the place and made an offer then and there: $75,000. It happened that the Bangs had recently lost their son, and the once-happy home had turned into a storehouse of melancholy souvenirs. They were willing to sell—at a price $10,000 higher than Lucy's initial offer. Fine with me, said the buyer, mentally eliminating the agent's fee. Mrs. Bang and Mrs. Arnaz made a handshake deal on the spot; then Lucy drove home and presented Desi with the details. He accepted the deal without question. The couple peddled their house in the Valley to the aging former child star Jane Withers, and headed for the Hills.

In doing so they tried to find their bearings in an industry—and a society—that was redefining itself by the day. Nineteen fifty-six was one of those pivotal years that can only be understood in retrospect. Two hundred thousand Soviet troops and tanks crushed a Hungarian rebellion, and Premier Nikita Khruschev of the U.S.S.R. told Western ambassadors, "History is on our side. We will bury you!" newly alarming the Pentagon. As if to answer Khruschev, that year the Dow Jones Industrial Average marked a new high of 500 points, the Gross National Product reached a new high of $434 billion, and unemployment dipped to 4.2 percent. No one could be sure whether the Cold War would heat up again. The Korean War had ended in a truce in 1953. But what if fighting broke out in Western Europe? Would U.S. soldiers go forth in another battle? Was this to be a century of total war? Schoolchildren underwent air-raid drills, and their parents tossed in their beds at night, wondering about the country, about their jobs, and most of all about the Bomb. Many of them spent what they earned—what was the point of saving for tomorrows they might not be alive to see?

Lucy and Desi were no different from their countrymen, only richer and more unhappy with each other than most husbands and wives. They spent what they had, too.

Desi acquired additional acres in Palm Springs, facing the green swaths of the Thunderbird Country Club. No one had bothered to tell him that in addition to being one of the most beautiful clubs in the state, the Thunderbird was also one of the most biased. It did not admit Jews, Negroes, or Latinos. Desi may have been a celebrity of means, but he was barred from membership. In response he began construction on a luxury motel nearby. "We won't discriminate against Gentiles, Jews, or Cubans," he proudly informed reporters. (By the time all the additions were made he would spend close to $1 million on his forty-two-room hostelry—a price that worked out to $24,000 per rental unit.)

Lucy was no less manic and extravagant: "I ordered new contemporary living room and bedroom suites from—where else—Jamestown, New York. The order was flown to Los Angeles in a special chartered plane." For the front hallway of her new home she chose a Japanese silk print that went for $90 a roll. Only after the wall covering was up did she notice the flaw: shadowy birds were a subtle part of its design. Lucy's neurotic dread of feathered things, present since the death of her father four decades before, reasserted itself. There was a brief, unpleasant scene and the silk print came down. And then, for the sake of appearances, and for her own stability, life resumed, as if nothing untoward had happened.

When everything was finally installed to their liking, Lucy and Desi moved out of the Beverly Hills Hotel and prepared to take up residence at 1000 North Roxbury. Lucie, Desi IV, and DeDe, Lucy's devoted mother, stood by beaming as Desi ceremoniously carried his wife across the threshold. Then there was a collective gasp. During the night, some water pipes in the eighteen-year-old house had burst. The thick white wall-to-wall carpet, Lucy recalled, was a stained, sodden mess and the newly plastered walls were disintegrating. "Desi really flipped. As the children huddled against me in terror, he ranted, raged, stormed, kicked the walls, and then began tearing them down with his bare hands." DeDe gathered the children and took them outside: "Come, dears, your father is rehearsing."

The leakage was stopped, the carpet replaced, the stains removed. Insurance covered a lot of the damage and the Arnazes made up the rest. It was only money, after all, and money was not the cause of Desi's flare-up. Nor were the scandal sheets; he had too hard a carapace to be distracted by gossip. What pushed him to the edge was worry about the future—if indeed there was to be a future—and overwork at the office. In addition to *I Love Lucy*, Desilu owned and supervised half a dozen television shows. The Western series *Wyatt Earp* and the hillbilly comedy *The Real McCoys* were filmed on the studio lots; so were *December Bride* and the Danny Thomas, Eve Arden, and Red Skelton shows. Not so long before, Desilu had had a total of seven employees. Now it was a preeminent symbol of the American dream, with more than a thousand people on the payroll. Desi tried to keep on playing the part of *patrón*, a father figure who knew the name and needs of every man and woman at Desilu, but these days it was impossible. Success had taken away his favorite role. And then there was his self-image, something he rarely spoke about. As a producer, as the husband (and straight man) of a great television personality, Desi had been accepted rather than embraced by the Hollywood establishment. He sensed the difference: in the end they were Anglos and he was a Latino. There was no getting around it; his accent was a permanent reminder of his outsider status, a status, ironically, that made him a demigod in the barrios with which he had long ago lost touch.

In *The Mambo Kings Play Songs of Love,* Oscar Hijuelos's luminous novel of expatriate Cuban life, Desi and Lucy drop into a New York nightclub. The narrator speaks of a fictive evening when, chatting with the expatriate Cuban musicians, Desi seemed

> all business, with the fatigue of responsibility showing on his face. Or perhaps he had an air of weariness and exhaustion about him that reminded Cesar and Nestor of their father, Don Pedro, down in Cuba. Perhaps he had sadly yawned and said, *"Me siento cansado y tengo hambra"*—"I am tired and hungry." Whatever happened, he and his wife accompanied the brothers uptown to the house on La Salle Street.

From that visit comes an invitation for the musicians to make a guest appearance on *I Love Lucy.* It is the zenith of their lives—the greatest Cuban of their time bestowing a favor they can never pay back. Desi's affect and the powerful iconography of his program are so strong that years later the nephew of one musician has a dream of his uncle's funeral, the deceased's

> heart swelling to the size of the satin heart on the *I Love Lucy* show, and floating free from his chest over the rooftops of La Salle. . . . the organist starts to play, except, out of each key,

instead of pipe-organ music, instead of Bach, what sounds is a mambo trumpet, a piano chord, a conga, and suddenly it's as if there's a whole mambo band in the choir stall, and so when I look, there is a full-blown mambo orchestra straight out of 1952 playing a languid bolero, and yet I can hear the oceanic scratching, the way you do with old records. Then the place is very sad, as they start carrying out the coffin, and once it's outside, another satin heart escapes, rising out of the wood, and goes higher and higher, expanding as it reaches toward the sky, floating away, behind the other.

In Hollywood, the place where those symbols had been manufactured, Desi was not so highly regarded. Every day new demands were made on his already jammed schedule, and at the same time his support system began to give way. After the 1956 season two faces would vanish from the Desilu crowd, and they were among the most important of all. First, NBC made Jess Oppenheimer an offer he could hardly wait to accept; after the years of wrangling with Desi he was leaving to develop new shows for the network. At the farewell party, Desi tried to put a good face on the defection: "We're not losing a producer, we're gaining a parking space." But he and everyone else knew what industry watchers were predicting: *I Love Lucy* could not run without its mainspring. Oppenheimer retained a percentage of the show, so he had mixed feelings about it now that he was going. As Bob Schiller put it, "He was hoping that *Lucy* would fall on its ass, and yet he stood to make a lot of money if it didn't." Karl Freund was also calling it quits; the old pro had worked longer and harder than he had ever expected to, and this seemed the right time to say farewell. More dire predictions were heard around Hollywood.

With the stalwarts gone or going, the average age of the Desilu employees was thirty-two, and Desi had trouble remembering all their names. He continued to do his gung ho act at company picnics and trips to Disneyland, but there was something sad about his bonhomie, something that seemed to suggest another farewell in the offing.

It was time to clear the air with Lucy, to speak about their marriage and their future. "We have two alternatives," Desi told her. "Now that we have two wonderful children, after waiting all these years, it'd be a shame not to be able to spend more time with them, enjoy watching them grow. Desi will be two and a half and Lucie four this summer. We could teach them to fish, ride a horse, and I could take all of you to Cuba to meet your thousands of relatives. What do you think?"

"You said we had two alternatives. What is the other one?"

To stay as they were, in Desi's view, was to drown. Therefore, if he and Lucy were not to get out they had to grow. They had won awards, made money, achieved national recognition. Yet he could not let go of the idea that the town still considered him a pushy Cuban, a bonito swimming with the sharks. In *A Book,* his candid memoir, Desi recalls his feelings, summarized in a warning to Lucy: "Unfortunately there is no such thing as a nice little company surviving anymore. You don't see many individually owned grocery stores or the little drugstore on the corner. They're all gone. Big Fish eats them all up."

Lucy's rhetorical question said it all: "How do you quit a number-one show?"

There was more to her decision than staying at the top of the heap. To retire meant that she and Desi would be forced to share each other's company day in and day out, month in and month out. Something of the fantasist lingered in Lucy; on rare occasions she caught herself wishing for an intimate and comfortable middle age with her husband, shuttling casually between Palm Springs and Los Angeles, visiting Europe when the spirit moved them, watching the children grow and learn. But the realist in her knew better than to batten on a dream. "I still preferred to spend my weekends resting, playing cards, and sitting on the floor with the kids," she was to write. Sad to say, Desi was "too keyed up and restless for such pleasures." Typically, after the last business was completed on Friday night, chauffeurs drove the Arnazes home in a limousine and station wagon. Once Lucy and the children were settled in, Desi would take off. "It was go, go, go, all the time," she added resentfully, "to the golf links, to his new motel, the gambling tables, or his yacht."

Yet she could often be enough of an irritant to drive her husband away. The script man Maury Thompson recounted Lucy's aggressive behavior off the set: "She loves to hurt a man. She's kicked Desi in the nuts several times. Just bowled him over. She laughed about it. If he's stooped over, she'll kick him in the butt, and she'll aim low and she'll hit him right in the balls." On another occasion, Desi insisted on remaining at the country club to watch the Kentucky Derby. Lucy wanted to go home, and when he refused she got in a golf cart and furiously drove off. Thompson happened to be there that day as well, and she took him home to look after the children. He, Lucie, and Desi IV were in the swimming pool when Lucy joined them. "You're the only one in the world I would ever show myself to in a swimming suit," she told the guest. "Well, you look marvelous," Thompson responded. "And she did. She was tight, thin, no stomach, long legs, just freckles on her legs. She got in the water, and she swam the breaststroke, always keeping her head above water. I treasure that moment. Because she was thoroughly relaxed and enjoying it. Then Desi got home, and she got mad again. There were only those few moments that there was no one to worry about."

As the year drew on, Desi found it impossible to play the genial Latino around the office. His smile turned into an unconvincing rictus, and casual conversations took on a metallic edge. The higher he rose, the greater became his fear of falling. "Failure is the most terrible thing in our business," he observed. "When we fail, the whole world knows it. When a Fuller Brush man fails, does the whole world know it? That's why we break our ass not to." Assurances from Lucy were not enough to put him at ease anymore. He lost his temper at home, often over trivial matters. "He stopped discussing any of our personal problems," she was to say. "I had to dig and dig to discover what caused his rages, and generally it had nothing to do with anything I'd done. I wanted to help him, find out where I was at fault. But as soon as I started questioning, he'd stalk angrily out of the room. Or the house."

Edgy and unwell, Desi consulted his physician. What Dr. Marcus Rabwin learned could hardly have been a surprise. The patient's colon was full of diverticula, inflamed by continuous mental pressure and tension. Untreated or exacerbated, this was the kind of ailment that could kill. The doctor advised Desi to rent a house on the beach and get away from the studio the minute he finished filming. "Have somebody drive you to the beach and stay there until Monday morning," he prescribed. "Have Lucy and the children join you there for Saturday and Sunday and don't even think about the business. During the summer take six or eight weeks off, and even if they offer you the entire CBS network to come back to work during those weeks, tell them to stick it."

Looking back, Desi agreed that this was "wonderful advice and it helped a lot, at least for a while." A very short while. Then other panaceas took over: booze, women, and intense labor. You had to work pretty goddamn hard if you were going to be a Big Fish.

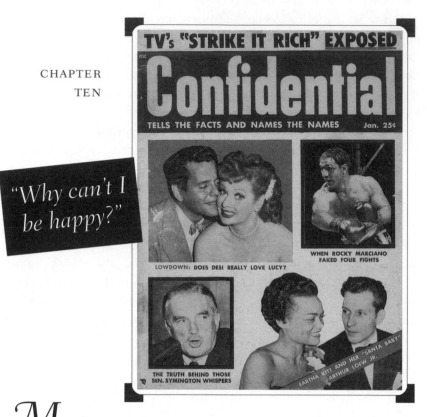

"Why can't I
be happy?"

$\mathcal{M}$ORE THAN one industrialist has acquired a movie studio in the hopes of diversifying his holdings and maybe meeting a few starlets along the way. Almost all have unloaded the investment within a few years, victimized by circumstance, bad timing, and the Hollywood operators who always manage to fleece "civilians"—their pejorative term for those outside of show business.

Howard Hughes was just such a civilian, entering major motion picture production with the purchase of RKO in 1948. At first he enjoyed the glamour; columnists coupled his name with actresses including Linda Darnell, Yvonne De Carlo, Elizabeth Taylor, Ava Gardner, and Terry Moore (who later claimed to have been secretly married to him). His reputation for eccentricity took another leap when he paid particular attention to Jane Russell's *poitrine* during filming of *The Outlaw*. Noticing that the leading lady's lavish bust rose and sagged unpredictably, he asked for a drawing board and a pencil. "This is really just a very simple engineering problem," he told a designer. He sketched a brassiere that would stabilize the focal points of the picture and saw to it that it was manufactured and worn. Extensively hyped, the Western made Russell a star, and established the name of Hughes in Hollywood. Unfortunately for him, the rest of RKO's movies could not be treated as engineering problems; what followed *The Outlaw* was a string of undistinguished failures.

By 1955 Hughes wanted out. He sold the studio to the General Tire & Rubber Company; that company had no more luck than he did, and two years later it put RKO on the block. General Tire's intention was to take a loss, offsetting capital gains for the past fiscal year. For $6.5 million a buyer would get all assets of properties in Los Angeles and Culver City, including sets and office equipment. "Everything," said the company representative when he waved the offer before Desi, "except unproduced scripts and stories and unfinished films."

The sum was more than Desilu had, and perhaps more than it could borrow. Before Desi dismissed the idea out of hand, however, he called the Great Eccentric himself and told him about the prospective sale of his old studio's properties.

"What do they want for them?" barked Howard Hughes.

Desi gave him the details.

"Grab it! Even if you tear them down and make them into parking lots, you've gotta make money."

Hughes's argument not only convinced Desi, it persuaded a lender; the Bank of America advanced $2 million after he negotiated the selling price down to $6.15 million. One key individual had been deliberately shut out of the bargaining—Lucy. Leery of her reaction, Desi asked his chief financial officer, Edwin E. Holly, to break the news. According to Holly, Desi "wasn't going to go out and tell Lucy she was going to have to mortgage the house, the kids, and everything else. This was, in effect, putting everything they and the company had on the line." Holly approached the *I Love Lucy* set with trepidation, keeping out of the star's way while she filmed a scene with Vivian Vance. When the two women took a break he hustled Lucy into her dressing room, briskly went through highlights of the RKO acquisition, and waited for the explosion. "Is this your recommendation?" was her sole question. Holly nodded. "Then go do it," Lucy told him. He responded with a mix of awe and dismay. Lucy "walked out of the dressing room right onstage with Vivian—she had just made the biggest decision she'd ever make in her lifetime from a business standpoint, and went right back into the routine they had been doing."

To a degree, she was protecting herself. It was true that *I Love Lucy* was an autocracy. Desi liked to tell the writers that whenever there was a disagreement about stories or gags, there would be a simple vote: "We'll do it democratically. Lucy wins." To underline her value, when she tripped and fell over a cable, he ran over, ostentatiously helped her up, and said to the room, "Amigos, anything happens to her, we're all in the shrimp business."

Yet much of this deference was for display, and Lucy knew it. As Desilu's vice president she had become little more than an ornament. Desi and his executives bought and developed the television programs going out under the company name; they were the ones who met the payroll and ran the day-to-day operations. It was an arrangement Lucy could live with; as an administrator Desi still had her full faith and credit. It was only as a husband that he had crucially diminished his wife's trust.

For the 1956–1957 season, Lucy rubber-stamped a decision to relocate the Ricardos and the Mertzes. The quartet moved from New York City to suburban Connecticut in order to refresh the series and give the writers new plot lines, and Ricky moved up in his professional world—he was now the owner of his own nightclub, the Babalu.

The changes could be effective; a classic episode, "Lucy Does the Tango," was produced during this period. The two couples decide to earn money by raising chickens in their backyards. When the hens fail to produce, Ricky threatens to sell the house and move back to the city. But now Lucy and Ethel have fallen in love with country life; retreat is unthinkable. To foil Desi they buy dozens of eggs, conceal them in their clothing, and proceed to the chicken house, where they plan to stuff the nests. Before they can get to their destination, however, Desi interrupts them. He needs Lucy right now, to go over a tango for an upcoming PTA fund-raiser. Lucy and Vivian deliberately rehearsed without eggs, and their reactions at show time were authentic and explosively funny. Indeed, the dodging and writhing, and the final crunching of eggs in her costume, brought Lucy a sustained sixty-five-second laugh—the longest of her career. "No matter what we wrote for the scene with the eggs," recalled Robert Schiller, "Lucille did it better than we could have imagined it." His partner Robert Weiskopf added: "And that bit where Frawley opens the door and hits Viv in the ass, cracking the eggs, was the topper."

As usual, Desi struggled to maintain his composure when scenes like that were under way. Several weeks later—and for very different reasons—his façade broke down when he was one of the hosts at the Ninth Annual Emmy Awards. "Usually Arnaz, despite personal problems, was completely professional," recalls Geoffrey Mark Fidelman in *The Lucy Book.* This evening, however, Desi's manner was "forced and overdone." It was the only time in Desi's career when his drinking was detectable onscreen. Formally attired, sweating profusely, he kept telling bad jokes to an unresponsive audience, and weaving in and out of focus, flummoxing the cameramen.

During this period, no one knew which Arnaz would appear on the set or in the office, the high Desi and or the low one, the gregarious glad-hander or the irresponsible alcoholic, the great straight man or the distracted executive, the affectionate family man or the driven womanizer. Yet throughout it all, he remained one of the best talent scouts and developers in the business. One evening, as he and Lucy idly watched bandleader Horace Heidt on his NBC show, a five-year-old percussionist debuted. Billed as "the World's Tiniest Drummer," Keith Thibodeaux possessed stage presence, musical ability, and that great desideratum, a fleeting resemblance to Desi IV. Within days Desi Sr. signed the child and hired Keith's father as a Desilu publicist, thereby assuring his loyalty. Under the name Richard Keith, the little musician appeared on *I Love Lucy* in the part of Little Ricky. The cast welcomed him aboard—with the exception of Frawley, who did his customary curmudgeon act. As the boy amused himself by drawing on a scratch pad during breaks, someone asked, "Richard, what are you doing?" From the sidelines, Frawley grumbled, "He's writing me out." To the Cuban community, as to many other Latinos, Thibodeaux actually served to widen the cultural separation between father and son. In *Life on the Hyphen,* a study of Hispanic-Americana, Gustavo Pérez Firmat observes: "[Little Ricky's] appearances in the show make clear that, his father's bedtime stories notwithstanding, the cultural identity is *papi*'s alone. Little Ricky couldn't speak accented English even if he tried. There is a healthy continuity between father and son, but there is also a healthy distance. When Ricky gets old enough to play an instrument, he follows in his father's steps by choosing drums. But instead of the Afro-Cuban *tumbadora,* little Ricky plays the American trap drums."

Offscreen, young Thibodeaux played another kind of role as he quickly became absorbed into the Arnaz family. "It was as if we had three children instead of two," Desi wrote proudly. The truth was not quite so benign. Although Keith was two years older than Desi IV, the boys did become fast friends, and under Desi's tutelage they learned how to swim, fish, and ride horses. From the outside, it seemed an idyll—a little boy turned into a TV star, and enjoying the benefits of two happy families. In reality, Keith's father and mother later divorced, and the elder Thibodeaux married a Desilu secretary. Chez Arnaz, Keith remembered, "Desi was a really great guy when he wasn't drinking." Unhappily, those occasions grew more infrequent as the seasons went by: "As kids, we'd definitely stay away from him when he was drunk." One evening when Keith was sleeping over, the boys were awakened by a ruckus outside the bedroom. Desi had heard that his son's tutor had called Desi IV "spoiled" and later, Keith recalled, "caught the guy talking to a girl in the living room and just beat him badly. Desi IV and I hid in the maid's quarters."

Marcella Rabwin, wife of Dr. Marcus Rabwin, Desi's physician, recollected the Low Desi. When he imbibed heavily, "there wasn't a personality change, but an intensification of all the worst things about him—the swearing got much worse. His language was always offensive. He used the worst language I've ever heard. It would get even worse when he got drunk. But it took a lot of liquor to make him drunk—he drank all evening long."

At the same time, the High Desi operated his business with an amalgam of luck, instinct, and acuity. It was he who saw dollar signs upon reading *The Untouchables* by retired G-man Eliot Ness, leader of the group that nailed Al Capone. Warner Brothers had taken an option on the book, but never got around to developing it. Desi ordered his legal department to stay on the qui vive: the day Warner dropped its option they were to grab the project for Desilu. Warner let the contract lapse, and Desilu acquired *The Untouchables.* Desi assigned a writer, Paul Monash, bounced the first draft, got the cops-and-robbers scenario he wanted, and made plans for a two-part series bankrolled at a half-million dollars. His top executives were against this extravagance, but the matter was settled with a Lucy-style vote: the opposition made their case and Desi overruled them.

There were more obstacles. Desi's childhood friend, Sonny Capone, called when he learned of the undertaking. "Why you? Why did you have to do it?" he demanded. Desi gave his standard rationale: "If I don't do it somebody else is going to do it, and maybe it's better that I'm going to do it." Sonny replied with a million-dollar nuisance lawsuit claiming defamation of character.

And that was the least of the worries. Desi entertained a brief fantasy about playing Eliot Ness himself, but his first serious choice of leading man was Van Heflin. When that actor turned it down, Desi went to another Van, Johnson, who readily agreed to do the pilot film for $10,000. Desilu proceeded with arrangements, ordering sets to be built, contracting for cameras, crews, and the requisite technicians. Less than forty-eight hours before the shooting was to begin, Evie Johnson phoned. Speaking in the dual role of Van's wife and his manager, she demanded a 100 percent salary increase. After all, Evie reminded Desi, *The Untouchables* program was going to be in two parts. Upon reflection she'd decided the right price would be $10,000 per episode.

"It was Saturday night," Desi rancorously noted. On Monday morning the first scene to be filmed "was the one in which Eliot Ness took a truck, busted into a brewery with his men, and proceeded to tear it apart. We had about 150 union people—and you can't cancel a call on a weekend.

"Evie knew this, so she was putting a gun in my back. 'Either give him $20,000,' she said, 'or he won't be there Monday morning.'"

Desi slammed down the phone and called his chief of production. The advice: pay the $20,000. "It's going to cost you $150,000 if you don't shoot on Monday."

"Maybe it will," replied the boss, "but I am not going to kiss this lady's ass." So saying, Desi began to comb through the Academy Directory. He settled on the name and image of Robert Stack. The former juvenile lead was best known for having given Deanna Durbin her first kiss more than ten years before; nevertheless, at that moment Desi professed to see in him an "Alan Ladd kind of quality and the same even-toned performance." Operating on adrenaline and coffee, he tracked the actor down at Chasen's on Saturday night, made an offer via phone: $10,000 for the two-part *Untouchables,* with a guarantee of $7,500 per episode plus 15 percent of the profits if the show became a weekly series. By the time Stack got home, a script was waiting for him. He read it and before dawn agreed to the conditions without a written contract—Desi's word was good enough.

With the cast in place, Desi went to William Paley and announced Desilu's series for the fall: *The Texan,* with Rory Calhoun, *The Ann Sothern Show,* starring Lucy's old friend, and *The Untouchables.* The CBS chief agreed to run the first two, but passed on the third. In the first place, Paley grumbled, "What the hell are you going to do after you do Capone?"

Desi replied: "Don't you know how many crooks you had in this country? We can go on forever telling the stories about all the gangsters."

"Well, Chico, there is another problem. Paramount is doing a pilot for us about gangsters."

Insisting emptily that his was better, Desi went hunting for a new home for *The Untouchables.* He found it at ABC. There was yet another hurdle. Desi sensed that an authoritative voice-over, someone from the Capone era, was needed to make the program work. Walter Winchell seemed ideal for the role—except that he was involved in a lawsuit with the network. Moreover, Lucy had never forgiven Winchell his cheap scoop, nearly wrecking her career with news about the Communist Party registration. Yes, she acknowledged, the columnist had backtracked and apologized. But that was only after the public and the President had come to her rescue. Operating under the classic Hollywood motto "I'll never speak to you again—until I need you," Desi pointed out, "Look, honey, this is business, so let bygones be bygones." She allowed herself to be persuaded. ABC grumbled about Winchell, but had no voice in casting.

In the end, everything went Desi's way. The two-part *Untouchables* performed so well in the ratings that ABC agreed to do it as a series, underwriting thirty-two hour-long episodes, each one bloodier and more violent than the one before. In another extension of the Desilu family, the show would be produced by Quinn Martin, the husband of Madelyn Pugh.

All this time Desi was rolling sevens as a high-stakes gambler and genially telling the press he was a "verry locky Cuban." He believed that his dark side was out of view. Only occasionally would an article hint that things were less than ideal at Desilu. In one issue *Life* commented, "Sometimes the old worry over playing second-fiddle to Lucy's fame shows beneath his brashness." For instance, the story continued, when he bought a champion racehorse the papers paid more attention to Lucy. With derisive attention to Desi's accent, the magazine offered a quote: "Geez, how do you like that? I pay 31,000 bucks for dees horse, and who gets her peecture on zee front page—my wife." This was accompanied by a wide smile, as if to indicate that it was all in fun. It was not.

As the anger and resentment mounted, so did the need to go on long alcoholic binges. Desi got too many calories from liquor, and began putting on pounds that he could not diet away. His face was frequently flushed, and instead of making him appear youthful, the hair dye only seemed to accentuate his onrushing middle age. Important documents were brought to Desi in the morning when he was clearheaded. The drinking could begin as early as 10 a.m., and after lunch it was useless to talk to him seriously about contractual matters. That meant involving Lucy in the process, if only to rubber-stamp decisions that had already been made. Not that it mattered; for the most part she was content to leave the big Desilu matters to others. Only on trivial items did she exert her authority, ruling on the commissary menus, and choosing the sites for company picnics. It was another manifestation of her deference to men, something that she could not shake even now. And besides, whenever matters got too complicated, whenever the alcohol and abuse became too much to bear, she could always retreat to the character she had invented: television's own Lucille Ball.

*A*t the conclusion of the 1956–1957 season, Lucy, Desi, and CBS agreed that they ought to go out on top. There had been a few tight moments: Charles Van Doren's last two weeks on *Twenty-One* (rigged, as it turned out) had topped Lucy in the ratings. And there were other moments when Desi regretted selling all the past *I Love Lucy* shows to CBS for $4.5 million, a sum that was beginning to look like a bargain for the network. But overall Lucy and Desi had exceeded their most exaggerated hopes. Almost every aspect of popular culture had been influenced by the show. Licensing fees brought them dividends from a syndicated "I Love Lucy" comic strip running in 132 newspapers, and from the sale of a million Little Ricky dolls. Between the Arnazes and the cast there had been more than two hundred awards, including five Emmys and twenty-three Emmy nominations. Only so many changes could be wrung out of the same half-hour format, with the same conniving couples. *I Love Lucy* had even run out of ideas for amusing guest shots, like the visit from Orson Welles, playing Orson Welles, egomaniest magician and Shakespearean ham, or the appearance of George Reeves, TV's Superman, at Little Ricky's birthday party. Yet because the public still loved Lucy, Desi devised a scheme to take advantage of this profitable affection: the Ricardos would carry on in semimonthly hour-long episodes. The notion of giving the Mertzes their own spinoff comedy was quickly chloroformed by Vance. She refused to make a half-hour pilot because it would extend her on-camera relationship with Frawley. "Whenever I received a new *I Love Lucy* script," she declared, "I raced through it, praying that there wouldn't be a scene where we had to be in bed together." Desi offered a $50,000 bonus if she would change her mind, but Vance was adamant.

Undeterred, he proposed a dozen new hour-long *Lucy* shows to CBS. The network allowed him to produce five. Each would be sponsored by the Ford Motor Company, which insisted on—and ultimately received—top billing. The first *Ford Lucille Ball–Desi Arnaz Show,* subtitled "Lucy Takes a Cruise to Havana," was partially filmed in Cuba only a week before the Castro revolution. Built around a flashback, the program begins with columnist Hedda Hopper grilling the Ricardos and the Mertzes in Connecticut. How did it all begin? asks the news hen. In a dissolve to the past, Lucy McGillicuddy and her friend Suzy McNamara (Ann Sothern) are seen on a vacation cruise to Havana. Onboard they meet singer Rudy Vallee, and in Cuba Lucy is introduced to the man who will be the love of her life, musician Ricky Ricardo. At a café Lucy tries to persuade Vallee to hire Ricky for his band, thereby bringing him to New York. Lucy's sales talk is lubricated with booze, and before the evening is finished she and Suzy are arrested for being drunk and disorderly. They just barely get up the gangplank before their boat departs for the States.

Seasoned though they were, the four writers had script trouble. The weekly continuity of the half-hour *Lucy*s had build up an audience of devotees over the years. It needed no "back story" to explain the characters. The one-hour format had to start from square one. Over thirty minutes, observed Bob Schiller, many episodes could be built on one large comedy scene. Not true of the long form, where shows had to have two or three to sustain the humor. In his view, "these were never as successful as the shorter ones, despite larger budgets and longer rehearsal time."

That was not how Desi saw it, however. To him, the cruise show was a triumph from start to finish: "It was beautifully written and it played great." The comment was more than hyperbole. He approved the story line and the gags, played straight man with his usual cunning and enthusiasm, oversaw the editing, and pronounced the finished product too impressive to be further reduced. When William Paley called to find out how the show had turned out, Desi assured the CBS chief that it was the best work he and Lucy had ever done. "There's only one little problem," he added. "We got an hour and fifteen minutes." Not to worry, Paley assured him. Simply cut the seventy-five minutes to the appropriate length. No, Desi protested, that wouldn't do. Paley was willing to meet him halfway: "We'll make your opening show an hour and a half and the rest will be an hour."

"I tried that, too, but it also louses it up. It slows it down here and there. What we've got is a great hour and fifteen minutes."

"Now, Chico, let me explain something to you. Television has fifteen-minute shows, half-hour shows, hour shows, sometimes even hour-and-a-half or two-hour shows, but it does not have any such thing as an hour-and-fifteen-minute show."

"Well, that's what we've got. Why can't we get fifteen more minutes from whoever follows us?"

"Right after your hour special comes *The United States Steel Hour*."

"So tell them to give us fifteen minutes of their time."

There followed a sulfurous exchange, after which Paley concluded, "You want me to call United States Steel, tell them they've got such a lousy show it wouldn't hurt them any if they give you fifteen minutes of their time."

"Would you mind if I called them?"

"No, do whatever you want, just make sure you keep me out of it."

Now all Desi had to do was convince U.S. Steel and Ford to accede to his wishes. Operating with maximum chutzpah, he located the vice president in charge of TV for U.S. Steel. Aware that *The United States Steel Hour* had languished in the ratings, Desi proposed: "You give me fifteen minutes from the front of your show. Instead of you going on at ten o'clock, you go on at ten-fifteen. At the end of our show, at ten-fourteen exactly, I will come on, in person, as Desi Arnaz, not as Ricky, and thank *The United States Steel Hour* for allowing Lucy and me to cut into your time period, tell the audience we have seen your show and it is one of the best dramatic shows we have ever seen, and to make sure to stay tuned for it."

"Who pays for those fifteen minutes we are going to give up?"

Improvising fluently, Desi declared: "Our sponsor, the Ford Motor Company."

"You got yourself a deal."

That he did. And on November 6, 1957, U.S. Steel doubled its rating in the bargain.

The second show, broadcast a month later, did not enjoy the same smooth transition. Originally, Bette Davis was scheduled to be the guest on the program subtitled "The Celebrity Next Door." She was still lording it over her former classmate from the John Murray Anderson school thirty years before. The movies' grand dame demanded a $20,000 fee, return airfare to her home in Maine, and, in case anyone doubted her enduring star power, equal billing with the Arnazes. She got them all—and then suffered a horseback riding accident, which aggravated a back injury, broke her arm, and put her out of commission.

Second choice was Tallulah Bankhead. The casting seemed appropriate: Bankhead's hooting, extravagant style was widely considered the source of Davis's performance in the 1950 film *All About Eve.* Asked about that movie, Bankhead claimed to bear no ill feelings. "Bette and I are very good friends," she purred in her distinctive whiskey drawl. "There's nothing I wouldn't say to her face—both of them." This malice, coupled with her dependence on alcohol, made rehearsals a running psychodrama. The actress would arrive at the set promptly at 9:30 a.m. But, complained Desi, "she wouldn't really wake up until eleven. Between eleven and twelve she was fine. But one p.m., right after lunch, we'd lose her again."

Lucy was not used to having her orders questioned on the set. Only a few times had she backed down when challenged, and then only when a director asserted himself. Performers never dared to disobey her.

The condition was about to change. Lucy had a way of snapping her fingers and giving line readings to cast members; when she tried that on her guest, Tallulah grabbed her hand and responded before the cast in a distinctive throaty bellow, "Don't ever do that to me!" Shocked at such a mutinous reply, Lucy could only mumble, "Well, I want you to read the lines right." "I have been acting for a long time," Bankhead reminded her. "I know how to read my lines. Don't give me readings." With that she walked off the set. The move was just another stagy tantrum; later in the day Bankhead came back and rehearsed as if nothing had happened. But tensions rebuilt over the next week as Tallulah showed up late, blew her lines, and bumped into the furniture.

The night before the actual filming, Desi invited principals, writers, and selected personnel into his office for a drink. There, he felt, last-minute notes could be given in an atmosphere of conviviality, and past difficulties could be smiled away. As the group sat in a circle chatting amiably, Lucy made a special effort to charm. She indicated the crocheted garment Bankhead wore around her shoulders: "I love that sweater."

"My dahling, take it!" Tallulah practically threw the thing in Lucy's face, despite her protests. There was a moment of icy silence, broken by Vivan Vance's cheery remark: "Well, for me, the slacks. I love the slacks." Tallulah promptly stood up and peeled off her slacks. Anything to oblige. She was not wearing any panties.

Madelyn covered her eyes. Bob Weiskopf jumped from the couch and headed out the door. "Desi, get her a robe!" Lucy yelled. "Get her a robe!"

"Tallulah was all set to sit there with her legs crossed on the floor for the rest of the evening," recalled Maury Thompson. "Here came Desi with a dressing gown and put it on her and she condescended." It was no wonder that Lucy chain-smoked up to the time she went on camera for the real performance, and that Desi planned to go on a bender as soon as they wrapped—after the inevitable retakes, of course. What possessed them to hire this aging egomaniac lush in the first place? he wondered.

Tallulah surprised them all. When it counted, she knew every line cold, hit every mark, elicited every laugh. She was so professional that it was Lucy who flubbed words so badly a scene had to be reshot. Later Tallulah told the press, "I've got not even one picayune derogatory thing to say about those wonderful people." That sentence alone should have warned the Arnazes to duck. "Of course," she went on, "I *did* have pneumonia at the time. And someone nearly blinded me one day at rehearsals with hairspray. But Lucy? She's divine to work with!

And Desi? He's brilliant. He has a temper, however. But that's because he's fat. It worries him."

The Ford Lucille Ball–Desi Arnaz Show outrated all other programs the week the episode was broadcast, and *Variety,* like many another paper, found the leading ladies "an irresistible combination." Nevertheless "The Celebrity Next Door" was a program that Lucy found hard to watch in later years: "It reminds me how I allowed Bankhead to mop up the floor with us." There would be no more mopping-up from the guests. From here on, misery would be an inside job.

*T*he odd thing was," said a veteran of the one-hour shows, "that while Desi was going downhill personally, he remained at the absolute top of his game professionally." Bert Granet, who produced those programs, agreed: "Desi was a very, very bright man. And a wonderful boss." However, he added, that wonderful boss "would sometimes go away for two or three weeks at a time. He loved to play. Desi was really a silent-picture star at heart."

His flamboyance, coupled with a gambler's instinct and a seducer's charm, had brought Desi every material object he could have desired. And he was not parsimonious with his fortune. When one of the hour-long programs was in trouble, Bob Schiller and Bob Weiskopf came up with a saving idea. Recollecting that comedian George Jessel had made a long-running routine out of phone calls to his mother, the writers created "tag scenes" in which Lucy telephoned Desi and made funny comments about the show she (and the audience) had just seen. It extended her airtime without involving her in any of costume changes or story lines, and, incidentally, saved the show. Lucy showered the men with praise, but Desi had a more dramatic way of showing his gratitude: he gave each of them a Jaguar sports car.

Generous though his gesture was, there were not enough Jaguars in London or, for that matter, writers in Hollywood to keep the Lucy-Desi program from going stale. Under new sponsorship for the 1958–1959 season, it was given a new and ungainly listing: *The Westinghouse Desilu Playhouse Presents the Lucille Ball–Desi Arnaz Show.* Looking back, Granet regretfully acknowledged: "Every comedy show reaches a point where it has outwritten itself. So you do the best you can to keep the thing afloat. Of these hour-long shows, five or six of them are really memorable. The rest are probably better left forgotten." One of the most memorable featured Lucy's great admirer, Red Skelton. The comedian had performed his Chaplinesque pantomime, "Freddy the Freeloader," for decades. It was never quite the same from performance to performance, delighting his fans, who found something new every time they watched the sketch. But that very mutability was what drove Lucy to distraction. She wanted every take to be exactly like the one before—except a little bit better—and ultimately she showed Skelton how to do his own material. Professional to his fingertips, Red followed her instructions. But they were never to work together again.

The most forgettable episode featured the acting couple Ida Lupino and Howard Duff. Lucy warned her director, Jerry Thorpe, that Lupino had no gift for comedy, and the result bore her out. The scene is a summer cabin in Vermont. A travel agent has booked the Ricardos in for the week, forgetting that he has already leased the place to the Duffs. The two pairs ultimately agree to share the place, and so begins the familiar, and no longer very risible, boys-against-the-girls routine, with a worn-looking Desi and an acerbic Lucy throwing lines in a game with no catchers. Offscreen, matters were every bit as grim. Desi made some verbal passes at Lupino in the presence of his wife and her husband; Lucy reacted coldly. This was followed by a greater drop in temperature when Lupino learned of Lucy's misgivings about her acting skills. The gelid relations between the couples was enough to wreck the timing and ruin the program. *Variety* remarked that "Lucy's Summer Vacation" was the only episode that "falls flat most of the way," and Bob Weiskopf later admitted, "This was not our finest hour."

As the 1950s wound down, both William Frawley and Vivian Vance took advantage of their national celebrity. Frawley recorded an album on the Dot label. *Bill Frawley Sings the Old Ones* presented the actor in a serious mode, crooning with surprising control and a mellifluous voice. The numbers included several that he had helped to popularize in his vaudeville days, including "Melancholy Baby," "Carolina in the Morning," "For Me and My Gal," and "I Wonder Who's Kissing Her Now." Vance filmed the pilot for a half-hour situation comedy based on the Patrick Dennis novel *Guestward Ho!* The show was not, strictly speaking, a spin-off of *I Love Lucy,* but Vance would play a very similar character. This time out, however, she would be the lead. On the first take, the star seemed to freeze in her tracks. A second and third take found her equally immobile. The director asked her what was wrong.

Vance explained: "This is the first time in eight years I've been in my own light." She had been dominated by Lucy for so long she scarcely knew how to move on her own. (The show did not find a buyer until 1960, when Joanne Dru took the part. The latter-day *Guestward Ho!* ran for thirty-eight episodes.)

Meanwhile, Lucy made herself as busy as possible, if only to keep from obsessing about the continuing failure of her marriage. Much of her thought and energy went into the establishment of the Desilu Workshop, an homage to the school Lela Rogers had set up for young hopefuls in the RKO days. Abetted by Maury Thompson, Lucy auditioned some 1,700 applicants and chose 22 to take lessons and, eventually, to perform in the company's two-hundred-seat theater. Lucy took great pains to explain that her classes were strictly nonprofit. In fact, she said, Desilu lost money on the deal: "We pay them sixty dollars a week—the Actors Equity minimum—and they're free to work wherever they want. They're not tied to us at all." She bemoaned the catch-22 of show business: "You can't get a job unless you've acted, and you can't act unless you've had a job. We're just trying to give them exposure."

As a teacher and adviser, Lucy had no rivals. She was an unquestioned authority, the biggest name in television comedy. The students cared little about the imperfect hourly shows, and had no notion of their teacher's collapsing personal life. They regarded her as a goddess, and their adoration helped to salve a severely damaged ego. But it was not enough. Lucy had always flirted with superstition and numerology—she had been convinced, for example, that the letters A and R, as in "Arnaz" and "Ricardo," brought good luck. Now she turned to astrology, accompanying Arlene Dahl, another unhappily married redhead, to the lectures of Carroll Righter.

The man who called himself "the Gregarious Aquarius" had risen to the status of Astrologer to the Stars. Among his clients were Cary Grant, Marlene Dietrich, Susan Hayward, and Charlie Chaplin. Dahl was especially impressed; she attended many of Righter's "zodiac parties," given for his favorites. The fete he gave for her had a Leo theme, complete with lion. The big cat was so drugged he fell into the swimming pool and had to be hauled out, but no one saw this as an embarrassment. Righter was much too important to be mocked. It was common knowledge that he had told Hayward the best time to sign a film contract was at exactly 2:47 a.m. She set her alarm for 2:45 so that she could obey his instructions. Like the others, she agreed with the astrologer's self-appraisal: "They need me here. Just like they need a doctor."

The stargazer traced the roots of the Arnazes' difficulties to the constellations. Lucy was a Leo and her husband a Pisces. Soon other astrologers summed up the fate of the union. One report read: "Desi is emotional, tender, sentimental, easily swayed by moods and appeals to sympathy. Lucille is as committed and loyal as Desi is, but Lucille is uncomfortable feeling or expressing softness, neediness, vulnerability, and emotion in general. She can easily dominate or trample over Desi's feelings, and this can be a source of considerable unhappiness."

When the unhappiness persisted, Lucy turned away from the heavens and sought earthly help. She turned to the apostle of self-esteem, the Reverend Norman Vincent Peale. In his heyday from the late 1940s to the early 1980s, the pastor of Manhattan's Marble Collegiate Church was the most popular minister in America. His book *The Power of Positive Thinking* sold in the millions (he wrote forty-six books in all), and his sermons were mailed to 750,000 adherents every month. A believer in "positive imaging," a mixture of religious philosophy and motivational psychology, Peale had special appeal for middle- and high-level executives. In a typical speech to Merrill Lynch real estate associates, he declared: "If you see yourself as inferior in any way, and you hold that image in your conscious mind, it will presently, by the process of intellectual osmosis, sink into the unconscious and you will be what you visualize. If, on the contrary, you see yourself as organized, controlled, studious, a thinker, a worker, believing in your talent and ability and yourself, over a period of time that is what you will become."

Here was a philosophy Lucy could apprehend. She had been reading Peale's words for some time, and when he visited California on a speaking tour, she sought him out and invited him to her Palm Springs home. Actress and singer Sheila MacRae, then suffering from her own marital tribulations, remembered: "We kneeled in front of her new fireplace and prayed with him for about an hour, and we both cried and hugged each other." More could be gleaned from this inspiring figure, Lucy decided, and invited Dr. and Mrs. Peale to dinner sans Desi. Peale asked if he might bring his brother along. She was only too glad to oblige. The brother, as it happened, was an obvious alcoholic, and when Lucy tried to steer the conversation around to her current difficulties, Dr. Peale thrummed, "If only you knew what a role model you two are—a marriage with love."

Lucy followed that unsatisfactory meeting with another. She wrote to Peale "in heartbreaking terms, and so he invited her to come to New York." Psychiatrist Smiley Blanton "was Dr. Peale's right-hand man. Norman wanted it known that she could talk to Smiley—whose wife just 'happened' to have a script for her to read." (Lucy did read the script of Mrs. Margaret Gray Blanton's best-seller, *Bernadette of Lourdes,* and persuaded Desi to have a look. He signed the author to adapt the book for television.) Deliberately ignoring evidence that she was being courted for her fame, Lucy devoured Peale's and Blanton's books. Surely these wise men would show her the way to tranquillity.

While she was researching, she obtained more immediate help from her cousin Cleo, who flew into town and listened to Lucy's litany of sorrows. "Why can't I be happy?" Lucy cried. Cleo replied with another question: "What is it you want more than anything in the world?" For a woman supposedly wracked by domestic woes, Lucy gave an answer that was astonishing to both of them: "My career."

Later in the week she bought a ticket to the Broadway comedy *The Marriage-Go-Round* starring Claudette Colbert, an old acquaintance from the war bond days. Backstage, she ran into another Hollywood veteran, Greer Garson, appearing down the street in *Auntie Mame.* Instead of being mobbed, the three actresses were alone and unsought. They wound up in Colbert's apartment for a late-night meal. "So here we were," Lucy wistfully remembered, "three old broads making scrambled eggs at two o'clock in the morning and bored to tears with each other!"

By now nothing seemed to work. Lucy remembered the words of Humphrey Bogart when he was slowly dying of cancer. He and his wife Lauren Bacall had no financial problems. In fact, he lamented, "Money is about all we do have." That had become the Arnazes' story. Desilu was booming. In addition to the *Lucy* programs, the studio owned a group of top-rated hits including *The Ann Sothern Show, The Walter Winchell File, The Texan,* and, of course, *The Untouchables.* In addition, Desilu provided the facilities and talent for such successful TV series as *The Betty Hutton Show, The Danny Thomas Show, December Bride, The Millionaire,* and *Wyatt Earp.* These were all manufactured in a place that had become, in terms of real estate and number of projects, the largest television studio in the world. Desilu boasted twenty-six sound stages and forty-three acres of back lot, far in excess of what such old giants as Warner Brothers, MGM, and Twentieth Century–Fox had.

Lucy and Desi were always mentioned as a pair, but their sole link these days was a monetary one. The affection had drained away. They were sleeping in separate rooms and barely communicating with each other, appearing together in public principally to maintain the corporate image of Desilu. *Cosmopolitan* sent Frederick Christian, one of its writers, to interview them; he came away with a very different image from the one he expected to see. In his view, Desi had the aspect of "a Latin American dictator, relaxing in sports clothes." Christian continued: "He behaves rather like a dictator, too—not a relaxing one, but a hardworking, demanding one." The only constant in his onscreen persona and the real thing was "the strong Cuban accent, which many believe is affected for the TV role but which is authentic. In life, the accent is liberally embellished with American profanities, but they constitute a kind of working language and are used mainly for emphasis and for release.

"Desi's accent is so strong that there are times when even Lucy cannot quite understand him.

" 'What do I say here?' she asked one day during a rehearsal.

" 'You say, 'I "can't." ' '

" 'Can?'

" 'Can't.'

" 'Are you saying "can" or "can't"?'

" 'I'm saying "can't," dammit! Can't!' "

Christian knew the separation rumors and asked about them. At first Lucy denied everything: "Desi and I have been in this whole thing long enough to be accustomed to them. We've got through that kind of thing before and, we'll get through it again. Maybe it's good for some couples to be separated for a time—maybe it can renew and refresh a relationship."

"Or wreck it completely," the journalist suggested.

"Yes, there's always that chance," Lucy conceded. Her face was grave—so grave that Christian concluded, "Driving back to my hotel, I kept seeing their faces: Desi's lined and intense. Lucy's drawn, tired, and worried." He considered *I Love Lucy* and "thought of Bing Crosby's comment: 'This show's got a lot of heart.' It does. And some of it may be broken."

Members of the Friars Club took a lighter approach to the Arnazes' dissolution. When Lucy and Desi were being honored by twelve hundred club members, Milton Berle warned Desi not to get a divorce because "she'll get the kids and you'll get Olivera Street"—an unsubtle reference to the L.A. barrio. He went on to refer to the honored couple as "the Cuban Leopold and Loeb." Lucy and Desi dutifully broke up on cue, as they did at the gags of Harry Einstein, a.k.a. the Greek radio comedian "Parkyakarkus." Einstein reminded the audience that when the guest of honor started out he had been introduced as "Dizzy" and "D. C.," before citing "Danny" the Cuban as one of his best friends. Milton Berle described the next moments: "Harry had been sick and a lot of people said, 'Don't do it,' but he was really the smash hit of the evening. He got a standing ovation. As he sat down I looked at him and his face was turning colors. I'm sitting to his right. He took a breath and went boom and hit my shoulder, dead. I heard a lot of 'oohs' and 'ahs' from the audience. They guessed what happened. I never saw so many pillboxes thrown. I said, 'Ladies and gentlemen, take it easy; just a little accident here.' Backstage about eight top physicians were in a tumult, working on him. They used scissors, knives, forks, I don't know, and they tried to revive him and they couldn't. Desi was crying. He was so beside himself, and so was Lucy. He said, 'We're grateful for this wonderful tribute, but we can't go on.' " Comedians in attendance, among them Eddie Cantor, George Burns, Sammy Davis Jr., and Berle himself, tried to restore some lightness to the evening.

A reporter from *Variety* was there, and in the next issue summed up the occasion: "A great and funny dinner had become veiled with the pall of a mortuary." For Lucy and Desi, things were not to improve. In the late 1950s, honors and dividends came at a price that neither of them had calculated.

*I*n December 1958, Desilu became a publicly held company. Desi claimed that new money was necessary to help expand the business, and to some extent that was true. But he had more pressing financial obligations just then: seven-figure gambling debts. Shares went for $10 per at the initial public offering, and since Lucy and Desi were major stockholders, they each stood to make some $2.5 million, after taxes.

Lucy kept every cent and invested it in blue-chip companies. Desi paid his creditors and wound up with less than $100,000. Only his ability to find and develop hit shows kept him solvent; he was hitting the bottle harder than ever, spiking his tomato soup with liquor, and attending meetings with a cup of 7-Up laced with vodka. Alcohol may well have been what prompted him to sell the old films of *I Love Lucy* to CBS for the bargain price of $4.5 million. "Even forsaking *Lucy*'s potential as a syndication entry," observed *Variety*, "CBS estimates a $6,000,000 annual bonanza in sales of quarter-hour network segments across-the-board." Certainly alcohol acted as the main solvent of the Arnazes' marriage.

A few last efforts were made to save their union. Lucy persuaded Desi to accompany her when she visited a psychiatrist; perhaps a specialist could get to the roots of their trouble. It was a futile venture. "Desi and I would scream and yell in front of the doctor," she told a friend, "because we weren't screaming and yelling in front of the children. I felt sorry for the poor guy, he'd ask a question and the two of us would jump down his throat." After a few sessions Desi stopped coming, and a short time later Lucy gave up as well.

A trip to Hawaii produced similar results. The couple argued for much of the time, and once, to cool off, Desi took a dip in the Pacific. He body-surfed for a while and emerged minus a glittering gold chain that held a St. Christopher medal and his wedding ring. Lucy was to categorize this as "Kind of symbolic. Our marriage was gone—so why shouldn't his ring be, too?"

But the marriage was not quite gone—not yet. A few more painful moments had to be endured, a few more nerves rubbed raw. In early May 1959, Lucy consented to perform at a Kiwanis Club youth rally against juvenile delinquency in Oklahoma City. Lucy arrived at Taft Stadium expecting the twelve-thousand-seat arena to be overflowing with ticket-holders. At most, two thousand people showed up. It was a hot day and she decided that if this was the best Oklahoma could do, the program could jolly well go on without her. A widely syndicated Associated Press account stated that Lucille Ball "refused to leave her air-conditioned Cadillac for a scheduled comedy routine and a talk on juvenile delinquency." Lucy's explanation failed to convince her disappointed audience. It wasn't just the size of the crowd, she maintained. "I've played to thirteen people in a dugout. It doesn't matter to me how many there are. But when they don't care enough to publicize the affair, it's high time they stopped getting people to go thousands of miles to perform."

She had a few thousand more miles to travel in the next fortnight. In a last, desperate attempt at reconciliation, the Arnazes agreed to exchange the stresses of California for the vistas of Europe. As a holiday à deux, the trip might have worked a temporary miracle. But the inclusion of the children, Lucy's cousin Cleo, and Cleo's husband just about guaranteed failure. On May 13, 1959, the Arnaz party boarded the *Liberté* in New York City and settled into six staterooms. A week later Lucy sent Hedda Hopper a letter from France. "I don't know if Paris is ready," she wrote, "but we sure are. . . . Forty bags, two trunks and look out, here we come—Capri, Rome, Paris, London. Everyone loves our kids—that makes us happy."

"Happy" was, in fact, the antonym for their situation. Cleo remembered that "Desi was falling-down drunk everywhere." In her memoir Lucy summoned up the image of a man who, "when he wasn't drinking, spent most of his time on the phone with the studio checking the Del Mar racetrack." She continued: "I was completely disenchanted, bitter, and unforgiving, and the kids saw and heard way too much."

Lucy's spirits were not aided by a London press conference. She was unfamiliar with the London gossip reporter, a species lower down the evolutionary scale than its Hollywood or New York counterpart. The questions were relentless and impolite: "How much money do you have?" "How old are you? . . . Well, if you admit to that, you must be five years older." One paparazza took hold of little Lucie and maneuvered her behind a potted palm. "What's it like to be rich?" she grilled the eight-year-old. "Is it true your father and mother fight all the time?" Nor was Desi bolstered by a package that came to their hotel addressed to "Mr. Ball." He hit the bottle harder, and by the time the family visited Maurice Chevalier he was flushed and incoherent much of the time. The elderly Frenchman, living in retirement outside Paris, had done a guest shot for one of the hour-long shows in 1958; he could see what was going on between the husband and wife. Chevalier took Lucy aside and advised, "the end of a love affair is more painful than anything else on earth except for staying in a love affair that has no love left." She assigned him the temporary role of Daddy: "He was like a father telling me it was all right to go. We cut the trip short and came back on the *Île de France*."

There could have been no more appropriate vessel; this was its final voyage as an ocean liner—and the last trip the Arnazes would take as a couple. As soon as she unpacked, Lucy began to reckon how soon she could initiate divorce proceedings.

Lawyers and friends told her to proceed slowly, not only for the sake of the children but for the future of Desilu. "You and Desi signed the Westinghouse contract as partners," a counselor reminded her. "If you walk out now, they could cancel and sue you." In addition, Desilu was now a corporation, responsible to its many investors. To scotch rumors of an impending divorce, and to bolster an image of financial stability, Lucy and Desi sat together at the first annual stockholders' meeting, in July 1959. Assembled at a Desilu sound stage, investors were given the official word. "We now estimate that our gross income during the current television season will be not less than $23.5 million," company president Desi Arnaz declared, reminding them that this was "an increase of 15 percent over the last fiscal year." In fact, as he was later to write, the company had realized a *net* profit of only $250,000 for the year. "We could have done better," he admitted, "if we had put our money in a savings account." Later in the week he and Lucy discussed a sale of the corporation. If the right bidder could be found they could probably sell at $14 or $15 per share. Everyone, he argued, would wind up richer—especially Desi and Lucy. She refused to countenance a sale.

The days of denial were growing short, and they ended when Desi took off for Europe that fall. On October 28, 1959, United Press International scooped its competitors with the story: "Desi Arnaz left for Europe today aboard the liner *Queen Mary* without a bon voyage from his wife, Lucille Ball, amid reports that their marriage was breaking up." Desi denied the rumors; he was going to Rome and North Africa to scout locations and oversee some productions. Lucy had to stay stateside to edit a script. "We're working too hard, that's the only trouble. Probably someone heard we had an argument, but we have lots of arguments." He added a line that had grown stale through the years: "When a redhead and a Cuban get together we argue pretty good." Reporters who turned to Lucy got some more of the company line. Scuttlebutt about an impending breakup was, in her words, "cruel and absolutely false," as were stories that Desilu was up for sale.

Lucy was always an orderly person, but in this period she became a demon of organization. Lucy told friends she looked upon her life as a chest of drawers: she opened one drawer, tended to whatever needed attention, closed it, and moved to the next drawer—comedy, children, Desilu, shopping, friends, each in its own time. She plastered memos to herself on the dashboard, peeling them off as soon as the assignment was done.

Desi ran his life in precisely the opposite manner. He returned from his holiday looking puffier and older; his hair, when he failed to dye it, was shot with gray. Lucy, on the other hand, had settled gracefully into her forties. She was quick to play into self-deprecation: on the show Desi's uncle inquires, "Where did you get your beautiful red hair?" The answer: "I get my red hair every two weeks—(*gasp*) oops!" But the long bones and bright blue eyes were permanent gifts of nature, and her still-shapely legs and model's carriage gave her the aura of a woman ten years younger. Nobody who met Lucy for first time believed that she was already forty-eight, whereas newcomers who encountered Desi had trouble accepting the fact that he was only forty-two. The once-boyish husband now seemed older than his wife, rather than six years her junior. The drinking had gone from self-indulgence to sickness, and in early fall he was stopped for "weaving down Vista Street," a place known to the police as a red-light district. The arresting officers were roundly cursed on their way to the station, and while he was booked Desi threatened to call his friend J. Edgar Hoover. After half an hour in a jail cell he posted bail of $21 and was released. No harm done—except that his habit had been entered in the official record.

In the wake of this arrest, it was all but certain that the Arnazes would separate and that Desilu would be put on the block. One financial reporter noted that National Theaters & Television was interested in buying the company. It seemed a logical step; the conglomerate of movie theater owners and operators had already invested in several profitable Desilu shows, among them *Grand Jury* and *U.S. Marshal*. But negotiations never had a chance; as soon as Desi expressed interest Lucy put a stop to the talks by again refusing to sell. Four Star Production, a company headed by Dick Powell, offered to merge with Desilu. Here Desi was responsible for a breakdown in negotiations. The new company, he maintained, needed a single guiding vision. Powell agreed. The problem was that both of them wanted to be president. In the end, neither got the job.

Although those talks went nowhere, the press confirmed that Desilu was in play and concluded, not unreasonably, that Lucy and Desi were about to divorce. A story in the *Hollywood Reporter* suggested that battle lines had been drawn: "We hear Lucy may align with Martin Leeds so there would no longer be a solid Arnaz block of stock."

Lucy and Desi kept nursing separate grievances: she resented his descent into alcoholism and his driven womanizing—why, at this stage of his life, when he was rich and famous, did he have to go slumming to prostitutes? He thought of her as a woman who had suddenly become a prig in middle age. The final confrontation came on an autumn evening in 1959. They agreed to attend a formal party at Dean Martin's house. As they entered a chauffeur-driven limousine, he threw her a compliment: "Lucy, you look like a doll. I'm going to have the best-looking date at the party."

Coldly she inquired, "Are we going to be the last ones to leave the party again?"

"For Chrissakes, Lucy, we haven't even left the fucking driveway yet and you're worrying about whether we're going to be the last ones to leave the party. I've got to be the last one to leave the party now. There ain't no way I can miss. You know, in Cuba, when we have a party and it doesn't wind up with everybody having breakfast the next morning, we consider it a lousy party. And now, if I'm having fun and want to stay a little longer than the other people, you consider me an asshole."

It was only a question of who would be the first to crack. The answer came in late November. Another argument had occurred at the Desilu offices, and this time Desi followed Lucy down the hall. When she stopped to have a drink at the water cooler he asked her outright for a divorce. They were both miserable—why not end it now?

Lucy later claimed, "I had a lawyer in his office in twenty minutes." That was not the case. She walked away, enraged. Whether she was angry because he had jumped the gun and asked for a split before she did, or because this was just the latest in an endless line of insults—how dare he confront her at the water cooler instead of in the privacy of their house?—was never made clear. She got home before he did, and when Desi entered she confronted him with her own question: "You meant what you said?"

"Yes, I'm very sorry, but I did. I cannot keep on living this way."

All the misery poured out. "Why don't you die then?" Lucy cried. "That would be a better solution, better for the children, better for everybody."

"I'm sorry, but dying is not on my immediate schedule."

Her tirade continued. "I'll tell you something. You bastard, you cheat, you drunken bum, I got enough on you to hang you. By the time I get through with you you'll be as broke as when you got here." Now she ran completely off the rails. "You goddam spic, you . . . you wet-back!"

Desi broke away to find a cigarette in his dressing room. Lucy ran after him, and there occurred a scene that could have come straight out of *I Love Lucy* in its early years. She grabbed an ornamental dueling pistol that lay on his desk, aimed it at his face, and pulled the trigger. She knew very well that it was a cigarette lighter, not a real firearm; she had used the movement and the prop before, usually to conclude whatever argument they were having at the time. But this time was different; behind her gesture were years of resentment and hostility, and behind *that* was a lethal intent. The end of the barrel ignited and Desi lit his cigarette on the flame. After an aching silence he conceded. Lucy could be the one to sue for divorce; he would not stand in the way of a fair financial settlement. He ended by asking, a little too theatrically, "Please, don't ever threaten me again." After that, there was nothing to do but make an exit.

That their parents were not getting along was no secret to Lucie or Desi IV. Their anxiety and depression were reflected in poor school-work and in temperamental outbursts. Yet both continued to deny what everyone else knew was true. To be sure, their father was not around the house much. These days he spent a lot of evenings at the office, and frequently lived away from their L.A. home, usually at their Palm Springs house, but also at the Circle JR Ranch, a Thoroughbred stock farm, where he owned some racehorses. Still, other daddies were just as busy, just as scarce. And if Mommy seemed distressed much of the time, other mommies were similarly unhappy. They remained secure in the knowledge that their parents were married, that their house was not run by stepmothers and stepfathers, as were the houses of so many of their schoolmates.

The denial ended on the afternoon Lucy and Desi took the children to Palm Springs. She broke the news gently: "I have to tell you that Mommy and Daddy are not getting along and I know the unhappiness you see is affecting you. And I want you to know that it has nothing to do with you. We love you very much."

An embarrassed silence ensued. Lucie broke it. She had an intense air, even at the age of eight, and her question bore in on her parents: "You don't have to get divorced, do you?"

The six-year-old Desi chimed in: "Can't you take it all back—and make up?"

No, both parents informed them, they could not. The next moments were almost unbearable. More than thirty years afterward Lucy still heard "the sound of those two kids weeping. That really stays with you. I never thought they would go to pieces like that." She and Desi tried to assure the children that he would be around as often as they wanted to see him, but their grief was not to be assuaged. As much as Lucie and Desi IV had heard and overheard, it was not enough to make them understand their parents. "I thought they knew what was going on, but they were little kids . . . and so it was like a bomb dropped."

In retrospect, Lucy reflected, perhaps she should have told her daughter and son their parents were splitting because "he's a drunk and he lays every broad in Hollywood." She continued: "It was important for me that they know that I didn't cause the divorce. That it wasn't me who failed. I wanted to tell them, 'It's all your father's fault. Blame him!'" But she couldn't make herself say the words. "I knew that if I told them to blame him, they'd only blame me anyway. I had to let them find out for themselves what their father was like. And unfortunately, they did."

$\mathcal{F}$ILMING of the last Lucille Ball–Desi Arnaz show on March 2, 1960, coincided with Desi's forty-third birthday. This time around, no one on the set expected a celebratory spirit, so none were disappointed—except for the program's guest performers, Ernie Kovacs and his wife, Edie Adams. The comedian and the singer had just arrived in town and knew little of the impending divorce. They learned the hard way. Edgy and querulous, Lucy insisted that Kovacs, whose specialty was improvisation, read his lines exactly as written. She also demanded that Adams lose her pageboy hairstyle. No sooner had Adams complied than Lucy decided that the old look was better. "I just couldn't seem to please her," the singer remarked. "If I concentrated on learning my blocking, she'd say, 'Stop! That's no way to read that line!' So, I'd do it full out as if I were on Broadway, and she'd say, 'Stop! You're not in your light!' So it went, back and forth. And not just with me, but with all of the cast and crew."

Desi had taken over direction of the show at the beginning of the

1959–1960 season, and he carried out his chores with a professional sangfroid as if to stay above the battle. Nonetheless, conceded Adams, long experience at watching others at the helm made Desi "a marvelous director because he knew what was funny and what was not." Moreover, "he was a hands-on floor director, as opposed to someone who just sat up in the booth and talked over a microphone." But Desi kept his hands off when dealing with Lucy. He addressed her through others—"Would you please tell Miss Ball to move over?" She responded in kind—"Will you tell Mr. Arnaz I *can't* move over there?" The plot of the show concerned Ricky's inability to find work as a bandleader. In order to get a gig for her husband, Lucy entices Kovacs to pay a visit to the house. Her plans are thwarted when Kovacs is charmed by the boy and decides to hire Little Ricky rather than the big one. Lucy refuses to give up. She pastes on a mustache and tries to worm her way into Kovacs's confidence by disguising herself as his chauffeur, a masquerade foiled when Desi gets invited along for a ride.

Except when they acted, Vance and Frawley looked at the floor or the ceiling, loath to watch the pair uncoupling before them. Between takes Lucy went into her dressing room, emerging each time with wet eyes. The final lines had a subtext no one wanted to contemplate too closely:

> LUCY
> Honest, honey, I just wanted to help.
>
> RICKY
> From now on, you can help me by not trying to help me. But thanks, anyway.

The script called for a kiss and embrace, with Lucy removing her mustache at the last moment. "This was not just an ordinary kiss for a scene in a show," Desi was to write. "It was a kiss that would wrap up twenty years of love and friendship, triumphs and failures, ecstasy and sex, jealousy and regrets, heartbreaks and laughter . . . and tears. The only thing we were not able to hide was the tears.

"After the kiss we just stood there looking at each other and licking the salt.

"Then Lucy said, 'You're supposed to say "Cut." '

" 'I know. Cut, goddamn it!' "

Those words seemed to draw a curtain down on the proceedings and the marriage and, quite possibly, the whole Desilu enterprise. Backstage, everyone choked back tears, including the curmudgeon Frawley. Not once, in all the years he worked for the Arnazes, had he been disabled by drink. True to the agreement he had made with Desi, he never missed a show or blew a line because of booze. But that night he went on a well-earned bender. In the past, his hands sometimes shook; from here on the tremor was so visible that whenever he acted he jammed them in his pockets, unless a scene called for gestures.

Right after the farewell Desi picked up his belongings from the house and departed for Las Vegas. The next day, March 3, 1960, outfitted in a modest black-and-white tweed silk suit, Lucy chatted with waiting reporters before entering a Santa Monica courtroom to file for divorce. Before Judge Orlando H. Rhodes she charged Desiderio Arnaz, her husband of nineteen years, with having caused her "grievous mental suffering," and went on to lament Desi's "Jekyll-and-Hyde" personality. When Hyde was in the ascendant, she said, there were "temper tantrums in front of the children; there was no discussing anything with him. . . . We could have no social life for the last three or four years." Called on to corroborate her cousin's testimony, Cleo stated that Desi did indeed exhibit "completely irrational behavior." Desi made a brief denial through his lawyer, Milton A. "Mickey" Rudin. A little while later he admitted to the charges, but did so, maintained Rudin, to keep this an amicable divorce in accordance with promises made to the children. "Did you try to work things out?" Lucy was asked in the courtroom. "There's no discussing anything with him," she replied, Lucy Ricardo–style. "He doesn't discuss very well."

The *San Francisco Chronicle* headed its front-page story: LUCY—"I JUST CAN'T GO ON." The *Los Angeles Times* went into detail—"Life With Volatile Cuban Was Nightmare, Court Told"—and reported on the agreement worked out by Rudin and Lucy's counsel, Art Manella. *Time* summed up the settlement: "For Lucy, their two children, half of their $20 million Desilu interests, the leaky mansion, two station wagons, a cemetery plot at Forest Lawn. For Desi: the other half of the $20 million, a golf cart, a membership in a Palm Springs Country Club, a truck, and several horses." There were other considerations. Desi agreed to pay support of $450 a month for each child. The income from his 210-room Indian Wells Hotel would be divided between the exes—

until 1966, when Lucy would buy out Desi and place the money in a trust fund for Lucie and Desi IV.

With everything so neatly buttoned up, Lucy professed herself astonished by the negative public reaction. Some eight thousand letters came in, urging her to reconsider: surely there was a way of patching things up. In the minds of Americans the Arnazes were the nation's Ideal Married Couple. And besides, they had split in 1944, only to reconcile. Wasn't a rerun possible, even now? Her monosyllabic answer, "Nope," satisfied no one but the speaker. "Even when I was called a Communist," she complained, "a few nuts called me terrible things, but in general everybody was so supportive. But when Desi and I got divorced, it was unbelievable. They called me everything in the book. Others just begged for us not to do it. Everybody asked us to think it over. I couldn't believe that everybody in the United States had an opinion about our divorce."

Desi put on his game face and went out in public, attempting to assure everyone that he had done the right thing. Those who knew him were unconvinced. During the hearing he sulked at the Desert Inn, drinking heavily and using such foul language that the management asked him to go someplace else. Returned to Los Angeles, he set up a dwelling at the Château Marmont on Sunset Boulevard. There he was more orderly, playing the host at parties and lavishly tipping the help. But he laughed a little too hard and drank a little too much, and he had trouble remembering little things and kept forgetting big ones. Disturbed and frightened, he checked into a Los Angeles hospital, where he dried out and followed a strict diet. Ten days later Desi checked himself out, determined to show everyone that the old spring was back in his step. When he returned to his office at Desilu, the vice presidents and assistants gratefully acknowledged that the boss did seem extraordinary cheerful and lucid. In the afternoons he was as sensible as he had been in the mornings, and on the golf links he shaved several strokes off his game. Moreover, he made a fresh start by moving to a forty-acre ranch in Corona.

In the coming months Desi would need to be in good shape; the company he headed was beginning to lose its place as a major factor in TV production. Warner Brothers, Columbia (Screen Gems), Four Star, and Revue had entered the race, and Desi, used to being numero uno, looked up to see Desilu outclassed, outspent, and outdistanced. Only

The Untouchables remained in the Top Ten; Desilu's new sitcoms *Harrigan and Son* and *Guestward Ho!* would not make it past their first seasons, and even the once-popular *Ann Sothern Show* was beginning to falter. To be sure, the studio could make money by renting out space for such programs as *The Jack Benny Show, Lassie,* and *The Barbara Stanwyck Show,* but as a production house Desilu seemed to be losing its touch. To regain it, Desi went after big Hollywood names, hoping to star them in television vehicles: he had meetings with Burt Lancaster, Eva Gabor, Tony Curtis, Jane Wyman, John Wayne, and Mickey Rooney, among others. Nothing came to fruition.

As her ex-husband pushed on, Lucy made plans to trade the small screen for the big one, and the sound stage for the Broadway boards. The film was *The Facts of Life,* a comedy costarring Bob Hope. The theater piece was originally supposed to be an adaptation of "Big Blonde," a Dorothy Parker short story to be produced by Kermit Bloomgarten and directed by Morton Da Costa. The script displeased her, however. While it was being rewritten, she turned to another project, *Wildcat,* a musical created by an extraordinary confluence of talents. The book was by N. Richard Nash, writer of the 1954 smash *The Rainmaker.* Music and lyrics were by the new young team of Cy Coleman and Carolyn Leigh, who had written such Frank Sinatra favorites as "Witchcraft" and "The Best Is Yet to Come." The director would be Michael Kidd, who had choreographed the megahits *Guys and Dolls* and *Can-Can. Wildcat* was being touted as the story of "the Annie Oakley of the Oil Fields," and Lucy was reminded of another musical about another Annie Oakley. By playing the original Annie in *Annie Get Your Gun,* Ethel Merman became the biggest musical comedy star of the 1940s.

Coleman spoke about an early meeting with Lucy, a huge star who, he was dismayed to find, "sang like Jimmy Durante." He said: "I had a lot of trouble writing the opening number. Finally, one day Carolyn said, 'If it was for anybody who wasn't as famous as Lucy, if it was just somebody who sang like her, what would you write?' and I wrote 'Hey, Look Me Over,' right there." The day came when Coleman and Leigh played and sang Lucy the full score. "She was as nervous as I was," said a surprised Coleman. "In a strange way, we were auditioning for her, but she was auditioning for us. When we got to 'Hey, Look Me Over,' she jumped from her seat and said, 'I can sing that!' In our mutual fear we got into one of those eye locks, and through terror we got through the song for the first time. When she finally got through it, she said, 'Let's not do that again—my eyeballs hurt.' " Actually she did it again and again, and when she was certain that the notes were not out of her limited range, agreed to do the musical as soon as she finished her movie. Moreover, she promised to stay in the show for a minimum of a year and a half.

The Facts of Life had a ten-week shooting schedule, Lucy told a *TV Guide* reporter. "Then I go to New York with the two children, my mother, and two maids. We have a seven-room apartment on Sixty-ninth Street at Lexington. I'll start rehearsals right away for a Broadway show, *Wildcat*." Her emotions seesawed as she discussed the project. "I've never been on the stage before, except in *Dream Girl* years ago. But we always filmed *I Love Lucy* before a live audience. I knew a long time ago that I was eventually going to go to Broadway and that's one reason why we shot *Lucy* that way. But I'm still terrified. The contract for the play runs eighteen months. Maybe it will last that long. Maybe longer. And maybe it will last three days." Lucy chain-smoked through the interview. "Nervous habit. I don't inhale, never did. Just nerves," a reaction from the divorce. She picked up a framed picture of Desi in her dressing room. "Look at him," Lucy said in a throaty, wistful tone. "That's the way he looked ten years ago. He doesn't look like that now. He'll never look like that again."

Everything about the revised *Facts of Life* seemed to resonate with Lucy. The script not only gave her a chance to trade gags with Bob Hope, it recounted the sorrows and yearnings of middle age. In Hope's quip, *Facts* was "the story of two handicapped people who fall in love. Their handicaps are his wife and her husband." Supported by fine character actors (including Philip Ober, then in the process of getting divorced from Vivian Vance), Lucy played Kitty, the middle-aged wife of a genial bore, Jack Weaver (Don DeFore). Hope was Larry Gilbert, husband of the ennui-producing Mary, played by Ruth Hussey. Kitty and Larry enjoy each other's company and make many adulterous plans, all of which go amusingly awry. "Am I really doing this?" Kitty asks herself en route to an assignation. "Me? Pasadena housewife, secretary of the PTA, den mother of the Cub Scouts. Have I really come to Monterey to spend a weekend with the husband of my best friend?" Their desires unconsummated, the frustrated and guilt-ridden lovers finally forsake their schemes and philosophically return to their respective spouses.

To demonstrate that he harbored no hard feelings toward Lucy, Desi agreed to coproduce the United Artists movie along with Hope. The official production company was headed by writer Norman Panama and director Melvin Frank. On June 2, 1960, just before filming began, the studio hosted a luncheon for the press. The head of Desilu made an appearance, wished the project well, and planted a kiss on his ex-wife. She returned his smile to generous applause. An aura of good feeling enveloped the project. It was not to last.

On July 1, during a boating scene, Lucy lost her footing and fell hard. An ambulance whisked her to Cedars of Lebanon Hospital to be treated for disfiguring leg and facial bruises. Desi heard the news, sped to her room, and refused to leave until doctors assured him that Lucy's injuries were not life-threatening. That evening he sent Hope a telegram: "I played straight man to her for nine years and never pushed her—why couldn't you control yourself?" One day after Lucy's accident, Melvin Frank broke his ankle during a golf tournament. A few weeks later, Don DeFore strained his back. Returned to work, Lucy complained about the crowded sound stage. "How do you get out of this firetrap?" she cracked. Several nights later the set went up in flames. Several more minor disasters occurred, including a hand injury to Hope. He concluded, "This film should have been shot at Cedars." Nevertheless, disasters and all, *The Facts of Life* managed to conclude on schedule.

As soon as she shook off a case of pneumonia, Lucy headed east with Lucie and Desi IV. Whenever she appeared in public, reporters continued to ask personal questions, and she continued to resent them. A journalist who demanded to know whether she would marry again was met with a glare, a long pause, and a monosyllabic "No!" Another, who inquired whether she was happy, received a curt answer: "Not yet. I will be. I've been humiliated. That's not easy for a woman."

Yet the man who had humiliated her was also one of her bulwarks when the *Wildcat* team went looking for producers. One night, said Nash, Desi called from Los Angeles after reading the script: " 'I love *thees thin!* I want to produce it!' It was all packaged and literally taken out of my hands. The final product had *nothing* to do with what my original intentions had been." *Wildcat* had started out as the tale of a nineteen-year-old oil prospector, supported by her elder sister in a comic role. The day that director-choreographer Michael Kidd first brought up the name of Lucille Ball, Nash naturally assumed that she would play the smaller part. Desilu's $400,000 altered conditions and forced the author back to his desk, where he made intensive rewrites, changing the focus and excising any references to age. The star playing Wildcat Jackson, a pretty oil speculator costumed in blue dungarees and bright red hair, would need a special kind of leading man. He must either be (A) famous enough to attract ticket buyers on his own, or (B) obscure enough to cede the marquee to Miss Ball. First the producers tried A, offering the role to Kirk Douglas, who was both too short and too expensive, and Gene Barry, who was committed to his hit TV series, *Bat Masterson.* Then they tried B, securing the services of a tall, good-looking song-and-dance man, Keith Andes. The actor had played opposite Marilyn Monroe in *Clash by Night,* but could hardly be considered a box office draw. Lucy, and Lucy alone, would have that distinction.

With everything bubbling along to her satisfaction, she settled into Imperial House on East Sixty-ninth Street with her son and daughter and their nanny, Willie Mae Barker. Lucy had the apartment decorated in vivid colors, California-style. She placed the children in private Catholic schools—Lucie in Marymount, Desi IV in St. David's—and described them to the press as "happy, adjusted kids" grateful to be in New York. She went into rehearsals, "mad for everyone in the company of *Wildcat.*"

For Lucy to see the children in this light required an extraordinary amount of self-deception and denial. Of all people, the fatherless girl should have known the importance of paternal figures. She should also have known how vital it was to keep and maintain roots in a young child's life. Instead, she thought mostly in terms of career rather than motherhood. She pulled Lucie and Desi IV along in her slipstream, scarcely considering what they might need or feel. In the ensuing months, Desi IV became the target of school bullies; neighbors could hear him in the evenings angrily banging away on his set of drums. Lucie was happier at Marymount, but described the experience of relocation as "very traumatic, leaving my friends, being ripped away from my father." She noted: "I only remember those New York months as gray. The trees were gray, the sky was gray, the buildings were gray."

Work on *Wildcat* had scarcely begun when Lucy read a disturbing item in *Variety.* Martin Leeds, who had been the real force behind the daily operations at Desilu, was leaving the company. However unwittingly, Lucy had a hand in this breakup. During the first weeks of her

New York sojourn Desi backslid to alcoholism. Leeds had complained via phone to Lucy, who agreed, "We've gotta do something about it." The "something" was a de facto takeover, with Leeds going around Desi to make corporate and financial decisions. Lucy confided as much to friends who leaked like a colander, and word got back to Desi. He telephoned Leeds one morning at three, totally inebriated, and asked why the executive had reversed a decision Desi had made earlier in the week. "Because you were wrong," came the irritable reply. "Then," said Desi, "you're fired." Nothing further needed to be said; their business relationship was finished. Leeds had helped Desilu to its glory days, but that was when he esteemed his employer. Now he regarded him, with sorrow, as an irresponsible drunk. The vice president in charge of production had four years left on his contract. He took half of his entitlement—"I could never hurt this man," Leeds said defensively—and never looked back.

But Lucy was too far away to have much influence on the company's future, and she was too exhausted to spend much time worrying about it. Through the long run of *I Love Lucy* she had worked a four-day week; in New York she was on her feet—learning lines, lyrics, melodies, steps—six out of seven days, and sometimes Sundays as well. The demands of rehearsal are difficult enough for young Broadway gypsies; for a newcomer nearing fifty they were nearly insuperable. Kidd felt that for all of Lucy's inexperience and flaws, she had "an amazing ability to know what was going on onstage at all times." Lucy failed to return the compliment. The director, she was to say, "didn't direct me into the show, he directed the show around me." For other actresses this might have been a flattering idea; for Lucy it was disconcerting, and for *Wildcat,* destructive.

The Philadelphia tryout was met with tepid laughter and mild applause, except when Lucy stepped out of character and reverted to the Ricardo persona: on one occasion she asked a supporting player in funny costume, "Say, do you know a fellow named Fred Mertz?" Recalled the star, "The slightest bit of *Lucy* that I would throw in would get the reaction I was looking for." But this triumph of personality came at a cost; the show's "through line"—its plot and drive—were leached away. Lucy blamed Nash: "Nothing that man wrote got any laughs, and I was getting desperate and Kidd didn't tell me not to, so I did." The out-of-town *Variety* review helped to buck up her spirits: "Miss Ball sings acceptably, dances with spirit, shines as a comedienne, and even does a couple of dramatic scenes with ease and polish." But Philadelphia was a long way from New York and there was much work to be done on the book and score.

Still under treatment for the contusions she had received on *The Facts of Life,* Lucy remained on antibiotics. They depleted her physical and mental energies when she needed them most. Changes had to be memorized on a nightly basis, and as if these were not complicated enough, the choreography called for her to be vigorously whirled and tossed by Andes and members of the chorus. On more than one occasion the dizzy, disoriented star held up her hand and stopped in mid-performance to let the audience know she had lost her place in the dialogue or the lyrics, and needed to begin the scene again. Ironically, the one stalwart friend she had was Desi, who journeyed to Philadelphia, watched the show, and gave advice to Kidd and Nash. The writer reluctantly allowed that Desi "had good dramatic instincts." On Thanksgiving Desi thrilled theatergoers by going to the apron of the stage and throwing Lucy an orchid as she took her curtain call. "The least you could have done was take the pins out!" she shouted, pleased with herself for the first time in weeks.

But Desi could not memorize Lucy's new numbers or boost her flagging energies. Each night the exhaustion seemed to be getting harder and harder to shake off, and by the time the show was deemed ready for Broadway Lucy had grown impatient with almost everyone—especially members of the press. Don Ross, a reporter for the *New York Herald Tribune,* considered her "hard-boiled" when the unsmiling actress showed up for his interview at the 1918 Restaurant on Chestnut Street. Under her mink coat Lucy wore a black jacket and pants, and the famous red hair was hidden beneath a blue kerchief. Hardly had she begun her chianti on the rocks when she complained to the management, "Goddam it, why don't they make tables so you can put your legs under them?" Ross thought it "difficult to detect any spiritual qualities in the Ball public personality." Happily, she had brought along DeDe and the children and mugged at them during the interview, forcing the concession that "when she looks at Lucie and Desi IV and listens to their gabble, her hard public face turns almost soft and misty."

What Ross did not know, and did not care to investigate, was Lucy's backstage personality. The cast of *Wildcat* saw an entirely different side of Lucille Ball, a woman who never pulled rank, and who cared extravagantly for her coworkers in the theater, as she had for her Desilu family. Television star Valerie Harper, starting out as a chorus girl in the musical, remembered the day that Lucy checked out the dressing rooms for the lesser players. "She said, 'Oh my God, what a dungeon! This is terrible! We gotta fix up the chorus dressing room.'" And when Lucy said "we" she included herself. "She had the place painted. She fought it through. She was very direct, very warm, very giving."

The critics felt that warmth on opening night, December 16, 1960, and almost to a man they showed affection and respect for the star. And almost to a man they held the show at arm's length. "As one who has loved Lucy even before she was Lucy," wrote Walter Kerr in the *Herald Tribune*, "—back in the days when she looked like a raffish but elegant sea horse in many an RKO picture—I'm deeply, deeply confused. Is it simply the unsmiling libretto of N. Richard Nash? Can it be that director Michael Kidd hasn't been able to find a big enough outlet for Miss Ball's zanier talents? There's a moment in which we catch a glimpse of the pop-eyed clown we know best: a moment in which she takes a big slug of tea and comes out of it with the spoon in her mouth. But these cartoon-like goodies are few. . . . It's the time, it's the place, where's the girl?" In the *Times*, Howard Taubman complained of a "tame *Wildcat*," noted the boisterous enthusiasm of Lucy fans in the opening-night audience, praised the song "Hey, Look Me Over," and then excoriated what he had just seen: "*Wildcat* went prospecting for Broadway oil but drilled a dry hole." At the end Taubman went soft, as if he needed to reassure the poor woman who played Wildcat Jackson: "Don't you care, Miss Ball. They all still love Lucy—and you, too." *Variety* called the show a "failure" and predicted that its duration depended entirely on "how long Miss Ball and the advance sale can keep *Wildcat* running at the Alvin." *Variety*'s reviewer also threw a bouquet to accompany his brickbats: "One further word about Lucille Ball: she should come again another time."

Desi answered the critics in the revered Broadway tradition: he ran a full-page ad in *Variety* using unattributed quotes ("Hoopla and boffola to satisfy the millions who love Lucy." "*Wildcat* proves a gusher!") along with a photograph of avid patrons waiting in line to buy tickets. The promotion worked. After nearly every show hundreds of fans waited for Lucy to show up. She never disappointed them; their collective energy and affection kept her engine running. Indeed, they may have caused her to go into overdrive. She stayed up for hours after every performance, unable to relax. On Wednesdays, instead of taking a break between matinee and evening performances, she went out to cocktail parties and dinner. Nothing seemed to calm her down. Was the script still inadequate? Did Nash let her down by failing to supply enough gags? Well, then, Bob and Madelyn could fix it. She brought them in with Nash's permission. "Anything to keep Lucy happy," he said. "I know she is up there suffering." Madelyn Pugh Martin and Bob Carroll Jr. came to town and supplied a dozen opening jokes. "She had the most appalling experience," Nash recalled, not without some satisfaction. "Not one of the lines got a laugh." He and Michael Kidd went backstage to inform her: "It's a different medium, Lucy. It's early in the show, they can hardly hear you, they haven't accustomed themselves to the acoustics of the theater, to your voice coming over the orchestra." Nash observed: "She took out the lines instantly. That was a bad shock for her. In television, those lines had worked."

Other new lines did work, however, especially when she ad-libbed them. The show had one nonhuman actor, a Yorkshire terrier named Mousy. During a matinee, Mousy lost control onstage. Mops and brooms happened to be featured in that number, so Lucy kept singing and dancing as she acted the part of pooper-scooper. "It's in the small print in my contract," she told the audience in her best Lucy Ricardo mode. "I have to clean up the dog shit!" The explosions of laughter were like the ones she used to get on *Lucy.*

For the most part, though, the yocks were hard to come by. Lucy got colds easily and couldn't shake them off. The slightest difficulty drove her to tantrums and crying jags. She began, rather irrationally, to miss Desi, to wonder whether even now a reconciliation was possible. Evidently he felt the same way; there was a tentative proposal of remarriage. Her yearning intensified until a retired couple came backstage and introduced themselves. Instead of wanting an autograph, they had something to give Lucy. During a recent vacation in Hawaii they came across an object shining in the sand. "The lady opened her purse and pulled out a gold chain with a Saint Christopher medal and a wedding ring," Lucy told a friend. "I looked at the ring and it read, 'To Desi with love from Lucy.' I thanked them, kissed them both, and then closed the door and wept. Just closed the door and wept. It's funny, but it was then that I knew it was really over. Having that ring in my hands didn't bring the good times back to me, it brought the terrible times back, and I knew it was right. I knew Desi and I could be friends, but that we shouldn't be married."

Early in February, *Variety* stated what the rest of Broadway already knew: *Wildcat* had to shut down for "an abrupt fortnight's layoff to permit star Lucille Ball to take a Florida rest on the advice of her doctor. Miss Ball has been suffering from a virus and chronic fatigue." Lucy returned to the show as promised, after appearing on *The Ed Sullivan Show* to sing *Wildcat*'s best number, "Hey, Look Me Over," but she was not the same woman who opened the show a couple of months back. On Sundays, to bolster her flagging spirits, she attended services at Marble Collegiate Church. There the celebrity-hunting Norman Vincent Peale dispensed commonsense advice. Lucy supplemented it with readings from *The Art of Selfishness,* by the self-styled psychology writer David Seabury. Students of Ayn Rand would recognize the similarity to that author's approach: "Here is a mysterious contradiction. Those who toil for the good of others often lose the respect of those for whom they sacrifice. As we change, under the stress of helping, others may blame us for the lessening of our strength, health, ability to cope and our charm." For Lucy's bruised ego, here was the perfect salve, the assurance that she had no reason to feel guilty about taking care of Number One. "This little book revolutionized my life," she would maintain. "It taught me to worry less about all the outside factors in my life and take command of *me.* I learned to subject everything in my life to these questions: is this *good* for *Lucy?* Does it fill my needs? Is it good for my health, my peace of mind? Does my conscience agree, does it give me a spiritual life?" A paragraph in which "my" comes up seven times, "me" three times, and "Lucy" and "I" on each indicates that altruism was not very high on her agenda just then. Yet all this self-absorption did little to fend off the terrors of ill health, of encroaching age, of the feeling that she was losing her place on the board. In the past she had been bolstered by her Los Angeles circle. New York offered no such intimates; she had to make do with her mother and with members of the *Wildcat* cast. Keith Andes served as an escort for a brief time; the fling concluded as fast as it began. A more lasting relationship was forged with supporting actress Paula Stewart, who played *Wildcat*'s younger sister. Stewart thought about appropriate gentlemen for Lucy and struck oil the evening she and her fiancé, comedian Jack Carter, brought along their friend Gary Morton. Morton (né Morton Goldaper) was a well-built, genial third-tier comedian who had come up the traditional route. He began spouting one-liners in Brooklyn, where his father drove a truck, then graduated to the Borscht Belt and small nightclubs, and finally appeared in larger venues including the Palace and Radio City Music Hall, where he was then performing. Morton usually sported a tan and a toupee, and on this night he sat back smoking and watching his date with some amusement. In between postures she loudly advertised her fatigue. He thought she needed to be taken down a peg or two, and when Lucy tossed a cigarette in his direction and ordered, "Light me," he threw the thing back in her direction and told her to light it herself. No one had spoken to Lucy like that in years. She laughed with a grudging admiration and asked how he earned his salary. "I'm a nightclub performer," Morton said. "What's your line?"

As the evening progressed, Lucy found herself intrigued more than attracted. "When I fell in love with Desi," she was to recall, "it was at first sight—my love for Gary was slow growth. I liked him before I loved him." They continued to see each other and to correspond in the winter of 1960–1961 without commitment on either side. Morton had out-of-town engagements, and Lucy continued to struggle in the role of Wildcat Jackson, unable to shake off exhaustion and various ailments. DeDe, who customarily kept her own counsel, felt obliged to speak out. "Lucille!" she advised her daughter. "The Man Upstairs is trying to tell you something!"

As usual, Lucy ignored the warning. She also paid no attention to another omen. In order to keep their star— and their show—going, the producers ordered an oxygen tank to be kept waiting in the wings. Lucy took hits from it between acts. Since she also took hits on cigarettes before, after, and sometimes during performances, however, any help she received was immediately neutralized. Hedda Hopper wrote about the night William Frawley attended a performance: "He created a minor sensation. 'It's Fred Mertz!' they all said. I went backstage to see Lucille when Bill came in. When he saw how thin Lucy was there were tears in his eyes."

On April 22, 1961, in the middle of a vigorous dance number called "Tippy Tippy Toes," Lucy collapsed onstage. Dancer Edith King reached out to break Lucy's fall—and fractured her own wrist in the process. From then on, every realist in the company of *Wildcat* knew that the end was near. Lucy's understudy, Betty Jane Watson, finished out the week while the producers scrambled to find a replacement star. They approached Gwen Verdon, Mitzi Gaynor, even Ginger Rogers. The women gave a uniform response: "Follow *Lucille Ball*. Are you *crazy?*" On May 24, Lucy gave her final Broadway performance. The next day a press release went out, guaranteeing ticket buyers that the star would rest up for eight or nine weeks, then reenter *Wildcat* on August 7. Lucy's return was crucial; at the time of the shutdown the advance sale was larger than it had been on opening day. Few personalities could have accomplished her feat: by dint of fame and grit she had made the critical barbs irrelevant; audiences came to the Alvin to see Lucille Ball, not Wildcat Jackson. For the first time, a television personality had proved to be an outsized box office draw.

*B*ut there would be no resumption. Lucy resigned in June, returning $165,000 of her own money to the box office. The sum would compensate for tickets that had been bought and would have to be returned. She had lost twenty-two pounds during the run and was now in a state of psychological depression and physical exhaustion. Upon hearing of Lucy's situation, Hedda Hopper wrote: "Let's hope Lucy stays in the hospital until she regains her health, strength, and peace of mind. Lucy's one of the most vital girls I know but so weak now she can scarcely hold a teacup."

Hedda was misinformed. Lucy was not in the hospital. She had settled on a new panacea. The way to escape trouble, she had concluded, was not merely to quit Hollywood or New York, but to leave the whole country behind her. She would set up residence in Switzerland, settle there for a while with the children. There was plenty of money in the bank. She was nearing the half-century mark. Who needed all this show business madness, this sickness of the body and soul? "I felt so awful," Lucy wrote in her autobiography, "I honestly thought I was going to die. I flew to London and eventually to Capri and Rome, determined to die in a scenic atmosphere."

She returned to Beverly Hills with DeDe and the children, slightly improved but still dispirited, determined to sell the houses and get the hell out of town. Somehow, though, she could not break away. Friendships were resumed, parties attended. And then there was Gary Morton, who showed up one day and settled into the guest house for several weeks. Lucy took him to a series of social gatherings where he said he felt like "some strange lamp" with people circling around and examining him from every angle. One of them was Desi himself, who annoyed his ex-wife by expressing approval of her new man. Other reports were not so favorable. Friends noted that, like Desi Arnaz, Gary Morton was younger than Lucy by six years; unlike Desi, however, he was very much a second banana who made a decent living but hardly the kind of income Lucy earned just by collecting dividends from Desilu. And he was Jewish; that would bring additional complications in the unlikely event that they married. It was widely assumed that this would be a short-lived affair, a rebound Lucy needed after the depressing divorce and the abrupt close of *Wildcat*.

Minds were changed after several weeks, when Lucy began to perk up and regain the weight she had lost—and even put on a few extra pounds. Clearly she was recovering, and Gary seemed to be the main cause of her happiness. His stay at the guest house lengthened. Speculation began. Lucy did a good job of pretending to be a truly independent soul, ordering friends not to mention the word "marriage" in her presence. A canny reporter heard the scuttlebutt and cornered her one day: "I'd like to bet that you will marry Gary Morton." Lucy countered: "You'll lose your money. Don't bet. It's nice this way." Lucy was kidding the journalist, and herself. She dreaded the approach of fifty and of finishing her life, as she had once confided in cousin Cleo, "loaded and lonely."

DeDe had very little use for men; one had died on her, the other had been a crank and a loser. Yet she knew Lucy was not quite her mother's daughter: she needed a man around, a reliable one this time, someone whose ego could be subordinate to a star's. No more famous men; no more egotists; no more boozers. Gary looked to be a viable candidate, and he might just be Lucy's last, best chance. Here was a comedian who was neither a loser nor a headliner, who had never met a payroll, never run a studio, never dominated a scene. He had been peripatetic since early manhood; his sole attempt at marriage had lasted less than a year and ended in an annulment. He was not much of a drinker or seducer and had no particular interest in the business end of things. Amiable, honest, a good listener, and something of a recessive personality, Morton was, in essence, the anti-Desi. If only some way could be found to make certain that the suitor wasn't a fortune hunter, he just might make a fine second husband for Lucille Ball.

The first time Gary brought up the idea of marriage Lucy deflected his proposal. DeDe surprised her by saying, "You shouldn't let that guy get away." The second time he proposed was on a plane headed to New

York. Gary was booked to play the Copacabana, and Lucy planned to make her first TV appearance since *Wildcat,* doing a turn with Henry Fonda.

"Lucy, what are we waiting for?" Gary asked.

"Well, are you prepared for any swipes that they might take at you? What if they call you Mr. Ball?"

"Who are *they*?"

She sat silent. Perhaps "they" were just an insubstantial fear, like so many of her recent worries. Straightening up, she said in a determined voice: "All right. If Dr. Norman Vincent Peale is free to marry us this week, we'll go ahead."

The reverend was of course free, and on November 19, 1961, Lucille Ball and Gary Morton exchanged vows at Marble Collegiate Church in a ceremony attended by DeDe and the children, flown in for the occasion. Informed about the imminent nuptials, Desi IV asked, "Will Daddy like it?" Lucy answered truthfully, "He wouldn't mind." The couple who had brought Lucy and Gary together, Paula Stewart and Jack Carter, were matron of honor and best man. (DeDe's concern about gold-digging was put to rest when Morton signed a prenuptial agreement and set up a separate bank account for his own expenses.)

Much symbolism, and not a little irony, attended the service. Lucy and Desi had also been married in November—twenty-one years before. When she and Gary applied for a license, Lucy wore the same outfit in which she had divorced Desi the previous year. She had done a little numerology when adding up the figures on her new marriage license and found that they equaled nineteen—"My lucky number!" she exclaimed to a reporter. It was not as lucky as she claimed; the nineteenth (and final) year of her first marriage had been one of unrelieved misery. She told other reporters, "I look forward to a nice, quiet life." Leaving the church, she and Gary had to follow in the wake of a flying wedge of New York City policemen. The cops protected the couple from a crowd of fifteen hundred fans who wanted a glimpse, a touch, or a piece of clothing from their favorite.

The Mortons started out separately. He went off to Palm Springs, where he was booked to play a nightclub. Lucy stayed in New York to rehearse for *The Good Years,* a CBS special costarring her old colleagues Henry Fonda and Margaret Hamilton and featuring the new comedian Mort Sahl. Based on *The Good Years: From 1900 to the First World War,* the nostalgic history by Walter Lord, the program looked back with affection on silent-movie serials, prohibition, and vaudeville. In various sketches Lucy sang and danced with and without Fonda, and acted the part of a reprobate, hauled into court as a public nuisance.

The show aired on January 12, 1962. It was hardly her finest sixty minutes. Geoffrey Mark Fidelman speculates that Lucy was not producer Leland Hayward's ideal: "It is most likely that Mary Martin was the first choice, as she had appeared in several of Hayward's productions." But Martin was doing eight shows a week as the centerpiece of *The Sound of Music* on Broadway, and Ball and Fonda were pals. (Fonda liked to joke that had the two Hollywood hopefuls gotten along back in the 1930s he could have co-owned a studio called Henrilu.) So Lucy was chosen, and she gamely went along with Franklin Shaffner's direction. In the words of her hair stylist, Irma Kusely, "This was a dreadful show. Both Fonda and Lucille hated it. Lucille did not look well. She was still battling weight." She was also fighting the clock, and makeup artists could hide only so much. Yet she stayed away from the route so many middle-aged film and television stars had chosen. "Few people know it," Kusely added, "but she was not a candidate for plastic surgery due to her skin type. She literally had very thin skin which bruised easily. Surgery was out of the question."

But no one seemed to care about Lucille Ball's appearance or about the mediocrity of *The Good Years.* The news, as expressed on the cover of *Life,* said it all: LUCY'S BACK ON TV. Nothing else counted to the network or the viewers. Lucy wasn't so easily impressed. After all, she had been here before. To a publicist who asked about her future on the tube she responded: "I will never do another TV series. It couldn't top *I Love Lucy,* and I'd be foolish to try. In this business you have to know when to get off."

S he had already been the undisputed First Lady of TV, and, for better or worse, a Broadway diva. She had even starred in radio. Only one medium remained for Lucy to dominate. She had never come close to the first rank of film stars, and it was much too late for ingenue parts. But there was still time for her to be a character lead, the comic equivalent of Bette Davis or Joan Crawford. Several ideas were batted around. Columbia offered a costarring role in *The Great Sebastians,* a

Broadway hit when the Lunts appeared in it. An independent producer had the notion of casting Lucy as a congenital liar opposite James Cagney as her psychiatrist in the comedy *Here Lies Ruthie Adams*. Lucy's favorites, Bob Carroll and Madelyn Pugh Martin, were preparing the script for *Full House,* concerning the romance of a widow with eight children and a widower with ten. And James Kirkwood's *There Must Be a Pony,* a drama about his mother, a silent-movie actress, briefly exerted some appeal. Lucy considered all projects, then opted for a Bob Hope vehicle, *Critic's Choice.* Ira Levin's comedy was based loosely on the conflict of theater critic Walter Kerr and his wife, playwright Jean Kerr, who had written the vastly successful *Mary, Mary*—a play he was forced to review.

The decision did much to restore Lucy's morale, as did her new husband. Gary Morton was assiduously attentive at home and at social events. At the same time, he tried to maintain a distance financially, playing club dates and feeding a personal bank account with his earnings. (That money, however, was soon supplemented by unsolicited contributions from a generous wife.) Though Gary settled into Lucy's home and circle, he made a point of asserting his own style and personality, even imposing some of it on the household cuisine—Lucy was making the trip, said her friends, from Cuban to Reuben. In fact, this voyage was not as new as it seemed; in a strange way she had always been subject to Jewish influence. Way back in the Celoron days there were the owners of Lerner's department store; in Manhattan there was Hattie Carnegie, née Henriette Kannengiser. In the early Hollywood days there was Eddie Cantor, then the studio heads like Sam Goldwyn and David Selznick whom she regarded as "papas." In television there were Jess Oppenheimer and William Paley. In the first few decades of the twentieth century, the provincial towns of upstate New York were not know for their philo-Semitism. Yet Lucy had never shown the slightest bias against any group, no matter what the feelings of her friends and neighbors. "My mother," observed Lucie Arnaz, "was a rebel wherever she went, and if she sensed prejudice around her she always went the other way." And then, of course, there was the example of Grandpa Fred. Lucy's dissidence was a matter of both nature and nurture.

In this intricately structured household Morton would remain Jewish, Lucy would identify herself as Protestant, and Lucie and Desi IV would continue to be Catholic. The separation of church and family worked for the adults; for the children it was no guarantee of happiness. Lucy entered her younger child in St. John's Military Academy in Los Angeles, only to find that the boy was totally out of his element. "He was having nightmares. He couldn't sleep. I said, 'What's the matter with you?' And he said, 'They gave me detention for tying a shoelace during drill when I was supposed to be at attention.'" Lucy learned that "thirteen-year-old 'generals' were giving these bullying orders." She took Desi IV out of yet another school and mentioned the move to reporters, exacerbating the situation. This was the time to address her son's resentments, but other matters and other people had priority. In a way, Morton was Lucy's newest child now. In the coming years he would receive more and more attention from her; his toys were the expensive watches (Rolex, Patek Philippe) and cars (Mercedes-Benz, Rolls-Royce) formerly out of his price range. But what did that matter, she responded when a critical friend pointed out the vast discrepancy between his finances and hers. Gary didn't chase girls, didn't booze, was unfailingly polite, a real gentleman. She had had the other kind, and enough was too much, thank you just the same.

Lucy's high income was not guaranteed. As vice president of Desilu she did almost nothing. But she was kept abreast of the company's fiscal condition, and in 1962 it was not exactly robust. The company had peaked in 1957, when its shows dominated the television schedule. Now Desilu had but one dominant series, *The Untouchables,* which had recently come under fire from parents for its graphic violence, and from Italian-American groups for its stereotypical Mafia villains. The Federation of Italian-American Democratic Organizations had boycotted the show's sponsor, and eventually the Liggett & Meyers Tobacco Company succumbed to pressure and withdrew its sponsorship. After that, no less a personage than Frank Sinatra expressed his displeasure. In one of its let's-you-and-him-fight pieces, *Variety* noted that Sinatra and Arnaz almost came to blows at Desi's Indian Wells Hotel when Frank looked him up at midnight to discuss the depiction of Italians as ruthless mobsters on the *Untouchables* programs.

The truth was a little more graphic and a lot more absurd. On an April evening in Palm Springs, Sinatra told friends, "I'm going to kill that Cuban prick." With that aim in mind, according to his hostile biographer, Kitty Kelley, Sinatra drove to Indian Wells, accompanied by actress Dorothy Provine, composer Jimmy Van Heusen, and Van Heusen's date. Desi, flanked by two large Italian-American bodyguards, entered the lounge. Obviously drunk, he spotted Sinatra and yelled, "Hi ya, dago." Desi assumed that Sinatra was at the place to have a good time, and blithely wove his way to the table. Tight-jawed, Sinatra told Desi what and his friends thought of *The Untouchables* and its ethnic bias. Desi exploded: "What do you want me to do— make them all Jews?" A muttered argument began. Sinatra admitted that he had never actually seen the program, but maintained that he was correct because, "I *always* know what I'm talking about. That's how I got where I am."

Desi gave a derisive laugh. The Cuban accent was more pronounced when he was liquored up. "Oh, yeah? Well, I remember when you couldn't get a yob. Couldn't get a yob. So why don't you forget all this bullshit and just have your drinks and enjoy yourself. Stop getting your nose in where it doesn't belong, you and your so-called friends."

"Unruffled," Kelley maintains, "Desi meandered back to the bar with the two bodyguards, leaving Frank full of unspent bluster. Obviously embarrassed, he looked around the table and said, 'I couldn't just hit him. We've been pals for too long.' " Sinatra eventually expressed his hostility in a nonviolent manner, relocating his production company from the Desilu lot to the Samuel Goldwyn studios.

In this fallow period Desilu's real estate holdings seemed more valuable than the company's television products—weary programs like *The Texan* and *Guestward Ho!* So it was not a surprise to see the former Arnazes in conference, not to discuss the sunny days of their marriage but to plan a new program using the talents of Lucille Ball. "They asked me to save the studio," Lucy was to claim with permissible exaggeration. "I wondered if there was anything to save. The only salable product we had was Lucy."

Desilu boasted quite a few assets besides its cofounder, but none with her universal appeal. Still, she could no longer represent herself as Mrs. Ricky Ricardo. How should she be made presentable to a public still unsettled by her divorce and remarriage? Many consultations later, it was announced that Lucille Ball would star in a new half-hour series, *The Lucy Show.* It would be based on *Life without George,* Irene Kampen's novel woven around the life of a suburban divorcée. By the time the writers finished with it, Madelyn Pugh Martin and the three Bobs, Carroll, Schiller, and Weiskopf, had turned the star into a widow. The change of her status was vital; the public knew the fictive Lucy as a happily married woman. In real life the only way she could divest herself of Desi was to divorce him; in her screen life the only way to get rid of her husband was to bury him. Lucy retained her Christian name, but her surname was now Carmichael. "Lucille could be very superstitious," said actress Carole Cook. "She liked the letters 'ar' together. That's part of the reason for the name 'Carmichael.' . . . I reminded her once that she had done pretty well with the name Lucille Ball, but she said, 'Yeah, but I didn't do *really* well until my name was ARnaz and RicARdo.' "

Lucy's Mrs. Carmichael is a somewhat ditsy inhabitant of Westchester, New York, who rents rooms to her friend, divorcée Vivian Bagley. (Vivian Vance, who had foresworn Hollywood upon marriage to her fourth, and much younger, husband, the editor–literary agent John Dodds, was enticed out of Connecticut retirement to play the part. William Frawley had left Desilu to appear as a regular in the sitcom *My Three Sons*.) Both women have children: Lucy a teenage daughter, Chris, and a younger son, Jerry. Vivian has a preteen son, Sherman.

In the first episode, broadcast October 1, 1962, Lucy bounces around on a trampoline. Subsequent adventures involve the widow Carmichael in her son's school football game, acquiring a sheep to trim the lawn, attempting to become an astronaut, and climbing into a kangaroo outfit. The show had the female ingredients of *I Love Lucy*, but that was all it had. Audiences knew that Lucille Ball was not Lucy Carmichael. They were keenly aware that she was not a widow and that she was too old to be repeating 1950s shtick, mugging and flashing her innocent blue eyes whenever plans went awry. With each show Lucy's worries intensified. Was she was on a fool's errand, trying to induce lightning to strike twice at the same studio? Candy Moore, who played Chris, described her screen mother: "I would talk to her sometimes before the show. It was scary—she'd be looking at me, and she wouldn't hear a word I said. She was tuned in to her own thoughts, and she'd be looking right through me." The fear was infectious: "Vivian was a nervous wreck, too. They were buzzing on adrenaline, they were so scared."

Given these terrors, the first batch of episodes proved to be much better than Lucy expected, although things went downhill rapidly from there. Broadcast the same night of the week as *I Love Lucy* (though a half hour earlier), *The Lucy Show* acquired an audience of nostalgia buffs and new viewers. *Variety* spoke for them: "Lucille Ball is back and welcome." Playing the good sport, Desi placed an institutional ad in the show-business paper, using snippets of favorable reviews surrounding a caricature of himself making a mock complaint: "How do you like that—they didn't even miss me!" The *Hollywood Reporter* spoke for the disappointed fans: "It's going to take a lot of getting-used-to-Lucy without Desi." His absence was being felt with every show, "tribute indeed to any comedian." A vague attempt was made to replace Desi with Lucy Carmichael's drop-in suitor, an affable, ineffectual airline pilot played by Dick Martin. It was not convincing. As the program went on, wisecracking insiders, noticing the lack of significant males, used *The Dick Van Dyke Show* as a reference. They called Lucy's program the "Dyke Sans Dick Show" and, more explicitly, the "Dyke Show Sans Dicks."

The production values were not all they could have been, either. The camera work was professional enough, as were the backgrounds and costumes, most of which not only flattered a heavily made-up Lucy but allowed Vivian to exhibit a little glamour of her own. The chief difficulty lay in Desilu's (i.e., Desi's) shortsightedness. In Desi's opinion, comedy was "all black or all white" anyway: "It's either funny or it's not." Why would an audience laugh any harder because a show was in shades of yellow, red, and blue? Like many others in the industry, he failed to realize that after Walt Disney's *Wonderful World of Color* debuted in the fall of 1961, a revolution was under way. *Fortune* magazine predicted that one in three homes (18 million viewers) would soon own a color set, and the year Lucy came back to prime time, RCA's board chairman predicted that "it won't be very long before color television will be a mass item of commerce." Yet at a Desilu stockholders' meeting in 1962, Desi informed investors that he had no intention of filming *The Lucy Show* in color. In his opinion, "she's just as funny in black-and-white."

In point of fact, he was correct. As we will see, Desi's commercial misjudgment turned out to be the ultimate making of Lucille Ball. But he could not know that; at the time, his statement seemed symptomatic of a general picture of inattention, for once again drinking had taken over his life. In *Desilu,* their detailed history of the company, Coyne Steven Sanders and Tom Gilbert cite several occasions on which Desi couldn't control his behavior, even with the children. "At Del Mar, he was teaching little Desi how to shoot a gun. The poor kid wasn't doing it right. His dad just lit into him, yelling, 'You motherfucker, can't you do anything?'" And Lucie remembered the times when her father "wouldn't understand things clearly. He would misunderstand situations. He would think people were talking about him. He would hear something and think he heard something else. When it was at its worst, he would blow up. If the TV was on too late, and it was bedtime, instead of saying, 'It's bedtime,' doors would crash. It was awful. It was terrible. Then he'd be terrifically sorry and feel awful. After I got a little older, I stopped going down there."

In a complicated chicken-and-egg situation, it was impossible to tell whether Desi drank because his company was faltering, or whether Desilu was in a slump because its president was an alcoholic. All that was certain was that something had to change.

Newton Minow, appointed chairman of the Federal Communications Commission by President John F. Kennedy, had warned that U.S. viewers were facing "a vast wasteland" every night. Even so, he had to concede, "When television is good, nothing—not the theater, not the magazines or newspapers—nothing is better." The early 1960s offered an opening for creative producers to flourish in the week-wide desert of *The Jetsons, I've Got a Secret, I'm Dickens—He's Fenster, Dennis the Menace, Laramie,* and *Sing Along with Mitch.* Many of them did, but not Desi, who had lost his focus and attention to detail. He was ill and burned out, an old man at forty-five. He had a last hurrah, billboarding his plans for the upcoming 1963–1964 season. Desilu would produce a game show; a TV series based on Cecil B. DeMille's all-star circus spectacular, *The Greatest Show on Earth;* spin-offs of *The Untouchables;* and more situation comedies starring the likes of Ethel Merman and Glynis Johns.

That was the reason why an announcement from Desilu on Friday, November 9, 1962, shocked the industry. Desi was abruptly leaving the company he had founded, selling out to his ex-wife and heading for retirement. Insiders knew that the drama could have ended no other way. The stock had fallen from a high of $20 per share to $7. The company was in debt, and in a literal and figurative sense Desi no longer had the stomach to engineer a turnaround. In point of fact, he was responsible for the current status of Desilu Productions. When the company went public in December 1958, the Arnazes had signed an agreement. Should the time come when either wanted to quit, one partner would have the right buy the other out. Desi, embittered but weary, and in a much steeper decline than Desilu, was ready to go. But he needed money to live in style once his regular income was gone.

With the help of Mickey Rudin, Lucy, the vice president, borrowed $3 million from City National Bank and bought the president's shares—52 percent of the total outstanding stock. Depressed as it was, Lucy's advisers believed she was still getting a bargain.

Desi insisted that he had been planning on early retirement all along, and he posed for the press wearing a tight smile. All feeling seemed to have vanished from his face and from his outlook. And, indeed, when he left the company for the last time he paused only long enough to take a picture cube with photos of Lucie and Desi IV from his desk. Everything else was left in place. He wanted no part of the studio anymore. But Lucy still felt sentimental; she couldn't bear to think of Desilu without him. She worked out a rationale for the press. "Desi has wanted to sell out for five years," she claimed, "and I had first refusal on the stock. It's a big and wonderful company—the real estate alone is worth six million—and I didn't want to close up shop and hand over my shares to a stranger." Besides, she added, "if I get in a jam I can always call up Desi and ask him what he'd do." Even now, remarried and resettled, the first woman to head a major Hollywood studio since Mary Pickford produced her own pictures in the silent era, Lucy could not cut the cord.

"What are you trying to do, ruin my career?"

SHE HASN'T even got her name on the door," wrote the admiring *New York Times* reporter Gilbert Milstein after a tour of Desilu. Essentially, Milstein found, the new president, Lucille Ball, planned to get along and go along with the company's top executives—every one of them installed by Desi. Ed Holly remained in charge of finance and administration; W. Argyle Nelson, of production; Jerry Thorpe of programming. As in the past, the *Times* man continued, Lucille Ball "will turn up at the irregular meetings of her executives, listening a lot, saying little, signing papers, and making it known if she has definite ideas on anything."

Stockholders heard that Lucy was just hanging back, waiting for the right moment to turn into a hard-driving administrator. She put that rumor to rest in an interview: "I'm mad about this idea that I'm a workaholic. I spent some time researching words like 'workaholic' and 'perfectionist.' Workaholic is not what people think." She invited the press and the public to examine her history. "For God's sake, I always took long vacations, eight weeks at a time in Europe, with the kids, and I always had three-day weekends." The fact is, though, that those holidays were not for relaxation. As she inadvertently admitted, they were for delusion: "I thought that time away could save the marriage to Desi."

"My mother was uncomfortable with it all," Lucie Arnaz remembered. "Basically she was a performer, not a businesswoman. The trappings of power meant very little to her. She was happy to delegate authority." Privately Lucy hoped that everything and everyone would go on as before, leaving her with no decisions to make. But irrevocable changes had already occurred, and more were on the way. This was the season of divorce, for example. After the splits of the Arnazes and Vivian Vance and Philip Ober, cousin Cleo and her husband Ken Morgan separated, as did Madelyn Pugh and Quinn Martin. Lucy sometimes wondered, unhappily, if these breakups occurred because she and Desi had led the way.

Other seismic shifts served to make her days long and uneasy. Two Desilu shows were brought on with an avalanche of publicity. *Be Careful, My Love,* a comic mystery series starring Glynis Johns and Keith Andes, was produced by Jess Oppenheimer and looked to be a winner. And the long-awaited television adaptation of *The Greatest Show on Earth* seemed ideal for family viewing. Neither made it out of the 1963–1964 season. Moreover, *The Untouchables* was coming to the end of its historic run, and none of the spin-offs was working out. *Critic's Choice,* the movie Lucy made with Bob Hope upon her return from New York, was supposed to announce her triumphant reentry into cinema. Instead, the picture was a perfunctory and shallow version of the stage play, of more interest to curious Broadway fans than to filmgoers. It was met with yawns from the critics and indifference from a nationwide audience, even though Lucy outshone the script and the costar. Reluctantly she came to the conclusion that her professional life had been a restatement of children's tales from Aesop to *The Wizard of Oz.* In the end, all the wandering through various media had taught her that there was no place like home, and for Lucille Ball that home was the sound stage of a television studio.

Whatever Desi's personal shortcomings, he had always been a shrewd judge of scripts and a sage career counselor. His advice would have been welcome. But he was out of the picture now, emotionally and geographically distant, with little apparent interest in the business he had foresworn. In the tradition of playing up birthdays, he celebrated his forty-sixth in Las Vegas by taking a new wife, Edie Hirsch, a striking redhead who reminded many of Lucy. The best man was Dr. Marcus Rabwin, the physician who had rescued Desi from many incidents of ill health; Jimmy Durante's wife, Marge, served as matron of honor. To show the world there were no hard feelings, Lucy sent the couple a huge bunch of roses in the shape of a horseshoe. The card read, "You both picked a winner." That message contained more irony than Lucy knew.

Edie was the ex-wife of Clement Hirsch, who had made his fortune manufacturing and selling Kal Kan dog food. Suspicious that his wife was carrying on with Desi, Hirsch had hired detectives to follow the pair. Desi heard about the move and employed detectives of his own to follow the men who were shadowing *him*. The farce ended when Desi persuaded Edie to leave her husband and join him in a new and luxurious life. It was new all right, but far from luxurious. On their wedding night Desi spent more time at the roulette table than with his new wife. That was only the beginning; he was soon to squander thousands at casinos and racetracks. "He was a real addicted gambler," lamented Dr. Rabwin's wife, Marcella. "It was impossible to stop him."

Desi's reputation as a troublemaker stayed with him in the post-Lucy days. One day he received notice that he was being sued for thousands of dollars. The plaintiff was an old man who said Desi had punched him at the Thunderbird Country Club during an argument. Melvin Belli had been hired to represent the plaintiff, and Desi appeared to be in deep trouble. Then he discovered that there was an eyewitness to the argument. That person was willing to swear Desi had not thrown a single punch. Now confident, Desi refused to settle out of court and retained a local lawyer, Donald Brown, to defend him. "I knew he was explosive," said Brown, "and I knew he was an actor. And I told him that if I were Melvin Belli, I'd put him on the stand and try to get him to lose his temper in front of the jury. He said to me, 'Don't worry. When I get on the stand, I'm Ricky Ricardo.'" True to form, Belli did try to provoke Desi: he asked if he had cursed out the old man's wife, and used an expletive for illustration. "I am a Cuban gentleman," Desi responded. "I would never call a woman that. *You* I would call that." The answer brought down the house. Brown then summoned the star witness. "State your name," the bailiff directed. "James Francis Durante," came the hoarse reply. That, too, brought down the house—everyone recognized comedian Jimmy Durante. Just in from Las Vegas, he completed his exculpatory testimony and exited. The jury deliberated for seventeen minutes. The old man and his wife went away without a cent.

Lucy heard about this from afar, relieved for Desi's sake, and glad for herself—she was beyond the reach of a man who seemed to draw trouble the way he used to attract women. Logically, she should have installed her new husband at Desilu, as a welcome Desi Arnaz substitute. She astonished the employees, to say nothing of the town, by refusing to do so. Gary Morton went on doing what he did best, appearing at nightclubs, until Lucy realized that in one respect the second marriage was repeating the first—the man would be on the road too much of the time. During the first months of their marriage, Lucy had been only too happy to edit Gary's routines, encouraging him to emphasize a word to elicit a bigger laugh, fine-tuning his timing and approach. Now she demanded that he put a stop to his road shows, and he complied. His performances would be confined to audience warm-ups before the *Lucy* shows were filmed, and occasional appearances on the show.

A scratch golfer, Gary began to develop a course in the San Fernando Valley. The rest of the time he spent as a substitute father, attempting with some success to befriend Lucy's children, staying discreetly out of the way, and making sure that Lucy was treated with great deference. His first anniversary present to her was a tiny gold watch and matching gold pocketbook.

A tougher, less malleable Lucy went public in August of 1963 when, as Desilu's new president, she ran the stockholders' meeting. More than one of those present must have recalled Bob Hope's quip, "Who would have ever thought I'd kiss a company president—on the lips?" Lucy's informal outfit—purple-and-white-flowered dress and open-toed sandals—clashed with her cool demeanor and prepared statements. The company had experienced some hard times, she stated: it had lost money the previous year. Now, however, things were looking up. For the first quarter of 1963 Desilu enjoyed a gross income of $4.8 million, up $1.5 million for the same period in 1962. And there were big plans for the upcoming season, with a heavy emphasis on situation comedy, the genre Desilu knew best. At the end, a few attendees asked pro forma questions; one wanted to know whether she could handle her executive duties and still star in her own program. Assuming the authoritative tone of a woman capable of having it all, she assured everyone that she could do several tasks at the same time and succeed in all of them.

Only afterward, when the listeners and the press had gone, did Lucy drop her guard. Those who knew her best could see evidence of the humiliated child as she went around collecting pencils distributed to the stockholders when the meeting began. Gathering up writing instruments was an old habit; she did the same thing after board meetings. "I could never find out what she did with all those pencils," recalled Ed Holly.

Sitting atop her empire, Lucy remained just as threatened now as she was in the days of the HUAC hearings. The only difference was that back then she was bothered by the past; today she was threatened by the future. Who knew if any of these gaudy plans would really work? You could assure your investors and wow the networks, but in his own ungrammatical way Sam Goldwyn had it right: if people don't want to watch you, you can't stop them.

𝒲henever Goodman Ace was asked about Lucille Ball, his eyes rolled. The veteran writer had been hired by Desilu Productions to create a special for TV comedians, sponsored by General Foods. The 1963 experience was so unpleasant that he made detailed notes about it, and later published a vengeful piece in the *Saturday Review*. The program, he noted, ran in September, just before the second season of *The Lucy Show*. But it aired only after many revisions demanded by Lucy.

Ace had come up with the premise that General Foods was going to drop one of its five stars—Jack Benny, Danny Thomas, Garry Moore, Andy Griffith, and Lucille Ball. Onscreen, the comedians' nerves would be on edge, competition would ensue, and jokes would abound. Or so it was expected when the sponsor approved the script. Then, Ace wrote, "in the purified vernacular of television, all heck broke loose. Miss Ball found it highly incompatible with her public image to pretend that she would worry about losing her job . . . because everybody knows she is president of Desilu Productions. She wanted a slight change—the script to state explicitly that she is president of Desilu and she wasn't worried." The changes were of course made, much to the detriment of the show. Grumbled Ace, "If I play my cards right, I may never have to write for her again."

He was not the only writer to make Lucy an object of derision in 1963. At the end of the year, *Nobody Loves an Albatross* opened at the Lyceum Theatre in New York. The Broadway comedy was written by Ron Alexander, who had extensive experience in television. Essentially, his was a revenge play about demanding producers and the employees they overpaid and then humiliated. Robert Preston starred, with strong support from veteran actress Constance Ford in the telling role of Hildy Jones. The script describes Miss Jones: "She is one of those incredible women who, despite her 47 or 48 years, looks better than anybody else who is 30. Add to this the fact that Hildy has the talent of a clown and the steel trap mind of a tycoon, and you have a general picture."

In a typical exchange, a writer pleads for his job:

> NAT
> Hildy, darling, I created and wrote the private eye show for you.
>
> HILDY
> That's all you've come up with in a year and a half, it's not enough for all the money I'm paying you, Baby. (*Smiles*) The difference between you and me is you're a man of five-minute loyalties and I'm a woman of no loyalty at all. I'm staking your reputation on this show, Nat, and if it doesn't work, you won't either.
>
> NAT
> You're very kind.

To New York critics and audiences, Hildy was just an amusing character—she could have been any female executive. Hollywood insiders had a specific boss-lady in mind.

Without offering an apology for Lucy's behavior during this period, her daughter thought she knew the reasons for it. "The worst thing you can do is suppress pain," observed Lucie, "and she made a career out of suppressing all her pain." Lately the miseries of childhood had been supplanted by the very public divorce and the assumption of responsibility Lucy had never wanted. To be famous, yes, she had always desired that, and to be respected. But to be responsible? That was something else, something unplanned and intimidating. But if that was the hand she had been dealt, so be it. She would intimidate back. Small wonder that director John Frankenheimer seriously considered Lucy for the part of Laurence Harvey's lethal, oedipal mother in the thriller *The Manchurian Candidate,* before awarding it to Angela Lansbury.

On the set, a different person began to show up. Through the *I Love Lucy* years, the star had been difficult and querulous, particularly at first readings, seeking the right tempo and takes. But the persona she displayed at the filming of *The Lucy Show* was quite unlike what had gone before.

Vivian Vance, whom Lucy regarded as a reliable script doctor as well as a friend, was not immune to harsh critiques from the boss. For "Lucy and Viv Play Softball," the two actresses were to choose up sides with a bat. Lucy kept throwing the bat in a way that made it impossible for her partner to catch it cleanly. "I could catch it right if you threw it right," was the very reasonable complaint. Lucy walked off the set and Vivian started to cry. When Lucy returned she simply said, "Now, where were we?" refusing to recognize that anything untoward had taken place.

Others came under fire and were not let off so easily. Lucy made a point of challenging authority figures who were working for her. Candy Moore thought it was "unprofessional for her to yell at people in front of others—particularly the director Jack Donohue. It undermined his authority." But that was Lucy's aim. After the first day on any episode, everyone knew who was in charge.

The only actor immune from Lucy's barbs was Gale Gordon, her old companion from radio days, when he had played innumerable haughty, pompous bosses. Gordon was written into *The Lucy Show* during its second season, in order to supply Lucy with the foil she lacked in the first thirty-three episodes. For the next five seasons he played Theodore J. Mooney, manager of the local bank and trustee of Lucy's money. In a better part, or with different direction, Gordon might have given the show some depth and satiric bite. The skilled farceur had learned his trade from the cradle onward, watching his father, an American vaudeville quick-change artist, and his mother, a British actress. Born with a cleft palate, Gordon had worked on his diction until it was perfect for radio, and on his appearance until it was ideal for television. Lucy's affection and regard for him were absolute, so much so that she failed to see the shortcomings of the Mooney character—or of the character actor who portrayed him.

In the first place, Gordon was never encouraged to vary his interpretation. "When you are at full tilt right from the beginning," noted Maury Thompson, "you have nowhere to build to—nowhere to go." When Gordon consulted Thompson about his acting, the camera coordinator leveled with him. "He said, 'You know, other people have told me that. But I can't seem to help myself. I'll try to temper it.' But he couldn't." In the second place, through no fault of his own Gordon was incapable of filling the vacuum left when Desi departed. "A husband is a funny authority figure," Bob Schiller pointed out. "A banker, although certainly an authority figure, doesn't have any of the warmth, humor, or sex of a husband."

Very occasionally that season, Lucy relaxed, allowing comedy to imitate life. In the *Lucille Ball Comedy Hour* special "Mr. and Mrs.," she and Bob Hope played two actors hired for a job because the producer believes they're married. When Lucy falls in love with another man, and Bob with another woman, they contrive to get a bogus divorce. There was enough similarity between the fiction and the Lucy-Desi story to make Lucy play the part convincingly. Decked out in Edith Head costumes, she looked elegant and surprisingly young. The years fell away—at least temporarily—thanks to makeup expert Hal King, who used surgical tape and elastic foundations to provide the effects of a face-lift without the anguish of surgery. In "Lucy Conducts the Symphony," Jack Donohue relinquished his usual assignment as director in order to play a hapless orchestra conductor. When his percussionist comes down with stage fright, Lucy stands in, hilariously overriding the man on the podium. She was absolutely convincing in the role, and why not? Offscreen, she had been doing much the same thing to Donohue whenever he directed her.

The nadir of the season came in April 1964, with "Lucy Enters a Baking Contest." The episode was written by her longtime favorites, Bob Carroll Jr. and Madelyn Pugh Martin. Desilu had made them affluent, and both wished to retire while they were on top. Lucy had coaxed them back, only to savage their work on the final show of the season. "What are you trying to do," she demanded, *"ruin my career?"*

In a gesture she would come to regret, Lucy threw the script to the floor. The writers gathered up the papers and exited, speechless. To Lucy, this was outright insubordination; she assumed that they were walking out on the job, and more significantly, on her. Nobody walked out on Lucille Ball. The next morning, Bob and Madelyn found their possessions neatly boxed outside their office door. In another era Desi would have stepped in and broken the tension with a joke and a compliment and they all would have pretended nothing had happened. But there was no one capable of making peace, and the best writers Lucy would ever have took their leave of Desilu. It was as if she was trying, both consciously and unconsciously, to erase Desi's fingerprints from every door and desk no matter what the personal cost.

The cost, it developed, would be prohibitive. Not long after the writers left, there came other crucial exits. Among those to leave were producer Cy Howard, who had created the long-running comedy *My Friend Irma;* executive producer Elliott Lewis; and programming vice president Jerry Thorpe. Replacements were found—for example, network veteran Oscar Katz was hired away from CBS to replace Thorpe. But Desilu would never be the same, and other signs indicated that personal trouble lay ahead.

In May, Lucy, Gary, and the two children, Lucie and Desi IV—or, as he was now billed, Desi Jr.—performed together for the first time on the game show *Password.* It should have been a minor triumph. Lucy and Gary were predictably fluent and funny on the show. Desi Jr. was easy—a little too easy—before the cameras, saying, "This is one of my favorite experiences of all time." Lucie, on the other hand, was hyper and self-conscious. "I can't even watch the tapes of that show," she was to tell Geoffrey Mark Fidelman, historian of the *Lucy* shows. "It makes me sick. I was trying to copy-cat comics. It's sad. I was trying too hard. I want to go to that little girl to say, 'You don't have to do this!' I wanted to be like Mom and Gary—snap my fingers to the music and have snappy patter."

In the meantime, Vivian Vance let it be known that shuttling from Connecticut to Hollywood was getting to be more of a strain each time out. This was not a ploy; she planned to ask for half a million dollars to sign for another season. It was an unrealizable demand, and she knew it.

At the 1964 stockholders' meeting Lucy was a little too ebullient when she discussed all the new series planned for Desilu—twenty-two in all. There would be programs for Ethel Merman, a hit when she appeared as herself on one of the *Lucy* episodes; for comedienne Dorothy Loudon; for Dan Rowan and his partner Dick Martin, who for a handful of episodes had played Lucy's romantic interest; and for comedians-dancers Dan Dailey and Donald O'Connor. None of these would sell. Lucy could not know that another genre, drama, would be the company's salvation, when MGM veteran Gene Roddenberry was signed to create and produce a police program, *The Lieutenant,* and a science fiction series he called *Star Trek.*

While the company made its way into the 1960s, one exploitable commodity carried it through bad times and good: Lucy. Her various series, including the current highly rated one, were syndicated in forty-four countries and more than a dozen languages, and her name was as famous as the President's. The public relations department saw to that, arranging a special "Lucy Day" to take place at the 1964 World's Fair in New York City. Accompanying her to the fair were the expected Gary and DeDe, and the unexpected Hedda Hopper, all flown out at the expense of General Foods, sponsor of the most recent Lucy shows. The columnist had been a protector and fan for decades, and in New York, while thousands of fans looked on, she knelt side by side with Lucy as they put their handprints in cement at the fair's Hollywood Pavilion. With the most powerful gossip columnist in her corner, Lucy seemed ready for renewed popularity and a resurgent home life. Things did not work out in quite the way she intended.

$\mathcal{R}$eturned to home ground, Lucy agreed to take a step backward in her career. She would make regular broadcasts on the old medium of radio, starring in *Let's Talk to Lucy.* Produced by Gary Morton, the ten-minute show would showcase guest performers and give Lucy a chance to get paid just for talking. According to authors Coyne Steven Sanders and Tom Gilbert, who kept the closest track of Desilu, Lucy told friends she took the job in order to give her husband "something to do." Evidently he did not know how to do that something: *Let's Talk* sputtered from the beginning, failed to attract sponsors, and was not renewed at the end of the season. Not that the misfire bothered Morton; it would give him more time on the golf course.

When Gary was at the links Lucy sat at home playing countless games of solitaire, a portrait of the poor little rich girl, except that she was neither little nor a girl. She was only rich. And money was not enough to keep the fashion police at bay. Earl Blackwell Jr., notorious for his bitchy evaluations of movie stars' outfits, continually placed Lucy on his Worst Dressed list. One year he put her down in three sentences: "If you can't wear it, carry it. Lucy buys her clothes without any planning, then lugs around most everything else she owns. Her appearance is absolute confusion." Another time Blackwell wrote: "Despite her great comedy flair, offstage she is a clown caricaturing an actress who borrowed her wardrobe from the studio costume department." Recently he had called her a "Halloween trick without the treat. Lucy, dear, shoulder pads went out with the black bottom." It was not a good season for Lucy to be left alone, brooding about her image, or about life in general.

All the while, Lucie and Desi Jr. had been nourishing a fantasy. Both had seen *The Parent Trap*, a Disney feature about children successfully reuniting their separated parents. It had become their favorite movie, and they insisted that Lucy see it. She saw it. Four times. The year before, Desi Jr. had even inquired, "Can't you say you're sorry and go back?" As gently as possible Lucy tried to convince them that the divorce was final, that Gary Morton was here to stay. "People change," she kept repeating. It was an uphill struggle. Morton did what he could to win over Lucie and Desi Jr. Affable and low-key, he made a special effort to be friendly with their real father. Perhaps in addition, as Lucie Arnaz suggests, he wanted to learn about the television business from Desi. But that was not going to happen. Desi acted as a subversive influence; within the children's hearing he kept referring to his replacement as "Barry Norton," as if he couldn't quite recall Morton's name, and he shared nothing with him but an occasional handshake and small talk.

Then, in 1966, after blowing a good portion of his savings, Desi returned to the only arena that had given him satisfaction and recognition: television. What better place to work than Desilu, the company that still bore his name? Said an executive, "He was older, heavier, his hair had gone pretty gray, and if you looked at him in the wrong light he looked a hell of a lot older than a man in his fiftieth year." There were intimations of mortality—Bill Frawley was the first of the great quartet to go, dead of a heart attack. "I've lost one of my dearest friends," said

Lucy when she heard the news. Desi did her one better, He took out an ad in the *Hollywood Reporter,* complete with a picture of the deceased and the exit line, *"Buenas noches, amigo!"*

Even so, as old as Desi appeared when he was caught off-guard, another executive conceded, "when he checked into the studio at Culver he lost about a decade. His smile was wider and his gait was younger. He forgot about his troubles. He was home." From that home he began to develop properties for Carol Channing, an extravagant Broadway entertainer who was hard to contain on the small screen, and for Western star Rory Calhoun, Eve Arden, and Kaye Ballard. The last two were the title characters of *The Mothers-in-Law,* a bright situation comedy written by the exiled Bob and Madelyn. Wary at first, Lucy came to regard her ex-husband as an office asset. The passions and resentments had diminished, if not dispersed, and the two were able to work together without arguing, Lucy turning thumbs up or down when certain performers were mentioned for shows, Desi advising her on scripts and creative people.

She would need all the help she could get. As Vivian Vance expected, her salary terms would not be met and she would be replaced for the upcoming season. After some soul-searching, Lucy placed a call to Connecticut: the program wouldn't be the same without her old sidekick, she said. It might not even survive. "Lucille," Vance said, "with your talent you mustn't feel that way about anybody." Yet, Vance wrote in a memoir, "I was sure she felt I was deserting her. She had a tremendous fear of rejection, and unless she thought it through, it could seem that I was rejecting her, giving her up after fourteen years of closeness and clowning, for a husband and a home I wanted to share with him. She and I would go on chatting together, seeing each other, staying friends, but the relationship inevitably changed." What changed most was the two actresses' attitude toward show business itself. Vance had seen too much of Lucy's insecurity and took a jaundiced view of fame and its concomitants. She even tried to talk the mother of her onscreen son, Ralph Hart, into taking the boy out of show business altogether.

For Lucy, entertainment was the only way to go. It was all she knew and all she wanted to know. Marriage, motherhood, leisure—all were subordinated to the main concern of putting on a good show and turning a profit for the Desilu stockholders. Though she determined to get along without her feminine foil, Vivian's departure did made an enormous difference, not only in the scripts but in Lucy's outlook. In her view, she had been dropped twice, by her husband and by her closest professional friend. The moat around her grew wider and contained more alligators.

"On the set she could be a holy terror," said one of the technicians who watched Lucy in action. She summarily fired a New York Method actor who mumbled his lines; intimidated directors and cameramen; and sought confrontations, even when the star was as big as she was. When she gave Danny Kaye instructions on how to do humor, he snapped, "Just who the hell do you think you are?" Lucy shot back, "You're full of shit, that's who I am." She was not smiling. Joan Blondell, who had known Lucy since their starlet days in the 1930s, had become a first-class film and stage comedienne in middle age. Lucy booked her on the show, then expressed dissatisfaction with the way Blondell read her lines. After one take, her friend Herb Kenwith reported, the director yelled "Cut" and "Lucille pulled an imaginary chain . . . as if flushing an old-fashioned toilet." Blondell turned away but caught the tailend of the gesture. " 'What does *that* mean,' she demanded. Lucille said, 'It means that stunk!' Joan looked her right in the eye and said, 'Fuck you, Lucille Ball!' and left. The studio audience was stunned. You didn't hear words like that in those days." Kaye and Lucy were to make up their differences in later years. Blondell never came back.

Lucy's mood was not improved by events at the 1966 stockholders' meeting, held at Desilu's Workshop Theater. As president of Desilu, she had to inform investors that after a long period of stability, Desilu's net income had plummeted 42 percent from the previous year. There were compensating factors, she argued: her company was cutting back on expenses; it held valuable rental spaces, and other studios were using them as never before. This time the Ball glamour could not mask the distressing statistics. If Desilu was tightening its belt, asked one shareholder, then why did its president draw such a high fee for her work? (Lucy was getting $100,000 in executive salary and $130,172 in acting fees.) Another stockholder pointed out that Lucy's income was just a little less than the company's annual loss. Gary Morton intervened on his wife's behalf, and board members attempted to defend the president: she was "about two hundred percent underpaid."

Lucy, flustered, could only stammer that she was a fiscal conservative who made "honest reports," and would stay in the job "as long as I

can afford it." She lit cigarette after cigarette as the meeting degener-
ated into accusations from the floor and posturing on the part of the
executives. Lucy tried to leaven the proceedings with a little humor,
offering free Bufferin and water to everyone, on the house. But by now
the audience smelled blood, and an angry member spoke out. Why did
Desilu's top advisers get such big money and produce such meager dividends? Why weren't they dollar-a-year men like the counselors in
Washington? That way their salaries could be plowed back into the
company coffers and stockholders could get a decent return for their
money. Lucy's exasperated response: "How long could I keep these valued advisers at a dollar a year? This isn't *war*—it's the *TV business*." As
the tumultuous meeting ended, one of the questioners shouted: "This
has been a real show. Too bad it wasn't shown on television. It might
have increased our revenues."

Lucy had been protected from the rough-and-tumble of finance for
too many years. She had no way to handle this kind of criticism. It
made her feel vulnerable and strangely isolated: a loyal husband, a
phalanx of executives, a carapace of celebrity could not insulate her
from attack. The past was of very little use in Hollywood—particularly
in the severe world of television. It was the old case of "What have you
done for me lately?" and clearly Desilu hadn't done enough for its
stockholders.

*W*earing one of several hats, Lucy the performer dickered with
CBS, as she usually did at the end of a season, claiming that she was
tired of acting on television and ready to retire for good. *TV Guide,* a
watcher of Lucille Ball since her earliest television days, called this
"the Lucy Game." It consisted, said the magazine, "of Lucy casually
announcing she was tired of doing *The Lucy Show* and just might skip
the whole thing in favor of 'more time with Gary and the kids.' When
she did this, the whole CBS Television network shook. It could not
afford to lose a show with the popularity of Madame President." The
result never varied. She was always "wooed back" with a large raise—in
this case a $12 million package with a budget of $90,000 per half hour,
two one-hour specials financed by the network, and a deal for future
work. Once the Game was concluded, Mickey Rudin, the architect of
Lucy's contract, made an official, if disingenuous, statement: "I do not

deny that Lucy's contractual right to say yea or nay at any time has had certain business advantages. But I don't think it's what motivates Lucy. It is important to her to be reminded every year how much she is loved and wanted."

When her CEO hat was on, however, Lucy showed quite a different negotiating technique. Actors who demanded top dollar from Desilu found her cold and unyielding. "They priced themselves out of the business," she would explain to the press. "I was the first to say 'I'm not worth it' when my agents told me what they were asking for me." And yet Lucy was ultimately the performers' benefactress, backing shows that provided them with new opportunities. She not only encouraged films that emulated the Disney formula for its live-action movies—clean, sentimental stories aimed at a family audience—she also green-lighted two series quite unlike anything Desilu had ever underwritten, *Mission: Impossible* and *Star Trek*.

During its development, the bracing half-hour adventure show called "Briggs Squad" had its name changed to "IMF" (for "Impossible Mission Force") and finally pared down to *Mission: Impossible*. CBS was unimpressed by the initial pitch, and Desilu's production chiefs appealed to Lucy: they needed funds to create a pilot to demonstrate what a dry presentation could not. The company had $600,000 in its development fund, but it was not earmarked. Lucy could easily have diverted the money elsewhere; it was hers to begin with. Instead, she read the script, agreed that *Mission: Impossible* needed to be seen, and allowed the money to be allocated for a pilot. It starred Steven Hill, one of the charter members of the Actors Studio, and Martin Landau, then beginning his career. "When I first became an actor," Landau was to recall, "there were two young actors in New York: Marlon Brando and Steven Hill. A lot of people said that Steven would have been the one, not Marlon. He was legendary. Nuts, volatile, mad, and his work was exciting." As repulsive as Lucy found the Method, she admired Hill's work, and with good reason. The second time around, CBS bought the show.

Mission was to become one of the most successful programs in the Desilu stable—and one with more than its share of woes. Due to technical problems, the production schedule started to run late. Expenses quickly mounted. Recalled supporting actor Peter Lupus: "Those checks were amazing, thousands of dollars for going over. And we always went over." As if this were not enough, Hill caused some new,

and eventually insurmountable, difficulties. He had become an Orthodox Jew, and his contract specified that he would not work Friday
nights or Saturdays. There was no doubt of his sincerity; Hill spent a
good deal of time organizing prayer meetings for the Jews working at
Desilu. But refusal to work on the Sabbath, coupled with spectacular
outbursts of temperament, were more than the show could bear. In the
second season, Steven Hill was unceremoniously replaced by Peter
Graves. (For the next ten years, Hill abandoned acting and settled in
an Orthodox community in Rockland County, New York. He was not to
become a performer of note until his much-lauded appearance as a
district attorney on *Law & Order* in 1990.)

It took a season for *Mission: Impossible* to catch on; not until its second year did the show develop a fanatical following. *Star Trek* was different in every respect. Its creator, Gene Roddenberry, had a
philosophical turn of mind, as well as a skill for writing episodes of TV
Westerns. He conceived of *Star Trek* as an intergalactic *Wagon Train*
leading its cast to various exotic locales in space. Desilu executives
found the idea intriguing but unaffordable; Ed Holly and W. Argyle
Nelson recommended against development. Lucy overruled them, and
Holly later allowed: "If it were not for Lucy there would be no *Star Trek*
today." In essence that would mean no first and second series, no animated version, no film versions—in other words, none of the billions of
dollars generated in America and across the globe on both sides of the
Atlantic and Pacific oceans.

In exerting her authority, Lucy made some enemies, and executives
in and out of the company referred to her as "the lady who became a
man." Not so, Lucy said when she learned of the sobriquet. "If I was
going to turn into a man, I would have done it a long time ago," she told
journalist Rex Reed. "I've been in awe of men most of my life. It never
occurred to me how an executive should be. . . . The rules were here
before I took over. I never wanted to be an executive, but when my
marriage to Desi broke up after nineteen years I just couldn't walk
away from my obligations and say forget it. We were an institution. So
I took on all the responsibilities."

As influential as *Star Trek* and *Mission: Impossible* were to be, Desilu
still revolved around the *Lucy* shows, and here the strategy went awry.
With the great writing teams gone, Lucy hired Milt Josefsberg, Jack
Benny's head writer for many years. At the time, Josefsberg was the
most experienced and competent sketch writer in the television busi-

ness. The trouble was that Lucy was not a sketch performer. She needed credibility and a recognizably feminine persona to go along with her comedy. Josefsberg hired male writers who gave her gags— good gags, but not organic ones that rose out of her personality. As her assistant Thomas Watson noted, "these guys did not understand how to get a housewife into physical stunts, so, essentially, she stopped being a housewife." Where Lucy Ricardo was a blithe and endearing schemer, the character on the *Lucy* shows of the late 1960s was unpleasant and argumentative, out to embarrass and humiliate Gale Gordon. The comment of former *I Love Lucy* writer Bob Weiskopf is germane: "I don't want to sound mean, but where was Lucy in all this? Why didn't she demand better writing for herself? She certainly was in charge. If Desi or Jess had been there, this would have been handled much more smoothly and with greater humor."

To add to this unstable mix, the fifty-something Lucille Ball was taking visible losses in her battle against age and worry. A face-lift remained out of the question; her skin remained too sensitive to bear knifework. She did have her eyes tucked, and even that relatively minor operation took more than a year to heal. During the long period of recuperation, Hal King had to conceal the redness around her eyes with heavy pancake makeup. She edged toward the glamorous but unreal—a star, rather than the endearing zany that viewers had adored for the last fifteen years.

I Love Lucy had been syndicated in Europe for more than a decade. Lucy decided to try her luck overseas. *Lucy in London,* broadcast in the fall of 1966, did not receive the hoped-for response. "What had promised to be one of the season's major specials," said *Variety,* "turned out to be a major disappointment."

While these distresses gathered, Lucy reached out for a confidant. Gary Morton was appointed to the role. He tried to be modest about it at first, quietly sitting in on meetings and deliberately playing down his significance. "Lucy can't run a company by herself," he said. "Maybe with me around, when she walks on the set, her mind is at peace. I pop in from time to time, on conferences, rehearsals. I can tell from her if things are going well, if the laughter is there." As the months went on he insinuated himself into the corporate workings of Desilu. Agreeable as always, he tried to ingratiate himself with the higher-ups, who rarely responded in kind. Desilu program executive Herbert Solow regarded Lucy's husband with a mixture of wariness and disdain. His view was,

"Don't take from your spouse and use that as your importance. Gary did that. Constantly." Cousin Cleo felt that Morton gave in to his wife too easily, and that the deference reinforced her worst instincts. Desi, who put on a public show of friendship, resented his replacement and was especially irritated by Morton's collection of expensive cars, obviously underwritten by Lucy. Others at Desilu felt that Morton was an embarrassment. "He tried to be Mr. Nice Guy," said one staffer, "and in a way he was—always smiling, always trying to grasp what was going on. But he was resented and, to be perfectly frank, he wasn't capable of taking over the company, which is clearly what he was aiming to do." Bernard Weitzman, one of the top Desilu executives, agreed, saying that Gary "tried to be what Desi was, without having Desi's authority." Or, for that matter, his skills.

There were times when Morton's inadequacies were apparent to Lucy, and those occasions could be unpleasant for him and for onlookers. Geoffrey Mark Fidelman notes that during the filming of one episode Morton indicated some steps leading to a doorway. "Lucy doesn't like them and she wants them out," he instructed the director. Maury Thompson was surprised at the order; the steps had been there for several previous shows. "I tried to stall Gary," he remembered, "telling him how much manpower and money it would take to redo the set." As he was speaking Lucy entered and looked at the tableau. "What's going on here?" she wondered. "Why is everybody standing around?" Thompson repeated what Morton had told him. "She looked at me," he recalled, "then turned to Gary and said, 'Gary, go buy a car, but get outta here.' Gary just hung his head and left. She never asked any more questions; she knew what Gary had tried to do. Lucille wanted him to be another Desi, but he just couldn't cut it." (Thompson would go on to receive an Emmy nomination for his work on the *Lucy* shows—the only director so honored—but perhaps because he had seen too much, he was fired at the end of the season.)

*I*n later years, Desi Jr. was fond of quoting fans who "thought I was Little Ricky." But, he said, "I knew Fred and Ethel didn't live next door—Jack Benny did." That sentence encapsulates his childhood and adolescence. In an environment where most of the neighbors were famous and all of them were wealthy, a normal childhood would have been extremely difficult; for Desi Jr. and Lucie it was impossible. Not only were their parents celebrated, rich, and divorced, their father was an alcoholic and their mother a deeply conflicted figure whose treatment of the children alternated between discipline and indulgence. "You're not special because you're famous" was one of Lucy's ongoing instructions to her son and daughter. Both had to make their beds and pick up their clothes; neither ever received an allowance that exceeded five dollars a week. Yet on one of Desi Jr.'s birthdays, a carnival was set up in the backyard, complete with Ferris wheel, clowns, and a live elephant. With mixed messages like these, confusion was bound to result, and it was exacerbated by their mother's long workday and the resultant guilt for time spent away from them.

Their father was not much of a role model during this time. There was, for instance, the summer night in 1966 when fifteen-year-old Lucie and a friend were visiting Desi at his beach house in Del Mar. Late at night some youths began making noise and cursing within earshot. It happened that Desi owned a .38 revolver—and this one was not a cigarette lighter. He fired two shots into the sand. They only added to the noise. The next thing he knew, the Del Mar police had arrived, arrested him for assault, and hauled him off to the station. He claimed that he had only fired blanks, but when the cops dug in the sand they found no evidence of such shells. They released Desi after he posted $1,100 bail, and he went home to sleep off his drunkenness.

Customarily, several years after a divorce an emotional distance opens up between the former husband and wife. Lucy had convinced herself that she could be indifferent about Desi's life and loves and vagaries, but the fact was that she could never turn her back on him. They had been too close in ways that neither of them fully understood. When she learned of Desi's arrest, instead of shaking her head and responding with a wry smile, she managed to get hold of some blanks and had a chauffeur drive them over to Desi's house in case the investigation continued—he could plant them as needed. Happily, the cops never returned. The incident made the papers, however, and the implication was that Lucy's ex, rather than protecting two teenage girls, had simply been on yet another binge.

Each child had a way of dealing with this kind of stress. Lucie, who inherited her father's exotic aura and her mother's long silhouette, led an active social life and performed in school plays. Desi Jr. played rock music with two young friends from the neighborhood: Dean Martin Jr., son of the singer-actor, and Billy Hinsche, son of a prosperous real estate developer.

In the beginning the boys composed songs to amuse themselves. Their amateur status was not to last long. First, Lucy indulgently booked the trio to warm up her audience before the show went on. When they were sufficiently rehearsed and polished, Dean Martin invited to them to perform for one of his close friends. Frank Sinatra was no fan of rock 'n' roll—he was subsequently to call it "the most brutal, ugly, desperate, vicious form of expression it has been my misfortune to hear." In those days, though, he found himself amused by the style and rhythms of the group called "Dino, Desi & Billy." Sinatra and Desi Sr. had long since reconciled, and as a lark he invited the trio to cut a disk for his label, Reprise Records. The mid-1960s was the time of global "youthquake," when newcomers like the Beatles and the Byrds let their hair grow, radiated insouciance, and performed their own material. The harmonies and attitudes of these groups changed the course of popular music, and the directors of Reprise, anxious to tap into the youth market, arranged for a contract. At the age of twelve, a round-faced Desi, with his thinner thirteen-year-old pals, went on tour and composed two songs that made the Top Forty. The first had a pleasant melody and banal lyrics with a tincture of something less felt than seen:

> You treat me just like dirt
> You have all the fun
> I stay home and hurt.

Other entries in their first album included an exuberant version of Willie Dixon's "Seventh Son," Bob Dylan's "Like a Rolling Stone" and "It Ain't Me, Babe," and two songs written by the boys' producer, Lee Hazelwood, "Not the Lovin' Kind" and "Rebel Kind"—quite a statement for a group whose combined age was thirty-eight. Hazelwood was later to say that working with Dino, Desi, and Billy was "hell on this earth." After one year he walked away from his contract because "I didn't want those little leg biters around me anymore."

Whatever their behavior in the studio, the trio were catnip to squealing groupies wherever they played. Lucy was heard to complain that she wanted Dino, Desi, and Billy on her show and was waiting for an appropriate script. "By the time it came along," she later said, "I couldn't afford them." (Her budget only allowed $400, whereas Dean Martin paid $1,000 for a single appearance on his show.) During the group's first flush of success, a journalist asked each member what he liked best about his sudden prominence. "The privilege to wear long hair," stated Dino. "The travel," was Billy's favorite. "The money," said Desi Jr. And therein lay much of the trouble.

Desi Jr. had never received a generous allowance from his mother. Now thousands of dollars were rolling in every month. On the cusp of adolescence he was not only getting rich, he was becoming famous. The proof was the adoration he received from the crowds wherever he went. He acted with such self-assurance that Lucie claimed her brother "had been thirty-four since we were kids." In the next few years that assurance would become arrogance, and the appetite for applause would turn into a need for greater stimulation. If there is, as some researchers believe, a substance-abuse gene, he surely inherited it from Desi. The phrase "sex, drugs, and rock 'n' roll" was to apply to his life and times for a longer, sadder period than anyone could possibly have predicted—least of all Desi Jr.

He was to remember experiments with marijuana, mescaline, quaaludes, cocaine, LSD, all the while questioning himself like someone in a song: "Is this all there is?" The query, he said, "terrified me. I told myself all I needed was something else—more money, another girl, a different kind of drug." At the age of fifteen he was financially independent. Lucy's criticism of his low grades had little effect, and her attempts to ground him went nowhere. "I felt indestructible," her son remembered. Mother and son argued, and then, when the wounds were raw, went for days without speaking to each other. Desi sought refuge at his father's place. Desi Sr. knew what Desi Jr. was doing to himself. He made some acid comments but generally refrained from confrontations. "His own drinking problem," Desi Jr. observed, "prevented him from coming down too hard on me."

Desi Jr.'s belongings, his instruments, his main emotional life were with Lucy, and it was to her house that he would return, only to have more fights about his indifference to school—and indeed to anything that didn't feed his ego. A young actor, Robert Pine, was on the set of a

Lucy show when a call came in from Desi Jr. Pine recalled: "He wanted to buy an expensive car. I think he was about to turn sixteen. She didn't put it off on an aide or a maid. She took the call like any mother and said, 'Goddamn it, I don't want you doing this, so don't do it.' Then she turned to me and said, 'Can you believe this kid?' It was very human." All too human, it seemed. Desi Jr. was, as he himself put it, "already independently wealthy from my work with Dino, Desi, and Billy." He went on: "I wasn't asking her permission; I just wanted an opinion about the car."

Aware of his son's emotional distress (and of his own inability to alleviate it by example), Desi offered guidance via mail. A sad irony attended this act. For the letter sent Desi Jr. was a copy of one Desi Sr. had received from his own father, back in 1933:

> Well, pardner, you are now sixteen, and in my book you are no longer a child; you are a man. . . .
>
> A note of warning about driving, particularly about driving on the road that lies before you—the one we all have to travel—the road of life.
>
> It is very much like the road from Santiago to El Cobre. There are stretches that are so smooth and beautiful that they take your breath away, and there are others that are so ugly and rough that you wish you had never gotten on the damn thing, and you wonder if you will ever get through.
>
> Somewhere along the way, you will get into a particularly bad spot that presents a very difficult problem, and you may not know exactly what to do. When that happens, I advise you not to do anything. Examine the situation first. Turn it upside down and sideways as many times as you have to. But then, when you have finally made up your mind, do not let anything or anybody stop you. If there is a mountain in your way, go through it.
>
> Sometimes you will make it; sometimes you will not. But, if you are honest and thorough in your decision, you will learn something either way. We should learn as much from our mistakes as we do from our successes.
>
> And when you do come up with a minus, try to convert it into a plus. You will be surprised how many times it will work. Use a setback as a stepping stone to better times ahead.

And don't be afraid to make mistakes; we all do. Nobody bats five hundred. Even if you did, that means you were wrong half of the time. But don't worry about it. Don't be ashamed of it. Because that is the way it is. That is life.

Remember, good things do not come easy, and you will have your share of woe—the road is lined with pitfalls. But you will make it, if when you fail you try and try again. Persevere. Keep swinging. And don't forget that the Man Upstairs is always there, and all of us need His help. And no matter how unworthy you think yourself of it, don't be afraid to ask Him for it.

Good luck, son.

Love,
Dad

Each letter was assiduously read and preserved. Neither had the desired effect. Something in the blood, maybe.

Whatever the case, the conflict between Lucy and Desi Jr. could not long endure. It came to a head one day when the youth pulled up at the house at 6 a.m. His mother and stepfather were at the front door to greet him. The two had been up half the night; in the small hours Lucy had dialed the police asking them to search for her son. Desi Jr. got out of the car and tried to explain: he had been out with his latest girlfriend and they had completely lost track of time. "I'm in love," was his lame excuse. Lucy exploded: "Don't you see that your actions affect other people? How could you be so irresponsible?" When her temper had cooled, Lucy tried to have a conversation with Desi Jr., stressing duty and accountability. They were not concepts he wanted to hear, and she found herself laying down the law. It was one thing to go off early, as she did, seeking a career. It was another thing to hurt the family; young Lucille had never done that to *her* family. Quite the contrary, her grandparents and brother and mother and cousin had leaned on Lucille and she had not let them down. "You can either live here and follow the rules, or you can leave," she concluded. "But if you go, you're entirely on your own."

Desi Jr. rose to the challenge: "I can take care of myself." It was a poignant moment, and a deeply painful one for Lucy. At the time, her son embraced his freedom eagerly. Later he conceded: "A part of my life was ending. I already belonged to the adult world and I couldn't go back to being a regular teenager. So although I was only sixteen, I chose to move into my own apartment. Over the years I drifted farther and farther away emotionally."

$\mathcal{A}$s busy and conflicted as she was, Lucy found time to act in Gene Kelly's film *A Guide for the Married Man,* a cheerful, flawed compilation of sketches about adultery in the 1960s. Several TV celebrities starred in the movie, including Sid Caesar, Jack Benny, and Art Carney, who appeared in the skit with Lucy. Playing an aggressive male anxious to go out on the town, Carney engendered fewer laughs than he did on *The Honeymooners.* Lucy wasn't funny at all. Her takes were obvious, her upswept hairdo was unflattering, and her pancake makeup was heavy and obvious. She was fifty-six, and for the first time in her life truly looked her age.

The reasons were manifold and complicated. The unhappy upstate girl had invented herself over and over again; she had built several careers, reconstructed her family and created a second one. The walk-on had become a superstar; the nobody, a mogul; the childless woman, a mother. In other arenas, this would have been a recipe for satisfaction; in the great tradition of Hollywood, it was a prescription for misery. The children were going their own ways more rapidly than she had anticipated, the *Lucy* show was nowhere near as funny as it should have been, and as a result the president of Desilu was walking around with an abstracted air, unable to focus on the company. According to one of the company's key executives, Herbert Solow, Desilu was "a dying studio." He would recall: "Lucy was still puttering away, doing the same thing over and over again. I explained at a meeting that I wanted to get some new things going." He sent a copy of a modernized Desilu logo for her approval. "As usual, I never heard from her."

Ever since the day Desi left, rumors had circulated about Desilu: a consortium of investors wanted to buy Lucy out; Paramount, recently swallowed up by Gulf + Western, had its eye on the company; Desilu's top executives wanted to pool their resources and take over. After a few years the fuss died down, only to be revived shortly after the 1966 stockholders' meeting, when investors were informed that for the first time ever, the company was declaring a 5 percent dividend, due to some adroit accounting. All well and good, but the gross revenue announced at that meeting had told the real story. In 1965, Desilu had brought in $18,997,163. In 1966 the figure was $18,797,502, and much of the income was due to sales of *I Love Lucy* to forty-eight countries overseas. According to Solow, "The professional Desilu was awful. Because it had nothing. It was all *Lucy.* Everyone loved to watch *Lucy.*" Many of the old programs were thriving, but Desilu had lost the ability to develop new ones—the lifeblood of dominant studios.

Otto von Bismarck once remarked that he never believed anything until he heard the official denial, and this time out, the Hollywood smart money all seemed to have studied the Iron Chancellor. No sale, Lucy kept assuring the press. Meantime, reliable insiders spoke of her wavering in Miami, where she had gone to consult with Jackie Gleason about a movie—or so she claimed. He would play Diamond Jim Brady, she said; she would be Lillian Russell. The real reason she had gone south was to avoid the calls of her lawyer, Mickey Rudin, who was anxious to close a deal with Charles Bluhdorn.

Through a combination of drive, avarice, and cunning, Viennese immigrant Bluhdorn had made an art of acquisitions, takeovers, and mergers. He was currently chairman of Gulf + Western, a conglomerate whose competitors called it "Engulf and Devour," and one of his prize acquisitions was Paramount Pictures. Frank Yablans, who was to become the head of Paramount, once characterized his boss as "an uncivilized pig." As if to live up to his billing, Bluhdorn announced that he wanted Desilu as another trophy and he wanted it *now.* No stalling or the deal was off.

Rudin flew down to Florida and confronted Lucy at her hotel. Bluhdorn needed an answer in twenty-four hours. Would she sell, or would she stay in a company that offered her only headaches and overwork? The era of independent production was drawing to a close, couldn't she see that? The big companies, the networks, were taking over. What chance would she have swimming with sharks? Lucy's reaction to a crisis remained the same from childhood to adolescence to maturity, from actress to comedienne to powerhouse—she cried. She mentioned the head of Gulf + Western: "Do you know, Mickey, I haven't even *seen* this man?" Rudin offered to make a call. She refused. "I like to see a man's eyes, shake his hand." She settled for a phone conversation. Bluhdorn turned on the charm: "Miss Ball, one of the things I am prepared to like about you is that you care." Lucy cried again.

Bluhdorn had great powers of persuasion, but these alone would not have won the day. The fact was that Lucy, owner of a paper fortune, was deeply in debt. She had managed to acquire another block of stock and now held 59 percent of Desilu. But those shares, valued at some $6 million, were held by the City National Bank of Beverly Hills. The stock was security for the loan she took out back in 1962 to buy out Desi. In order to get rid of the debt Lucy *had* to sell. And in order to enjoy a whopping profit, she had to sell to Bluhdorn. The clock began to tick down. Lucy cried one last time. Then she said yes.

And just like that, the long climb to the top was over. The years of struggle, the small victories, the big triumphs were in the record books. The minority stockholders agreed to go along with Lucy, and in February 1967, for the price of $17 million, Gulf + Western consumed Desilu. Of that sum, $10 million went to Lucille Ball as the principal stockholder. The day of the transaction, the rich retiree sat up in bed with her breakfast tray. When Lucie entered, Lucy informed her daughter unemotionally, "We sold the studio today," as if she had just unloaded a burdensome country house. To be sure, she would stay on in some official capacity, but everyone knew this was largely a ceremonial assignment. When she finally met Bluhdorn, all Lucy could say afterward was: "He was charming. He travels fast, talks fast, and acts on impulse. I just hope he stays alive." (He would survive for another sixteen years, then die as he had lived, in passionate overdrive, succumbing to a heart attack on his private plane at fifty-six, the same age that Lucy was when she sold Desilu.)

Once the sale was official, Lucy was free to put her feet up, relax, travel, do whatever struck her fancy. With a fortune in the bank, very little would have been out of reach. But if she had ever known how to take things easy, she had lost the knack long before the buyout. She peppered her speech with "kiddo," like some survivor from vaudeville days; went around town in a gray Silver Cloud Rolls-Royce, her head held high like Norma Desmond in *Sunset Boulevard;* stuck notes to herself on the dashboard and steering wheel; bragged about her pets (one watchdog was so dedicated, she told Rex Reed, "I've seen her sit for seven hours guarding an avocado seed"). She also clucked about the moral backslide in America. She allowed Gary to show the James Bond thriller *Thunderball* on their home screen. "Well, the blood is spurting, the bullets are flying, the sharks are biting, and then this 007 guy climbs into bed with this dame," Lucy remembered. "I yelled, 'Stop the film! What the hell kind of picture is this?' " Lucie protested,

"Oh Mother, my God—we've seen it three times." At the next private screening Lucy opted for *Blow-Up*. The import had received good reviews—but it did not get one from Lucy, who labeled it "that awful Italian thing." The only reliable genre was the Western. She acquired one. "And so help me they're in the fort, see, with the Indians coming through the gate, and I'll be damned if the girl doesn't make the sign of the cross, rip her clothes off, and climb on top of this cowboy, and they're crawling over each other in bed like there's no tomorrow! Ugh! Everybody's taking their clothes off but me. You'll never catch me in the buff, kiddo."

Where she would be caught was in a film she had wanted to do for years. *Full House,* the true-life account of a widow with eight children who married a widower with ten, had been acquired by Desilu seventeen years before. Madelyn Pugh and Bob Carroll had adapted the story for the screen, titled it "The Beardsley Story," and tailored the lead roles for Lucy and Desi. Years later, Lucy vainly attempted to enlist Fred MacMurray as her costar, and when that fell through she approached James Stewart. Still later, Lucy bounced the Pugh-Carroll version and signed Leonard Spigelgass, scenarist of *The Big Street,* for a rewrite. After that she thought of John Wayne, Art Carney, and Jackie Gleason as possible members of the cast. Other actors were considered, other rewrites prepared. Finally, in 1967, Melville Shavelson, writer-director of Bob Hope movies (*Seven Little Foys, Beau James*) and Mort Lachman, Bob Hope's head writer, came up with a script that everyone liked. Shavelson agreed to direct Lucy, playing opposite her old costar Henry Fonda. Lucy had a last-minute request: she wanted Desi Jr. and Lucie to be cast as two of the couple's eighteen offspring. Shavelson refused; the children were wrong for the roles. For a moment Lucy considered arguing with her director—who was paying for this film anyhow? The moment passed. What the hell, Lucie and Desi Jr. were under contract to her for her new TV show, *Here's Lucy.* She could use them on that program. For all her display of temperament, Lucy was a realist. She knew she was not the "lu" of Desilu anymore; she was just a performer who needed to get laughs. Could she still provoke them on the little screen? The odds were good. But what about the big screen? Was there any heat left in the old Ball of Fire? She was afraid to find out, and more afraid not to.

"Tough, very tough"

𝒜FTER *I Love Lucy* went off the air in 1957, Lucille Ball was never again to glow with such intensity—save on one occasion. In *Yours, Mine and Ours,* she played opposite Henry Fonda on the big screen for the first time in twenty-five years. As Helen North, a middle-aged widow with a large family, Lucy develops a crush on Frank Beardsley, a similarly burdened widower. The career naval officer is intrigued with her; his ten children are not. At a crucial moment the youngsters try to sabotage the romance, spiking Mrs. North's mild drink with heavy doses of vodka, gin, and scotch. At the dinner table she becomes cockeyed drunk, uncoordinated, batting her false eyelashes, spilling food, laughing raucously at the wrong moments.

The scene was not a simple replay of the "Vitameatavegamin" routine. In that episode, as in all of Lucy Ricardo's classic moments, there was never really anything at stake. The audience knew that no matter how the TV heroine was embarrassed, she would always extricate herself and be forgiven by Desi—even if she had some "'splainin'" to do.

In *Yours, Mine and Ours* the future of North, Beardsley, and their eighteen children depends on her stability, and her inebriation is nearly
fatal to the relationship. Many comedians could do impersonations of
sots—indeed, two celebrated performers, Jack Norton and Foster
Brooks, rarely played anything else. But as Lucy goes through her pivotal scene, Helen is not merely falling-down funny, she is deeply
poignant—at first amused, then bewildered, and finally appalled by
her own behavior. To be simultaneously attractive, hilarious, and
melancholy is a gift given to few, and Lucy was probably the only
actress of her generation who could have played Helen North with
such conviction. It was as if she were finally able to shake loose from
the past and become a grand dame of American cinema, fit company,
at last, for Katharine Hepburn, Bette Davis, and Joan Crawford.

Shooting the film had been difficult for Lucy and formidable for
Melville Shavelson, who impatiently battled his star's attempts to control the lighting, the camera work, the tempo of dialogue. Toward the
close of filming the director pointedly informed Lucy that it was the
first time he ever directed *nineteen* children—a comment that caused
her to cry and afterward to cut him dead. Six months later the hostility
ended when *Yours, Mine and Ours* was released to extraordinary critical
and popular acclaim. In its customary jargon, *Variety* said what other
papers expressed more traditionally: "Socko family entertainment.
Based on actual characters, the film is marked by uniform excellence.
Literate scripting, excellent performances, and superior direction are
underscored by top-notch production." Made for less than $2 million,
the movie grossed $25 million in 1968, one-quarter of which went to
the female star. Lucy had almost forgotten what raves could do to
restore the spirit. She could hardly be blamed for mistaking the dusk
for the dawn.

Setting up as president of a smaller operation, Lucille Ball Productions, Lucy installed Gary Morton as vice president and went to work
in a space provided by Paramount. The relationship with Paramount
did not endure. Bluhdorn's emblematic phrase was, "Well, what is the
bottom line?" and he turned out to be as bad as his word. Within a few
months he saw to it that much of Lucy's old staff was dismissed or
phased out. Callers to Desilu's phone number were greeted by operators chirping, "Paramount Gower." Perhaps fancifully, Lucy complained that when she called the office and asked for herself she
received the answer, "Lucy *who?*"

It was not a question that the public ever put to her. CBS had been running the old *I Love Lucy* shows during the daytime, and when CBS news director Fred Friendly wanted to use the time slot to show a Senate committee hearing on U.S. Vietnam policy, he was overruled. His superiors at the network opted to stay with an *I Love Lucy* rerun instead. "It was not a matter of deciding between two broadcasts," Friendly was to write in his memoirs, "but a choice between interrupting the morning run of the profit machine—whose admitted function was to purvey six one-minute commercials every half hour—or electing to make the audience privy to an event of overriding importance." Friendly was advised that "housewives weren't much interested in Vietnam," and he resigned over the controversy. He was backed by an unexpected ally: Lucille Ball. The newsman had a legitimate gripe against the network, she said. "They throw in the old *I Love Lucy*s instead of something vital."

Altruism is always laudable. Nevertheless, the profit-motivated network sensed something Lucy did not: a revolution in popular culture. Even the greatest pictures were revived only after long intervals, or at festivals confined to universities and clubs. Television was different. In the 1960s the business of reruns started in earnest. TV became a repository of popular culture, the storehouse of national memory. From its very beginnings, *I Love Lucy* had been designed as a family show. Thus adults could enjoy a half hour of nostalgia as they watched the old images of Lucy capering on the little screen. The children looked on, introduced to the woman they had only heard about from their parents. Lucille Ball now existed in two time periods, in black-and-white and color, with Desi and without him—television's first schizoid superstar.

Lucy was grateful for her unique position but wary of becoming an antique in the public mind. She opted to look through the windshield rather than at the rearview mirror. *The Lucy Show* was renamed *Here's Lucy,* and it took off without Desi or the Mertzes. With an eye to the ratings, the producers did invite Vivian Vance to appear on one of the early programs, but Lucy pointedly stayed away from references to the original series. *I Love Lucy,* she said, was from "another era," and Lucille Ball was going to be as relevant as the 11 p.m. news.

She was also going to be totally in charge of her life and art. Accordingly, she bided her time, then abruptly moved her outfit off the Paramount lot—"Eat *that,* Charlie Bluhdorn," cheered a colleague—and went with Universal, where she had the respect of studio head Lew Wasserman. (She also had the backing of Bernard Weitzman, the former Desilu executive, who had moved to Universal months before.) Universal set her down in a place dubbed "Lucy Lane" with a private dressing room for herself and a public dressing room for tourists to visit. Performers who worked with Lucy during this period saw a newly confident persona—perhaps a little too confident. Booked onto *The Lucy Show*, Joan Crawford, always a formidable personality, showed up late for a rehearsal. Lucy telephoned her ultimatum: "If you're not here tomorrow morning at ten on the nose, you're fired. You get that? Fired!" Next day Joan Crawford came in on time—and promptly regretted it when Lucy made her go through a dance number again and again, faulting her rhythm and tempo. When it was all over, an exhausted Crawford allowed that Lucy could "outbitch" her any day of the week. As a lark Lucy appeared in a minor role on *The Untouchables*. There she tried to tell Robert Stack how to play his part—and would have taken over the program had Stack not politely reminded his boss that he had played Eliot Ness longer than she had played Lucy McGillicuddy, the name of her character on *The Lucy Show*. And then came the Burtons.

In 1970, Welsh superstar Richard Burton and the former child actress Elizabeth Taylor, sometimes referred to by her sobriquet "violet eyes to die for," were the most famous couple in the world. Eight years before, they had been cast in *Cleopatra*. While filming it, the two began an epic affair that crowded other news from the papers and eventually led to two divorces, Burton's from the former Sibyl Williams, and Taylor's from singer Eddie Fisher. The publicity continued as the lovers battled openly, split up, came together again, and then married in 1964. Burton was famous not only for his histrionics but also for his fondness for alcohol, and Taylor for her beauty and her affection for the mirror. Anyone could have predicted the couple would bring trouble with them, but Lucy was hell-bent on having Liz and Dick appear on her program. At that point she was up against the NBC show *Rowan & Martin's Laugh-In*, and the younger, hipper rival had become a ratings front-runner. Lucy needed some punch, and for that reason she had made peace and rehired Bob Carroll and the recently remarried Madelyn Davis (formerly Madelyn Pugh Martin). The Burtons, never averse to publicity or a big payoff, agreed to appear in the opening show of the 1970–1971 season.

The premise of the show was simple: Burton gets mobbed at his hotel and dodges the fans by donning Sam the Plumber's overalls. Lucy mistakes him for a real plumber and hires him to take care of the office plumbing. He does the job while reciting Shakespeare. When he leaves, Lucy discovers a large diamond ring in his abandoned overalls. She tries it on, and can't get it off—just as the press arrives to examine the jewel. Taylor appears and Lucy hides behind a curtain near her, thrusting out her hand as if it were Liz's.

Filming was hell from day one. Amid all sorts of publicity, Burton had presented his wife with that now-notorious ring. It held a diamond of 69.42 carats, ostentation incarnate. Wherever Elizabeth appeared, the insurance company was sure to follow, and the premiums were gigantic. Richard insisted that if Lucy wanted the Burtons (and, of course, the Ring), she would have to pay not only for the team, but for their jewelry insurance. Lucy agreed.

Perhaps to gall his employer, Burton kept mumbling in rehearsal. Taylor followed suit. "Richard kept throwing away comedy lines in that British 'drawing room' way of his," Lucy claimed. She counted six big laughs he was failing to get, drew his attention to them, and forced him to change his timing and diction. "He didn't take too kindly to it," she went on, "but after the filming he came over to me and said, 'There were eight!' " Privately the actor was not so conciliatory. His diaries speak to the situation: "Those who had told us that Lucille Ball was 'very wearing' were not exaggerating. . . . She lives entirely on that weekly show which she has been doing and successfully doing for nineteen years. Nineteen solid years of double-takes and pratfalls and desperate upstaging and nervously watching the 'ratings' as she does so."

In *Richard Burton: A Life,* the actor's sympathetic biographer, Melvyn Bragg, theorizes that the Burton and Ball were programmed for a collision course. Richard "waited for his gift to materialize: if it did not, he was helpless. Lucille Ball worked on her talent like an engineer, forever shaping and restructuring, driving the machine of her shows to performance *whatever.*" Vastly experienced in stage and film, Burton had never been cast in a situation comedy before. He was totally unprepared for the schedule and the pace, and grew more impatient by the hour. His discomfort, writes Bragg, may well have been fueled by guilt. "Why, after all, was he doing it? For exposure? (Did he fear he might need it?) For money? (Surely not. He was very wealthy by now.)

For fun? That is most likely. In which case it back-fired badly." Days of discomfort preceded Burton's final appraisal of Lucy, written just before shooting wrapped up: "I loathe her today but now I also pity her. After tonight I shall make a point of never seeing her again. . . . She can thank her lucky stars that I am not drinking. There is a chance that I might have killed her."

Burton found it fascinating to watch Lucy's reaction to his wife. Lucy sent Elizabeth a dozen roses a week before rehearsals began. Elizabeth returned the compliment by sending Lucy eighteen roses. Lucy replied with a gift of two dozen. The one-upwomanship continued until both dressing rooms looked like flower shops. Burton was amused to find Lucy calling Liz "for the most part Mrs. Burton or Miss Taylor and occasionally Elizabeth but [she] corrects it to the more formal immediately." (Taylor, whose tendency toward the scatological was kept from the public, returned the favor by referring to Lucy as "Miss Cunt.") Burton himself was addressed in the third person as His Highness, Mr. Burton, or sometimes Mia. "This is a joke that E. made on the first day when she, E., said that I had become so thin—I am now about 160 lbs—that sleeping with me was like sleeping with Mia Farrow, who is first cousin to a matchstick."

Actually Burton, appalled as he was by Lucy's insistence on giving him line readings, acted like a gentleman for most of the week. He complimented Gale Gordon and expressed sympathy for the second banana, Cliff Norton. That comedian was indignant because Gary Morton had tried to cut his salary—the Burtons had consumed too much of the budget, he said. Only once did Burton become irascible, and then he did it privately, advising director Jerry Paris to warn Lucy that if she tried to pull any rank on Elizabeth "she would see, in person, what a Thousand Megaton Hydrogen Bomb does when the warhead is attached and exploded." The detonation never took place, and for all the little insults Lucy had no reason to regret booking Liz and Dick— "Lucy Meets the Burtons" pulled the highest ratings *Here's Lucy* ever received.

Other episodes showed flashes of brilliance, and during this period several veteran comedians saluted Lucy's way with a script. Norton, for example, called her "a walking, living authority on comedy," and actor-director Charles Nelson Reilly remarked: "Lucille Ball taught me one of the most important things I've ever learned about comedy. We were sitting around the table, and she said, 'Great joke—wrong place!' I can't tell you how many shows I've done that I have made better by remembering her wisdom." And Tony Randall, who had vast experience in every medium from stage to film and TV, praised Lucy even as he acknowledged that many people found her difficult to work with. "She bossed everybody around and didn't spare anybody's feelings. But I didn't mind that because she knew what she was doing. If someone just says 'Do this!' it's awful if they are wrong. If they are right, it just saves a lot of time. And she was always right."

About comedy, he might have added. Not necessarily about anything else. Show business aside, the years 1970 and 1971 would have to qualify as *anni horribiles* in the life of Lucille Ball. Desi showed up on the set from time to time, engaging in banter with his ex-wife. She kidded him along and stayed away from the obvious: he was a seamed and puffy figure who had already undergone a colostomy yet still struggled with alcohol and smoking addictions. Desi once said he looked forward to the end of his acting career because he could relax and get old and fat. He had done exactly that. These days he was just a well-off retiree in short sleeves, wearing thick-soled shoes to give himself stature. In the old days no one noticed how tall or short he was—as president of Desilu he had all the stature he needed. And when Desi looked at Lucy he saw a different woman from the one he had known so intimately; now she was a take-charge person who still smoked too much and who needed a lot of help from the makeup department. He noted, a little sadly and more than a little egocentrically: "She'd been boiled hard by the hatred of me. She needed the hatred yet."

Actually, Lucy was fueled more by insecurity than by animosity. "With all her talent," Bernie Weitzman testified, "she didn't really believe she had that much talent." The doubt caused her to observe, "When you're Number One there's only one place you can go." She resolved that no one was going to push her downhill. In fighting to maintain her place she began to lose friends, or to distance herself from them. Jayne Meadows, whose husband, comedian Steve Allen, had always complimented Lucy on her style, was treated like a piece of furniture, and was made to pay for her own wardrobe when she appeared in a *Here's Lucy* episode. "Lucy was *very* cheap," Meadows said afterward. "She *was* what Jack Benny *played*." And Jack Benny himself, a man who made a point of never criticizing anyone in the business, stated privately after an appearance on *Here's Lucy* that the boss-lady was "tough, *very* tough," and suggested that she ought to get herself to a good psychiatrist.

If Lucy knew about these opinions she refused to recognize them. She was too preoccupied by the inadequacies of her show, and by the problems of the next generation of Arnazes. Desi Jr. had begun to drink in secret at the age of eleven. From alcohol he had gone on to experiment with drugs, particularly when the trio Dino, Desi & Billy was on the road. The trio had run its course by 1970, but he was an addict at that point—a skilled one who hid his habit from public and family view. Lucy and her seventeen-year-old son had since reconciled, but a tension remained and it was impossible for either of them to break it. For Desi Jr., like Lucie, had been incorporated into *Here's Lucy*, playing roles that featured them almost every week. So they were with their mother not only at home but on the set. Lucy, recalled Desi Jr., "would treat us—rightfully so—as cast members at work, but we would still take things personally that probably weren't intended that way. When most people are hassled at work, they can blow off steam when they get home. But it didn't work that way for us because we just continued the same arguments when we got home."

At the age of eighteen, Lucie moved out of the house and got her own apartment, much to Lucy's distress. The following year, 1970, she began dating Phil Vandervort, an actor-director, and she announced her intention to marry him. Lucy, who tended to characterize her daughter's dates as "fishheads," thought Lucie was too inexperienced—she needed to date other men, gain some knowledge of herself and the world. Still, Lucie's problems paled besides Desi Jr.'s.

As his sister declared her love for a disapproved man, the seventeen-year-old Desi Jr. began a romance with the twenty-three-year-old Patty Duke. The actress's résumé read like something from a Zola novel. The child of alcoholics, Anna Marie Duke had been abused psychologically and sexually by her managers, a couple who lived off the earnings of their young client. At the age of sixteen, Anna (now called Patty) landed the part of the young Helen Keller in *The Miracle Worker* and won an Academy Award. She also married at that age, at least partly to get away from the people who were driving her to the brink of madness. Several years later the gifted actress was the centerpiece of *The Patty Duke Show*, in which she played identical cousins. All the while, she drank and experimented with drugs. Currently she was separated from her husband but not divorced, a volatile young woman who squandered money, bit her fingernails down to the quick, had a history of suicide attempts, and was dependent on chemicals, alcohol, and tobacco—in short, a mother's nightmare.

Lucy did what she could to break up the affair; as Duke noted in her memoir, Desi's mother "felt she was in a crisis situation, and her attitude was efficient and cold, with barely a veneer of politeness." The attitude had no effect. Late in the year Patty gave out the news that she was pregnant, and that Desi Jr. was the father. Desi Sr. was apparently unperturbed at the thought of becoming a grandfather; "boys will be boys" seemed to be his view of the matter. Lucy was not so sanguine. She said Duke was "living in some fantastic dreamworld, and we're the victims of it. Desi being the tender age of seventeen when they met, she used him."

Sean Duke was born in February 1971, and the tabloid press closed in. Lucy visited the infant, wearing a heavy veil so that reporters wouldn't recognize her, but she refused to acknowledge the child as a blood relative. Thinking back to the beginnings of the romance, and noting Sean's birthday, she said, "none of the dates made sense to me." Her math was correct. Much later Duke admitted that the father was John Astin, a married actor who eventually left his wife in order to marry Patty. Desi Jr. promptly took up with Liza Minnelli, almost seven years his senior.

In the meantime, Lucie had gone against her mother's wishes and wed Phil Vandervort. The marriage would be over in a year. After that she began to date Jim Bailey, a female impersonator and ex-boyfriend of Liza. Bailey was to tell Lucy biographer Charles Higham: "Lucy liked me very much. But when I started my involvement with her daughter she told me she used to lie awake nights trying to figure it all out. She kept asking herself, 'Isn't he? Is he? Is he gay? Isn't he? If he wears a dress, which is he? How could he be having an affair with my daughter?" Some evenings, the obsession with her children's affairs got completely out of hand. At a screening of Woody Allen's cheeky *Everything You Always Wanted to Know about Sex but Were Afraid to Ask*, Lucy did her Queen Canute act, erupting in fury: "Am I seeing a man making love to a *sheep*? Am I seeing a man who is married with children wearing a *gown*? Am I seeing a *breast* appearing over the horizon? Has civilization come to an end? Take this picture off! Now! Immediately! This is filth!" It was as if by an act of will she could push time backward, past the Vietnam War, the youthquake, the clanging music of the Doors, the lyrics of Bob Dylan warning his older listeners about what was blowing in the wind, the experiments with drugs, the sexual revolution, the bumper stickers reading QUESTION AUTHORITY—as if she could re-create 1952, when she and Desi ruled the airwaves and all things and all people were in their places and the music was good and the laughter did not come out of a can and the world was as stable as Twentieth Century–Fox.

*T*here were times when Lucy must have wondered why fate had turned against her with such a will. Even in small matters she seemed to be rolling snake-eyes. Jess Oppenheimer, the father of *I Love Lucy* and in many ways a father figure for Lucille Ball, threatened a lawsuit. He charged that the character Lucy played in *The Lucy Show* and *Here's Lucy* was basically Mrs. Ricky Ricardo. As such she derived her humor from his conception of a scheming, though genial, ditz. Lucy's lawyers knew he had a case and advised her to settle out of court. She did, to the tune of $220,000, and avoided him thereafter. (Gary Morton quietly continued to play golf with Oppenheimer, without mentioning the fact to his wife.) The payout, and various wrangles with Desi Jr. and Lucie, coupled with reminders of advancing age, seemed to accentuate Lucy's eccentricities. On cross-country flights she would suddenly unbuckle her seat belt and begin compulsively cleaning the floors and the toilets, distressing the stewardesses who recognized her and astonishing the passengers who didn't. She raised hell in rehearsals when things went wrong, and anyone and anything that contradicted her anywhere got the full force of her wrath. Actress Kaye Ballard remembered biking alongside Lucy when a dog appeared from a yard and barked at them ferociously. "Get back in those bushes, you son of a bitch!" ordered Lucy. The dog turned tail and ran off. DeDe, vigorous in her eighties, warned director Herbert Kenwith that her daughter was the bitch everyone said. Lucy, who heard the remark, protested, "I am not! Only when I'm working." Countered her mother reasonably, "But that is when people see you."

The only pleasant news—or so it seemed at the time—was Lucy's continuing popular appeal. Jerry Herman's arch, campy musical *Mame* opened on Broadway 1966 and ran for 1,508 performances. Two years later Warner–Seven Arts bought the film rights for $3 million plus a percentage of the remaining theatrical grosses. Several high-powered actresses were rumored to be up for the role, including Elizabeth Taylor, and also Angela Lansbury, who had played the original Mame Dennis onstage and who made the mistake of saying, "If they're going to do my *Mame,* then I'll have to do the film." Lucy got the part.

All these years, Lucy had relied on Desi's advice, but this time when he told her to pass on the role she ignored him. Author Patrick Dennis had made a fortune when he introduced the world to his quotable aunt—"Life is a banquet and most poor suckers are starving to death"—in the 1955 best-seller. Rosalind Russell took the title role in the 1958 film, *Auntie Mame;* she got fine notices and for most moviegoers became the definitive Mame. Lucy thought she could top Roz; playing the extravagant Mame Dennis would be the capstone of her career and no one was going to talk her out of it.

As usual, Desi's instincts were on the money. It was not only a question of age—for much of the play and film Auntie Mame is supposed to be a woman in her forties, as indeed Angela Lansbury was when she played her in New York. Lucy was also an inappropriate choice because her comic persona was that of a naïf, a sweet conspirator undone by her own strategies. Mame Dennis was a sharp-tongued, sophisticated *professoressa* in the school of life.

The film was still in the planning stage when Lucy took a break and traveled to Snowmass, Colorado. She had found a new retreat in the white-capped mountains, where she bought three condominiums, one on top of the other, for herself, the children, and any visitors who might drop in. Gary had no use for cold weather; golf was his game, not skiing. Lucy sometimes went there on her own, happy for a little solitude after so much family tsuris. However, in an extended celebration of the Christmas season, Gary was there early in January 1972, as were DeDe, Lucie, and Desi Jr. and Liza Minnelli. Lucy had begun to take up skiing. She had mastered stilts when one of the *Lucy* shows called for her to walk on them, and done somersaults on a wire in her fifties. To a natural athlete, what was the big deal about going downhill on a couple of boards? So what if she was sixty years old? In hindsight, Lucy's insouciance seemed to have tempted fate, for as she was standing and talking, a female skier lost control and collided with her. There was the confusing sound of a snap, much louder to Lucy than to the onlookers, and she collapsed in agony. Her right leg had been broken in four places.

Medical help arrived almost immediately, and Desi Jr., Liza, and Lucie followed the ambulance to the local hospital. Lucie remembered her mother screaming, "not from the pain, but because of the hundreds of people she thought would be thrown out of work because of her condition. She thought it was over." "It" was not only *Mame* but *Here's Lucy* and Lucille Ball Productions. Almost as soon as Lucy came out from under the anesthetic, depression set in. "I'll never work again," she was heard to say. "To hell with it. To hell with it all." A few days later she changed her mind, ripping off the leg-length cast twice before she got something that allowed her more freedom of movement. "It was hell," she remembered. Then she added philosophically: "Of course, things always happen to me like this. All my life it's been arms legs arms legs arms legs." Flown to Palm Springs for convalescence, she received Robert Fryer, producer of *Mame.* He guaranteed that she would not be replaced; preproduction of the movie would stop in its tracks until she had made a total recovery.

Here's Lucy employees were astonished and gratified to find their president back in the saddle less than a month after the accident, filming the next episode. "For Mom," Lucie said, "it was like doing *Whose Life Is It Anyway?*" That play concerned a paraplegic whose only moving part was his face. Lucy was luckier; the scripts, rewritten to accommodate her disability, put her in bed or in a wheelchair, where she could at least use her torso. As Geoffrey Mark Fidelman remarks in *The Lucy Book,* the accident turned out to be a plus for the series. It provided a continuity and focus previously absent from the program. Because Lucy was in a wheelchair or leg cast it would have been unseemly for her boss to yell at her, so the writers gave Gale Gordon a more agreeable persona. The former antagonists became emotional equals rather than simply boss and employee, and the Lucy character, at long last, was allowed to grow older. No one referred to her as a young lady anymore.

$\mathcal{D}$esi's show business career was not quite finished. "I was tired," he claimed, "of seeing Ricardo Montalban and Fernando Lamas in all those Mexican roles." He was also tired of being television's forgotten man. And so he appeared in an episode of *The Men from Shiloh,* a Western series, some twenty-five pounds heavier but looking none the worse for his bouts with severe diverticulitis. He had sold his horse-breeding farm and now spent almost all his leisure hours fishing in Mexico or relaxing on the grounds of his Del Mar house. If no new money was coming in, he had plans to produce several new series. And perhaps he would do some more acting now that he had gotten his feet wet again. Lucy wasn't the only one with talent, the networks were continually reminded.

True enough, but Desi's greatest gifts lay in his uncanny ability to put writers on the appropriate properties, and to cast the ideal actors in the right roles. Thus he could not help but feel a great sadness and frustration at the start of 1973, when the cameras began to film Lucy in *Mame.* For Desi it must have been like watching a train wreck in slow motion. The skiing accident had caused a sixteen-month postpone-ment, and George Cukor, who had directed Judy Garland in *her* sensa-tional comeback film, *A Star Is Born,* dropped out to fill other commitments. Cukor was replaced by the inexperienced Gene Saks, director of the Broadway *Mame.* Leonard Gershe, who had adapted the Gershwins' *Funny Face* and Cole Porter's *Silk Stockings,* was announced as the scenarist, but the script was eventually done by Paul Zindel. That writer's main credits were for stage works, most notably the off-Broadway play *The Effect of Gamma Rays on Man-in-the-Moon Marigolds.* Bette Davis, who made no secret of her desire to play Vera Charles, Mame's "bosom buddy," was passed over in favor of Beatrice Arthur, the original Broadway Vera—and, not coincidentally, Gene Saks's wife. The comic actress Madeline Kahn had been signed to play Agnes Gooch, the terrified spinster who becomes liberated by Mame's lust for life. Five weeks into rehearsals Lucy challenged her, "When are you going to show us Gooch?" Replied Kahn, "I have." It was the wrong answer. Kahn later claimed, "The producers explained a few things, and let me go, wishing I could have stayed." Lucy thought there was more to the dismissal than that: Madeline "got them for fifty grand, and she knew all she had to do was play it cool—she would get paid off and go to work immediately on [Mel Brooks's comedy] *Blazing Saddles.* She had no intention of giving me Gooch." Jane Connell, who had played the part on the stage, took Kahn's place.

For most of the nineteen weeks of shooting, Lucy suffered from anxiety and leg pains. The tension manifested itself in an argument with her longtime makeup man, Hal King, who had been using a liquid adhesive to conceal the actress's wrinkles. The device hurt, and Lucy's temper was short anyway; she slapped him during an argument and he walked off the picture.

As soon as the doctors gave her the green light to begin rehearsals, Lucy began to rise at 5 a.m. and spend ninety minutes every morning stretching and bending before she drove to the set. With all this preparation, choreographer Onna White could do only so much with an actress whose great versatility had never included terpsichore. When writer Charles Higham visited her on the set, Lucy exploded: "Why am I doing this? I must be out of my mind. Dancing for a whole hour, exercise, the vocal coach, Jesus. Movies! The *hours*! It's like running backward!" As a friend remarked, "Lucy knew very well why she was working her tail off: it was in the hope of firing the last stage of her rocket—becoming a movie diva in her sixties."

When the filming concluded, Lucy gave out interviews pushing *Mame* as a family movie. She made it, she insisted, "because I don't want the industry to go down the sewer, and I mean *sewer*! There are too many lines around the wrong movie houses these days." She cited the Bernardo Bertolucci film *Last Tango in Paris* as a prime example of sex gone wrong. "I don't know why Marlon Brando would lower himself to do a film like that. I think there are a lot of dirty old men making a fast buck—and confusing young people." She kept making that point wherever she journeyed, and, as the New York opening approached, turned an episode of *Here's Lucy* into a half-hour plug for the upcoming *Mame*.

All the plans, all the promises and aspirations crashed in March 1974, when *Mame* had what was called a World Premiere at Lincoln Center for the Performing Arts. (The film then moved on to Radio City Music Hall.) Desi proved to be right in all respects. Lucy was miscast and unprotected; everything had slalomed downhill from there. Worse musicals had preceded it in the 1970s, among them the tuneless *Song of Norway,* starring an unconvincing Florence Henderson, and the plodding *Lost Horizon,* which contained Bert Bacharach and Hal David's worst score. But this one seemed to irritate the critics in a new and different manner, and most of them went out of their way to be unkind. It was as if they were personally affronted by a TV personality who dared to criticize the film business, and who had the effrontery to go above herself. In *Newsweek,* Paul D. Zimmerman wrote: "There she stands, her aging face practically a blur in the protective gauze of softer-than-soft focus, her eyes misting, her remarkably well kept figure gift-wrapped in the fashions of the twenties, looking alternately like any one of the seven deadly sins and a decorator wing chair." In *Time,* Jay Cocks observed: "Miss Ball has been molded over the years into some sort of national monument, and she performs like one too. Her grace, her timing, her vigor have all vanished." Cocks wrote that only Bea Arthur brought the film to life: "She tucks *Mame* under her arm and walks away with it, although not far enough." In the *New Yorker,* Pauline Kael made the cruelest assessment, giving the project a homosexual spin: "Why did Lucille Ball do *Mame?* After more than forty years in movies and TV (and five years of chorus work and assorted jobs before that)—after conquering the world—did she discover in herself an unfilled ambition to be a flaming drag queen?" The audience, looking at the star, is "not thinking of fun," Kael goes on, "we're thinking of age and self-deception. When Mame's best friend, Vera Charles (Bea Arthur), asks her, 'How old do you think I am?' and Mame answers, 'Somewhere between forty and death,' one may feel a shudder in the audience. How can a woman well over sixty say a line like that, with the cameraman using every lying device he knows and still unable to hide the blurred eyes?"

Lucy called the critical response "a shellacking" and never really got over it. She put up a cheery front, pointing out that *Mame*'s first weeks had broken box office records at Radio City. As time went on, though, she kept rereading the knocks, like a casualty whose fingers keep straying to the wound. *People* magazine reporter Jim Watters was less than friendly about the way she was "regally apportioning her time" during a publicity trip to New York: "ninety minutes with prestigious if low-rated Dick Cavett to an evening accepting a 'Ruby' (named after Keeler) award hosted by a homosexual-oriented magazine." When he confessed that he was less than enthusiastic about *Mame,* she should have stayed away from the subject. Instead she gave Watters a ten-minute diatribe on the deterioration of American cinema: " 'Don't you think there is a need for pictures that won't strain to the nth degree every bone in your body? Don't you have enough reality so that in a theater you should be entertained? I suppose you like covering the waterfront. I bet you even liked *Last Tango,*' she asserted in her best basso tones." In Chicago Lucy broke down during an interview with *Sun-*

Times critic Gene Siskel. "It's not that I'm tired," she said as tears rolled down her face. "Why do the newspapers have to send people just so they can take ugly pictures of me?" she wailed. "So I look my age— what's wrong with that? These stories make me feel wrong and old."

*I*n a sad synchrony, the rest of her career wound down in 1974. *Here's Lucy* had slipped badly in the ratings; for the first time in her life, a Lucille Ball program failed to make the Nielsen Top Twenty. CBS statisticians had been charting her waning popularity for months, but the network's management had not dared to intervene because Lucy was still a beloved figure all across the United States. But by the winter of 1974 it was decided that *Here's Lucy* had turned into a liability. Meeting upon meeting followed, until an announcement confirmed the water-cooler speculations. After twenty-three years as a television superstar, Lucille Ball would ring down the curtain on weekly comedy. A CBS press release hastily added that Miss Ball and the network were still great friends. To demonstrate that affection she would be in an "undisclosed number of specials" in the 1975–1976 season.

Here, at least, the press was indulgent. The *New York Times* noted that the various *Lucy* shows were running in seventy-seven countries. In a valedictory, the paper saluted Lucy, saying she "was to CBS what Milton Berle had been to the National Broadcasting Company during the early days of television, and she was credited by CBS with winning an audience to make it competitive." The *Los Angeles Times* saw Lucille Ball as an international figure on the order of Chaplin. Her works were "playing in so many countries that a salesman once said that he knew when *Lucy* had reached a new nation of Africa or Asia by finding babies named Lucy."

The subject of this adulation was unwilling to call it a day, to put her feet up, take stock of her career, and organize her scrapbooks. DeDe was still around, and watching the spry old lady with the dyed red hair allowed Lucy to feel that she herself was in an extended period of middle age. And since neither Desi Jr. nor Lucie had settled down yet, she could compare herself with women decades younger, whose children were in much the same fix.

In his twenties, Desi Jr. embarked on a new career as a film actor, appearing as Marco Polo in the comedy *Marco,* and as a young half-

Indian in the Western *Billy Two Hats,* costarring Gregory Peck. The years of performing on the stage and television had given him a professional sheen. In addition, the now lean and attractive young man had inherited great measures of his father's charm and his mother's drive. Still, he never quite caught on. There were new romances after Liza Minnelli became distracted by Peter Sellars when she was off filming in England. And there were more drug trips and more alcohol.

In contrast, Lucie was beginning to carve out an independent show business career. A tall, striking young woman, she developed a cabaret act, did regional theater, then landed her first major role, as the neurotic dancer Gittel Mosca in the 1974–1975 national tour of the musical *Two for the Seesaw.* In 1975, she played the title role in NBC's *Who Is the Black Dahlia?,* based on the true story of an unsolved Los Angeles slaying. The same year she starred in *Death Scream,* an ABC drama inspired by the murder of Kitty Genovese, whose screams for help were ignored by her New York City neighbors.

Lucy kept almost as busy in 1975. She was the lodestar of *Grand Ole Opry*'s farcical "Lucy Comes to Nashville," and of the CBS seriocomedy *Three for Two,* opposite Jackie Gleason. Lucy had long nourished the idea of playing Lillian Russell to Jackie Gleason's Diamond Jim Brady; this was the closest she was to come. In the first vignette, Lucy, wearing a black wig with silver highlights, impersonated a neglected wife. In the second, as a plain hausfrau having an affair, she wore an upswept blonde wig and a feather boa. In the third, sporting an upswept brown wig and a close-fitting gown, she played a manipulative mother and wife. Lucy's versatility was not enough to save the show. Too few of the lines were moving or funny, and *Three for Two* found no favor with the critics—*Variety* judged it a "dismal trio of one-act plays about unpleasant and stupid people." Despite this assessment, the paper held no grudge, praising her work in the semiautobiographical *What Now, Catherine Curtis?* on CBS. For the first time since her pregnancy Lucy had gained noticeable weight. Nevertheless, under a well-made brunette wig she looked more attractive than she had in years, and she acted with unaccustomed subtlety and poignance. Miss Ball, maintained *Variety,* gave "an outstanding performance as a middle-aged divorcée emotionally shattered by the end of a twenty-year marriage."

One show broadcast that year was notable for Lucy's absence. "NBC's Saturday Night," shot in New York, employed its young *Satur-*

day Night Live stars—plus Desi Arnaz Sr. and Jr.—to send up *I Love Lucy* and Desilu's *The Untouchables*. Desi Jr. was to look back benignly on the program. "*I Love Lucy* had never been satirized by anyone," he told Geoffrey Mark Fidelman. "It was groundbreaking in a strange way." His sister was not so sanguine. "I remember watching that show in my mother's condo in Aspen and thinking it was dreadful. I had a feeling they were making fun of my father, and fooling him into thinking they were tributing him. It really bothered me that they never even let him finish singing 'Babalu.' I felt really sad for him afterward, like he had been used."

Desi got his own back, and more, when his autobiography, *A Book*, was published the following year. It was a candid, oddly appealing work, done without a ghostwriter. The author enjoyed a little self-mockery, as in the account of his sexual initiation: "I was obviously anxious and noticeably ready for action, and getting more and more frustrated by the minute. We had tried a number of ridiculous experiments and were working on a new one when there was a loud knock on the door. It was her mother, the cook, asking her to come out. I didn't have any trouble putting on my trunks in a hurry. The small proof of my anxiety had disappeared. I wish I could have done the same."

But for the most part *A Book* was a straightforward account of the romantic, financial, and familial relationship of Lucille Ball and Desi Arnaz, from Desi's point of view. Desi summoned up the grand beginnings, the exciting heyday of *I Love Lucy*, the building of the studio, the children as youngsters, and finally the arguments, the split, and the paradise lost. "The irony of it all," he concluded, "is how our undreamed-of success, fame, and fortune turned it all to hell." Only a few books have been encapsulated by the pictures on the dust jacket. Desi's was one of them. On the back, a handsome young Cuban flashed a brilliant smile as he hammered a set of conga drums. A lifetime later, Desi squinted out from the cover, gesturing to an audience with cigarillo in hand. The younger man hadn't a line on his face. The older man was seamed and weary, battered by life and circumstances and—as he ruefully acknowledged in his memoir—by too damn many self-inflicted wounds.

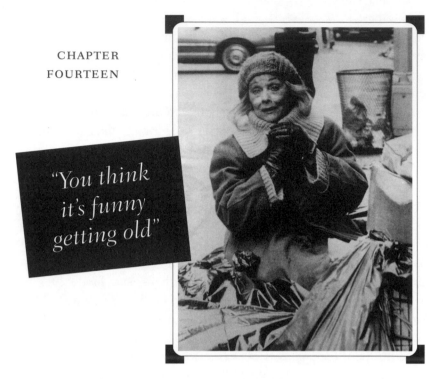

"You think
it's funny
getting old"

IN THE MID-1970S and beyond, the losses went on. Lucy's onetime neighbor Jack Benny, the man who had taught her so much about timing, died in 1974. Early in 1977, DeDe, aged eighty-five, suffered a stroke that confined her to a house in Brentwood. Lucy had bought the place to provide DeDe with the illusion of independence, but she called in every morning, dreading the day when no one would pick up the phone. It came on July 22.

DeDe had been in the audience for thousands of broadcasts, and Lucy remained shocked and disoriented long after her mother's death. Two months later, as taping began for the special "Lucy Calls the President," the star abruptly shouted: "Cut!" She explained to the onlookers: "I'm sorry, I got off to a bad start. My DeDe is usually in the audience, and damn it, that threw me at the top. That was my Mom. She's made every show for all these years and it suddenly dawned on me as I was coming down the stairs. Forgive me! I'm glad I got that out of my system and I'm awfully glad you're here. It was maudlin, but I just couldn't help it."

In the cast of that special was Vivian Vance, making what was to be her last public appearance. She had suffered a minor stroke, and Lucy sent her to a specialist. Back came Vivian with the news: "Your fucking doctor says I have cancer!" The diagnosis was correct. She immediately went off to northern California to receive radiation treatments.

During this time Lucy appeared in a number of other specials, ranging from *Circus of the Stars* to the *Mary Tyler Moore Hour,* the latter an experience she preferred to forget: "I'd say something to Mary and she'd smile that big toothy smile and walk away." Lucy became notorious for her crankiness on the set, no doubt a reaction to all that was going on around her, and to her consciousness of encroaching age. Late in 1977 she sat for an unpleasant interview with Barbara Walters, during which she retailed what had already become a standard cascade: "Desi is a loser. A gambler, an alcoholic, a skirt chaser . . . a financially smart man but self-destructive." She characterized Gary, who sat beside her, as a welcome contrast. All the pent-up bitterness began to affect her performances. On a *Steve Allen Comedy Hour* special, for example, Allen resurrected an old hospital routine he had written with comedian Gene Rayburn. Originally, Rayburn had played a patient swathed head to toe in bandages; Jayne Meadows had played the man's wife. "Jayne got screams," Allen recalled, "doing it perfectly as she grabs at him in innocence, concern, and hysteria. We were looking for something strong for Lucy to do on this show. Yet, to our surprise, when she did it there were no laughs at all. We had to sweeten the laugh track later. She didn't do the right kind of hysterics. There was no believability to what she did." The irony of all this was that in 1977 Lucy had been named one of the ten most admired women in a Gallup poll, coming in ahead of Mamie Eisenhower, Barbara Walters, and Queen Elizabeth II.

To many of her colleagues it seemed that Lucille Ball had suddenly become obsolete—reason enough for the Friars Club to give her a tribute. It was their way of acknowledging comedians who were passé without being senile. An extraordinary group of performers and politicians attended, including the opera diva Beverly Sills, comedian Carol Burnett, and Los Angeles mayor Tom Bradley. They were joined by a parade of movie stars, among them John Wayne, James Stewart, and

Henry Fonda. When the accolades were over, Lucy stood up and said wistfully: "I must have done something right, but I cannot be as great as everyone's said. So I'll just accept a third of the compliments, gratefully."

*E*xcept for appearances in the occasional special, compliments were about all Lucy was to receive for the next year and a half. To pass the time she taught a course in television film and aesthetics at California State University, Northridge. Essentially, she said, she would instruct those majoring in communications in the practical, get-you-through-the-day basics of survival in the TV and film industries. "They [the students] are thrown out with what they think are all the ingredients, but sometimes they have to start from scratch. I emphasize self-preservation."

Self-preservation was something Lucy had majored in all her life, but at that moment she could have used a little help. Character actress Mary Wickes tried to supply it. The *I Love Lucy* stalwart was acting in summer stock in 1979 when she persuaded Lucy to fly to San Francisco for a sentimental journey. Together the two old friends called on a bedridden Vivian Vance. Most of the stay was spent in happy reminiscence between Lucy and Vivian, with Mary off in a corner. The laughter lasted for two hours; afterward the visitors cried all the way to the airport. Vance died that August.

In the following year came an event that seemed a reproach—until Lucy realized how much it would change her daughter's life for the better. In 1979 Lucie Arnaz had truly emerged from the family shadow to star in the Neil Simon–Marvin Hamlisch Broadway musical *They're Playing Our Song*. *Time* enthusiastically noted that Lucie "hurdles the barricade of being the daughter of Lucille Ball and Desi Arnaz by imitating neither, but she has inherited their incomparable comic timing." Down the street, Laurence Luckinbill was making his own mark in another Simon production, the autobiographical comedy *Chapter Two*. The actors met at Joe Allen, a restaurant in the theater district, fell in love, and announced marriage plans. Not only had Luckinbill previously been married and fathered two sons, he was also seventeen years older than Lucie—a marked difference from Lucy, whose two husbands were each six years her junior. Desi had no trouble accepting his prospective son-in-law, and Lucy soon came around. (And wisely so: the Arnaz-Luckinbill marriage was to prove successful and durable, and made her the grandmother of two boys and a girl.) Both Lucy and Desi showed up for the wedding in upstate New York. Lucy surprised no one when she cried during the ceremony. Afterward her ex-husband, always a crowd-pleaser, sang the *I Love Lucy* theme.

Back in Hollywood, Lucy made only one significant comedy special in 1980: *Lucy Moves to NBC.* She had been with CBS for almost thirty years, and the broadcast signaled that her old network no longer needed or wanted her. In theory, Lucille Ball Productions would be creating comedies at her new home; in reality, very little would come from the association, and that little was not to be popular.

Discomfort seemed to follow Lucy these days. She hit the white wine bottle a little harder than usual, and sometimes the clear fluid in her water glass was vodka. Richard Schickel had written the narration for a special, *High Hopes: The Capra Years,* an homage to director Frank Capra. The critic-scenarist provided a picture of Lucy at that time when he journeyed out to her house one afternoon and found her "slightly in her cups." He reported: "She was nice and slightly vague and uninterested in the niceties of the hostly prose I'd drafted for her to speak. On set, I noticed she was wearing those little weights behind her ears that older actresses sometimes use to pull the skin on their faces tighter. But basically she came, did her brief job, and departed. What she had to do with Capra I'll never know. Probably just the network seeking stars—any stars—to perk up a show they eventually played just once (on Christmas Eve)."

That year was not a good one for her ex-husband, either. When Jimmy Durante died in 1980, his widow asked Desi to help with the funeral. According to comedian Jack Carter, "He was so out of it that he kept inviting people who were dead. He kept calling that old race-track crowd, and they were all gone. He was thinking of people from thirty years ago when they were all kids. At the funeral Desi stood in the back, stammering. He didn't know where he was. He was even bombed that day."

In 1981, rehearsing for a Milton Berle special for HBO, Lucy saw Gary Morton attempting to provoke the host. "Hey, Uncle Miltie," Morton asked loudly. "Why don't you relax and let everyone do their jobs?" Berle rose to the bait: "And what did you ever direct, you son of a bitch, that your wife didn't arrange for?" The seventy-year-old Lucy was clearly uncomfortable with the argument that followed, and with the resolution—sullen laughter on the part of both comedians. Two years later she and Gary took an apartment in Manhattan at 211 East Seventieth Street in order to spend more time with the grandchildren—Lucie and Laurence Luckinbill then lived across town. The place was decorated with much more formality than her California house, and the little Luckinbills sensed it. They were not comfortable there, nor was Lucy with them. Mainly, when she got the urge to see grandchildren, she went to their place. Lee Tannen, Gary Morton's cousin, grew very close to Lucy in her last years. He observed that the family visits were infrequent and later wrote that he found the situation "sad, because it seemed to me like it was always such an obligation for Lucy to be with her children and now with her grandchildren as well."

She seemed to take more solace in the handful of ceremonies arranged in her honor. One occurred in 1984, when at a televised *All-Star Party for Lucille Ball,* Sammy Davis Jr. gushed before a crowd of fellow performers: "God wanted the world to laugh, and He invented you. Many are called, but you were chosen." Davis went on to analyze Lucy's talent. "Clown you are not. All of the funny hats, the baggy pants, the moustaches and the wigs, the pratfalls and the blacked-out teeth—they didn't fool us for one minute. We saw through the disguises, and what we found inside is more than we deserve." More accolades came her way: the Television Hall of Fame made her the first female inductee in 1984, and the Museum of Broadcasting in New York staged an evening in her honor.

Grateful as Lucy was for such tributes, they gave her the feeling that she was being eulogized rather than saluted. The things that were said were the kind one said about the dear departed. And, indeed, it was not until 1985 that she was again welcomed back on television as an actress. At the age of seventy-three she appeared in *Stone Pillow,* playing a homeless crone wandering the cold Manhattan streets. Lucy was still a star, and certain script changes were made on her insistence. The protagonist's name, for example, became Flora Belle, in honor of Lucy's maternal grandmother. She also decided that the character would be a vegetarian—"because it's healthier. I'd just need one carrot." And she devised Flora Belle's makeup and costume. What she did not choose was the weather—*Stone Pillow* was supposed to take place in February, but was shot in the middle of an unexpectedly sweltering

New York spring. Suffering under layers of clothing, Lucy lost twenty-three pounds over the course of the six-week production. In addition, she suffered periodically from dehydration, and as if that were not enough, she tore a tendon during a rehearsed fight when an actress held on to her too long. All this failed to bank the fire of her performance. Lucy was tough on herself and tougher on the staff. Even a bunch of street rodents, trained for the purpose, were reviled for being too tame. "These are sissy rats," she proclaimed. "I want real ones." *Stone Pillow*'s scenarist and coproducer, Rose Leiman Goldemberg, was amused by Lucy's confrontation with a supposedly stray canine: "The dog they hired didn't want to come. In the final cut, she just grabbed that dog and pulled him down. She was gonna have him whether he wanted to come or not."

Precious few pleasures could be derived from the making of the TV movie, but anonymity was one of them: Lucy liked to walk a few blocks in her costume, trying it out on the public to see if anyone would recognize her. No one ever realized that the hunched old woman was Lucille Ball. She related the experience to Katharine Hepburn, when they met on the East Side. Instead of being amused at the bag lady role, Hepburn warned, "You know, of course, darling, you'll be inundated with those." Hepburn was right: the only scripts that came Lucy's way that summer were about pathetic old folk. Yet Lucy remained optimistic about the work; as she saw it, good reviews were just about guaranteed. Goldemberg's spousal-abuse drama, *The Burning Bed,* had impressed critics the year before, and the director would be George Schaefer, winner of numerous awards for his elegant *Hallmark Television Playhouse* productions.

If Lucy was impressed by these résumés, the critics were not. Their appraisals were almost uniformly negative. The *New York Times* was among the most lenient when its reviewer observed, "Anyone in search of biting, or even illuminating, social insights in *Stone Pillow* can look elsewhere, perhaps only as far as the streets outside the window." The *Boston Globe* fumed: "At a recent press conference, Ball said she gave up on television comedy because it was all filth—'sex, sex, sex.' But there aren't many situation comedies as obscene as a television movie that would exploit the plight of the homeless for the sake of the ratings envisioned from resurrecting a faded comedian's career." The *Washington Post* added: "What Ball does with the character of Flora the bag lady qualifies more as an appearance than an actual performance."

Looking back, Lucie Arnaz remarked on just how difficult *Stone Pillow* had been for her mother: "She wasn't well. She kept getting these attacks where she got very hot and couldn't work. She had a bad heart. It was in the middle of summer, and here she was dressed in these layers of clothes. She had always been claustrophobic anyway. And the script was not that strong. I think at this time in her life it was almost too much for her to learn a script and create a character that was different from 'Lucy.' She just wasn't up to it physically." Lucy took some comfort from the Nielsens: that season *Stone Pillow* earned the second-highest rating for TV films. But it was not enough to make her forget the situations of the two Desis.

Desi Jr. had married an aspiring actress, Linda Purl, in 1979. She had appeared with him on a couple of TV movies, and Lucy had come to accept her as a daughter-in-law. At times she appeared to think that Linda might be marrying beneath herself, if only because she seemed so organized. "If there's anyone in the world who isn't organized, it's my son," said Lucy to a *People* magazine reporter. "I hope she rubs off on him and he doesn't rub off on her." Neither rubbing occurred; a year later Desi Jr. and Linda divorced, and several columnists hinted that the cause of the split was the young man's problems with substance abuse.

Desi Sr. continued to have his own bouts with alcoholism, spurning friends who refused to give him a drink, and sinking deeper into despair, intensified by the news that his second wife, Edie, was dying of cancer. Then, through an act of will and the counsel of the family physician, Marcus Rabwin, Desi Jr. checked into the recovery center at Scripps Memorial Hospital, determined to overcome his addictions. When he walked out he was clean, and he stayed that way. Convinced that he could serve as an example to others, Desi Jr. persuaded his father to come to the recovery center. There the gray-haired, sallow figure stood next to his son and daughter, who came along for moral support, and in the time-worn manner addressed the assembled addicts: "I'm Desi and I'm an alcoholic." For two months the stoicism worked— then the backsliding began. Desi Sr. missed meetings, stayed home, and finally drugged himself with painkillers. In the year of *Stone Pillow* Edie passed away, and Desi moved into a small house in Del Mar with his old and ailing mother. The money, once so plentiful, was ebbing along with his health. Conditions were to get worse. In 1986 his persistent cough was diagnosed: he had lung cancer.

The encroachments and reminders of age were too painful for Lucy to contemplate, and too close to ignore. The only salvation was work. But who would have her? She had already been rejected by CBS, and the arrangement with NBC had not been satisfactory. Of the big networks, only ABC was left. It was all she needed. Executives at the American Broadcasting Company were impressed with the ratings of *Stone Pillow,* and they convinced themselves that Lucy's celebrity was still viable.

Their belief was born out of desperation. At the National Broadcasting Company, comedian Bill Cosby had broken racial barriers with his family-centered *Cosby Show,* and a new comedy series about older women, *The Golden Girls,* was reinforcing NBC's reputation as the network to watch. As ABC programmers saw it, Lucille Ball's credentials would make her the ideal candidate for a rival sitcom—after all, the woman had made her fortune with family comedy, and she certainly qualified as a golden-ager. So anxious was the network for her services that Lucy was given full creative control over her new series. With the writers and producers, she decided to build it around an ornery widow who had inherited one-half of a hardware store. Gale Gordon would be her disputatious partner. Together the two would display their familiar knack for getting into, and out of, comic catastrophes.

Gary Morton was listed as executive producer along with Aaron Spelling, but it was the latter who would do the heavy lifting. Spelling had a unique history with Lucy. Close watchers of *I Love Lucy* reruns could spot him as the young performer who played the foil to "Tennessee Ernie" Ford when the singer made guest appearances. Spelling had forsaken his acting career to become a producer—one of the most successful in television history. He was the creative force behind *Charlie's Angels, Dynasty, The Love Boat,* and other hit series, and when he signed on to produce *Life with Lucy* ABC confidently booked the series for Saturday nights. It was expected to dominate the evening.

The show was bought without a pilot. Network programmers assumed that Lucy knew all there was to know about making a Lucille Ball comedy—what was the point in wasting money on a tryout? Lucy began on a note of triumph. From his bedside, Desi cheered her on: "What took you so long to get back to work?" Buoyed by his spirit and by happy memories of the old days, she hired Bob and Madelyn. Gale Gordon happily clambered aboard. "He'd try anything," she remarked to her friend Jim Brochu with admiration. "Do anything we asked him to. He was always taking chances. He was eighty years old, and he could still turn a cartwheel."

Gordon proved to be the show's only asset. Lucy had trouble memorizing lines and depended heavily on cue cards. These completely threw off her comic timing. Moreover, no makeup could disguise the fact that she was more than threescore and ten, and her physical bits caused anxiety rather than amusement. The first episode pulled well; ratings went precipitously downhill from there. As Steve Allen saw it, "Lucy's comedy did not age well, meaning the things she did weren't as funny as she got into her late sixties and seventies. She couldn't handle the physicality or pull off being so cutesy." Allen found himself agreeing with Pauline Kael: "Like most attractive women in show business, Lucy eventually wound up looking a little like a drag queen."

The critics closed in. Lucy tried to harden herself against negative reviews, but the appraisals of *Life with Lucy* were more than pans, they were condemnations. In *Channels* magazine, William A. Henry III summed up the general feeling of hostile disappointment: "That wasn't Lucy up on the screen. It was some elderly imposter. Caked with makeup, she looked mummified." The article went on to describe the protagonist's voice as akin to "a bullfrog's in agony," and added: "She gamely attempted her old style of slapstick but her impeccable timing had fled. Worse, what used to be cute and girlish in a younger woman, and in a male chauvinist era, turned out to be embarrassing in a senior citizen. . . . Her new impossible dream of agelessness only saddened audiences with its intimations of mortality."

Lucy appealed to Desi for counsel; he was too ill to help, and in any case *Life with Lucy* was already on life support. When the Nielsens listed it in seventy-first place, ABC pulled the very expensive plug. In all, thirteen episodes were filmed and eight were aired. However, the network had agreed up front to fund all twenty-two, and it paid in full. Each segment was worth $150,000 to Lucy, $100,000 to her husband, and $25,000 to Gordon.

The money, good as it was, did not assuage Lucy's misery. Whatever her experiences in film and theater, she had always been able to dominate the electronic media. This was the first time she had ever failed on television, and the flop was a very public one. Ann Sothern remembered the phone call from her old friend: "She said, 'Ann, I've been fired. ABC's let me go. They don't want to see an old grandma. They want to see me as the Lucy I was." Alas, that lady was available only on reruns.

*I*llness had weakened Desi severely. He never would get around to writing volume two of his autobiography, provisionally entitled *Another Book.* But in his decline he found several moments of grace: Lucie had grown close to her father in his last years. Her children were to remember the old man in the baseball cap, hobbling down the inclined walkway in Del Mar and leaning on their station wagon for support as he kissed them good-bye. Desi had lost much of his hair because of the radiation treatments, and he had lost a good deal of weight. His son and daughter and their spouses and grandchildren were all welcome. But he had no wish for Lucy to see him in such a reduced state. Lucie persuaded him to change his mind, and she brought her parents together in Desi's final months.

On the first occasion he was in parlous shape and the visit was brief and inconclusive. On the second he was vigorous but edgy, until Lucie ran some videotapes of *I Love Lucy.* She left her mother and father chatting and laughing like kids, she said, on their first date. As Lucy got up to leave, Desi asked, "Where are you going?" She told him, "I'm going home." "You *are* home," he replied. It was Lucy's most difficult exit.

Later Lucy and Desi Jr. and Lucie walked on the beach, reminiscing. Lucy was to speak to her ex one more time, on November 30, 1986, repeating the words "I love you, I love you, Desi, I love you" on the phone. He assured her that he loved her, too. Had they stayed together, it would have been their forty-sixth anniversary. Two days later he died in his daughter's arms.

The news went out over the radio that morning. Lucy heard it on the set of the quiz show *Super Password* and turned to the other guest. Actress Betty White recalled the moment: "She turned to me and said, 'You know, it's the damnedest thing. Goddamn it, I didn't think I'd get this upset. There he goes.' It was a funny feeling, kind of a lovely private moment." Lucy issued a statement to the press, carefully scrubbed of references to their marriage: "Our relationship has remained very close, very amiable over the years, and now I'm grateful to God that Desi's suffering is over." Like Willie Loman, Desi had expected his funeral to be well attended by members of his own profession. In fact, except for Lucy and Danny Thomas, who gave the eulogy, there was no one from the television business Desi had so powerfully influenced.

As the 1980s dwindled down, Lucy's main comforts came from her children. Desi Jr. had remained clean and had remarried, to Amy Bargiel, a recovered addict he had met at the New Life Foundation. The organization, dedicated to physical and spiritual renewal, turned the couples' lives around. Desi Jr.'s second marriage, like his sister's second, was to endure.

In other ways, though, Lucy's days were not happy. She regarded her enforced retirement as a living death; her only hobbies were games like Scrabble and backgammon. She played endless contests with younger friends, among them Jim Brochu, a scenarist, and Lee Tannen, an aspiring writer; they saw her loyally through the last years. Brochu was to remember her induction into the Television Hall of Fame: after a film clip of Lucy's historical career, Lucie Arnaz came onstage and sang the *I Love Lucy* theme. "At the end, she looked out front, and with her voice breaking said, 'I love you, Mom.'" Lucy stepped up to the podium to receive the award. "The mascara was running down her face in rivers as she finally managed to say a few words: 'This tops 'em all!'"

The expression Lucy wore on that occasion was a welcome contrast to the face she presented to her daughter in talking about plans to write her own autobiography. She was worried about what to write concerning people she had known and worked with through the years. Should she tell all, or omit some telling incidents? "What the hell," she burst out. "Half of them are dead already." Lucie reminded her that Desi had written the very candid *A Book,* and Lucy snapped, "He didn't tell all the stuff he could have." Lucie offered some advice: "You've never done this. Why don't you sit down with a therapist and talk about the stuff you're afraid of and see what comes out? Maybe you won't feel so bad about everything." Lucy was having none of that. "She called therapists every name in the book," Lucie would recall. "I was offended, because at the time I was having tremendous success with a therapist who was helping me be a mom and a wife. She said, 'What do you need to go to a therapist for?' And I thought, here we go. She wigged out. I ended up having to pack up my kids, leave Palm Springs. It was a nightmare. We didn't speak for weeks and weeks." If you were in therapy in Lucy's day, "it meant you were crazy, and word would get out to the Hedda Hoppers and Louella Parsonses that you were seeing a shrink, and it was a no-no."

In the mid-1980s tributes began to come in bunches—there was the Life Achievement Award at the Kennedy Center, the Lifetime Achievement Award in Comedy from the American Comedy Awards, the Woman of the Year from Harvard Hasty Pudding Theatricals, the Eastman Kodak Second Century Award, the Emmy Governor's Award from the Academy of Television Arts and Sciences. How much they meant may be gauged from an exchange reported by Lee Tannen in his memoir, *I Loved Lucy*:

"She said, 'God, it seems like only yesterday when I was with Roosevelt at the White House.'

"Without missing a beat I asked, 'Which Roosevelt, Franklin or Teddy?'

"Gary Morton looked up from his magazine and laughed out loud. 'Hey, Luce, that's funny,' he said.

"But I knew a split second after I said it that I had said the wrong thing. Lucy's whole face turned to flame. She started ranting, almost foaming at the mouth. 'You think it's funny getting old. Just wait until you're old and nobody wants you around, and they throw awards at you when they know you're gonna die soon anyway. You think it's funny to lose your job and the people you love? You think it's funny when you can't do a thing for yourself anymore? Well, you can all go fuck yourselves!' Then she stormed into her bedroom and slammed the door behind her."

For Lucy to say she could not do things for herself was something of an exaggeration. True, she suffered from high blood pressure and angina; Onna White, who had been the choreographer of *Mame,* helped her work out the kinks in a painful shoulder; and in January 1988 she had a cyst removed from her thyroid gland. But Lucy still managed to get around by herself, and she had sufficient energy to clean the house and straighten the drawers over and over, as if she were marking time, waiting for a new job offer to come in. In May, one opportunity did arise: Lucy's old pal Bob Hope asked her to do a song-and-dance number on his eighty-fifth-birthday special. Entitled *Comedy Is a Serious Business,* the piece of special material was written by Cy Coleman and James Lipton, and was performed with considerable difficulty. Supporting actress Brooke Shields remembered the tall lady with the dyed red hair "frustrated, and embarrassed that she was having trouble with the steps." Lucy collapsed soon after the performance.

A week later she woke up in the middle of the night and went to the bathroom. She had just seated herself on the toilet when a heavy object seemed to fall into her lap. For a moment she thought a piece of the ceiling had broken off. Then she looked down. The object was her lifeless right arm. Gary drove Lucy to Cedars-Sinai Medical Center, where an examination revealed that she had suffered a stroke.

Lucy was a terrible patient and, ironically, crankiness is what kept her indisposition out of the papers. For she had been at the hospital for only a few hours when she began to hallucinate, probably due to the drugs she had been given intravenously. Roaches appeared on her stomach, marching, she was to recall, to the tune of "Seventy-six Trombones." She screamed. Nurses strapped her down, but they failed to stop her protests. "Get me out of this goddamned place," she yelled. "I want to go home." Lucy happened to be directly under a microphone broadcasting to nurses' stations all over the hospital. The authorities acceded to her wishes. Hours later they sent Lucy back to Roxbury Drive for convalescence.

Lucy's powers of recuperation were still in force. A private nurse, Trudi Arcudi, was hired, and was immediately nicknamed Trudy-ArcudiPrivateDuty. Working with her, and with Onna White, the sufferer was cured of her facial paralysis, and in about three months the numbness in her right side went away. To prove to herself, as well as to the family and the public, that Lucille Ball was still a big-time entertainer, she agreed to appear on yet another *Super Password*. She would be playing for the John Wayne Cancer Center along with other celebrity guests including Betty White, Carol Channing, and Dick Martin. It was a mistake. Lucy's diction was uncertain and the most casual onlooker could see that she was unable to concentrate on the questions. "She had been a sharp game player," Martin said wistfully, "but was now very slow on the pickup. She wanted to do it so badly. But she couldn't keep up. It was kind of sad." All the same, those who counted her out had one more surprise coming.

She was asked to be a presenter at the Academy Awards on March 29, 1989, along with Bob Hope. The pair would salute the "Oscar Winners of the Future"—a nod from the seasoned pros to the promising newcomers. Without hesitation Lucy agreed, but then she had second thoughts. "I hate the way I look," she told Tannen. "That goddamn wig with all that goddamn netting gives me a goddamn headache." Hope called to cheer her up, and once again she agreed to be his co-presenter, only to complain afterward, "Goddamn Hope, nobody cares what the hell he looks like, but everybody cares what I look like—God, I'm so tired of myself."

Perhaps she was, but her public was not. The designer Ret Turner fashioned a black sequined evening gown with a slit that went all the way up her left thigh. She wore it with confidence—until she was about to go on. "Do my eyes look baggy?" she asked Hope's publicist, Frank Liberman. "Don't worry about it," he replied. "You and Hope have a way of straightening up and dropping thirty years when the lights hit you and you hear the applause." He was not flattering her. Gasps issued from the audience when Lucy came out. At the age of seventy-eight she was still radiant, with the gait and gams of a showgirl. The ovation lasted for several minutes while she and Bob Hope exchanged smiles and inaudible ad-libs. The applause died down and she picked up her cue—only to stumble over the names of some of the newcomers. Later Lucy complained that she looked terrible, that her teeth had pained her, that she was deeply disappointed in her performance. If she felt that way she was alone. At Irving "Swifty" Lazar's post-Oscar party, celebrities stopped by her table to praise her affect and her wardrobe. When she and Gary exited, a group of fans cheered Lucille Ball and she lifted her hem to show off the legs once more, threw kisses to the crowd, got in the limousine, and went home beaming.

For the next two weeks, though, she seemed abstracted and depressed, and on April 17 she felt excruciating chest pains. Gary and Lucie drove her to Cedars-Sinai, the hospital she hated. She was rushed to an operating room for nearly seven hours of open-heart surgery: her aorta had ruptured. Again she bounced back; eight days later, doctors gave permission to have her moved from the intensive care unit to a private room.

Bouquets and flower baskets had arrived by the score and more than five thousand well-wishers had called from across the United States, Europe, and Australia. Entire towns sent get-well cards. Lucy's private room overlooked the Hard Rock Café. In consideration, the trendy youth hangout put up a sign reading GET WELL LUCY. She waved at it from her bed. The hospital fax machine and switchboard became overloaded, prompting a Cedars spokesman to burble: "On a scale of one to ten, this is an absolute ten. Before it's over the hospital will look like a combination of the U.S. post office and the botanical gardens." To protect herself, and Cedars-Sinai, Lucy employed a code name. The only way to get through was to call "Diane Belmont"—the monicker Lucy had used a half-century before, when as a gangly novice she tried to convince Broadway producers that she hailed from Montana. With her son and daughter, Lucy watched footage of the overwhelming response on the local news. "Can you believe what's going on here?" she chirped. "It's *wonderful!*" Lucie and Desi Jr. left in high spirits; their mother was regaining strength. And why not? DeDe had lived to eighty-five; if genes told the tale, Lucy would have at least another eight years.

Early the next morning the patient's back seemed to be acting up. She tried to raise herself, then sank back, unconscious. Her aorta had ruptured again. More than a dozen emergency doctors and nurses labored to undo the damage. It was irreparable. The heroic measures stopped at 5:47 a.m. when Lucille Ball was pronounced dead.

Word went out immediately. The *New York Times* ran an immense obituary, "Spirited Doyenne of Television Comedy Series Is Dead at 77," and followed that with an unprecedented editorial. Under the heading "We Love Lucy, Too," it posited: "If a clown's face is humanity's writ large, then Lucille Ball was born to her work. The red of her hair came out of a bottle, but who else would have chosen a shade so fiery? And who in this world ever had bigger, bluer, rounder eyes, or a mouth that slid so quickly into smiling? Hers was the mask of comedy." *Variety*'s tribute ran over five pages, with a heavy emphasis on money: in syndication, said a headline, "Lucy Will 'Run Forever'; Grossed $75-mil So Far." The front page of the *Hollywood Reporter* read: "Thanks, Lucy, We Had a Ball!" Every major newspaper in the country printed a large, lyrical obit; most had been written months before when word circulated that Lucille Ball was seriously ill.

That Lucy had been hospitalized for over a week, that she was elderly and somewhat infirm, was no secret. Even so, her death came as a kind of national shock. Much of the populace had grown up with Lucy in their living rooms; to them she was a member of the family and the grief was personal. *Entertainment Tonight,* as might be expected, devoted its entire half-hour program to Lucy; so did ABC's *Nightline.* CBS hastily assembled footage from the best *I Love Lucy* shows and presented the clips in an hour-long format hosted by the network's former anchor, Walter Cronkite. The surprise was an appearance by William S. Paley, the eighty-eight-year-old chairman of CBS, going on camera to state that Lucy "was in a class by herself." He followed that up with a press release claiming that Lucille Ball would "always be the first lady of CBS," and adding that her "extraordinary ability to light up the screen and brighten our lives is a legacy that will last forever." Unmentioned was the fact that the network had allowed "the first lady" to go to NBC in 1980 because her usefulness appeared to be at an end. Business, after all, was business, and in lapidary inscriptions one was not under oath.

The following week, *Time* ran a full-page eulogy, comparing Lucy to a quartet of men: "Lucille Ball was as deft and daring as Harold Lloyd, as rubber-faced as Bert Lahr, as touching as Chaplin—and more lady-like than Milton Berle. In reruns, she is eternal." *Newsweek* called her "probably the most popular woman in the history of show business." Tributes came from all over. In Los Angeles, fans pasted condolence letters on the door of her house. Two presidents saluted Lucille Ball: ex-President Ronald Reagan called her "an American institution," and his successor, George Bush, defined her as "a legendary figure." In Paris, Sammy Davis Jr. called her "a great artist—one of the world's great clowns." And in Boston, comedian Lily Tomlin said: "It's a sad day. She was a great role model for me, and a great funny woman." Comedienne Kaye Ballard could not speak about Lucy without mentioning Desi. Despite their remarriages, she maintained, "She was in love with him until the end. And he was in love with her." Actress Paula Stewart agreed, privately quoting a comment made by Gary Morton: "I guess she's happy now. She's with Desi."

In a follow-up to the obituary, the *Los Angeles Times* ran two appraisals of Lucille Ball side by side. Charles Champlin, the paper's arts editor, observed that the star's "craft was invisible, the skills so perfected they concealed themselves totally. It was a brilliant illusion, generating a charm that hid the hard work and the artful writing and editing as well the performing. The result was probably the finest and certainly the most durable single series in television's history thus far." He went on to observe that "when Lucy began to commandeer our hearts on *I Love Lucy* in 1951, the movies were already in considerable trouble, their audiences staying home in large numbers to watch the likes of Lucy in their living rooms. As always, her timing was impeccable."

In an adjoining column Howard Rosenberg, the *Times* television critic, wrote: "The more you think about Lucy as an icon, the more remarkable she becomes, for her esteem has grown and grown despite Lucy Ricardo being in many ways the flighty, manipulative, narrowly defined female of her time, a stereotype far outdistanced by today's woman." A spokesman at the Museum of Broadcasting commented that Lucy "influenced almost every comic to come after her, whether it be Carol Burnett or Tomlin or the actors on *Saturday Night Live*. Her Lucy character is like Charlie Chaplin's 'Little Tramp' figure. It is a classic, and it is a reference point. There aren't a whole lot of characters like that, which have transcended their format." Perhaps the most vivid reminiscence came from Mike Dann, an NBC program executive when Lucy made her mark. "We had a show on the air called *Lights Out,* sponsored by Amident. Both the show and the toothpaste were tremendously popular—*everybody* watched *Lights Out*.

"Then Desi and Lucy came on the air opposite that show, and *Lights Out* was canceled. We at NBC were flabbergasted, we just couldn't believe it. Here was this girl who wasn't that famous, and this bongo player from Cuba—and it never lost its momentum. It was the first time we used the word 'runaway' to describe a show." Only the *Nation,* grumpy and scrubbed of humor, had anything bad to say. Speaking for the hard left, the journal recalled that Lucy had registered to vote as a member of the Communist Party in 1936, and when she appeared before the House Committee on Un-American Activities named no names and went back to work on Monday. The article went on, "Lucy told HUAC she had registered only to make her granddad, a lifelong socialist, happy. Was Lucy putting the committee on or kowtowing to it? Which mattered more to CBS, harboring a Red or being in the black? One can't find the answer in such mainstream media as the *New York Times,* the *Washington Post, Time,* or *Newsweek,* since none of their obits mentioned the HUAC encounter. That's at least consistent with their failure to report on the blacklist in the first place."

By the time these entries were printed, Lucille Ball had been laid to rest at Forest Lawn cemetery, her ashes set in a place next to her mother's remains. Gary Morton was alone at the interment; soon after, Lucie and Laurence Luckinbill, accompanied by their children, and Desi Jr. and Amy Arnaz gathered at the grave.

Lucie scheduled three memorial services: one in Los Angeles, one in Chicago, one in New York. On May 8, in their various time zones, they would start at exactly 8 p.m. on Monday night, the day of the week, and the hour, when *I Love Lucy* ran in its heyday. The Manhattan service took place at St. Ignatius Loyola Church, on Park Avenue at Eighty-third Street. Lee Tannen had asked Diane Sawyer to deliver the eulogy. Lucy had long been an admirer of the ABC anchor, even though they had never met. In her speech, Sawyer commented: "Isn't it funny. I cannot for the life of me remember how the furniture was laid out in the living room of the house I grew up in, but I can remember where every stick of furniture was in the Ricardo house." The comment could have been made by any one of Sawyer's two thousand listeners, and by any of Lucy's millions of devotees. In the end, credibility had been the secret of her comedy.

As sentimental as Lucy had been in life, she wanted no ceremony after her death. Instructions were left that her passing should be honored with a picnic and not a lugubrious testimonial dinner. According to Jim Brochu, Lucy was specific about the food and drink: ham, baked beans, potato salad, watermelon—all the dishes that she remembered from the delirious summers in Celoron when her only responsibility was making the beds, before she left to find a career and a life. The feast was held on May 14, Mother's Day, at an estate in Mandeville Canyon. A benign feeling enveloped some fifty guests, including Lucy's old comrades Mary Wickes and Onna White, as well as Lucie's and Laurence's former spouses, Phil Vandervoort and Robin Strasser. The press and much of the Los Angeles public had been informed of the picnic, but was barred from attending. No matter. Inside and outside the gates, the quotes were much the same. People spoke lengthily of the deceased's virtues, and briefly of her shortcomings. Almost everyone remembered one or another of Lucy's famous apothegms: "Knowing what you can *not* do is more important than knowing what you *can* do. In fact, that's good taste." "I don't know anything about luck. I've never banked on it, and I'm afraid of people who do. Luck to me is something else: hard work and realizing what is opportunity and what isn't."

At day's end, there came the wistful sentiments that customarily follow such memorials: final thoughts, a stressing of laughter over tears, and, inevitably, the pronouncing of the deceased as the last of her kind. It was, by general agreement, Lucille Ball's final curtain, finis, fade out, credits on a crawl, the end. No one at the picnic, or outside it, realized that the lights were actually coming up.

A Marx
Sister

O N JULY 6, 1989, the Presidential Medal of Freedom was awarded
to five Americans. General James H. Doolittle was heralded as "the
trailblazer of modern aviation," and Ambassador George F. Kennan as
"a visionary who foresaw the future of Soviet-American relations." Sen-
ator Margaret Chase Smith was "a bold achiever who stood alone
against the tide of extremism," Ambassador Clarence Douglas Dillon,
"an unparalleled public servant who shaped American foreign and economic policy." Among this highly placed group was an unexpected
name: Lucille Ball, given the medal posthumously as "The First Lady
of Television—one of America's greatest comediennes." The citation
went on: "her face was seen by more people more often than the face
of any human being who ever lived. Who can forget Lucy? She was like
everyone's next-door neighbor, only funnier. Lucille Ball was a national
treasure who brought laughter to us all. Love Lucy? Sure. This nation
is grateful to her, and we will miss her dearly."

The following autumn, Jim Brochu published *Lucy in the Afternoon,* a sentimental memoir of his friend's later years. On February 10, 1991, CBS broadcast a turgid biography, *Lucy & Desi: Before the Laughter*. Starring Frances Fisher as Lucy and Maurice Benard as Desi, the made-for-TV movie received the appraisals it deserved. *People*: "The acting (which consists primarily of vamping and exaggerated facial aerobics) is terrible. And the clumsy set pieces that make up the exposition are strident: Lucy explodes over Desi's constant philandering; Desi fumes over a career going nowhere. The two scenes where they do comedy together are totally torturous." Mocking Benard's put-on Cuban accent, the review concluded: "If ju goan to do something so tacky, at least make it funny. Grade: C–." Yet *Lucy & Desi* has a place in history alongside the Medal of Freedom and Brochu's book. For these three projects marked the beginning of the apotheosis, a phenomenon that was to make Lucille Ball unique in the history of American show business.

After Lucy's death, widower Gary Morton dated Eva Gabor for a short time; the couple broke up, the actress stated, because he was more dedicated to golf than he was to her. Gabor may have been correct: in 1994 Morton married golf pro Susie McCallister; the marriage lasted until his death from lung cancer in 1999. With Gary out of the family picture, the Arnaz children were exclusively in charge of their mother's image, and in the early 1990s Lucie Arnaz Luckinbill hosted a CBS program in celebration of *I Love Lucy*. Later she and Desi Jr. would produce and direct *Lucy and Desi: A Home Movie*, with candid footage of the couple made during their years together.

In 1993 the book *Desilu*, by Coyne Steven Sanders and Tom Gilbert, affectionately detailed the history of the studio and its founders. In 1994 Kathleen Brady's painstakingly researched *Lucille* covered new biographical details of her subject's life. In 1996 came *Love, Lucy*, Lucille's autobiography, made from tape recordings pieced together seven years after her death. When *TV Guide* selected the "50 Greatest TV Stars of All Time" in 1996, Lucy was Number One. Two years later *Time* magazine picked the dominant twenty artists and entertainers of the twentieth century, men and women "who enlightened and enlivened us." There was Lucille Ball again, this time in company with such illustrious achievers as Pablo Picasso, Charlie Chaplin, Martha Graham, Coco Chanel, and Louis Armstrong. As the new century began, the United States Postal Service issued a thirty-four-cent stamp honoring Lucille Ball. In 1999, she and Desi had been featured on a thirty-three-cent stamp celebrating 1950s television. No other civilian had ever been honored twice in so brief a period. Shortly after the new millennium began, the Public Broadcasting Service (PBS) paid tribute to Lucille Ball by including her in "Finding Lucy," an entry in its *American Masters* series. In writer-producer Thomas Wagner's judgment, "Lucy doesn't date." He added: "People who saw the show fifty years ago still remember magic moments, the way Lucy and her television family kept us laughing. But our seven-year-old watched a lot of *I Love Lucy* for the first time when we were making this film and she got it all: the characters, the situation, and she couldn't stop laughing either. Lucille Ball's inspired lunacy will outlast almost everything that's on television today."

There were poetic tributes as well. Poets Nick Carbó and Denise Duhamel, who are married, each acknowledged the universality of the Lucy image. Carbó, a Filipino-American, describes a cousin:

> She showed up on the doorstep of my apartment
> in Albuquerque just after the blizzard of '85
> in a fluffy tan fake-fur coat, an elevated
> I Love Lucy hairdo, and a twelve-year-old son.

Duhamel looks back at the immigrant experience:

> Please know that your would-be American girlfriend
> Still pines for you, José, somewhere in Nebraska or North Dakota.
> She has a slew of kids now and her red dress is in storage.
> She cries when she watches reruns of I Love Lucy.

In the *Journal of Popular Culture,* Louis Phillips remembered Lucy with the poem "A Summer Spent Watching Lucille Ball Perform":

> Philosophers insist
> No one laughs at a sunset,
> But nothing in my heart is breaking
>   (Old bones do not heal so fast),
> As Lucy mugs & grimaces,
> Pro that she is,
> Dives into a vat of grapes

With fractured Italian
   (substituted on the TV screen).
What is comedy
Philosophers ask,
But grass does not laugh
Nor the trees
Still, I am only human,
Broken hip & all.
In the sunset everything seems funny.

Simultaneously, a blending of comedy and commerce got under way. Jamestown, New York, determined to treat its first daughter with the utmost respect. Drivers entering the town of 36,000 were presented with green road signs honoring Lucille Ball and another celebrity born there, the artist and naturalist Roger Tory Peterson. Lucy received top billing. The signs are there today. The Lucy-Desi Museum, supervised by the Arnaz family, has been set up as a pop shrine. At the lilac-painted installation on Pine Street, presentations take no note of any past unpleasantness; it is as if Dwight D. Eisenhower were still in the White House and Lucy and Ricky Ricardo were still in love and living with their landlords, the inimitable Fred and Ethel Mertz. More than eighty thousand tourists from thirty-six countries have paid homage since the museum was founded in 1996, gawking at costumes, merchandise, correspondence, and family photographs. In 2002, the living-room set from *I Love Lucy* was added. Those who want to take home a souvenir—and that includes almost all who sign the guest book—drop in at the Museum Shop on Third Street. There they can purchase games, shower curtains, dolls, T-shirts, and a vast selection of other Lucy-centered merchandise to show the folks back in their own hometown, a locale that may be in America, Europe, Asia, or Africa—anyplace where *I Love Lucy* has been broadcast.

Each summer, the museum schedules events for Lucille Ball's loyal fans. In August 2002, for example, there were such activities as a "Vintage Memorabilia Collectors' Show," featuring movie posters, comic books, magazines, and a "Memorabilia Auction," with more than one hundred vintage properties for sale. These were supplemented with the kind of boosterish, small-town events Lucy had sentimentalized in later life—and from which she had fled three generations before.

("Jamestown is only a place to be *from*. To be from *only*.") Included
was a musical tribute to the First Couple of Comedy by the Jamestown Suzuki Strings Students and Middle School and High School
orchestras, and a candy-wrapping competition with three-person
teams re-creating Lucy's chocolate-factory routine.

With gratitude and affection for this outpouring of regard, the Arnaz
children announced plans to transfer their mother's remains, and those
of their grandmother DeDe Hunt Ball, from Forest Lawn Memorial
Park in the Hollywood hills to a modest, tree-shaded family plot in
Jamestown. Lucie also attempted to purchase the home in which Lucy
grew up, but she was outbid by one Elaine Thoni of Cooper City,
Florida, who apparently bought the place as an investment. "I have a
few Lucy curios," Thoni told *TV Guide,* "but I plan to get more. Before
this I was more of an Elvis fan."

The year 2001 marked the fiftieth anniversary of *I Love Lucy*'s debut.
In response there were farcical events (in Jerry Zucker's film *Rat Race,*
for example, Cuba Gooding Jr. gets trapped on a tour bus with more
than a dozen Lucille Ball imitators), as well as carefully calculated
salutes from TV Land, national cable home to the show's reruns. Later
came Lucie and Desi Jr.'s two-hour documentary. Predictably, the program was freighted with sound bites from enthusiasts and film clips
from the best-known episodes, including the Vitameatavegamin drunk
scene, the grape-stomping battle, and the pregnancy announcement.
Of greater interest was a recollection of Orson Welles, who did a guest
shot in the 1950s. During rehearsals he had sat in the wings staring at
the star. Asked what he was doing, Welles, enchanted with Lucy's skills
since the 1940s, explained, "I am watching the world's greatest actress."
In the *Washington Post,* the beguiled TV critic Tom Shales observed:
"As the camera zooms in on the two principals for the closing shot,
Lucy drops presents that have been piled into her arms and puts those
arms around her husband. At any given moment, it is stated on the special, people somewhere in the world are watching an *I Love Lucy*
episode, and what they're watching is more than high jinks, more than
slapstick and wacky routines and clowning around. They are peering
into a time capsule at another world that tempts and beckons. And
they are also getting a look at the operation of that most intricate and
delicate of all complex mechanisms, the human heart." *USA Today*
took a second look at the series and concluded: "Ricky symbolized how
the world was supposed to run. Lucy was that absurdist factor of mod-

ern American humor—the irrational force which cannot be anticipated."

The anniversary prompted encomia from unexpected sources.
Pulitzer Prize–winning novelist Jane Smiley remembered a childhood
of reruns that entered her house in the morning: "I associate it with the
feeling of being pleasantly not at school. Perhaps I saw the small
screen (which did not seem at all small to me, since I was sitting cross-
legged right in front of it) as a window through which I could look at
what people did 'at work,' where my mother was." The show made her
uneasy, because "Lucy never seemed to learn from one episode to the
next how not to get into trouble, and since I didn't understand comedy,
I never laughed at the incongruity of the situations." Still the little girl
watched intently, "no doubt because I identified Lucy not only as my
mother, but also as myself. Could I really get into that chocolate fix?
That wine vat mess? Why not? It was a frightening possibility." When
she got older, however, she "discovered Lucille Ball, Lucy's better half,
a woman of talent and ambition who had been around and knew how
to make something of her talents. Lucille Ball—now there was someone to pay attention to. I knew nothing of her personal life, only that
her demeanor in real life was utterly different from Lucy's, and that
was enough to say all there is to know about the difference between
life and art."

Historian Dan Wakefield, author of *New York in the Fifties*, asked,
"Why is Lucy so loved?" and offered two theories. "Maybe because she
was the first good-looking actress to throw her body around with abandon in the cause of comedy; compare her rubbery torso flings to Mae
West's statue-like stance as she shot one-liners from the side of her
mouth." Or "maybe she's loved so long and well because her problems
were as sunny as funny, unlike the darker shades of *The Honeymooners*." Jackie Gleason's domestic comedy, Wakefield went on, "gained its
faithful following later, when the dark side was more admitted in a
world become conscious of its own subconscious."

National Public Radio correspondent Susan Stamberg took a contrarian view. She found Lucy: "Hilarious, of course. A brilliant comedienne. Physically fearless, slapstick silly. Impeccable timing. A direct
descendant of Charlie Chaplin and Harpo Marx. I love her eyelashes
and her big bright mouth. I also love Ricky's theme song. And the
neighbors.

"But as for loving *I Love Lucy*, no. Because certain behaviors, funny as they were, were troubling to me, coming of age in the 50s. . . . On television, Lucy was no Good Girl, and I liked her for it—her spirit and her gumption. But I didn't like what she did to get what she wanted."

Social critic Susan Sontag thought she knew the reasons for the durability of *I Love Lucy*. The program invited its audience "to observe Desi's exasperated mutterings or Lucy's whines with an amused sense of superiority. This sanctioned voyeurism couldn't help but flatter the viewer it entertained.

"The show was built on an entrancing pseudo-effect of the real: that the very ordinary couple portrayed was played by a real couple, one of whom was extremely famous, successful, and rich. Lucille Ball, a real star, became a goofy housewife named Lucy Ricardo, but nobody was fooled. Didn't we smile when we saw the heart-shaped logo at the end: Desilu Productions?

"That was the fun of it—the confusion and mixture of televised fantasy and voyeuristically apprehended reality. A dose of fantasy. And the insinuation that we might be watching something real. Which has turned out, fifty years later, to be television's perennial, still winning formula."

Not all voices were so upbeat. During a seminar in Las Vegas, a member of the audience asked Jerry Lewis which female comics he admired. "I don't like any female comedians," Lewis said. Moderator and fellow comedian Martin Short brought up the name of Lucille Ball: "You must have loved *her*." "No," insisted Lewis, "a woman doing comedy doesn't offend me, but sets me back a bit. I, as a viewer, have trouble with it. I think of her as a producing machine that brings babies into the world."

A backhanded eulogy came from underground-film director John Waters, who claimed that Lucy Ricardo was a profound influence on *Polyester* and *Hairspray*. Waters remembered *I Love Lucy* as the show that changed his life: "At last, a female impersonator who dyed her hair orange, wore obviously false eyelashes and scary red lipstick at home, married a man of another race, got pregnant on television, hung out with her blue-collar neighbors, and ran away to pal around with Rock Hudson. As an eight-year-old voyeur, looking ahead to my teenage years was a lot easier because of *Lucy*. I knew you could break the rules."

Darker notes were sounded in *Talk* magazine, when Rex Reed compiled a set of interviews with some of Lucy's colleagues and relations. Her longtime friend Sheila MacRae remembered an occasion at the Arnazes. "We were all having dinner with William Holden and his wife and watching a movie, and Lucy said, 'Take it off. It's all about people having sex.' She started to cry and there was dead silence. It was very embarrassing. There were only six people in the room. Desi said, 'For Christ's sake, Lucy!' She said, 'I'm going to leave you.' He said, 'So go ahead. What do I care?' And he moved into the guesthouse."

Actress Carole Cook recalled: "I went to see her on the set of that last show that she did and she was in a tirade. I said, 'Gosh, Lucy, you're working again.' And she said, 'They just don't like women over fifty.' I said, 'You've been over fifty a long time, you know? If it's your first bad review, that's not such a bad deal.'

"I always thought it was sad that a woman like that—who could have done charity work, gone to the theater, traveled, read, held classes—spent her dumb days playing backgammon."

Actress Polly Bergen described her Roxbury Drive neighbor in very specific terms. Lucy's "outer persona as a performer was this cute, bubbly, zany character. But in her personal and social life she was a very tough broad."

Paula Stewart blamed Gary Morton for much of Lucy's downhill slide toward the end. "She was taking all these different medications and she was very sick. The high blood pressure was the killer. She was depressed and she was having a hard time with Gary. They were not getting along. But she still liked the margaritas with salt, and she'd sneak sardine sandwiches. You know, anything with salt. And Gary would say, 'Oh, let her have the salt.' " Several years later, during one of Lucy's hospital stays, "she needed a nurse to watch over her. Gary let the nurse go. He said it was too expensive. I said, 'What? She's one of the richest women around.' And not only that, but her insurance had to be paying for everything. What could that nurse have cost?"

Lucy's publicist, Thomas Watson, said: "She never raised herself to grow old gracefully. She used to tell me, 'I am not Helen Hayes.' She should have retired." When the last series failed, "she didn't know what to do. Gary never said, 'Show business is my life.' He always said, 'Show business is my *wife.*' "

Lucie Arnaz weighed the pros and cons of her mother's life and career. "On the positive side, she had tenacity, an amazing ability to keep going until she got it right. Bravery. She was the first to do things that women didn't do. She was gifted, she had genius, like Chaplin. Artistry of the top rank. On the negative side, she was tactless with some people. Brusque. She wasn't able to really be open, close, intimate with a lot of people. That was a negative—for her and for what we lost as a family."

Further details were added in London, where Lucie starred in a West End version of *The Witches of Eastwick*. Understandably, the *Daily Mail* interview was never reprinted in the States. By the time her mother had assumed the presidency of Desilu, said Lucie, Desi was gone and Lucy worked "from dawn to dusk. She didn't need the money, she had everything she wanted, from clothes to jewels to cars. Yet only work mattered. She could be very cold and although she told me she loved me all the time, I didn't feel loved. When children don't feel they deserve love they start feeling unworthy of love . . . and I felt like that most of the time." Lucie went on: "I never wanted to behave to my own three children the way my mother did with us, never being there to talk to us, to get our breakfast, to bathe us, to read us stories at night. We had people to look after us and my grandmother was there sometimes. But I couldn't wait to leave home and I did at 18. I got married to the first man I went out with." She assured Lucy, "I can make it work," but she found that she couldn't. "I'd made a terrible mistake and within a year it broke up. I'd made a terrible mistake." The three children she had with Laurence Luckinbill, plus the two from his previous marriage, caused some difficulties. "At first I used to be quite sharp with my kids because I had nothing to follow, nothing to learn from." Much as she admired her mother's talent, Lucie concluded, "I just wish she'd been there to give us the love that we so desperately needed."

But the sorrier aspects of Lucille Ball were more than counterbalanced by the perceptions of adoring fans and colleagues, who would hear no disparagement of the loved one. In an article on images that make men cry, the *New York Times* cited Douglas McGrath, the director of the movies *Emma* and *Nicholas Nickleby*. "I'll be in bed at night with my wife," he confided to a reporter, "and a rerun of *I Love Lucy* starts, and just as the heart is closing around the title, the tears well up in my eyes." According to the paper, McGrath thought it was "because of the contrast between the triumph of love of the fictional Desi and Lucy, and the fact that they broke up in real life." Added the *Times*, "Now that's a sensitive guy!" Likenesses—rather inflexible likenesses, it must be said—went on display at Madame Tussaud's Wax Museum in New York and at the Hollywood and Movieland Museums in California. Lucy's star was burnished on the Hollywood Walk of Fame. Statues, whose intent was more laudable than their execution, could be found in Jamestown; at the Academy of Television Arts and Sciences Hall of Fame Plaza in North Hollywood, where Lucy had worked; and in Palm Springs, where she had vacationed. In Dallas, her words were inscribed in the Women's Museum: "You really have to love yourself to get anything done in this world." In 2001 she was inducted into the National Women's Hall of Fame in Seneca Falls, New York, where the first Women's Rights convention was held in 1848.

In New York City, summer school students in the English as a Second Language program at Bushwick High School were presented with an unusual assignment. They were shown the job-switching episode of *I Love Lucy*, in which Ricky and Fred turn househusbands and Lucy and Ethel take jobs in the chocolate factory. They were then to write papers on what they had viewed. The purpose, said the Board of Education, was twofold: "to immerse students in the language, and to introduce them to cultural institutions." Elsewhere, Dr. Seth Shostak, an astronomer at the Search for Extraterrestrial Intelligence Institute, groped for a proper way to explain the reach of light and sound in space. "The nearest star is about four light-years away," he said, "and there are on the order of several thousand stars within the fifty-light-year range. So the earliest episodes of *I Love Lucy* are washing over a new star system at the rate of about one system a day."

All measuring devices agreed: the status of Lucille Ball was permanent, on Earth and beyond it. That being the case, entrepreneurs, indiscriminate fans, hypercritical scholars, feminists, and revisionists all moved in. The Internet, growing exponentially in the 1990s, offered more than one hundred Lucille Ball Web sites, and the number has grown since then. Some are electronic stores, offering every conceivable sort of souvenir connected with Lucy's glory days. The home page of Cathy's Closet displays a quote from Lucie Arnaz: "The only closet with more 'authentic' Lucy items than Cathy's was my mother's!" No one is likely to challenge that statement; Cathy's Closet offers some fifty categories of merchandise arranged alphabetically, including Ceramic Boxes, Figurines, Games, Mouse Pads, Snow Globes, Tote Bags, and Watches. Everything Lucy, a similar site, but bearing no Arnaz endorsement, sells such exotica as "I Love Lucy" Chocolate Factory salt and pepper shakers, a large "I Love Lucy" cookie jar in the shape of a car seen on the series, and an "I Love Lucy" bear. The items are not cheap; the cookie jar, for example, sells for $149.99. Collectors can buy dolls that range back to the 1950s and go up to the present, including a "Lucille Ball and Desi Arnaz Bobblehead Set" issued by Classic Collecticritters; "Celebrity Barbie" dolls by Mattel, featuring Barbie and Ken dressed as the Arnazes; and the "Lucille Ball Vinyl Portrait Doll" from the Franklin Mint, priced around $200.

The most dedicated fans, however, are less interested in accumulation than in making points about their favorite. Oxygen Media, whose television channel and Web site target a female audience, regards Lucy as an avatar of women's rights: "Generally, what she wanted was to play a less passive role, to be more actor than acted upon. She wanted attention and what's wrong with that? We all want it; Lucy was just very up-front and focused about getting it. Not one to repress her insecurities, Lucy tackled them head-on, and since her fears were our fears, we rejoiced in her flagrant disregard for propriety in her quest for inclusion."

Michael Karol, author of that compound of insight, fact, and trivia *Lucy A to Z,* conducts the serious, if worshipful, site www.geocities.com/Sitcomboy/. On it he examines the influence of *I Love Lucy* on situation comedies that followed in its slipstream:

I Love Lucy	*All in the Family*	*Just Shoot Me*
Lucy tries on a wig at a salon and is amazed at how different she looks in it. She buys it to see if she can fool Ricky and prove that he looks at other women. Ricky of course discovers what's going on and decides to teach Lucy a lesson.	Gloria buys a blonde wig to spice up her love life with Mike, only to find out that he likes her in it too much; "it's like sleeping with another woman," the dolt admits. After lots of screaming, the two run upstairs to make love, much to Archie's disgust.	Maya buys a long wig in an effort to make boyfriend Elliott notice her more, and gets upset when she finds out he likes making love to her in it. Solution: she likes him in uniform, so she's happy to wear the wig as long as he'll dress up for her.

Sitcomboy rushes on: "If you're a dedicated channel surfer, unique delights await you. Within the space of a few hours just recently, I saw 'Lucy' make an appearance on the Simpsons (as Lucille MacGillicuddy Ricardo, I believe): she turns up to help Lisa Simpson, who's having a problem managing Homer and Bart while Marge is in the hospital. And then, a bit later, I was passing through VH-1 when I noticed a familiar drummer: Desi Arnaz, Jr. Intrigued, I watched as Dino, Desi & Billy (the rock trio that had some minor success in the 1960s) played a forgettable love song, then went to be congratulated by Ed Sullivan (the show itself was a syndicated clip fest of rock moments from his Sunday night show). Ready to keep surfing, I stopped as Sullivan introduced one of the trio's mothers from the audience—none other than Lucy herself."

The feminist site Lucille Ball Is a Cool Woman! stresses the influence of Lucille Ball on female entertainers—and on American women in general: "One of the most important things that Lucy showed us was that women could be funny and attractive all at once—a groundbreaking concept for the day. This was particularly admirable given that Lucy was beautiful enough to be a conventional film star, and, in fact had become a Hollywood movie sensation as 'Queen of the B-Movies.' But she shrugged off the persona of a cool beauty, instead reveling in the chance to get a laugh. She was never afraid to look foolish, silly, or even ugly for the sake of a good gag and her public loved her for it. By proving this formula, she paved the way for generations of funny women to come. Think of Carol Burnett, Roseanne, Gilda Radner, and Candice Bergen—they all owe at least a part of their success to the amazing Lucy."

Floating above these fans' notes is the Higher Criticism—inquiries about, and analyses of, Lucille Ball as comedian, artist, and executive. Molly Haskell, one of the most prominent and discerning critics of popular culture, had her say in a piece entitled "50 Years and Millions of Reruns Later, Why Does America Still Love Lucy?" To Haskell, the answer lay in Ball's subversive approach. "Although the Lucy persona would disavow any connection with feminism," the author asserts, "in her own foot-in-mouth way, she cuts a wide swath through male supremacy, saying anything that comes into her head and taking down sacred cows and chauvinist bulls along the way. Trying to say 'thank you' to Ricky's pompous Cuban uncle, and garbling her Spanish, she calls him a fat pig before accidentally (?) shredding his foot-long, hand-rolled cigar—no mean symbol of Lucy's assault on puffed-up male potency."

Haskell is particularly fond of an episode in which Lucy pores over a *New York Times* want ad section. "Oh, this is terribly unfair," she moans. "You can't get a job in this town unless you can *do* something."

Lucy eventually lands a job tending two misbehaving brats, and this leads to a performance on a talent show emceed by Ricky. The baby-sitter enters in moustache and chaps; the two boys back her up as singing cowboys. While Lucy is distracted the brats place a frog under her shirt. The movements of the amphibian soon force her to pop and leap like a Nijinsky-inspired jumping bean. Haskell finds the routine "an incandescent moment of magical farce that also conveys a talent and determination that will be not be denied. The performance ends with the triumphant Lucy kissing Ricky, who, recognizing her, does one of his ineffable double takes. And so do we, since unbeknownst to him, her moustache has been transferred to his face—a nice visual metaphor for the restoring of the patriarchy, Lucy-style." Lucy may surrender at the final clinch, but "she is no 'surrendered wife.' In the final analysis, Lucy is a fireball who treads a fine line between inde-pendence and submission, the stay-at-home wife who wouldn't."

Haskell's affectionate tone was amplified by another pop culture critic. Writing in the *New York Times,* Joyce Millman argued that Lucy "waged an unspoken battle against Ricky's attitude of male superiority—you could feel her sense of injustice burning behind every scheme." How did *I Love Lucy* become television's most popular sit-com in a deeply conservative era? "It did not violate viewers' comfort zones, particularly female viewers' comfort zones. If Ball had been too assertive, too forthright, she might have turned women away from the show. So Ball couched her characters' bold ambitions in peerless phys-ical comedy. She looked silly and unglamorous; she played the clown. And as a clown, Ball was a radical, powerful figure; it was as if she was daring you to think it was unseemly for a woman to put on a putty nose or a fright wig and throw herself into a joke with body and soul. (Decades later, physical comedians like Lily Tomlin and Gilda Radner finished what Ball started, turning chaotic energy into a feminist state-ment)." Statements like these would have astonished Lucy, who had gone public with her view of the Movement: "Women's lib? It doesn't interest me one bit. I've been so liberated it hurts."

But Lucille Ball had long since passed from the scene, and her statements, like her properties, her shows, and even the events of her life, were now in the hands of others. The revisionists felt free to move in. In *Madcaps, Screwballs, and Con Women,* Berklee College of Music professor Lori Landay chooses Lucille Ball as a prime examplar of "the female trickster in American culture." Lucy, she holds, embodies all

three categories—madcap, screwball, and con woman—providing
occasions "for laughter and pleasure by creating comedy out of the
constraints of the postwar feminine mystique." The author quotes the
performer in order to set up her case: " 'We had great identification
with millions of people,' Lucy stated, long after *I Love Lucy* was in syndication. They could identify with my problems, my zaniness, my
wanting to do everything, my scheming and plotting, the way I cajoled
Ricky. People identified with the Ricardos because we had the same
problems they had. Desi and I weren't your ordinary Hollywood couple
on TV. We lived in a brownstone apartment somewhere in Manhattan,
and paying the rent, getting a new dress, getting a stale fur collar on an
old cloth coat, or buying a piece of furniture were all worth a story.

" 'People could identify with all those basic things—baby-sitters,
traveling, wanting to be entertained, wanting to be loved in a certain
way—the two couples on the show were constantly doing things that
people all over the country were doing. We just took ordinary situations
and exaggerated them.' "

Producer Jess Oppenheimer is brought on as a witness: " 'The
things that happen to the Ricardos happen to everyone in the audience. We call it "holding up the mirror." Whatever happens, they love
each other.' "

Landay sums up for the prosecution: "The only way to make sense
of Oppenheimer's explanation that the series holds up a mirror to
everyday life is if we recognize that it is a distorting mirror. . . . How
seriously can we take Ricky's injunctions that his wife can't be on television when Ball and Arnaz *are* a husband and wife on television? On
one level, the show does what on another level it says shouldn't happen. This contradiction illustrates the gap between the social experience of the women who were working in the public sphere and the
ideology that attempted to contain them within domesticity. The series
itself is a kind of trick that encourages the audience to participate in
the attractive image of the stars' happy marriage, a fiction representative of postwar behaviour and attitudes that obscures asymmetry in the
sex-gender system." Even so, the professor is forced to admit in the
end that Lucy has a way of outlasting the critics and the scholars. For
ultimately, "like Coyote, Brer Rabbit, the con man, and other American
incarnations of the trickster, Lucy can withstand historical cultural
changes." Her antics, "her ability to create possibility where others
would only recognize restraint, and her untiring optimism that this

time her scheme will succeed, above all, keep Lucy, and the trickster, alive and at the center of our popular culture."

In *High Anxiety,* University of Wisconsin history professor Patricia Mellencamp uses Lucy to underscore her investigations of 1950s America. Fred Mertz's definition speaks to prevailing conditions. "When it comes to money, there are two kinds of people: the earners and the spenders. Or as they are more popularly known, husbands and wives." To Mellencamp, "this 'ethos of gender' recognizes a key facet of postwar ideology, a cluster of ideals and expectations at the crossroads of mainstream representatives of gender roles, marriage, domesticity, and consumerism." Every week for seven years, she reminds us, "Lucy, the chorus girl/clown, complained that Ricky was preventing her from becoming a star. For twenty-four minutes, she valiantly tried to escape domesticity by getting a job in show business. After a tour de force performance of physical comedy, in the inevitable reversal and failure of the end, she was resigned to stay happily at home serving big and little Ricky. The ultimate 'creation/cancellation'—the series' premise, which was portrayed in brilliant performances and then denied weekly—was that Lucy was not star material." In one celebrated episode ("The Ballet"), Lucy throws a pie in Ricky's face during his solo at the Tropicana. But he gets the last laugh by rigging a bucket of water over the apartment's front door. When Lucy opens the door, she soaks her head, and at the fade-out pleads, "You were right all along, Ricky. Forgive me?" Notes Mellencamp dryly: "Laughter. Applause. Seven days later, Lucy repeats her break for freedom, her anarchism against wifery. To rephrase Freud, 'An action which carries out a certain injunction is immediately succeeded by another action which stops or undoes the first one.' The affect, drawn by Freud from war neuroses and for me from popular culture, is one of anxiety."

Frances Gray's *Women and Laughter* views the 1950s as a shadowed and contradictory time, for when "the older generation of women hung on to their jobs: for the younger, educated middle class, a problem developed." Gray say the problem was articulated for them by Adlai Stevenson, the former Democratic candidate for president, in his 1955 commencement address at Smith College: "Once they wrote poetry. Now it's the laundry list. Once they discussed art and philosophy till late into the night. Now they are so tired they fall asleep as soon as the dishes are finished. There is, often, a sense of closing horizons and lost opportunities. They had hoped to play their part in the crises of the age. But what they do is wash the diapers." But Stevenson, Gray insists, didn't unearth the root of the problem. To him, in common with most of his countrymen, the American woman had a unique opportunity to "inspire in her home a vision of the meaning of life and freedom . . . to help her husband find values that will give purpose to his specialized daily chores." This "opportunity" would undo many, says Gray, ominously dropping a name: "Sylvia Plath, like all the class of '55, applauded enthusiastically."

Had Lucille Ball been present, Gray implies, she too would have clapped and cheered. For when Lucy wasn't up on the sound stage she was a follower, not a leader, and she approved of the 1950s values. Onscreen she protested that her status was nothing to quo about, but that was only so that she could do her Sisyphus routine, making a grand effort—and then falling back to the starting point to begin again next week. The plots of her show set up "tensions rarely found when male slapstick performers are at work; we are invited to pity Harry Langdon, admire the stoicism or to rejoice in the subversive triumph of Chaplin's Little Man—but each of these had an existential integrity denied Lucy." Chaplin's hero may be downtrodden by society, "but he knows who he is and avoids social or economic thrall to another individual. The essence of Chaplin is that he is his own man. Lucy isn't her own woman; her triumphs are always partial, her power fragmented, her defeats always sanctioned by the narrative." A reference to Lucy's bag lady performance in *Stone Pillow* encapsulates the author's contrarian view: "It's understandable that in the world of the 1980s Ball chose to play Chaplin's symbol of existential freedom, a tramp."

Perhaps the most fascinating aspect of Lucille Ball's posthumous career is the continual association of her name with Charlie Chaplin's. The comparisons were first made in the 1950s and elaborated upon in 1963, when she paid homage to Charlie by donning a little moustache and twirling a cane on an episode of *The Lucy Show. TV Guide* praised this episode as the best of the lot "because it rose from a simple source: The daughter, giving her first boy-and-girl party, doesn't want mother at home. The party is a dud until Lucy does her Chaplin routine." At times, the piece concluded, "you have to wait between the great moments. But it isn't hard. After all, you can always look at Lucille." Others, including her family, also made the comparison between Charlie and Lucy. And some four decades after *I Love Lucy* went off the air, *The Dictionary of Teleliteracy,* compiled by New York *Daily News* critic

David Bianculli, mentioned the guest appearance of Harpo Marx on *I Love Lucy*, calling it especially fitting "because Lucille Ball did enough comedy, verbal and physical, to qualify as a Marx sister—or as TV's closest female equivalent of a Charlie Chaplin, Harold Lloyd, or Buster Keaton."

There have been many other slapstick performers since the Little Tramp capered on the silent screen. Why should Lucille Ball be esteemed so highly? In large measure the praise is due to her talent and grit. She was not only funnier than anyone else on TV; she was also more beautiful—a matchless combination. But there is another component in the mix.

Prior to the introduction of TV Land, *I Love Lucy*'s current cable venue, a Viacom executive complained: "The only problem with *I Love Lucy* is that it's not in color. That's why you never see *Lucy* reruns in early fringe or prime time. The stations believe that people buy color sets, so therefore they want to see color programs. So what happens is *Lucy* is relegated to the morning time periods when full viewership levels are not available." Ironically, those were the very conditions that solidified Lucy's reputation. The comedians to whom Lucy has been compared, those who achieved iconic status worldwide—Chaplin, Keaton, Harold Lloyd, Laurel and Hardy, the Marx Brothers—all capered before the Technicolor era. Even Bob Hope, who was still filming into the 1980s, is best remembered for his pre-color work in such films as *My Favorite Brunette* and the *Road* pictures. The clowns who came to prominence after 1960, when color became the norm rather than the exception, have by and large been supernovas, glowing brilliantly—and then vanishing in the void. There is something incompatible about humor and color; the palette calls attention to itself, instead of to the jokes. Lucy's contemporary Danny Kaye, for instance, was MGM's biggest comic star, clowning in vivid red, yellow, and blue. His range was wide, his abilities unquestioned. Yet his films are virtually unknown to the generations that followed him, and his television specials are rarely glimpsed. The episodes of *I Love Lucy*, from "Lucy Thinks Ricky Is Trying to Murder Her" through "The Ricardos Dedicate a Statue," have never stopped rerunning.

Lucille Ball was a festival of contradictions: a woman who yearned for her own family—and didn't know how to relate to her children; a demanding wife who allowed herself to be humiliated by a philanderer; a cold-eyed, exacting businesswoman who made others cry—and then retreated into tears when her authority was questioned. In the end, all the negatives will be forgotten or forgiven, as they usually are with performers—particularly funny ones, whose lives tend to be counter-weights to the laughter they engender. Whatever Lucy's private faults, her public accomplishments over a comparatively brief period are enough to guarantee her a lofty place in the history of popular enter-tainment. In W. H. Auden's indulgent words about another poet, "You were silly, like us: / your gift survived it all."

Lucy would have been the first to admit that she was silly; that she made profound and painful mistakes; that nothing else she did on radio, TV, film, or theater ever equaled *I Love Lucy* and its follow-up, *The Lucy Show;* that she simply fell into fortune—the right producer, the right writers, the right husband, the right decade, the right medium. In the end, though, that very improvisatory quality is what will make her endure as long as there are audiences to laugh at pranks and pratfalls.

Everyone has spoken of Lucy's gift of timing. Yet it was her late-ness—or, to be more accurate, Desi Arnaz's—that conferred immortal-ity. While others were disporting in a variety of rich hues and tints, she remained in stark, contrasting shades no different from those of the great silent-film comedians. So many other comedians, male and female, have come after her, enjoyed the tinted spotlight, and then slipped into obscurity. Lucy stays eternally comic because of the vital, frenzied, irreproducible years when the Ball of Fire got it all down in black and white.

Bibliography

The researcher for *Ball of Fire,* as well as for two of my other books, was John Bennett at Sterling Library, Yale University. In examining a life begun nearly a century ago, and a career that ended more than two decades ago, I found it necessary to ransack hundreds of long-forgotten personal papers, as well as thousands of periodicals, memoirs, books, and that newest form of communication, Web sites. These concerned not only the obvious subject of bygone show business personalities, but the more complex categories of politics and finance. Mr. Bennett's work was a model of nuance and scruple, with special attention paid to obscure records ranging geographically from upstate New York to Hollywood, Broadway, Europe, and the Caribbean. The writing of this book would not have been possible without his unflagging diligence, and persistence.

For additional research I am also indebted to Danielle Moon, Archivist, Manuscripts and Archives, Yale University Library; Jean Geist, Librarian, Popular Culture Library, Bowling Green University; Lyn Olsson, Acting Special Collections Librarian, Malcolm A. Love Library, San Diego State University; Brad Bauer, Archivist, Herbert Hoover Presidential Library-Museum; Nathaniel Parks, Senior Archival Assistant, Special Collections, Boston University; Sally McManus, Palm Springs Historical Society; Nancy Robinson, Librarian/Local History Indexer, Palm Springs Public Library.

Individuals who provided enormous aid include Lucie Arnaz Luckinbill, Daniel Melnick, Regina Kessler, the late Chuck Jones, Josh Greenfeld, Howard Weishaus, Stephen Becker, Kevin and Andrew Ettinger, Robert Rittner, Robert Tucker, Will Shortz, Robert Mankoff, Steven Zeitlin, Dr. Robert Spitzer, Richard Schickel, and others who prefer to remain anonymous.

Although all the works cited below bear on Lucille Ball's biography, several are particularly significant, for historians, scholars, and unabashed Lucy fans.

AUTOBIOGRAPHIES OF LUCY AND DESI

Arnaz, Desi. *A Book.* New York: Morrow, 1976. Desi's disarmingly candid appraisal of his private and professional life happily stresses his own virtues but never shies away from his liabilities, including his alcoholism and unbridled temper that eventually broke up a storybook marriage. Filled with engaging show business anecdota.

Ball, Lucille, with Betty Hannah Hoffman. *Love, Lucy.* New York: Putnam, 1996. A posthumously published, less-than-frank exercise in nostalgia. The tone is clearly that of a woman who would rather not bear any grudges—in print—but who is withholding a lot from the reader. Nonetheless, a valuable item because Lucy wrote so little about herself.

KEY BIOGRAPHIES AND MEMOIRS

Brady, Kathleen. *Lucille: The Life of Lucille Ball.* New York: Hyperion, 1994. The most recent of the biographies, this thoroughly researched, important work uncovers new material about Ball's early years in Jamestown, N.Y., and closely follows various stages of her career, from modeling in Manhattan to acting in minor and major Hollywood films, to the rise of *I Love Lucy* and Desilu, to the slow decline of marriage, family, vocation, and, finally, health.

Brochu, Jim. *Lucy in the Afternoon: An Intimate Biography of Lucille Ball.* New York: Morrow, 1990. A graceful, melancholy memoir of Ball in her final years, by a close friend who noted her recollections of triumphs, sorrows, and regrets, and saw her through the last illness.

Gregory, James. *The Lucille Ball Story.* New York: New American Library, 1974. An early and rather uncritical appraisal of the star after the breakup of her marriage, but well before her decline.

Harris, Eleanor. *The Real Story of Lucille Ball.* New York: Farrar, Straus & Young, 1954. The first biography of the star, shortly after *I Love Lucy* had risen from sitcom to phenomenon. A valuable indicator of television's power to amuse—and then to influence—its new audience.

Higham, Charles. *Lucy: The Life of Lucille Ball.* New York: St. Martin's Press, 1986. A short, intelligent biography of the actress–studio head, published three years before her death, by a veteran Hollywood biographer and journalist.

Morella, Joe, and Edward Z. Epstein. *Lucy: The Bittersweet Life of Lucille Ball.* Secaucus, N.J.: L. Stuart, 1973. An early account of, as the authors put it, "a super-talented woman with a super-fascinating life."

Oppenheimer, Jess. *Laughs, Luck—and Lucy: How I Came to Create the Most Popular Sitcom of All Time.* Syracuse, N.Y.: Syracuse University Press, 1996. Despite its subtitle, a disarming and bemused account of *I Love Lucy* from drawing-table idea to international phenomenon, by its inventor and first producer. The late author recalls his employers with affection, but does not shy away from less-than-flattering glimpses of the couple under pressure.

Sanders, Coyne Steven, and Tom Gilbert. *Desilu: The Story of Lucille Ball and Desi Arnaz.* New York: Morrow, 1993. A close, sophisticated look at Lucille Ball and Desi Arnaz, separately and together, with great emphasis on the formation and daily operation of the Desilu studios. With many interviews and photographs.

Tannen, Lee. *I Loved Lucy: My Friendship with Lucille Ball.* New York: St. Martin's Press, 2001. Another fan checks in, with his own chronicle of Lucille Ball in old age. Manifestly, she grew dependent on her young admirer, and it is to his credit that he not only treated her well, but saw to it that her meditations on life, love, and work were recorded in print.

OTHER BOOKS

Abbott, George. *Mister Abbott.* New York: Random House, 1963.

Ace, Goodman. *The Book of Little Knowledge: More Than You Want to Know About Television.* New York: Simon & Schuster, 1955.

Adir, Karin. *The Great Clowns of American Television.* Jefferson, N.C.: McFarland, 1988.

Altschuler, Glenn C., and David I. Grossvogel. *Changing Channels: America in TV Guide.* Urbana: University of Illinois Press, 1992.

Anderson, Christopher. *Hollywood TV: The Studio System in the Fifties.* Austin: University of Texas Press, 1994.

Andrews, Bart, and Thomas J. Watson. *Loving Lucy: An Illustrated Tribute to Lucille Ball.* New York: St. Martin's Press, 1980.

Arden, Eve. *Three Phases of Eve: An Autobiography.* New York: St. Martin's Press, 1985.

Babington, Bruce, and Peter William Evans. *Affairs to Remember: The Hollywood Comedy of the Sexes.* Manchester, U.K.: Manchester University Press, distributed by St. Martin's Press, 1989.

Bacon, James. *Hollywood Is a Four Letter Town.* Chicago: Regnery, 1976.

———. *Made in Hollywood.* Chicago: Contemporary Books, 1977.

Balio, Tino, ed. *Hollywood in the Age of Television.* Boston: Unwin Hyman, 1990.

Barlett, Donald L. *Empire: The Life, Legend, and Madness of Howard Hughes.* New York: Norton, 1979.

Barnouw, Erik. *Tube of Plenty: The Evolution of American Television.* New York: Oxford University Press, 1975.

Basinger, Jeanine. *A Woman's View: How Hollywood Spoke to Women, 1930–1960.* New York: Knopf, 1993.

Beauchamp, Cari. *Without Lying Down: Frances Marion and the Powerful Women of Early Hollywood.* New York: Scribner, 1997.

Beeman, Marsha Lynn. *Joan Fontaine: A Bio-bibliography.* Westport, Conn.: Greenwood Press, 1994.

Berg, A. Scott. *Goldwyn: A Biography.* New York: Knopf, 1989.

Berle, Milton, with Haskel Frankel. *Milton Berle, An Autobiography.* New York: Delacorte Press, 1974.

Bernardi, Daniel, ed. *Classic Hollywood, Classic Whiteness.* Minneapolis: University of Minnesota Press, 2001.

Billips, Connie J. *Lux Presents Hollywood: A Show-by-Show History of the Lux Radio Theatre and the Lux Video Theatre, 1934–1957.* Jefferson, N.C.: McFarland, 1995.

Billman, Larry. *Betty Grable: A Bio-bibliography.* Westport, Conn.: Greenwood Press, 1993.

Blesh, Rudi. *Keaton.* New York: Macmillan, 1966.

Blumenthal, Ralph. *The Stork Club: America's Most Famous Nightspot and the Lost World of Cafe Society.* Boston: Little, Brown, 2000.

Boddy, William. *Fifties Television: The Industry and Its Critics.* Urbana: University of Illinois Press, 1990.

Boller, Paul F., and Ronald L. Davis. *Hollywood Anecdotes.* New York: Morrow, 1987.

Boswell, Thomas D., and James R. Curtis. *The Cuban-American Experience: Culture, Images, and Perspectives.* Totowa, N.J.: Rowman & Allanheld, 1984.

Bragg, Melvyn. *Richard Burton: A Life.* Boston: Little, Brown, 1988.

Breslin, Jimmy. *Damon Runyon.* New York: Ticknor & Fields, 1991.

Brochu, Jim. *Lucy in the Afternoon: An Intimate Memoir of Lucille Ball.* New York: Morrow, 1990.

Brown, Les. *Television: The Business Behind the Box.* New York: Harcourt Brace Jovanovich, 1971.

Brunsdon, Charlotte, Julie D'Acci, and Lynn Spigel, eds. *Feminist Television Criticism: A Reader*. New York: Oxford University Press, 1997.

Bubbeo, Daniel. *The Women of Warner Brothers: The Lives and Careers of 15 Leading Ladies, with Filmographies for Each*. Jefferson, N.C.: McFarland, 2002.

Burns, George, with David Fisher. *All My Best Friends*. New York: Putnam, 1989.

Callow, Simon. *Charles Laughton: A Difficult Actor*. London: Methuen, 1988.

Carbó, Nick. *El Grupo McDonald's: Poems*. Chicago: Tia Chucha Press, distributed by Northwestern University Press, 1995.

Carrick, Peter. *Liza Minnelli*. London: R. Hale, 1993.

Carrier, Jeffrey L. *Tallulah Bankhead: A Bio-bibliography*. New York: Greenwood Press, 1991.

Castleman, Harry, and Walter J. Podrazik. *The TV Schedule Book: Four Decades of Network Programming from Sign-on to Sign-off*. New York: McGraw-Hill, 1984.

Ceplair, Larry, and Stephen Englund. *The Inquisition in Hollywood: Politics in the Film Community, 1930–1960*. Garden City, N.Y.: Anchor Press/Doubleday, 1980.

Chunovic, Louis. *One Foot on the Floor: The Curious Evolution of Sex on Television from "I Love Lucy" to "South Park."* New York: TV Books, 2000.

Clark, Tom. *The World of Damon Runyon*. New York: Harper & Row, 1978.

Clements, Cynthia. *George Burns and Gracie Allen: A Bio-bibliography*. Westport, Conn.: Greenwood Press, 1996.

Cobb, Sally Wright. *The Brown Derby Restaurant: A Hollywood Legend*. New York: Rizzoli, 1996.

Cohan, Steven. *Masked Men: Masculinity and the Movies in the Fifties*. Bloomington: Indiana University Press, 1997.

Davis, Ronald L. *The Glamour Factory: Inside Hollywood's Big Studio System*. Dallas: Southern Methodist University Press, 1993.

Dewey, Donald. *James Stewart: A Biography*. Atlanta: Turner Pub.; Kansas City, Mo.: distributed by Andrews & McMeel, 1996.

DiBattista, Maria. *Fast-Talking Dames*. New Haven: Yale University Press, 2001.

DiMeglio, John E. *Vaudeville U.S.A.* Bowling Green, Ohio: Bowling Green University Popular Press, 1973.

Doane, Mary Ann, Patricia Mellencamp, and Linda Williams, eds. *Re-vision: Essays in Feminist Film Criticism*. Frederick, Md.: University Publications of America, 1984.

Duhamel, Denise. *The Star-Spangled Banner*. Carbondale: Southern Illinois University Press, 1999.

Duke, Patty, and Kenneth Turan. *Call Me Anna: The Autobiography of Patty Duke*. New York: Bantam Books, 1987.

Eames, John Douglas. *The MGM Story: The Complete History of Fifty Roaring Years*. New York: Crown Publishers, 1975.

Eberly, Stephen L. *Patty Duke: A Bio-bibliography*. New York: Greenwood Press, 1988.

Edelman, Rob, and Audrey Kupferberg. *Meet the Mertzes: The Life Stories of "I Love Lucy"'s Other Couple*. Los Angeles: Renaissance Books; distributed by St. Martin's Press, 1999.

Eder, Shirley. *Not This Time, Cary Grant! And Other Stories About Hollywood*. Garden City, N.Y.: Doubleday, 1973.

Edgerton, Gary R., and Peter C. Rollins, eds. *Television Histories: Shaping Collective Memory in the Media Age*. Lexington: University Press of Kentucky, 2001.

Eells, George. *Hedda and Louella*. New York: Putnam, 1972.

Ehrenstein, David. *Open Secret: Gay Hollywood, 1928–1998*. New York: Morrow, 1998.

Ewen, David. *Richard Rodgers*. New York: Holt, 1957.

Eyles, Allen. *The Marx Brothers: Their World of Comedy.* Cranbury, N.J.: Barnes, 1966.

Faith, William Robert. *Bob Hope: A Life in Comedy.* New York: Putnam, 1982.

Fidelman, Geoffrey Mark. *The Lucy Book: A Complete Guide to Her Five Decades on Television.* Los Angeles: Renaissance Books, 1999.

Filmmakers on Filmmaking: The American Film Institute Seminars on Motion Pictures and Television. Edited by Joseph McBride. Los Angeles: J. P. Tarcher; distributed by Houghton Mifflin, 1983.

Fisher, James. *Eddie Cantor: A Bio-bibliography.* Westport, Conn.: Greenwood Press, 1997.

Fleming, Michael. *The Three Stooges: Amalgamated Morons to American Icons; An Illustrated History.* New York: Doubleday, 1999.

Fonda, Henry. *Fonda: My Life / As Told to Howard Teichmann.* New York: New American Library, 1981.

Forrester, Tom, with Jeff Forrester. *The Stooges' Lost Episodes.* Chicago: Contemporary Books, 1988.

Freedland, Michael. *Maurice Chevalier.* New York: Morrow, 1981.

Friedwald, Will. *Sinatra! The Song Is You: A Singer's Art.* New York: Scribner, 1995.

Gabler, Neal. *Winchell: Gossip, Power, and the Culture of Celebrity.* New York: Knopf, 1994.

Gehring, Wes D. *The Marx Brothers: A Bio-bibliography.* New York: Greenwood Press, 1987.

Gentile, John Samuel. *Cast of One: One-Person Shows from the Chautauqua Platform to the Broadway Stage.* Urbana: University of Illinois Press, 1989.

Gerber, Albert Benjamin. *Bashful Billionaire: The Story of Howard Hughes.* New York: L. Stuart, 1967.

Gilliatt, Penelope. *Unholy Fools; Wits, Comics, Disturbers of the Peace: Film & Theater.* New York: Viking Press, 1973.

Gil-Montero, Martha. *Brazilian Bombshell: The Biography of Carmen Miranda.* New York: D. I. Fine, 1989.

Goldman, Herbert G. *Banjo Eyes: Eddie Cantor and the Birth of Modern Stardom.* New York: Oxford University Press, 1997.

Gonzalez-Pando, Miguel. *The Cuban Americans.* Westport, Conn.: Greenwood Press, 1998.

Goodman, Ezra. *The Fifty-Year Decline and Fall of Hollywood.* New York: Simon & Schuster, 1961.

Graham, Sheilah. *The Rest of the Story.* New York: Coward-McCann, 1964.

———. *Confessions of a Hollywood Columnist.* New York: Morrow, 1969.

Gray, Frances. *Women and Laughter.* Charlottesville: University Press of Virginia, 1994.

Gregory, James. *The Lucille Ball Story.* New York: New American Library, 1974.

Guiles, Fred Lawrence. *Hanging on in Paradise. Selected Filmographies by John E. Schultheiss.* New York: McGraw-Hill, 1975.

Hadleigh, Boze, comp. *Hollywood Babble On: Stars Gossip about Other Stars.* Secaucus, N.J.: Carol Publishing Group, 1994.

Hadley-Garcia, George. *Hispanic Hollywood: The Latins in Motion Pictures.* Secaucus, N.J.: Carol Publishing Group, 1990.

Halberstam, David. *The Fifties.* New York: Villard Books, 1993.

Hannsberry, Karen Burroughs. *Femme Noir: Bad Girls of Film.* Jefferson, N.C.: McFarland, 1998.

Harris, Jay S., comp. and ed., in assoc. with the eds. of *TV Guide. TV Guide, The First 25 Years.* New York: Simon & Schuster, 1978.

Harris, Warren G. *Gable and Lombard*. New York: Simon & Schuster, 1974.

————. *Lucy & Desi: The Legendary Love Story of Television's Most Famous Couple*. New York: Simon & Schuster, 1991.

Haskell, Molly. *From Reverence to Rape: The Treatment of Women in the Movies*. New York: Holt, Rinehart & Winston, 1974.

Heide, Robert. *Home Front America: Popular Culture of the World War II Era*. San Francisco: Chronicle Books, 1995.

Heimann, Jim. *Out with the Stars: Hollywood Nightlife in the Golden Era*. New York: Abbeville Press, 1985.

Heldenfels, R. D. *Television's Greatest Year—1954*. New York: Continuum, 1994.

Helmick, Paul A. *Cut, Print, and That's a Wrap!: A Hollywood Memoir*. Jefferson, N.C.: McFarland, 2001.

Higham, Charles. *Charles Laughton: An Intimate Biography*. Garden City, N.Y.: Doubleday, 1976.

————. *Orson Welles: The Rise and Fall of an American Genius*. New York: St. Martin's Press, 1985.

Hijuelos, Oscar. *The Mambo Kings Play Songs of Love*. New York: Farrar, Straus & Giroux, 1989.

History of Chautauqua County, New York, 1938–1978: A Bicentennial History Project. Edited by Ernest D. Leet. Westfield, N.Y.: Chautauqua County Historical Society, 1980.

Holt, Georgia, and Phillis Quinn, with Sue Russell. *Star Mothers: The Moms Behind the Celebrities*. New York: Simon & Schuster, 1988.

Hoopes, Roy. *When the Stars Went to War: Hollywood and World War II*. New York: Random House, 1994.

Hopper, Hedda. *From Under My Hat*. Garden City, N.Y.: Doubleday, 1952.

Horowitz, Susan. *Queens of Comedy: Lucille Ball, Phyllis Diller, Carol Burnett, Joan Rivers, and the New Generation of Funny Women*. Amsterdam, Netherlands: Gordon & Breach, 1997.

Hoyt, Edwin Palmer. *A Gentleman of Broadway*. Boston: Little, Brown, 1964.

Hyland, William. *Richard Rodgers*. New Haven: Yale University Press, 1998.

Javna, John. *The Best of TV Sitcoms: Burns and Allen to the Cosby Show, the Munsters to Mary Tyler Moore*. New York: Harmony Books, 1988.

Jerome, Stuart. *Those Crazy, Wonderful Years When We Ran Warner Bros*. Secaucus, N.J.: L. Stuart, 1983.

Jones, Gerard. *Honey, I'm Home!: Sitcoms, Selling the American Dream*. New York: Grove Weidenfeld, 1992.

Josefsberg, Milt. *Comedy Writing for Television and Hollywood*. New York: Perennial Library, 1987.

Kael, Pauline. *Reeling*. Boston: Little, Brown, 1976.

Kanfer, Stefan. *A Journal of the Plague Years*. New York: Atheneum, 1973.

————. *Groucho: The Life and Times of Julius Henry Marx*. New York: Knopf, 2000.

Kanin, Garson. *Hollywood: Stars and Starlets, Tycoons and Flesh-Peddlers, Moviemakers and Moneymakers, Frauds and Geniuses, Hopefuls and Has-Beens, Great Lovers and Sex Symbols*. New York: Viking Press, 1974.

Kanter, Hal. *So Far, So Funny: My Life in Show Business*. Jefferson, N.C.: McFarland, 1999.

Keats, John. *Howard Hughes*. Rev. ed. New York: Random House, 1972.

Kelley, Kitty. *His Way: The Unauthorized Biography of Frank Sinatra*. New York: Bantam Books, 1986.

Kisseloff, Jeff. *The Box: An Oral History of Television, 1929–1961*. New York: Viking, 1995.

Kulzer, Dina-Marie. *Television Series Regulars of the Fifties and Sixties in Interview*. Jefferson, N.C.: McFarland, 1992.

Landay, Lori. *Madcaps, Screwballs, and Con Women: The Female Trickster in American Culture*. Philadelphia: University of Pennsylvania Press, 1998.

Langman, Larry, and Paul Gold, comps. *Comedy Quotes from the Movies: Over 4000 Bits of Humorous Dialogue from All Film Genres*. Jefferson, N.C.: McFarland, 1993.

Lasky, Jesse L. *Whatever Happened to Hollywood?* New York: Funk & Wagnalls, 1975.

Lawford, Patricia Seaton, with Ted Schwarz. *The Peter Lawford Story: Life with the Kennedys, Monroe, and the Rat Pack*. New York: Carroll & Graf, 1988.

Leaming, Barbara. *Orson Welles: A Biography*. New York: Viking Press, 1985.

———. *Bette Davis: A Biography*. New York: Simon & Schuster, 1992.

Levy, Shawn. *Rat Pack Confidential: Frank, Dean, Sammy, Peter, Joey & the Last Great Showbiz Party*. New York: Doubleday, 1998.

Leyda, Jay, ed. *Voices of Film Experience: 1894 to the Present*. New York: Macmillan, 1977.

Lichter, S. Robert, Linda S. Lichter, and Stanley Rothman. *Prime Time: How TV Portrays American Culture*. Washington, D.C.: Regnery; distributed by National Book Network, 1994.

Lowe, Denise. *Women and American Television: An Encyclopedia*. Santa Barbara, Calif.: ABC-CLIO, 1999.

MacDonald, J. Fred. *Television and the Red Menace: The Video Road to Vietnam*. New York: Praeger, 1985.

Mair, George. *Under the Rainbow: The Real Liza Minnelli*. Secaucus, N.J.: Carol Publishing Group, 1996.

Maltin, Leonard. *Carole Lombard*. New York: Pyramid Publications, 1976.

Manuel, Peter Lamarche. *Caribbean Currents: Caribbean Music from Rumba to Reggae*. Philadelphia: Temple University Press, 1995.

Marc, David. *Demographic Vistas: Television in American Culture*. Philadelphia: University of Pennsylvania Press, 1984.

———. *Comic Visions: Television Comedy and American Culture*. Boston: Unwin Hyman, 1989.

———. *Prime Time, Prime Movers: From I Love Lucy to L.A. Law—America's Greatest TV Shows and the People Who Created Them*. Boston: Little, Brown, 1992.

Marcus, Greil. *The Dustbin of History*. Cambridge: Harvard University Press, 1995.

Marill, Alvin H. *Samuel Goldwyn Presents*. South Brunswick, N.J.: A. S. Barnes, 1976.

Martin, Linda, and Kerry Seagrave. *Women in Comedy*. Secaucus, N.J.: Citadel Press, 1986.

Marx, Arthur. *Red Skelton*. New York: Dutton, 1979.

Marx, Samuel, and Jan Clayton. *Rodgers & Hart: Bewitched, Bothered, and Bedeviled: An Anecdotal Account*. New York: Putnam, 1976.

McCrohan, Donna. *Prime Time, Our Time: America's Life and Times through the Prism of Television*. Rocklin, Calif.: Prima Publishing, 1990.

McDougal, Dennis. *The Last Mogul: Lew Wasserman, MCA, and the Hidden History of Hollywood*. New York: Crown Publishers, 1998.

McLean, Albert F. *American Vaudeville as Ritual*. Lexington: University of Kentucky Press, 1965.

Meehan, Diana M. *Ladies of the Evening: Women Characters of Prime-Time Television*. Metuchen, N.J.: Scarecrow Press, 1983.

Mellencamp, Patricia. *High Anxiety: Catastrophe, Scandal, Age & Comedy.* Blooming-
    ton: Indiana University Press, 1992.

Metz, Robert. *CBS: Reflections in a Bloodshot Eye.* Chicago: Playboy Press, 1975.

Miller, Ann, with Norma Lee Browning. *Miller's High Life.* Garden City, N.Y.: Double-
    day, 1972.

Miller, Merle, and Evan Rhodes. *Only You, Dick Daring! Or, How to Write One Televi-
    sion Script and Make $50,000,000; A True-Life Adventure.* New York: W. Sloane
    Associates, 1964.

Modleski, Tania, ed. *Studies in Entertainment: Critical Approaches to Mass Culture.*
    Bloomington: Indiana University Press, 1986.

Montalban, Ricardo, with Bob Thomas. *Reflections: A Life in Two Worlds.* Garden City,
    N.Y.: Doubleday, 1980.

Mordden, Ethan. *Movie Star: A Look at the Women Who Made Hollywood.* New York:
    St. Martin's Press, 1983.

Morley, Sheridan. *Tales from the Hollywood Raj: The British, the Movies, and Tinsel-
    town.* New York: Viking Press, 1984.

Mott, Robert L. *Radio Live! Television Live!: Those Golden Days When Horses Were
    Coconuts.* Jefferson, N.C.: McFarland, 2000.

Nachman, Gerald. *Raised on Radio: In Quest of the Lone Ranger, Jack Benny . . .* New
    York: Pantheon Books, 1998.

Naremore, James. *The Films of Vincente Minnelli.* New York: Cambridge University
    Press, 1993.

Neibaur, James L. *The RKO Features: A Complete Filmography of the Feature Films
    Released or Produced by RKO Radio Pictures, 1929–1960.* Jefferson, N.C.: McFar-
    land, 1994.

Nolan, Frederick. *Lorenz Hart: A Poet on Broadway.* New York: Oxford University
    Press, 1994.

O'Dell, Cary. *Women Pioneers in Television: Biographies of Fifteen Industry Leaders.* Jef-
    ferson, N.C.: McFarland, 1997.

Paley, William S. *As It Happened: A Memoir.* Garden City, N.Y.: Doubleday, 1979.

Parish, James Robert. *The RKO Gals.* New Rochelle, N.Y.: Arlington House, 1974.

Parish, James Robert, and Lennard DeCarl. *Hollywood Players: The Forties.* New
    Rochelle, N.Y.: Arlington House, 1976.

Parker, John. *Five for Hollywood.* London: Macmillan, 1989.

Parsons, Louella O. *Tell It to Louella.* New York: Putnam, 1961.

Pegg, Robert. *Comical Co-stars of Television: From Ed Norton to Kramer.* Jefferson,
    N.C.: McFarland, 2002.

Pegler, Westbrook. *T Aint Right.* Garden City, N.Y.: Doubleday, Doran, 1936.

The Penguin Book of Hollywood. Edited by Christopher Silvester. New York: Viking
    Press, 1998.

Perez Firmat, Gustavo. *Life on the Hyphen: The Cuban-American Way.* Austin: Univer-
    sity of Texas Press, 1994.

Pilat, Oliver. *Pegler, Angry Man of the Press.* Boston: Beacon Press, 1963.

Pitrone, Jean Maddern. *Take It from the Big Mouth: The Life of Martha Raye.* Lexing-
    ton: University Press of Kentucky, 1999.

Press, Andrea Lee. *Women Watching Television: Gender, Class, and Generation in the
    American Television Experience.* Philadelphia: University of Pennsylvania Press,
    1991.

Putterman, Barry. *On Television and Comedy: Essays on Style, Theme, Performer, and
    Writer.* Jefferson, N.C.: McFarland, 1995.

Quirk, Lawrence J. *Bob Hope: The Road Well-Traveled*. New York: Applause Books, 1998.

Read, William H. *America's Mass Media Merchants*. Baltimore: Johns Hopkins University Press, 1976.

Roberts, John Storm. *The Latin Tinge: The Impact of Latin American Music on the United States*. New York: Oxford University Press, 1979.

Rogers, Ginger. *Ginger: My Story*. New York: HarperCollins, 1991.

Rosenfield, Paul. *The Club Rules: Power, Money, Sex, and Fear—How It Works in Hollywood*. New York: Warner Books, 1992.

St. Johns, Adela Rogers. *Some Are Born Great*. Garden City, N.Y.: Doubleday, 1974.

Samuels, Charles. *Once Upon a Stage: The Merry World of Vaudeville*. New York: Dodd, Mead, 1974.

Schatz, Thomas. *Hollywood Genres: Formulas, Filmmaking, and the Studio System*. Philadelphia: Temple University Press, 1981.

Sennett, Robert S. *Hollywood Hoopla: Creating Stars and Selling Movies in the Golden Age of Hollywood*. New York: Billboard Books, 1998.

Shipman, David. *Movie Talk: Who Said What About Whom in the Movies*. London: Bloomsbury, 1988.

Silverman, Stephen M. *Funny Ladies: The Women Who Make Us Laugh*. New York: Abrams, 1999.

Singer, Arthur J. *Arthur Godfrey: The Adventures of an American Broadcaster*. Jefferson, N.C.: McFarland, 2000.

Slater, Robert. *This—Is CBS: A Chronicle of 60 Years*. Englewood Cliffs, N.J.: Prentice-Hall, 1988.

Smith, Leon. *Famous Hollywood Locations: Descriptions and Photographs of 382 Sites Involving 289 Films and 105 Television Series*. Jefferson, N.C.: McFarland, 1993.

Smith, Sally Bedell. *In All His Glory: The Life of William S. Paley, the Legendary Tycoon and His Brilliant Circle*. New York: Simon & Schuster, 1990.

Sochen, June. *From Mae to Madonna: Women Entertainers in Twentieth-Century America*. Lexington: University Press of Kentucky, 1999.

Solow, Herbert F., and Robert H. Justman. *Inside Star Trek: The Real Story*. New York: Pocket Books, 1996.

Springer, John Shipman, and Jack Hamilton. *They Had Faces Then: Super Stars, Stars, and Starlets of the 1930's*. Secaucus, N.J.: Citadel Press, 1974.

Stack, Robert, with Mark Evans. *Straight Shooting*. New York: Macmillan, 1980.

Stein, Charles W., ed. *American Vaudeville as Seen by Its Contemporaries*. New York: Knopf, 1984.

Sterling, Christopher H., and John M. Kittross. *Stay Tuned: A Concise History of American Broadcasting*. Belmont, Calif.: Wadsworth Publishing, 1978.

Swindell, Larry. *Screwball: The Life of Carole Lombard*. New York: Morrow, 1975.

Tapia, John E. *Circuit Chautauqua: From Rural Education to Popular Entertainment in Early Twentieth Century America*. Jefferson, N.C.: McFarland, 1997.

Terrace, Vincent. *Television Specials: 3,201 Entertainment Spectaculars, 1939–1993*. Jefferson, N.C.: McFarland, 1995.

Thibodeaux, Keith, with Audrey T. Hingley. *Life After Lucy: The True Story of Keith Thibodeaux—"I Love Lucy's" Little Ricky*. Green Forest, Ariz.: New Leaf Press, 1993.

Thomas, Bob. *King Cohn: The Life and Times of Harry Cohn*. New York: Putnam, 1967.

Thomas, Tony. *Howard Hughes in Hollywood*. Secaucus, N.J.: Citadel Press, 1985.

Thompson, B. Dolores. *Jamestown & Chautauqua County: An Illustrated History*. Woodland Hills, Calif.: Windsor Publications, 1984.

Thompson, Robert J., and Gary Burns, eds. *Making Television: Authorship and the Production Process.* New York: Praeger, 1990.

Took, Barry. *Comedy Greats: A Celebration of Comic Genius Past and Present.* Wellingborough, Northamptonshire, England: Equation, 1989.

Unterbrink, Mary. *Funny Women: American Comediennes, 1860–1985.* Jefferson, N.C.: McFarland, 1987.

Van Heerden, Bill. *Film and Television In-Jokes: Nearly 2,000 Intentional References, Parodies, Allusions, Personal Touches, Cameos, Spoofs, and Homages.* Jefferson, N.C.: McFarland, 1998.

Vasey, Ruth. *The World According to Hollywood, 1918–1939.* Madison: University of Wisconsin Press, 1997.

Von Hoffman, Nicholas. *Citizen Cohn.* New York: Doubleday, 1988.

Weatherby, William J. *Jackie Gleason: An Intimate Portrait of the Great One.* New York: Pharos Books, 1992.

Wasserstein, Wendy. *Shiksa Goddess, Or, How I Spent My Forties: Essays.* New York: Knopf, 2001.

Wells, Robert V. *Facing the "King of Terrors": Death and Society in an American Community, 1750–1990.* New York: Cambridge University Press, 2000.

Wexman, Virginia Wright. *Creating the Couple: Love, Marriage, and Hollywood Performance.* Princeton: Princeton University Press, 1993.

Wilk, Max. *The Golden Age of Television: Notes from the Survivors.* New York: Delacorte Press, 1976.

Wilkerson, Tichi, and Marcia Borie. *The Hollywood Reporter: The Golden Years.* New York: Coward-McCann, 1984.

Williams, Esther, with Digby Diehl. *The Million Dollar Mermaid.* New York: Simon & Schuster, 1999.

Wilson, Earl. *The Show Business Nobody Knows.* Chicago: Cowles, 1971.

Winchell, Walter. *Winchell Exclusive: "Things That Happened to Me—and Me to Them."* Englewood, N.J.: Prentice-Hall, 1975.

The WPA Guide to America: The Best of 1930s America as Seen by the Federal Writers' Project. Federal Writers' Project of the Works Progress Administration, 1935–1941. Edited by Bernard A. Weisberger. New York: Pantheon Books, 1985.

Wyman, Ric B. *For the Love of Lucy: The Complete Guide for Collectors and Fans.* New York: Abbeville Press, 1995.

Yablonsky, Lewis. *George Raft.* New York, McGraw-Hill, 1974.

Young, Jordan R. *The Laugh Crafters: Comedy Writing in Radio and TV's Golden Age.* Beverly Hills, Calif.: Past Times, 1999.

Zimmerman, Tom. *Light and Illusion: The Hollywood Portraits of Ray Jones.* Glendale, Calif.: Balcony Press, 1998.

ARCHIVAL SOURCES AND DISSERTATIONS

Anthony Newley Collection. Special Collections at Boston University.

Arnaz, Desi. Papers. San Diego State Drama Department Collection, 1914–1996. Malcolm A. Love library, San Diego State University.

Conner, Patricia Sandberg. *Steve Mills and the Twentieth Century American Burlesque Show: A Backstage History and a Perspective.* Dissertation, University of Illinois at Urbana-Champaign, 1979. Ann Arbor, Mich.: University Microfilms International, 1991.

Crawford Theater Collection. Manuscripts and Archives. Yale University Library.

Genre Periodicals Collection. Popular Culture Library. Bowling Green State University, Bowling Green, Ohio.

Helen Deutsch Collection. Special Collections at Boston University.

Kilgallen, Dorothy. Papers and Scrapbooks, 1926–1965. Billy Rose Theater Collection. The New York Public Library for the Performing Arts.

Palm Springs Historical Society, Palm Springs, Florida.

Palm Springs [Florida] Public Library. Local History.

Pegler, James Westbrook. Papers. Herbert Hoover Presidential Library.

Reid, Ogden Rogers. Papers. Manuscripts and Archives. Yale University Library.

Weisblat, Tinky. *Will the Real George and Gracie and Ozzie and Harriet and Desi and Lucy Please Stand Up? The Functions of Popular Biography in 1950s Television.* Dissertation, University of Texas, Austin, 1991.

PERIODICAL SOURCES

Ace, Goodman. "Top of My Head: That Same Wax of Ball Again." *Saturday Review,* May 16, 1964.

Advertiser [New York]. "From Housewife to Heroine: An Evolution Before Our Eyes." March 16, 2002.

Alexander, Jeff. "Madeline Kahn Shone Best in Nutty Mel Brooks Flicks." *Jupiter Courier* [Vero Beach, Fla.], December 12, 1999, sec. A, p. 19.

Als, Hilton. "At the Galleries: So Very Hattie." *New Yorker,* March 11, 1996, 80.

American Film. "Freeze Frame: 1950—Lucille Ball and Eddie Albert; *The Fuller Brush Girl.*" March 1987, 72.

American Film Institute. "Dialogue on Film, 'Lucille Ball.' " Vol. 3, no. 6 (1974).

Anders, Gigi. " 'Luuu-cy!' Fifty Years Later, America Still Loves Lucy and Ricky." *Hispanic* magazine, November 2001, 42.

Anderson, Nancy. "Meet Desi's New Girl: More Dangerous than Liza." *Photoplay,* September 1973.

Archibold, Randal C. "In a Small Upstate City They Love Lucy." *New York Times,* March 23, 2002.

Arnaz, Desi. "This Is Lucy." *Look,* November 18 1952.

Arnaz, Desi, Jr. "My Mom, Lucille Ball." *People,* March 5, 1991.

Arthur, Allene. "How We Loved Lucy: How the Desert Loved Lucy—But Desi's Got Some 'Splainin' to Do." *Palm Springs Life,* January 2002, 166–179.

Badger, Elisabeth. "The Ball's a Rollin'." *Modern Screen,* May 1938.

Bankston, Douglas. Wrap Shot: "Unsatisfied with the Quality of the Kinescopes . . . I Love Lucy . . . Desilu Productions Opted to Shoot the Show on 35 mm Film. . . ." *American Cinematographer* (October 1999): 128.

Basinger, Jeanine. "Ladies Matinee." *Film Comment* (November/December 1999): 28.

Bellafante, Gina. "Here's Lucy—Kathleen Brady." *Time,* November 21, 1994.

Bergen Record. "NY Didn't Quite Love Lucy: Protests CBS Portrayal of City's Homeless." November 6, 1985, sec. A, p. 20.

Berger, Phil. "The New Comediennes." *New York Times,* July 29, 1984, sec. G, p. 27.

Bergquist, Laura. "Lucille Ball: The Star That Never Sets." *Look,* September 7, 1971.

Bernstein, Dan. "Desi Assault Cases." *Press–Enterprise* [Riverside, Calif.], December 7, 1986.

Betcher, Bob. "Lucy Ball Lives on in Larush." *Vero Beach* [Fla.] *Press Journal,* November 7, 2001.

Birmingham [Ala.] *Post.* "Lucille Ball Queen of Comedy." November 20, 2001.

Boston Globe. "Tomlin on Stage." April 30, 1989.

Bowers, Ronald. "Lucille Ball's Career to Date." *Films in Review* (June/July 1971).

———. Review of *Mame. Films in Review* (April 1974).

Brady, Kathleen. "The CEO of Comedy." *Working Woman,* October 1986.

Brazil, Jeff, and Sharon Morser. "They Love Lucy at First Convention." *Los Angeles Times,* July 21, 1996.

Bretcher, Bob. "Lucy Balls Lives On." *Vero Beach* [Fla.] *Press Journal,* November 17, 2001.

Brochu, Jim. "I Loved Lucy." *Ladies' Home Journal,* August 1989.

Brook, Danae. "The World Loved Lucy . . . But She Didn't Have the Time to Love Me, Her Daughter." *Mail on Sunday* [London], July 9, 2000, 38, 39.

Brown, James. "Lucy Moves to NBC." *Los Angeles Times,* February 8, 1980, sec. 6, p. 19.

Brownfield, Paul. "First and Still Funniest." *Los Angeles Times,* September 2, 2001.

Buck, Jerry. "Lucille Ball Pioneered Innovative TV Techniques." *Press–Enterprise* [Riverside, Calif.], April 28, 1989.

Buffalo News. "New Manager of Museum." December 11, 2001.

———. "Stars' Kids Cut Ties with Lucy-Desi Museum." December 20, 2001.

———. "Arts Council Direction Takes Job in Schenectady." January 5, 2002.

———. "Luci-Desi Museum Will Chart New Course." March 8, 2002.

———. "Accord Allows Lucy-Desi Museum to Reopen." April 11, 2002.

———. "Simmons to Headline 'Lucy's Day.' " June 25, 2002.

———. "Lucy-Desi Museum Gets New Owners." June 25, 2002.

Burke, Ann. "Lucy Fans Honor Comic Redhead." *Los Angeles Times,* July 17, 1997.

Burke, Tom. "Lucy Coaxing Blues Right out of the Horn as 'Mame.' " *Los Angeles Times,* January 14, 1973.

Burns, Howard. "Lucy Obit: Thanks Lucy. . . ." *Hollywood Reporter,* April 27, 1989.

Calgary Herald. "Lucy, I'm Home: *I Love Lucy* Soundstage Dedicated on 50th." August 19, 2001.

Carnsdy, John. "The TV Column: Nielson Results for *Stone Pillow.*" *Washington Post,* November 7, 1985, sec. C, p. 16.

Carson, Tom. "The Crystal Ball." *American Film* (July/August 1989).

Champlin, Charles. Review of *Mame:* "Lucy Starts as 'Mame.' " *Los Angeles Times,* March 27, 1974.

Champlin, Charles, and Howard Rosenberg. "Everybody Loved Lucy." *Los Angeles Times,* April 27, 1989, sec. 6, p. 1.

Christian, Frederick. "Lucille Ball's Serious Life with Desi Arnaz," *Cosmopolitan,* January 1960, 67.

Christon, Lawrence. "Tomlin Gets Jack Benny Award, 'No Loss of Words.' " *Los Angeles Times,* October 24, 1986, sec. G, p. 6.

Cocks, Jay. Review of *Mame:* "Maimed." *Time,* March 25, 1974.

Confidential. "Does Desi Really Love Lucy?" January 1955, 22–25, 46.

———. "Heard the Latest About the Lucy-Desi Split." May 1960, 10–13.

Cook, B. W. "William Asher—The Man Who Invented the Sitcom." *Palm Springs Life,* April 2001.

Crichton, Kyle. "Three Loves Has She." *Colliers,* August 16, 1941, 16–18.

Daily Variety. "Death of Ray Katz, Manager to Lucie Arnaz and Lily Tomlin." March 24, 2000.

de Crinis, Mona M. "He Loved Lucy: An Interview with Author Lee Tannen." *Desert Post Weekly* [Palm Springs], November 8, 2001.

Desert Business Journal [Palm Springs]. "The City of Indian Wells." June 1993.
Desert Magazine [Palm Springs]. "Desert Circus Queen." March 19, 1964.
————. "Obituary, Desi Arnaz." December 2, 1986.
————. "Obituary, Desi Arnaz." December 19, 1986.
————. "Heart Attack Forces Ball into Surgery." April 19, 1989.
————. "Fans After Lucy's Attack." April 20, 1989.
————. "Ruptured Artery Kills Lucille Ball." April 27, 1989.
————. "Lucy's Legacy: 193 Episodes of TV Classics." April 28, 1989.
————. "Smoking Played Role in Comedian's Death." June 3, 1989.
————. "Lucy Honored Again." June 21, 1989.
————. "Lucy Sells Desi's Indian Wells Hotel." October 4, 1991.
————. "Lucy Debuts on Palm Canyon Drive." October 12, 1995.
————. "Statue Deserves Much Better." November 14, 1995.
————. "Millennium Moments: Valley Legends, Lucille Ball—1911–1989." March 9,
    1999.
————. "Lucy Remembered." April 12, 2000.
————. "Lucy's Stamp Unveiled." July 22, 2001.
Doty, Alexander. "The Cabinet of Lucy Ricardo: Lucille Ball's Star Image." *Cinema
    Journal* 29, no. 4 (1990).
Enrico, Dottie. "Celebrity Endorsers—Lucy Models Blackglama." *Adweek,* June 3,
    1985.
Family Circle. "Lucy and Desi Make a Movie." September 1953.
Farber, Stephen. "Networks Are Juggling Lineups at Mid Season." *New York Times,*
    December 13, 1986.
Fessier, Bruce. "I Love Lucy." *Desert Sun* [Palm Springs], August 6, 1981.
————. "Morton Discredits Lucy-Desi Story." *Desert Sun* [Palm Springs], March 8,
    1993.
————. "Gary Morton, Husband to Lucille Ball, Dies in Valley." *Desert Sun* [Palm
    Springs], April 1, 1999.
Firmat, Perez. "Rum, Rump and Rumba: Cuban Contests." *Dispositio: Revista Ameri-
    can de Estudios Comparados y Culturales* 16, no. 4 (1991): 61–71.
Fleeman, Michael. "Fans Wish Ball the Best After Heart Attack." *Desert Sun* [Palm
    Springs], April 20, 1989.
Flint, Peter B. Lucy obituary: "Spirited Doyenne of TV Comedy." *New York Times,*
    April 17, 1989.
Folkart, Burt. "Desi Arnaz, TV Lucy's Loving Co-star, Dies." *Los Angeles Times,*
    December 3, 1986, sec. 1, p. 3.
Frank, Terry. "Ads Featuring Lucy, Desi to Go on Display." *Buffalo News,* May 1, 2002.
————. "Dispute Over Reins Closes Lucy-Desi Museum." *Buffalo News,* June 24,
    2002.
————. "Remains of Lucy, Mother to Be Interred in Home Town." *Buffalo News,* July
    3, 2002.
Frenry, Mark. "A Better Candidate—Lucy a Choice for Mom in *Manchurian Candi-
    date.*" *Boston Globe,* April 14, 2002, 19.
Garcia de Rosier, Tania. "Proctor's Power Broker." *Times Union* [Albany, N.Y.] May 5,
    2002.
Garner, Jack. "Lucy, We Had a Ball." *Desert Sun* [Palm Springs], April 26, 1989.
Gehring, Wes. "*I Love Lucy* Turns 50." *USA Today Magazine,* September 2001.
Gilbert, Tom. "'Splainin' New *Lucy* Episodes." *Daily Variety,* June 25, 1998.
Glenn, Larry. "Bob Hope Bounces a Ball Named Lucy." *New York Times,* April 19, 1964.

Gordon, John Steele. "The Business of America: What Desi Wrought." *American Heritage,* December 1998.

Gould, Jack. "The Case of Lucille Ball." *New York Times,* September 20, 1953, sec. 2, p. 1.

———. "TV: Corny but Clever: Hope-Ball Special." *New York Times,* April 20, 1964.

Greenway, Sue. "Why We All Love Lucy." *Bristol* [U.K.] *United Press,* November 21, 2001.

Greer, Gloria. "Desert Circus Queen, Lucille Ball." *Desert Magazine* [Palm Springs], March 1964, 45–46.

Gross, Linda. "First Awards by Women in Films." *Los Angeles Times,* June 20, 1977, sec. 6, p. 12.

Guardian [Manchester, U.K.]. "Funny Girls: Best of the 20th Century Comediennes." March 9, 1995.

Haber, Joyce. "Lucy in *Mame* a Chic Auntie." *Los Angeles Times,* October 1, 1973.

———. "Lucy to Win Golden Apple Award." *Los Angeles Times,* December 18, 1973.

Haithman, Gloria. "The Industry's Debt to Lucy." *Los Angeles Times,* April 30, 1989, Calendar section.

Harmetz, Aljean. "Lucille Ball Dusts Off Her Slapstick." *New York Times,* August 3, 1986.

Harris, Ron. "Little Ricky, Now 38, Remembers Lucy as Surrogate Mom." *Press–Enterprise* [Riverside, Calif.], April 28, 1989.

Harris, Warren G. "When Love Was New [excerpt from *Lucy & Desi*]." *Ladies' Home Journal,* May 1992.

Harrison, Diana. "Uninvited Party Brings Baby to Lucy's Doorstep." *Photoplay,* July 1971.

Hartford Courant. "Daughter in Bidding for Lucille Ball's Childhood Home." March 17, 2002.

———. "Retiree from Florida Buys Lucy's Childhood Home." April 7, 2002.

Haskel, Molly. "Why We Love Lucy: Wild and Crazy or Proto-feminist? Fifty Years After the Debut of *I Love Lucy,* the Wacky Redhead Is Still Red Hot." *Modern Maturity,* September/October 2001, 44–51.

Hastings, Julianne. "TV Pays Tribute to 'Famous' Seven." *Los Angeles Times,* March 3, 1984, sec. 6, p. 2.

Henry William A., III. "Private Eye: How ABC Dropped the Ball." *Channels* [New York], February 1987, 75.

———. Lucy obituary: "A Zany Redheaded Everywoman." *Time,* May 8, 1989.

Herrera, Dan. "List of Sources of Pride for Hispanics and Americans." *Albuquerque* [N.M.] *Journal,* September 23, 2001.

Higham, Charles. "Is Lucy Having a Ball as 'Mame'?" *New York Times,* February 18, 1973.

———. "Lucy: The Legend: The Birth of America's Favorite TV Comedy." *Los Angeles Herald Examiner,* April 30, 1989.

———. "Lucy and Desi's Stormy Marriage and Breakup." *Los Angeles Herald Examiner,* May 1, 1989.

———. "Hollywood Was Lucy's Destiny: After Shaky Start, Her Star Began to Rise." *Los Angeles Herald Examiner,* May 2, 1989.

———. "Lucy a Card-Carrying Member of the Communist Party?" *Los Angeles Herald Examiner,* May 3, 1989.

———. "Lucy Means Business: Comedian Becomes Corporate Star." *Los Angeles Herald Examiner,* May 4 1989.

Hingley, Audrey. "Life with Lucie." *Saturday Evening Post,* March/April 1994, 46.

Hinkley, David. "Why We Love Lucy." *Daily News Vue* [New York *Daily News* supplement], December 2000, 3–9

———. Series: "Big-Town Classic Characters—From *I Love Lucy*—Fred and Ethel Mertz." *Daily News* [New York], March 17, 2002.

Hirshon, Paul. "Who Did You Say Loved Lucy?" *Boston Globe,* January 12, 1990.

Holguin, Richard. "Lucille Ball Starring in Northridge Classroom." *Los Angeles Times,* December 16, 1979, sec. 2, p. 5.

Hollywood Reporter. "The Desilu Story." January 13, 2000.

Hollywood Tattler. "Who Loves Lucy Now?" November 1961, 38–41.

Hope, Bob. "Unforgettable Lucille Ball." *Reader's Digest,* March 1990.

Horn, John. "Ruptured Artery Kills Beloved TV Redhead." *Desert Sun* [Palm Springs], April 27, 1989.

———. "They Loved Lucy: Ball, Arnaz Wanna-Bees Flock to Film Audition." *Desert Sun* [Palm Springs], July 17, 1990.

House & Garden. "Is Lucy Still Lovable?" May 1957, 32, 41.

Hughes, Mike. "Reflection on Arnaz." *Desert Sun* [Palm Springs], December 4, 1986.

Inside Story [New York]. "Why Desi Took That Little Tramp." May 1960, 34–35, 46–47.

Johnson, Beth. "Encore: Desilu's Redhead Honcho Lucille Ball Took Charge of Her Fated TV Studio 34 Years Ago." *Entertainment Weekly,* November 15, 1996.

Jones, Charissa. "An Outpouring by Fans: They Really Do Love Lucy." *Los Angeles Times,* April 20, 1989, sec. 1, p. 30.

Jones, Jack. "Lucille Ball Stricken: Has Heart Surgery." *Los Angeles Times,* April 19, 1989, sec. 1, p. 1.

Jones, Liza. "Lucille Ball: First Ten Years of Marriage." *Photoplay,* April 1971.

Kaplan, Dan. "Oh Ricky, Lucy's Family Is Homeless." *New York Post,* March 30, 2002.

Keane, Dottie. "Funny Girls on Top: How Women Have Ousted Men as the Leading TV Comics." *Mail on Sunday* [London], August 29, 1993.

Kerr, Walter. Review of *Wildcat. New York Herald Tribune,* December 17, 1960.

King, Susan. "Q & A: Lily Tomlin." *Los Angeles Times,* August 9, 1992.

———. "Network Celebrates 50 Years of Emmys." *Bergen Record,* September 13, 1998, sec. Y, p. 1.

———. "TV Museum—Fountain of Youth Show." *Los Angeles Times,* March 31, 2000.

Kleiman, Dena. "Ball in a Dramatic Role Is Returning to TV." *New York Times,* October 21, 1985, 20.

Kroll, Jack. Lucy obituary: "Everyone Loved Lucy." *Newsweek,* May 8, 1989.

Ladies' Home Journal. "TV Star Wars / Talking with Lucy." October 1986.

———. "We Remember Mama—Sons of Liz and Lucy Look Back." May 1990.

———. "Barbara Walters' Best Interviews: Lucille Ball." July 1994.

Life. "More Girls. Fun and Romance Are New Trend to Offset War." August 5, 1940.

———. "Beauty into Button." February 18, 1952, 93–97.

———. Cover story: "Lucy's Boys." April 6, 1953.

———. "Arnaz and Ball Take Over as Tycoons: $30 Million Desilu Gamble." October 6, 1958.

———. "Sexy Eyes over Hope's Shoulder." March 17, 1961, 107–108.

———. "A Lusty Return by Lucy." January 5, 1962.

———. "The Show That Changed America: 60 Years of Network Television." April 1999.

Liverpool Daily Post & Echo [London]. "Pioneer Became a Top Star; Here's Why All TV Fans Loved Lucy." November 20, 2001.

Look. "Laughing Lucille." June 3, 1952.

————. "Lucy Goes Shopping." December 28, 1954.

————. "Fall TV Forecast." September 17, 1957.

————. "How *The Untouchables* Hyped TV's Crime Wave." September 27, 1960.

————. "Lucy: A New Outlook." October 9, 1962.

Lucille Ball: An American Film Institute Seminar on Her Work. American Film Institute Seminars, pt. 1, no. 12. Beverly Hills, Calif., 1977.

Lyons, Leonard. The Lyons Den: "Suit for Divorce." *New York Post,* March 6, 1960.

MacLeans. Lucy obituary. May 8, 1989.

McCarthy, Robert J. "Ball's Ashes May Return to Jamestown." *Buffalo News,* March 1, 2002.

Magill's Survey of Cinema. "The Long Trailer." May 15, 1995.

Mann, Roderick. "Lucie Arnaz Says It's Her Life Anyway." *Los Angeles Times,* August 26, 1980, sec. 6, p. 5.

————. "To New Yorkers, Lucy's Just Another Bag Lady." *Los Angeles Times,* October 20, 1985, sec. 5, p. 1.

Margulies, Lee. "Lucie Throws Her Series into the Ratings Ring." *Los Angeles Times,* April 17, 1985, sec. 6, p. 1.

Martin, Peter. "I Call on Lucy and Desi." *Saturday Evening Post,* May 31, 1958.

Martinson, Dan. "Whatever Happened to Stars of Television's 'Golden Age'?" *Los Angeles Times,* January 2, 1985, sec. 6, p. 10.

Mencum, Lauralee. "Valley Friends Share Memories of Lucy." *Desert Sun* [Palm Springs], April 27, 1989.

Michael, Christopher. "Public Art in the Valley: A Critical Tour." *Desert Sun* [Palm Springs], February 21, 2002.

Millman, Joyce. "The Good, the Bad, the Lucy: A Legacy of Laughs." *New York Times,* October 14, 2001, sec. 2, p. 30.

Millstein, Gilbert. "Lucy Becomes President." *New York Times Magazine,* December 9, 1962.

Morehead, Albert. "Lucy Ball: She Flunked Dramatic School, Was Fired as a Chorus Girl, but Today This Sexy Redhead Is TV's Top Comedienne." *Cosmopolitan,* January 1953.

Morris, Emily. "Secrets of an 'Ugly Duckling.' " *Life,* May 1938.

Nation. Editorial: "Postscript on Lucy." May 22, 1989.

Newsday. "Tributes." April 28, 1989.

————. "Lucie on Lucille: Less Than Rave Reviews." January 12, 1990, 11.

Newsweek. "Lucille Ball: Who Doesn't Love Lucy." January 19, 1953, 56–59.

————. Newsmakers. March 14, 1960.

————. "On Set—Calamity Lucy." August 22, 1960.

————. "Lucie on Lucy—Less Than Rave Review." January 12, 1990.

————. "The Lost Lines of Lucy." January 15, 1990.

New York Journal–American. "Fans Love Lucy and Coming Baby." September 15, 1952, 5.

————. "Probers Give Her Clean Slate: Lucille Ball Denies She Ever Was Red." September 12, 1953, 3.

————. "She Didn't Love the Comrades: Lucy No Red Party Member." September 13, 1953, 8.

————. "Fair Play for Lucy." September 14, 1953.

New York Post. "Hollywood Party Girl to Tell About Spying on the Stars for *Confidential.*" August 14, 1957, 5, 31.

————. "Desi Arnaz Blasts *Confidential:* Desi Arnaz Raps *Confidential;* State Calls Private Eye (a Lady)." August 14, 1957, 1, 3, 7.

————. "Opening—*Wildcat*." December 11, 1960.

————. "Lucy Would've Hated This Idea." March 20, 2002.

New York Times. Film reviews, 1913–1968.

————. "Near Birth of (?) Arnaz Is Engendering Interest of Fans of *I Love Lucy*." January 16, 1953.

————. "Lucille Ball Adheres to Television Script: Comedienne Gives Birth to 8½ Pound Boy." January 20, 1953, 27.

————. "Police Here Cited at Scandal Trial: Ex-editor Says *Confidential* also Obtained Data from a New York Law Aide." August 13, 1957, 53.

————. "Magazine Policy Cited by Witness: Admitted Ex-prostitute Says Publisher of *Confidential* Wanted Lewd Stories." August 14, 1957.

————. "Desilu: From Gags to Riches." October 20, 1958.

————. "Desi Held on Drunk Charge." September 20, 1959.

————. "Lucille Ball Sues Arnaz for Divorce." March 4, 1960.

————. "Lucille Ball Wins Divorce from Arnaz." May 5, 1960.

————. "Lucille Ball Injured." July 2, 1960.

————. "Miss Ball Named Desilu President." November 9, 1962.

————. "Miss Ball Views Desilu from Top." November 20, 1962.

————. "Desilu Appoints Director." March 22, 1963.

————. "Lucille Ball Reports Gains at Desilu." August 21, 1963.

————. "Desi Charged with Assault After Firing a Gun at Several Youths." September 1, 1966.

————. "Gulf & Western to Buy Desilu; Lucille Ball to Stay as President." February 15, 1967, 59, 65.

————. "Gulf & Western Plans to Sell Part of Desilu." July 26, 1967.

————. "Lucille Ball to Return to Fall Series on ABC." March 8, 1986.

————. "ABC Drops Lucille Ball and Ellen Burstyn." November 8, 1986, 50.

————. Editorial: "We All Love Lucy." April 27, 1989.

————. "A Star Who Stays in the Shade." May 26, 1994, 36, 89, 91.

New York Times Magazine. "Desi Paid Hush Money; *Confidential* Scandal." August 13, 1957.

————. "Lucy Becomes President." December 9, 1960.

O'Connor, John J. Review of "A Lucille Ball Special, Starring Lucille Ball and Jackie Gleason." *New York Times,* December 3, 1975, 90–91.

————. Review: "Lucille Ball Plays a Bag Lady on CBS." *New York Times,* November 5, 1985, sec. C, p. 21.

————. Review: "Lucille Ball Returns in ABC Comedy Series." *New York Times,* September 22, 1986.

————. "Women Who Have Made Viewers Giggle and Roar." *New York Times,* October 24, 1991, sec. C, p. 22.

Oppenheimer, Jess. "Lucy's Two Babies." *Look,* April 21, 1953.

Osborne, Robert. "Lucy Festgoers Should Love Forgotten Ball-Arnaz Movie." *Hollywood Reporter,* August 7, 2001.

Ostrow, Joanna. "Lucy Without Laughs; Comedienne Ball Stars as Bag Lady." *Bergen Record,* November 3, 1985, Lifestyle section.

Palm Beach Post. Interview with Bea Arthur. December 11, 2001.

Palm Springs Life. "Love Lucy." January 1997.

Parade Magazine [Los Angeles]. "Collector's Item: Lucille Ball." June 4, 1989.

————. "He Said, She Said." March 27, 1994.

————. Review of *Hollywood Babble On,* by Boze Hadleigh. March 27, 1994.

Parnell, Tony. "Last Night's View: Lovable Lucy Has Last Laugh." London *Daily Mirror,* November 21, 2001.

Pegler, Westbrook. As Pegler Sees It: "The Case of Lucille Ball and How to Treat Reds." *New York Journal–American,* September 22, 1953.

People. "Ask Her Anything About Desi Sr., Divorce, Drugs, Gay Rights—Lucille Ball Hasn't Become Bashful." February 11, 1980.

———. "Fan Review." March 4, 1985.

———. "TV's Rerun Madness." March 4, 1985.

———. "Top 25 Stars—Lucille Ball." May 4, 1989.

———. "Lucy: The Life Behind the Laughter." August 14, 1989.

———. "Casting a New Lucy." August 6, 1990.

———. "Lucy & Desi: Before the Laughter." September 3, 1990.

———. "The Untold Story of Lucy & Desi." February 18, 1991.

———. "The Greatest Love Stories of the Century." February 12, 1993.

———. "Readers Poll of Personalities and Their Impact 1974–1994 [inset on Lucy]." November 1, 1993.

Peterson, Peter. "So Why Love Lucy?" *Daily Mail* [London], November 23, 2001.

Phillips, Louis. "A Summer Spent Watching Lucille Ball Perform." *Journal of Popular Culture* 17 (Fall 1983): 99.

Phillips, Sidney. "Desi Arnaz Took His Show on the Military Road." *Desert Sun* [Palm Springs], December 10, 1986.

Phoenix [Ariz.] *New Times.* "Frankie with the Snarling Face." May 28, 1998.

Photoplay. "Stop Crying." February 1942.

———. "The Bouncing Ball." September 1946.

Pisetzner, Joel. "Life of a Glad Bag Lady; Lucille Ball in *Stone Pillow.*" *Bergen Record,* November 1, 1985, Lifestyle section.

Pittsburg Post–Gazette. "Bad Movies We Love. How to Ring in the New Year with a Festival of Flops." December 31, 1993, Entertainment, p. 2.

Pollio, Mark. "Fans of Lucy Have a Ball During Auction." *Buffalo News,* May 29, 1994.

Press–Enterprise [Riverside, Calif.]. "Lucy's Appearance at Claremont College." November 2, 1985.

———. "Question and Answer: Lucy with Gary Morton." July 10, 1988.

———. "The Fans Show They Love Lucy." April 20, 1989.

———. "Specific Diseases That Killed Lucy." April 24, 1989.

———. "How We Loved Lucy." April 27, 1989.

———. "Lucille Ball Dies." April 27, 1989.

———. "Entertainment Briefs: Fans Visit Sidewalk Star to Mark Lucy's Passing." May 2, 1989.

———. "Lucy and Gary in 1987." November 5, 1995.

Providence [Rhode Island] *Journal.* "For Sale: Lucille Ball Childhood Home." March 23, 2002.

Reed, Rex. "Lucy: I Ran My Studio Like My Home." *New York Times,* October 8, 1967.

———. "Lucy the Lioness: Steely Pride on Those Journeys." *Chicago Tribune,* February 17, 1974, sec. 2, p. 18.

———. "Secret History: Seeing Red." *Talk* [New York], June/July 2000, 114.

Riggs, Robert. "Where's Ricky Ricardo's Hollywood?" *Los Angeles Times,* January 7, 1983, sec. 2, p. 7.

Robertson, Nan. "Will Broadway Love Lucy?" *New York Times,* December 11, 1960.

Roeper, Richard. "Women Couldn't Get Arrested for Inciting a Laugh Riot." *Sun–Times* [Chicago], March 31, 2000.

Roraback, Dick. Review of *Lucy & Ricky & Fred & Ethel,* by Bart Andrews. *Los Angeles Times,* November 28, 1976.

Rosen, Jay. "*Love Boat* Goes to College." *Channels* [New York], October 1986, 67.

Rosenberg, Howard. "Hard to Sit Long for *Stone Pillow.*" *Los Angeles Times,* November 5, 1985, sec. 6, p. 9.

Rosenfield, Paul. "Lucy on the Platter of Honor." *Los Angeles Times,* November 7, 1977, sec. 4, p. 13.

———. "Compulsively Lucy." *Los Angeles Times,* October 12, 1986, Calendar section.

Ross, Don. "Oil on Broadway; Lucy on the Trail." *New York Herald Tribune,* December 1, 1960.

San Antonio Express. "Love of Lucy Keeps Fans Laughing, Buying." July 15, 1997.

San Francisco Chronicle. "*Confidential* Case: Trial Jury Told of Gable 'Affair,' He Issues Denial." August 13, 1957, 1, 6.

———. "Desi Denies 'Confidential Affair': Call Girl Names Desi Arnaz in *Confidential* Trial." August 14, 1957, 1, 4.

———. "*Confidential*'s Lurid Stories Read to Jury." August 15, 1957, 1, 4.

———. "Lucy Divorcing Desi: 'I Just Can't Go On.' " March 4, 1960, 1, 5.

———. "Lucy Tells Judge Desi Was a 'Jekyll and Hyde.' " May 5, 1960, 7.

———. "Lucy's Childhood Home for Sale on EBay." February 27, 2002.

Sann, Paul. "Lucy on Breakup." *New York Post,* May 8, 1960.

Schallert, Edwin. "Bromfield Seeks Desi Arnaz as Star—Hopes to Lure Brigitte Bardot." *Los Angeles Times,* October 14, 1957.

Schwarzbaum, Lisa. Review: "Ball and Chain Lucy, the Outrageous Queen of Comedy, Unfortunately Tethers to Mannered, Ladylike Pattern in *Love, Lucy.*" *Entertainment Weekly,* September 27, 1996.

Scott, John A. "How to Be a Success in Show Business." *Cosmopolitan,* November 1958, 67.

Selway, Jennifer. "On Last Night's TV—Lucille Ball." *Express,* November 23, 2001.

Shales, Tom. Review: "Lukewarm Lucy: A Bag Lady in CBS *Stone Pillow.*" *Washington Post,* November 5, 1985, Style section.

———. "Lucy Coming to Life: At 75 TV's Definitive Star Is Back at the Grind." *Washington Post,* September 19, 1986, sec. D, p. 1.

———. "The Laughter Lucy Gave Us Helps Us Wash Away the Tears." *Press–Enterprise* [Riverside, Calif.], April 30, 1989.

———. "Funny Women: The Ball Epoch." *Washington Post,* October 24, 1991, sec. C, p. 1.

———. "Lucy & Baba-luminous." *Washington Post,* November 11, 2001, sec. G, p. 1.

Shalit, Gene. What's Happening: "Arnaz Mother/Daughter Interview with Lucille Ball and Lucie Arnaz." *Ladies' Home Journal,* October 1979.

Shaw, David. "Celebrities Act in Many Ways to Gain Privacy." *Los Angeles Times,* September 5, 1973.

Shirley, Paula W. "Reading Desi Arnaz in *The Mambo Kings Play Songs of Love.*" *Melus* [Storrs, Conn.] (September 1, 1995): 20.

Siegel, Lee. "Disease That Hit Lucy Can Be Among the Most Painful Known." *Press–Enterprise* [Riverside, Calif.], April 24, 1989.

Silvian, Leonore. "Laughing Lucille." *Look,* June 3, 1952.

Siskel, Gene. "Tired Lucy: A Redhead Whose Dander Is Up." *Chicago Tribune,* March 13, 1974, sec. 2, pp. 1, 2.

———. "Put the Blame on *Mame,* Boys." *Chicago Tribune,* April 1, 1974, sec. 2, p. 10.

Smith, Cecil. "Lucy to Meet Stiff Foe: Her Movie." *Los Angeles Times,* November 4, 1973.

———. "Curtain Rings Down Lucy Show After Record 23 Years." *Los Angeles Times,* February 27, 1974.

———. "The Long Shots of Desi Arnaz." *Los Angeles Times,* March 4, 1976, sec. 4, p. 2.

———. "They Still Love Lucy." *Los Angeles Times,* May 23, 1977, sec. 4, p. 13.

———. "A Walking History of TV." *Los Angeles Times,* November 21, 1977, sec. 4, p. 14.

———. "Lucy: Truly a Child of the Tube." *Los Angeles Times,* January 3, 1980, sec. 6, p. 16.

———. "Looking Back on Life with Lucy." *Los Angeles Times,* October 14, 1981, Calendar section.

Smith, Dinitia. "The Newest Wasserstein Creation Comes Home." *New York Times,* December 23, 1999.

Sokolsky, Bob. "I Love Lucy: Television's Queen of Comedy Will Share Some Memories from Her Best Years." *Press–Enterprise* [Riverside, Calif.], November 2, 1985.

———. "Amidst Laughter, Few Tears, Audience Still Loves Lucy." *Press–Enterprise* [Riverside, Calif.], November 4, 1985.

———. "The Arnaz Way." *Desert Sun* [Palm Springs], December 4, 1986.

———. "She'll Always Be Lucy." *Press–Enterprise* [Riverside, Calif.], April 27, 1989.

Stack, Mary. Guardian Women: "As the Women Said After Smoking the Ashes of Her Husband." *Guardian* [Manchester, U.K.], October 19, 1984.

Starr, Shannon. "Celebrities Starred in Parade." *Press–Enterprise* [Riverside, Calif.], March 23, 2002.

Stoop, Norma McLain. "Here's Lucy as 'Mame.' " *After Dark* [New York], October 1973.

Strachan, Alex. "50 Years Later, We Still Love Lucy; Lucille Ball and Desi Arnaz Revolutionized Television." *Vancouver* [B.C.] *Sun,* November 10, 2001, sec. H, p. 9.

Sun–Times [Chicago]. "Hazelwood Screened and Other Stories." May 18, 1995.

Taubman, H. Review of *Wildcat. New York Times,* December 17, 1960.

This Week [New York]. "Television Producer Desi Arnaz Arrested." September 1, 1966.

Thomas, Kevin. "Second Thoughts: A Miscarriage." *Los Angeles Times,* March 11, 1983, sec. 6, p. 2.

Thompson, Carolyn. "Travel News: Jamestown Has Even More Lucy to Love." *Newsday,* August 2, 2002.

Thompson, Thomas. "Lucy—Having a Ball at 62." *Ladies' Home Journal,* April 1974.

Time. Review of *Five Came to Dinner.* June 20, 1934.

———. Review of *Too Many Girls.* November 11, 1940.

———. "Sassafrassa the Queen." May 26, 1952.

———. "The New Tycoon." April 7, 1958.

———. People. March 14, 1960.

Times Union [Albany, N.Y.] "And No, the Mertzes Didn't Own It." March 5, 2002.

Toronto Star. "Lucille Ball's Bag Lady Has Her Funny Moments." November 1, 1985, sec. D, p. 22.

TV Guide. "Lucy the Lecturer." October 31, 1959.

———. "A Visit with Lucille Ball." July 18, 1960.

———. Review of *The Lucy Show.* 1967.

———. "*I Love Lucy* 50 Funniest Moments." October 13, 2001, 18–40, 67.

———. "50 Greatest Shows of All Time." May 4, 2002, 22.

———. "50 Greatest TV Guide Covers." June 15, 2002, 14.

———. "In Jamestown, New York, They Love Lucy." July 6–12, 2002, 28.

———. "50 Worst Shows of All Time." July 20, 2002, 20.

TV Stage. "Lucy and Desi's New Ranch." June 1954.

Unger, Arthur. "Lucille Ball as a Bag Lady?" *Christian Science Monitor,* November 4, 1985, Arts section.

U.S. News & World Report. "Comedienne Lucille Ball on the Mess in Television Land." September 26, 1977, 88.

———. "Lucy Has Grown Up a Lot." September 22, 1986.

USA Today Magazine. "*I Love Lucy* Turns 50." September 2001.

Valentine, Leslie. "Lucy Today: Her Life of Love, Luck & Loneliness." *Photoplay,* September 1973.

Van Ryzin, Jeanne Claire. "Claiming Our History." *Austin* [Tex.] *American Statesman,* September 26, 2000, sec. E, p. 1.

Variety. Film reviews, 1938–1942.

———. "Harry Finstein (Parkyakarkus)." November 16, 1958.

———. "When in Trouble Call 'Lucy.'" November 19, 1958.

———. "Parkyakarkus Fatally Stricken." November 25, 1958.

———. "Martin Leeds Exits Desilu." September 28, 1960.

———. "Shows on Broadway—*Wildcat.*" December 21, 1960.

———. "Lucy Continues to Recover from Surgery." April 26–May 2, 1989.

———. "Tribute to Lucille Ball." May 3–9, 1989.

Vejnoska, Jill. "Lucy Lives On." *Atlanta Journal–Constitution,* October 15, 2001.

VeLocci, Tony. "Lessons of Leadership: The Real Lucille Ball." *Nation's Business,* October 1981.

Vogue. "$54,000,000 Bonanza—Lucille Ball." May 1968.

Wall Street Journal. "Desilu Stock Sale of 525,000 Shares, at $10.00 per Share." November 11, 1958, 15.

Ward, Patricia Biederman. "Family Attractions; Lucy—The Museum." *Los Angeles Times,* March 10, 1991.

Wasserstein, Wendy. "Rebel in a Housedress." *New York Times,* April 18, 1999.

Waters, Jim. "Lucy Is 'Mame.'" *People,* March 18, 1974, 34–45.

Waters, John. "A Career Colored by *Lucy.*" *Electronic Media* [Los Angeles], October 1, 2001.

Watson, Jenny. "When Lucy Was the Queen of the Ball." *Liverpool Daily Post & Echo* [London], November 21, 2001.

Weeks, Janet. "Annual Convention Pays Tribute to Lucille Ball." *Daily News* [Los Angeles], July 9, 1997.

———. "A Redhead Revival: Lovers of Lucy Launch Convention." *Press–Enterprise* [Riverside, Calif.], July 10, 1997.

Werts, Diane. "The Show That Changed TV Forever." *Newsday,* October 15, 2001.

Whisper. "The Night Desi Arnaz Wasn't Half Safe." August 1956, 19–21, 54.

Whitney, Dwight. "The President Wore a Dress to the Stockholders Meeting." *TV Guide,* July 15–21, 1967.

Wick, Ted. "Irrepressible Lucy Plays Again." *Alberta Report,* February 3, 1997, 41.

Wilson, Earl. It Happened Last Night. *New York Post,* December 19, 1960.

Wilson, Jeff. "Lucille Ball Survives Heart Attack, Seven-Hour Surgery." *Press–Enterprise* [Riverside, Calif.], April 19, 1989.

Wohls, Robert. "Angela: The 'Mame' Who Got Away." *Los Angeles Times,* April 14, 1974.

Zimmerman, Paul. Review of *Mame:* "On the Ball." *Newsweek,* March 18, 1974.

Zoglin, Richard. "The TV Star: Lucille Ball." *Time,* June 8, 1998.

WEB SITES/PROGRAMS

ABC Special Report. Barbara Walters and guests, "A Celebration: 100 Years of Great Women." April 30, 1999. http://abcnews.go.com/onair/DailyNews/sp990430_100women_promo.html.

AP General News. "Aussie Answer to Lucille Ball Farewelled in Sydney." June 11, 2002.

AP Spanish Online. "Contemplan Llevar los Restos de Lucille Ball a Nueva York." March 20, 2002.

AP Wire Service. Carolyn Thompson, "More Family Involvement Signals Bigger and Better Shrine to Lucille Ball." July 11, 2002.

Biography Channel. "American Classics: Celebration of Comedienne Lucille Ball." December 2001.

Craig's Big Bands and Big Names. http://www.bigbandsandbignames.com/.

eLibrary Photographs. http://www.encyclopedia.com/html/b/ball-l1uc.asp.

Glen Charlow's Lucille Ball Collection. http://www.lucilleball.net/collection/magcov.html.

Lucille Ball [computer file]. Washington, D.C.: U.S. Department of Justice, Federal Bureau of Investigation [1998?]. Mode of access: Internet from the FBI Web site. http://foia.fbi.gov/ball.htm.

Mr. Blackwell's List of Worst Dressed, 1960, 1961, 1962, 1965, 1966. http://www.mrblackwell.com/list/.

Nesi, Ted, comp. "Lucy's TV Appearances and Specials." http://www.geocities.com/TelevisionCity/6066/lucindex.html.

NPR Wire Transcript. David Hiltbrand & Scott Simon, "No Question What's Number One to TV Guide." May 29, 1996.

———. Renee Montague interview with Kathleen Brady. August 6, 2001.

———. Diane Hanses, "Profile: 'Skit Performed by Various TV Personalities—Slowly I turned. . . .' " July 7, 2001.

TV Guide Online. "Insider: Lucy's Darkside." May 11, 2000.

Variety.com. "Lucy Awards," June 24, 2002.

World News Tonight Transcript. Peter Jennings, "The Century on Friday." March 12, 1999.

Index

Permissions Acknowledgments

Photographic Credits

A Note About the Author

STEFAN KANFER'S books cover an extraordinary range of subjects. His nonfiction includes the widely praised biography, *Groucho*; *The Last Empire*, a history of the De Beers diamond company; *Serious Business*, a history of animated cartoons in America; and *A Journal of the Plague Years*, a history of the show business blacklist. His novel *The Eighth Sin*, which was about the fate of the Gypsies during World War II, was a selection of the Book of the Month Club and led to an appointment on the President's Commission on the Holocaust. Two other novels, *Fear Itself* and *The International Garage Sale*, also concern historical events. He has written for most major periodicals, including *Time* magazine, where he wrote and edited for more than twenty years. He currently serves on the editorial board of *City Journal* and as theater critic for the *New Leader*. Kanfer is a featured interviewer in two documentaries: the Academy Award–nominated *The Line King*, a biography of *New York Times* theatrical caricaturist Al Hirschfeld, and the PBS film *Extremes and In-Betweens*, a study of animator Chuck Jones. A Literary Lion of the New York Public Library and recipient of numerous writing awards, Kanfer has been a writer in residence at the City University of New York and the State University of New York at Purchase, and is currently Distinguished Author in the writing program of Southampton College, Long Island University. He lives in New York and on Cape Cod.

A Note on the Type

This book was set in Fairfield, a typeface designed by the distinguished American artist and engraver Rudolph Ruzicka (1883–1978). In its structure Fairfield displays the sober and sane qualities of the master craftsman whose talents were dedicated to clarity. Ruzicka was born in Bohemia and came to America in 1894. He designed and illustrated many books, and was the creator of a considerable list of individual prints in a variety of techniques.

Composed by North Market Street Graphics,
Lancaster, Pennsylvania
Printed and bound by Berryville Graphics,
Berryville, Virginia
Designed by Anthea Lingeman